HUMANS AND THE ENVIRONMENT

Humans and the Environment

*New Archaeological Perspectives
for the Twenty-First Century*

EDITED BY MATTHEW I. J. DAVIES
AND FREDA NKIROTE M'MBOGORI

OXFORD
UNIVERSITY PRESS

OXFORD
UNIVERSITY PRESS

Great Clarendon Street, Oxford, OX2 6DP,
United Kingdom

Oxford University Press is a department of the University of Oxford.
It furthers the University's objective of excellence in research, scholarship,
and education by publishing worldwide. Oxford is a registered trade mark of
Oxford University Press in the UK and in certain other countries

© Oxford University Press 2013

The moral rights of the authors have been asserted

First Edition published in 2013
Impression: 2

British Library Cataloguing in Publication Data
Data available

ISBN 978-0-19-959029-2

Printed in Great Britain by
CPI Group (UK) Ltd, Croydon, CR0 4YY

SAGES-ARCH

Preface

There is a growing feeling among professional archaeologists that their discipline should have something to say about the pressing global issues of climate change and environmental degradation (e.g. Anderson et al. 2007; McIntosh et al. 2000; Mitchell 2008); however, there is little consensus as to what this contribution might be. Moreover, it is even unclear what archaeological data might be relevant (for example, will data on the Maya Collapse really help us solve present day problems?) or, for that matter, how archaeologists might make their voices heard above the cacophony of natural and physical scientists clamouring for a piece of the 'action'!

While motivated by such questions this volume does not solve these issues, but it is intended as a first step toward this end. The basic approach is critical and reserved, with a particular reaction against those sources which have prophesied the 'predictive' powers of archaeology to draw grand lessons from the past and then solve the problems of the future without offering much that is concrete (Diamond 2003; Fagan 2004, 2008). Instead the papers presented here offer less grand but potentially more useful perspectives on the nature of human–environment relations through time, drawn from archaeological and related data. In particular they aim to break down some of the assumptions and propositions on which modern environmental debates are founded, to engage with environmental management in a practical way (not only at global but also local and community-based scales), and to engage with culturally constructed perspectives of the environment as a means of more effective contribution. While the papers by no means present a single unified point of view, they do share a basic commonality of approach which might be termed 'humanistic' in that the role of individual agency within a cultural framework is given precedence in mediating human–environment interactions. The papers generally aim to counteract simple models which see humans either as somewhat passive respondents to their environment or conversely as active destroyers or degraders of 'pristine' environments. They view the human–environment dialectic in much more dynamic ways with multiple cause and effect relations, stemming from the non-human physical world (climate, geology) and from the human realm, both physical (subsistence, material culture) and non-physical (such as cognitive and symbolic).

The general approach of the volume is 'archaeological' in the sense that all the chapters deal with long-term human environment interactions, but this does not limit them to discussions of data derived only from muddy holes in the ground! Indeed, archaeologists tend to be uniquely interdisciplinary in their approach. This has often been seen as a weakness, in that archaeologists are thought of as borrowers who cobble together theoretical and methodological tools from other disciplines without producing anything original. This is an academic stereotype which mirrors the various popular stereotypes of archaeologists as well meaning but generally unthinking wellington-wearing hobbyists, gentlemen explorers, or daring superheroes. Such stereotypes may explain why archaeologists are rarely invited to the fancy parties of 'proper scientists' (often held at flashy venues such as the UN or the G8!) and therefore why our unique interdisciplinary perspective has struggled to find a voice.

It is, we believe, time to begin celebrating, rather than lamenting, the strong interdisciplinary strengths of archaeology and the polymath abilities of archaeologists. Archaeologists must be both scientists and humanists: we must understand a little of everything, and this places us in a unique position to bring together diverse approaches and ideas as central, rather than ephemeral, to the environmental debates of the day. Throughout, this volume presents the integrated use of a wide range of sources including historical, ethnohistorical, palaeoenvironmental, and anthropological data alongside core archaeological data, and it attempts to do so without being overly technical. One aim then is to make accessible and introduce readers to a wide range of possible long-term environmental approaches focused around the core methods of archaeology. Another aim is to emphasize the fundamental centrality of long-term history and the application of archaeological techniques to any true understanding of human–environment relations in the present.

The volume aims to be inclusive by presenting papers from a wide geographical and temporal range. We believe that this illustrates archaeology's ability to communicate across a uniquely wide global and temporal span. Four papers focus on the Americas, three on Europe, two on Africa, one on Australia, one on the Pacific, one on the Tropics, and three ephasize the global scale. The communities considered include both farmers and foragers, living in a range of biomes from the sub-arctic to tropical forests and temperate highlands.

These papers were specifically selected from a much larger number of papers presented at the 6th World Archaeology Congress in Dublin in July 2008. Each of the papers was presented at one of five sessions (one being a plenary) within a broad Congress theme entitled 'Our Changing Planet: Past human environments in modern contexts', convened by the editors. In this volume the papers have been revised and re-arranged to reflect broad commonalities between them. Some papers are presented in newer contexts reflecting key 'cross-cutting' themes noted by the editors. In addition, three new papers are presented here; Davies' paper in section 1 (Chapter 1) was inspired by Crumley's 'history of Historical Ecology' given in a Congress plenary but bears no resemblance to the original; the paper by Fairhead in section 5 was specifically commissioned to provide a voice from outside of archaeology and to build on the calls for interdisciplinarity made by a number of the other contributors. Gosden's overview was initially intended as part of the congress but owing to prior commitments it was not presented there; it is included here as a concluding review.

The book is divided into five sections which partially mirror the key themes derived from the congress sessions. Section 1 deals with the history of approaches to the environment in Archaeology and emphasizes new developments as a point of departure for the rest of the volume. In Chapter 1 Davies outlines the implicit and explicit roles of 'environment' as a key explanatory tool within European and North American archaeology and points toward important points of intersection between diverse approaches. In Chapter 2 Smyntyna reviews environmental approaches in Soviet and post-Soviet archaeology and identifies fruitful Soviet-inspired research agendas.

Section 2, entitled 'Environment as artefact', deals with the ways in which most, if not all, environments are culturally constructed, both in a physical sense and in the way that humans perceive them. In particular, each of the chapters tends towards the view that environments might be treated as human artefacts that have been shaped and moulded by human action for millennia. This perspective acts to break down the Cartesian distinction between 'nature' and 'culture' and should be of interest to not only academics but also developers and policy makers interested in the complexity of human–environment interactions. In Chapter 3, Balée forcefully makes this point with reference to tropical forests worldwide. His discussion provides strong evidence for the widespread manipulation of tropical forests across the globe and demonstrates that forests which were once considered 'pristine' actually resulted from the manipulation of humans. Notably, in West Africa he shows that there are actually anthropogenic forests where once there had been none (a theme also picked up by Fairhead in Chapter 16). The most important point to take from Balée is that humans modify all environments but that this does not necessarily result in decreased biodiversity. In many areas humans have often acted to increase and promote diversity, and the diversity we so often try to conserve by limiting human activity is, in itself, a human construct. Balée further points out that these artefactual environments are signatures of past indigenous land-use which should be treated as markers of identity and heritage in the same way as more tangible archaeological sites. This has important implications for heritage management and land-use decision-making in the present.

In Chapter 4 Davies explores indigenous land management among the Pokot agricultural community in northwest Kenya. He argues that Pokot farming practices are not determined by or adapted to environment but rather caught up in a complex socio-cultural web. In particular he argues that while environmental conditions might constrain practices and environmental changes may precipitate technological and social change, they do not specify practices let alone the scale or nature of change. Rather it is people themselves who are active in defining environmental practices and the nature of change, such that the Pokot landscape might be thought of as an artefact produced in a field of choice. To understand both practice and change we therefore need to understand the range of practical choices open to individuals and therefore why one option, the 'good move', is chosen over other possible moves. This range of possible choices can best be explored through long-term approaches to landscape as evidenced in changing patterns of land-use and settlement.

In Chapter 5 Fiore et al. explore hunter-forager subsistence practices in Tierra del Fuego, utilizing both archaeological and historic data. The chapter strongly critiques models of hunter-forager behaviour that rely on concepts of economic optimality. In contrast Fiore et al. establish the proper use of 'optimality' models as the basis for a null hypothesis against which empirical data might be compared so as to identify 'non-optimal' culturally conditioned human–environment interactions. The result is a view of Tierra del Fuego hunter-foragers as inhabiting a culturally constructed environment composed of recursively overlapping ideological and ecological spheres in which species are considered as much for their symbolic potency as their nutritional value. Ultimately both Davies and Fiore et al.'s approaches demonstrate that present-day environmental management practices can only be understood, changed, or improved through a holistic approach grounded in long-standing local environmental perceptions.

In Chapter 6 Chevalier builds on the concepts identified by Fiore et al. by emphasizing the role of subsistence-based environment use with regard to cultural identity. Chevalier demonstrates how differences in botanical assemblages from two contemporaneous pre-Colombian centres on the central Peruvian coast might be accounted for with respect to the construction of different identities within a non-hierarchical social structure. Chevalier's analysis demonstrates how ecological practices are intricately interlinked with a community's deeply sedimented identity, even to the extent that communities will expend more energy on obtaining some food resources than those resources convey energetically. Once again, this emphasizes that human–environment relations cannot be managed solely on the basis of economic rationality because the environment is, in part, perceived as a cultural tool through which various 'non-economic' ideas and values are transmitted. Long-standing environmental practices can be integral to a community's whole being, irrespective of their energy efficiency and environmental 'impact'. Often community–environmental relations cannot be easily altered or modified without some social disjuncture or disruption.

In Chapter 7 Kost brings us from issues of ideologically constructed environments (as discussed by Fiore et al. and Chevalier) back to analysis of the physically constructed environment. She returns to the theme of modified vegetation regimes, but this time with respect to the temperate forests and grasslands of south-western Australia. Kost demonstrates how the vegetation of south-western Australia has been shaped by millennia of Noongar selective firing practices. Importantly, she demonstrates how those firing practices were altered by the onset of colonialism. She identifies two narratives, the first being the narrative of changing human impacts on vegetation composition through time. This narrative emphasizes the extent to which seemingly minor human actions (when viewed in the short term) act to radically shape environments over longer timescales. The second narrative relates to the uniquely Western concept of environmental conservation based on mythical notions of 'pristine' or 'untouched' environments. This narrative aims to preserve 'natural' environments by limiting human action. However, such narratives clearly stem from a short-sighted view of history which assumes that indigenous peoples lived in a 'state of nature' with a neutral impact on the world around them; in other words that the environment would exist in the same state with or without the presence of humans. This myopic historical perspective generally sees detrimental human action as commencing at some distinct time in the recent past and aims to reverse the effects of that action. However, as Kost shows through a long-term archaeological approach, modern interventions, including conservation efforts, are merely another phase in the long-standing human modification of any environment.

Section 3, entitled 'Environmental narratives and applied archaeology' takes its lead from Kost's paper and moves from theoretical considerations of the human–environment relationship into more practical applications of archaeological data to issues of environmental management in the present. Through four case studies this section provides explicit evidence of archaeology's ability to contribute to present environmental issues. Two core themes are addressed. The first is the concept of applied environmental archaeology (in this instance applied 'agro-archaeology'), whereby archaeology might contribute to the reestablishment or resurrection of past land-use and land-management as resilient practices for the present. Many archaeological possibilities might exist in this realm, not least the archaeogenetic analysis of resilient past crop species and cropping regimes as a remedy for the unpredictable climate of the future. Both of the papers presented here, however, focus on past Andean terrace and irrigation systems with the aim of producing more sustainable methods of soil and water management. In Chapter 8 Isendahl et al. neatly review the concept of applied archaeology before discussing agro-archaeological research in the Bolivian Yungas. Isendahl et al. explore effective applied agro-archaeology as a dialogue between archaeologists and present-day farmers, whereby archaeology supplies ideas, questions, and new possibilities derived from the past. In Chapter 9 Kendall reports on the highly successful work of the Cusichaca Trust over the more than thirty years that they have been working on the rehabilitation of agricultural terrace systems in Peru. She paints a vivid picture of archaeology's role in rehabilitating hundreds of hectares of Inca and pre-Inca terraces and irrigation channels and the successes of such schemes within integrated rural development initiatives. Kendall highlights the ability of archaeology to identify key design features (particularly relative to drainage and building materials) fully appreciated by Peru's pre-conquest inhabitants, but easily overlooked by modern planners. Another key, but often overlooked, aspect of Kendall's chapter is the role of archaeologists in demonstrating why past land-use practices came to be abandoned and therefore in establishing a logical rationale for why they might usefully be reinstated. In the case of Peru's Inca terraces, Kendall demonstrates that they were not abandoned through any technical inefficacy (in favour of 'better' practices); rather they were abandoned because of the revolutionary impact of the Spanish conquest. The terraces did not lose their inherent practicality; instead people lost the ability, will, and indeed simply the numbers to maintain the terraces under the social and economic regime established by the Spanish. In a new social, political, and economic climate the terraces once again make much more sense.

In Chapter 10 Stump identifies the critique of environmental narratives as another important applied environmental archaeology. He points out how present-day environmental interventions are often justified on the basis of an implicit historical narrative. He further notes that these historical narratives often take quite contradictory forms and fall into two basic types; those which view human societies as inherently degrading of natural environments and advocate modernizing intervention; and those which emphasize the strengths of indigenous knowledge (IK) and promote traditional land management. Using a range of case studies from Eastern Africa, Stump explores the role of archaeology in questioning and critiquing such development narratives. He identifies this process as a clear and very specific applied archaeology.

In Chapter 11 Armstrong Oma develops further the theme of environmental, particularly agronomic, narratives. She explores the reciprocal interaction between narratives of modern farming practice and archaeological narratives of past farming. In particular, she explores how modern forms of 'factory' farming have encouraged models of past farming based on economic optimality. These same archaeological models have then circularly reinforced and helped justify present-day farming practices. By way of challenging such narratives, Armstrong Oma considers the relationship between farmers and their livestock in Bronze Age Scandinavia. She shows how the Bronze Age may have witnessed a change in the terms of engagement between humans and animals as exemplified in the establishment of three-aisled long-houses in which humans and their animals lived side by side. She identifies this moment as the establishment of a partnership between animals and humans and a revocation of the idea of animals as simply an economic resource to be exploited. Her chapter makes us question how people viewed animals in the past and therefore how we view them today. This is an ideologically applied archaeology which challenges us to rethink our own views.

Section 4 takes the concept of environmental narratives further and explores the role of archaeology in framing both Western and non-Western perspectives of nature, particularly with regard to 'natural' disasters.

In Chapter 12 Holmberg begins the section by showing how archaeology itself is a discipline shaped by the influence of natural disasters. She points out how disasters often contribute to processes of loss and abandonment which act to preserve archaeological sites for future discovery. In particular, she points to the role of Pompeii as a site preserved by disaster which subsequently became (both practically and ideologically) a 'training ground' of sorts for the development of professional archaeology. However, Holmberg cleverly also points out the misleading way in which archaeology is often framed as a 'Pompeii premise'. In essence she argues that archaeological descriptions of Pompeii and other similar sites as the past 'frozen in time' have often led us to assume that dramatic occurrences in the past should be conceived of as single instantaneous events, rather than as processes in which human agency was active. This Pompeii premise has then encouraged archaeologists to view not only disasters but much of nature as independent and primary determinants of human action rather than an active process of engagement between humans and the world. As Holmberg notes, the eruptions that engulfed Pompeii occurred over several days with many residents fleeing and others choosing to stay. The eruption, as singular as it might at first appear, was not an instantaneous event, but rather a good example of ongoing human engagement with nature. Pompeii's residents had experienced earthquakes and eruptions before and they weighed their decisions to stay or leave based on various combinations of historical knowledge, intuition, and risk taking. Disasters, like the eruption at Pompeii, are therefore not so much unique events but rather are simply another aspect of the ongoing processes of human–environment interaction. They are distinctive only with regard to the speed at which they happen, not necessarily with regard to scale. More importantly, such disasters rarely preclude the space for humans to engage with them in some way, to partially mitigate their effects, to run and hide, or to find the psychological strength to reconstitute one's life following them. Holmberg's critically reflective view of the development of archaeology as a discipline therefore emphasizes the ways in which archaeology has played into popular but misleadingly deterministic views of past human–environment interactions—particularly disasters—conceived of as snapshots in time. Ultimately Holmberg's chapter speaks to the way in which past perceptions of nature are played into the present, and archaeology's role in this process.

In Chapter 13 Leckie takes the theme of environmental perception further by exploring Victorian perceptions of nature through the lens of antiquarian and archaeological narratives of the past. She identifies two explicit nineteenth to early twentieth century views of human–environment relations which continue to play into the present day. The first sees past societies romantically living in harmony with nature. The second sees past societies as living at the whim of nature, in constant peril of environmental disaster. This second view is contrasted with the idealistic self-perception that Victorian society had transcended nature—a misconception all too apparent in today's world of environmental disaster. As a counterpoint, Leckie draws on the archaeology of Bronze Age Swiss lake dwellings to rethink the ways in which communities live and deal with environmental risk. She shows how Swiss lake dwellings were regularly burnt to the ground with great loss of possessions if not life. She argues then that disaster was a common phenomenon for the inhabitants of these lake dwellings, one which they lived with, managed, and which ultimately may have formed part of their identity and solidarity as a community. The paper is a strong lesson for how communities today internalize environmental disaster and live with environmental risk. She shows how it is not these risks that are new, only the idea that we should no longer be exposed to them. This, of course, is a uniquely late-twentieth-century Western perspective which does not hold in other times and places.

In Chapter 14 Rudiak-Gould takes the discussion of environmental perception further through the analysis of flood disaster histories in the Marshall Islands. Rudiak-Gould's analysis shows how long-standing sequences of floods have shaped people's perception of the risk of floods and their seemingly unalarmed attitude towards impending sea-level rises caused by global climate change. Although Rudiak-Gould's analysis is primarily historical and anthropological he emphasizes the importance of long-term environmental histories, as analysed by archaeology, to deeper understandings of a community's environmental perception. As Rudiak-Gould suggests, as well as playing an important role in understanding why people take such attitudes to disaster, archaeology can also act to educate people as to differences between then and now. While past floods have perhaps predisposed the Marshallese to cope with the effects of flood, history combined with modern scientific prediction shows how different the floods of yesterday and tomorrow may be and why novel action is now required.

In Chapter 15 Anderson et al. take a broader perspective on the role of archaeology in elucidating long-term patterns of human–environment relations. In particular they emphasize the knowledge to be gained through the archaeological record of societal growth and collapse. They argue that environmental stimuli may spark radical social change but that such changes are not linear or predictable. Environmental change, especially non-anthropogenic 'disasters', may induce both increased and decreased social complexity, depending on the response of the community in question. The chapter then is a lesson for those who have simplistically pointed to past social 'collapses' as environmentally induced and as warnings for our own time. The archaeological record shows that the relationship between complex polities and their environment is never straightforward and that the response of any community to dramatic environmental change depends largely on the community's ability to solve problems, to weather difficulty, and to change and adjust accordingly. Some communities clearly have not fared well in the face of environmental crisis but others have responded more effectively, and some have radically reconstituted themselves. In light of Anderson et al.'s chapter we might ask what constitutes social collapse or disaster. If the material culture of a community radically changes in the face of disaster (for example, through changes in material objects and their consumption, or in settlement patterns and sizes) but the population itself remains intact, is this 'collapse' or simply reorganization? Is such change a positive or negative event? Although archaeology currently has no answer to such questions—and indeed they seem to tread into the territory of philosophy, ethics, and morality as much as archaeology—they are important questions which the archaeological record of past social changes reveals. In the face of global climate change today, what is our priority? Should we aim to cling to our present material and cultural values at all cost, even at the expense of loss of life, or can our material existence be sacrificed for the benefit of our physical well-being? This may be a false dichotomy and one which we may not have to face, but, like communities before us, these are questions that we would do well to consider. Archaeology may provide some advice, if not direct lessons.

Section 5 offers an overview of the previous papers and some ideas for new research directions. In Chapter 16 Fairhead provides a perspective from outside of archaeology and argues for the important integration of archaeological research with the results of ecological anthropology. Fairhead returns to work on West African tropical forests as introduced by Balée in Chapter 3. He re-states that many West African forests and soils are anthropogenically constituted and that archaeological research is essential to understanding the history of such environments. Archaeologically derived environmental narratives should, he argues, form the baseline for present-day environmental management and intervention strategies at a local scale. Fairhead's evaluation of the applied potential of environmental archaeology mirrors many of the previous discussions, especially those in sections 2 and 3 and particularly the chapters by Isendahl et al., Kendall, and Stump. Fairhead's chapter is a call to arms by an outsider who can perhaps see the potential of archaeological research better than we can ourselves.

In Chapter 17 Crumley takes a more global approach and discusses the contributions by archaeologists within the global climate change scientific community, particularly the work of the Integrated Histories of the People of Earth (IHOPE) project as part of the Integrated Geosphere Biosphere (IGB) programme. She details the ongoing collection of archaeologically derived data sets on long-term human–environment dynamics from around the world, and shows how archaeological data is becoming increasingly recognized by the broader scientific community. Crumley's chapter is a clarion call for archaeologists to integrate their data with projects such as IHOPE and to contribute more fully in the pressing environmental issues of today.

Between them Crumley and Fairhead offer two clear and mutually compatible ways forward for applied environmental archaeology. Fairhead points to the local or regional scale and the importance of archaeology for developing appropriate local environmental management. Crumley points to the way in which these local data sets may be incorporated into broader-scale analyses when combined with data from other regions. Archaeological research has the potential to contribute at both of these scales, but more importantly it has the ability to translate between them, to explore the interaction between the global and the local, and to translate the local effects of environmental change into global analyses and the effects of global change into local consequences.

In the concluding review Gosden usefully points out some of the intersections between the chapters and attempts to situate the volume more broadly within current anthropological thought. As he points out, the perspectives offered are complex and occasionally at variance, but he notes that what really brings them together is an emergent view of the world which breaks down the nature culture divide and recognizes the agency of both people and things. This interaction between people and things is ongoing. It exists in the present and plays into the future, but its trajectory is inherently historical and this is where archaeology finds itself an important role. As Gosden notes, the papers presented here all represent an engagement with the present and future *through* archaeology.

As Gosden also notes, there is much work to be done to truly understand humanity's place and future in the world and even more to change things; however, we hope that this volume is a step in the right direction.

Editors' Acknowledgements

The editors would like to express their deepest gratitude to the organisers of the Sixth World Archaeology Congress (WAC 6) held in Dublin in 2008 from which this volume developed. We would also like to express our thanks to the organizers of each of the individual sessions from which these papers were drawn. In addition, the editors would like to thank a number of anonymous reviewers for their useful comments on the volume structure and composition.

We would expressly like to thank the editorial team at Oxford University Press for their patience during the writing of this volume and to Professor Peter Mitchell for pointing us in the direction of OUP and providing continuous encouragement.

Matthew would personally like to thank the UK Arts and Humanities Research Council and St Hugh's College, Oxford for financial support to attend WAC 6. He would also like to thank the British Institute in Eastern Africa for allowing him to spend time editing this volume and for providing an excellent working environment and support.

Freda would personally like to thank the organizers of WAC 6 for their generous financial support which allowed her to attend. She would also like to thank the National Museums of Kenya for allowing her the time to participate at WAC 6 and for providing museum working hours to edit this volume. Finally she would like to thank family and friends for their continued support of her academic endeavours.

Contents

PART I: ARCHAEOLOGY AND ENVIRONMENT

PART II: ENVIRONMENT AS ARTEFACT

PART III: ENVIRONMENTAL NARRATIVES
AND APPLIED ARCHAEOLOGY

PART IV: ENVIRONMENT, DISASTER AND MEMORY

PART V: NEW DIRECTIONS

List of Figures

List of Tables

List of Contributors

David G. Anderson received his PhD in anthropology from the University of Michigan in 1990. He has conducted archaeological fieldwork in the Southeastern, Southwestern, and Midwestern United States, and in the Caribbean, work documented in some 350 publications and meeting papers and some 45 books and technical monographs. Professional interests include exploring the development of cultural complexity in Eastern North America from initial colonization onwards, climate change and its impact on human societies, teaching, and developing technical and popular syntheses of archaeological research.

Kristin Armstrong Oma is a postdoctoral fellow at the University of Oslo, in the Department of Archaeology, Conservation and History. Her work centres around human–animal relationships in the past, and she works within the cross-disciplinary field of human–animal studies. The working title of her current project is 'Prehistoric human–animal practices: social life, land use and economic strategies on the farm and their reciprocal impact upon natural systems'.

William Balée is Professor of Anthropology at Tulane University, where he has taught since 1991. He was earlier employed by the Goeldi Museum in Belém, Brazil (1988–91) and the New York Botanical Garden (1984–88). He has been doing fieldwork on or related to historical ecology in the Amazon region since 1980. He edited *Advances in Historical Ecology* (1998) and co-edited *Time and Complexity in Historical Ecology* (2006). His monograph *Footprints of the Forest* (1994) used an historical-ecological approach to understand Ka'apor ethnobotany in the eastern Amazon. His most recent research has focused on historical-ecological interpretation of inventories in old growth forests of archaeological sites in the Amazon regions of Brazil and Bolivia. His current and future research plans are to conduct comparative analysis of arboriculture and historical ecology in Amazonian forests with forests of south-east Asia.

Sergio Calla received a Licenciatura in archaeology from the Universidad Mayor de San Andrés, La Paz, Bolivia, in 2010 and has participated in numerous national and international field projects in the Andes and the lowlands of Bolivia. His main research interests are lithic technology, land use, and settlement patterns of Andean hunters and gatherers. He is the author of *Asentamientos prehispánicos en el Valle Alto de Tiwanaku: Contribuciones a la arqueología de la praxis humana en el Valle de Tiwanaku* (2012).

Alexandre Chevalier holds a PhD in prehistoric archaeology from the University of Geneva (Switzerland) with a complete training in vegetal biology (Geneva Botanical Garden and Conservatory), as well as in macrofossil identification (University of Missouri-Columbia) and microfossil analyses (UC-Berkeley and the Smithsonian Institutions). He has been working for more than fifteen years on past vegetal resources exploitation and the archaeology of food. He is currently a research fellow at the Royal Belgian Institute of Natural Sciences, applying macroremain (seed and charcoals) as well as microremain (phytolith, starch grain) analyses to South American and European archaeological contexts.

Carole Crumley is Professor emerita of Anthropology at the University of North Carolina, Chapel Hill. She is currently Executive Director of the Integrated History and Future of People on Earth (IHOPE) project, based at the Department of Archaeology and Ancient History, Uppsala University and also Visiting Professor at the Centre for Biodiversity, Swedish University of Agricultural Sciences (SLU), Uppsala. Her interests include historical ecology, European landscape archaeology (notably long-term regional change in Burgundy), and complex systems approaches to the social sciences. Among her publications is *Historical Ecology: Cultural Knowledge and Changing Landscapes* (ed. 1994, School of American Research). An example of recent work in global archaeology includes A Heterarchy of Knowledges: Tools for the Study of Landscape Histories and Futures in Plieninger & Bieling (eds.) *Resilience and the Cultural Landscape: Understanding and Managing Change in Human-Shaped Environments* (Cambridge 2012).

Matthew I. J. Davies is currently Fellow in East African Archaeology at the British Institute in Eastern Africa and the McDonald Institute for Archaeological Research, University of Cambridge. He completed his DPhil in 2009 on the later archaeology of Eastern Africa at the University of Oxford and spent the next two years as Assistant Director of the British Institute in Eastern Africa, based in Nairobi, Kenya. He currently directs a number of archaeological and ethnographic research projects in Kenya, Uganda, and the South Sudan.

James Fairhead is Professor of Social Anthropology at the University of Sussex and Chair of the Association of Social Anthropologists of the UK and Commonwealth. Much of his past research in West and Central Africa has examined how environmental and conservation sciences and policy articulate with existing perspectives and practices of land users concerning agro-ecology and the wider environment. His publications include a trilogy of books, *Misreading the African Landscape* (CUP), *Reframing Deforestation* (Routledge), and *Science, Society and Power* (CUP). His current research focuses on the significance of the enriched anthropogenic soils of ruined settlements in West Africa.

Danae Fiore is a researcher at CONICET (National Council of Scientific and Technological Research, Argentina) and a lecturer at UBA (Universidad de

Buenos Aires, Argentina). Her main research interests are related to the archaeology of hunter-gatherer societies from Patagonia and Tierra del Fuego, and her lines of research include the archaeology of art from economic, technological and visual-cognitive perspectives, archaeological theory and archaeometry.

Chris Gosden is Professor of European Archaeology, University of Oxford. He is a Fellow of the British Academy and a Trustee of the Art Fund. He has carried out archaeological and ethnographic work in Britain, central Europe, Papua New Guinea, and Turkmenistan. He has run projects funded by large grants from the AHRC, ERC, ESRC, and Leverhulme Trust. He has written a number of books and articles, including works on cultural property and issues of post-colonialism. His current interests concern the nature of human intelligence, late prehistoric and Roman period cultural change, art, and aesthetics. Recent works include *Archaeology and Anthropology: a changing relationship* (Routledge, 1999), *Prehistory. A very short introduction* (OUP, 2003), *Archaeology and Colonialism* (CUP, 2004), *Collecting colonialism: material culture and colonial change in Papua New Guinea* (with C. Knowles) (Berg, 2001), 'What do objects want?' (*Journal of Archaeological Method and Theory*, 2005), 'Social Ontologies' (*Philosophical Transactions of the Royal Society B*, 2008), and *A Technology of Enchantment? Exploring Celtic Art: 400 BC to AD 100* (with D. Garrow) (OUP, 2012).

Karen Holmberg received a Ph.D. from Columbia University in 2009; she taught as a postdoctoral fellow at Brown University from 2009–2010 and as a Lecturer at Stanford University in 2011. Her research and teaching interests include cross-cultural perspectives of nature, disaster and risk, and the intersection of natural and social sciences with art, film, and literature. She focuses primarily on volcanic regions as encapsulations of local environments that can change rapidly and catastrophically after long periods of perceived stability, but is interested overall in how people—past and contemporary—relate to changing environments and natural phenomena. She is currently on leave from teaching in order to work on several creative collaborations in New York City.

Marco Irahola is a student of archaeology at the Universidad Mayor de San Andrés, La Paz. Over the last decade he has participated in several national and international archaeological field projects in the Andes and lowlands of Bolivia. His main research interests are lithic technology and resource use of Paleoindian and Archaic hunters and gatherers in the south-central Andes.

Christian Isendahl is Associate Professor of Archaeology at the Department of Archaeology and Ancient History, Uppsala University, Sweden, and conducts fieldwork in Bolivia, Brazil, and Mexico. Among his main research interests are the historical ecology of urbanism, farming systems, and water management. He edited *The Past Ahead: Language, Culture, and Identity in the*

Neotropics (2012) and co-edited *The Urban Mind: Cultural and Environmental Dynamics* (2010) and *Ecology, Power, and Religion in Maya Landscapes* (2011). His most recent papers include 'The Weight of Water: A New Look at Pre-Hispanic Puuc Maya Water Reservoirs' (*Ancient Mesoamerica*), 'The Domestication and Early Spread of Manioc (*Manihot esculenta Crantz*): A Brief Synthesis' (*Latin American Antiquity*), and 'Agro-Urban Landscapes: The Example of Maya Lowland Cities' (*Antiquity*).

Ann Kendall has worked since 1968 in the Central Andes of Peru as an archaeologist, completing an MA at the University of California, Los Angeles, and a PhD at the Institute of Archaeology, University College London. She founded and is Director of the Cusichaca Trust, since 1977, carrying out interdisciplinary archaeological projects including landscape research in the Cuzco area in the Cusichaca and Patacancha valleys with an emphasis on developing applied archaeology in rural development projects. Also an archaeological Project at Juchuy Coscco contributed to early Inca archaeology. From 1997, in Ayacucho and Apurimac the emphasis has been primarily in the implementation of rural development projects, where the focus on applied archaeology in the rehabilitation of the pre-Hispanic terrace systems is resulting locally in commercialization and extensive food support. Currently she is an Honourable Senior Research Fellow at the Institute of Archaeology, UCL. In 1980 she was awarded an Order of Merit by the Peruvian Government and in 1994 the OBE in the U.K.

Fiona Kost graduated with honours degree in Archaeology and Zoology from the University of Western Australia in 2007. After completing a short stint at the Western Australian Museum as Assistant Curator in Anthropology, she returned to the University of Western Australia where she is currently completing a doctorate in Archaeology and teaching undergraduate classes. Her PhD project is an investigation of Aboriginal management practices as revealed in pollen and charcoal changes in sediments representing the last 6,000 years.

Katherine Leckie recently completed her PhD at the Department of Archaeology, University of Cambridge where her thesis explored the collection of Swiss Lake Dwelling artefacts in the UK between 1850 and 1900. Wider research interests include late nineteenth century archaeological collecting practices, archaeological visualization and the production of replicas, artefacts as historic archives, and how material culture is used as evidence in nineteenth century archaeology.

Freda Nkirote M'Mbogori is a Senior Research Scientist based at the Archaeology Department, National Museums of Kenya, Nairobi, with extensive fieldwork in the region spanning 3000 years to the present. Her principal interests lie in the relationship between material culture, economy/environment and identity, and how received concepts played into colonial and present day economic/environmental policies in Eastern Africa.

Kirk Allen Maasch is Professor in the Department of Earth Sciences and the Climate Change Institute at the University of Maine. He has over 20 years of experience using climate models and statistical methods to investigate the causes of climate change. These models range in complexity from simple low-order dynamical systems to complex three-dimensional models of the atmosphere. He is actively involved in modelling present-day and future regional scale climate change using a nested high-resolution climate model. His interests also include inter-annual to decadal scale climate variability in the Holocene and the relationship between climate change and human activities.

Peter Rudiak-Gould is a Mellon Postdoctoral Fellow in the Department of Anthropology, McGill University, with extensive fieldwork experience in the Marshall Islands. His research on public perceptions of climate change has appeared in *Global Environmental Change, Anthropology Today,* and *Public Understanding of Science.* He is the author of the ethnography *Climate Change and Tradition in a Small Island State* (Routledge), a Marshallese language textbook (WorldTeach), and an ethnographic memoir, *Surviving Paradise* (Sterling).

Dagner Salvatierra is a student of archaeology at the Universidad Mayor de San Andrés, La Paz, and studies Andean funerary practices. He has participated in archaeological fieldwork in the Bolivian Andes and is currently associated with the Museo de Metales Preciosos Precolombinos, La Paz.

Walter Sánchez received a PhD in archaeology from Uppsala University, Sweden, in 2008. His archaeological work focuses on landscape archaeology and is aimed at understanding: (1) the interrelationships between the lowlands and the highlands and (2) the dialectical relationship between human agents and environment in the humid Yungas of Cochabamba, Bolivia. He also carries out anthropological, ethnohistorical, and ethnomusicological research with indigenous groups in Bolivia. He has published widely on these and other topics in Bolivia and is the author of the book *Inkas, 'flecheros' y mitmaykuna: Cambio social y paisajes culturales en los Valles y en los Yungas de Inkachaca/Paracti y Tablas Monte (Cochabamba-Bolivia, siglos XV–XVI).* He is currently director of the Instituto de Investigaciones Antropológicas-Museo Arqueológico at the Universidad Mayor de San Simón (www.museo.umss.edu.bo), Cochabamba, and teaches history at the Faculty of Social Sciences at the same university.

Dan Sandweiss is an archaeologist who works in western South America, particularly on the Peruvian coast. He studies the role of climate change (especially El Niño) and maritime adaptations in the prehistory of the region, and he has complementary interests in extracting climatic data from the archaeological record and in understanding the influence of climatic and environmental change on past societies. Sandweiss is Dean and Associate Provost for Graduate Studies and Professor of Anthropology and Quaternary & Climate Studies at the University of Maine, where he joined the faculty in 1993.

Daryl Stump has just completed a Marie Curie Research Fellowship with the European Union-funded Historical Ecologies of East African Landscapes project, at the Department of Archaeology, University of York, and has particular research interests in east African agricultural history and in the potential application of archaeological knowledge. He gained his PhD in African archaeology from UCL in 2006, and currently has three active field-work projects in Tanzania and Ethiopia examining landscape change and the history of local resource management.

Olena Smyntyna is Professor and Director of the Institute of International Education and Head of the Department of Archaeology and Ethnology at Odessa National I.I. Mechnikov University (Odessa, Ukraine). Her principal areas of scientific expertise are Stone Age Archaeology with a specialty of Late Paleolithic and Mesolithic, environmental history and prehistory, the history of environmental thought, and nature–society interaction in historical retrospect. Her main research involves the reconstruction of human responses to global climate change during the Late Pleistocene to Early Holocene in the Northern Pontic region.

Juan Marcelo Ticona received a Licenciatura in archaeology from Universidad Mayor de San Andrés, La Paz, Bolivia, in 2006 and has participated in several national and international field projects in the Bolivian Andes. Among his research interests are the history and prehistory of Andean mining, farming systems and religion. He is currently research associate at the Instituto de Estudios Bolivianos, Universidad Mayor de San Andrés, and teaches at the Universidad Pública del Alto, Bolivia.

Angélica M. Tivoli has recently received her PhD from the University of Buenos Aires and has a CONICET (National Council of Scientific Research, Argentina) post-doctoral fellowship. Her main research concerns the role of birds in the socio-economic organization of prehistoric maritime hunter-gatherers of southern South America, especially subsistence and technology. She has done field work in the Beagle Channel (Tierra del Fuego). Her interests focus on zooarchaelogy, coastal and island archaeology, and methodology.

Atilio Francisco Zangrando is a full-time researcher at CONICET (National Council of Scientific Research, Argentina), and a part-time lecturer at the University of Buenos Aires. He received his PhD from the University of Buenos Aires. His current research focuses on the subsistence of maritime hunter-gatherers in Southern South America, analysing causes of economic and social changes. His lines of research include coastal and island archaeology, intensification of resources, zooarchaeology, and stable isotopes.

Part 1

Archaeology and Environment

This section introduces the volume by outlining the history of archaeological approaches to the environment. In Chapter 1, Davies begins with a discussion of Western perceptions of the environment before assessing how such perceptions have been applied throughout the development of North American and European archaeology. In conclusion Davies looks towards new trends in Landscape archaeology and Historical Ecology and their potential to contribute to our understanding of broader global environmental concerns. In Chapter 2, Smyntyna assesses Soviet and post-Soviet approaches to the archaeology of environment. These approaches display intriguing divergences and convergences with the Western approaches discussed by Davies and highlight new directions for future collaborative research.

1

Environment in North American and European Archaeology

Matthew I. J. Davies

INTRODUCTION

Environment has always been a central concept for Western archaeologists, although it has been conceived in many ways and its role in archaeological explanation has fluctuated from a mere backdrop to human action to a primary factor in the understanding of society and social change. Archaeology also has something of a unique position, for its base of interest positions it temporally between geological and ethnographic timescales, spatially between global and local dimensions, and epistemologically between empirical studies of environment change and more heuristic studies of cultural practice (See Crumley, Chapter 17 and Gosden, Chapter 18 in this volume; see also McIntosh et al. 2000; van der Leeuw and Redman 2002). Archaeology *should* therefore take on a prominent role when it comes to discussion of long-term human–environment interactions up to the present; however, archaeologists have not always been successful in promoting their data or consolidating a clear approach (Fisher and Feinman 2005; Mitchell 2008). As a point of departure, this introductory chapter aims to trace some of the fluctuating conceptions and applications of 'environment' within North American and European archaeology, with a particular emphasis on new trends and fruitful points of intersection between seemingly diverse paradigms. The history of concepts of the environment could take up a whole volume of its own and so this chapter is necessarily partial; however, I hope that it will raise a number of points of interest that can be explored further through the references given. The geographical range is also limited to broadly North American and European (especially British) archaeology. In the following chapter Olena Smyntyna will discuss the concept of environment in Soviet and post-Soviet archaeology, while it is hoped that future scholars may fruitfully write the history of such issues in other regional traditions.

The chapter is split into three parts. The first deals with diverse ways in which 'environment' has been conceived or defined in Western thought, particularly within archaeology. The second concerns itself with an examination of the changing historical role of environment as an aspect of explanation in the archaeological record, particularly differing perspectives on the ways in which humans interact with their 'environment' and how environments are both shaped by and come to shape human societies. The third section examines the current state of archaeological approaches to human–environment relations and outlines two diverse approaches, historical ecology and post-structural landscape archaeology, as important developments with significant and potentially productive points of intersection.

CONCEIVING CULTURE AND ENVIRONMENT

The term 'environment' is used widely in the social sciences and humanities. Nevertheless, understandings of the environment are highly contested and vary significantly from 'objective' understandings based on empirical observations of quantified species lists, climatic records, and geological typologies through to more abstract notions of perceived or cognitive environments as partial but meaningful social constructs. It is also almost impossible to define 'environment' without recourse to the concept of 'culture', with which it is commonly contrasted.

Cartesian concepts of environment

Common Western notions of the environment tend to derive from a position of Cartesian duality, whereby the environment is considered to be 'natural' (given) and distinct from human culture; a physical or material property, being subject to quantitative description and formal rules or laws derived from rational experimentation. In contrast, culture is viewed as an intangible property of the human mind which can be highly variable and difficult to characterize, let alone quantify. Such notions also often consider human impact on the environment to be minimal, and make a distinction between the 'natural' environment—relatively untouched by humans—and the 'built' environment as a construct of human culture. This 'natural vs built' perspective partially stems from the European imperial encounter and was enhanced by the industrial revolution, such that Europeans viewed themselves as having obtained the ability to transcend nature while the indigenous peoples that they met were characterized as constrained by—or even locked in—a perpetual battle with their natural environment (Ingold 2000: 62–6; Leckie, Chapter 13 this volume).

The twentieth century formulation of the Cartesian perspective is characterized by the influence of Darwinian evolutionism, key to which is the notion of human culture as an aspect of (evolutionary) adaptation to the environment (Ingold 2000: 27–39). Such ideas were common in the late nineteenth century and gained renewed vigour during the mid-twentieth century with the advent of the neo-Darwinian synthesis. Neo-Darwinianism became particularly prevalent in both the social and biological sciences, from where it has fed strongly into archaeology, particularly the processual or 'new' archaeology of the 1960s onwards. Two particularly important but divergent strands of thought were influential; the first, commonly termed 'cultural ecology' (Steward 1955a), considered human culture to be on the one hand 'extra-environmental' (that is, a product of the human mind rather than natural biology) but also to be humanity's means of adapting to the given or natural environment. Cultural ecology tended towards technological and environmental determinism, in that, while allowing that humans might shape an environment through their actions, it saw the ways in which that environment might be shaped as strongly constrained by environmental and technological limitations. At extremes this approach suggested that society, technology, and environment might be deterministically linked as a series of universal types—'equatorial foragers' or 'swidden cultivators'.

The second strand stems from behavioural ecology and sees human cultural behaviour as a natural characteristic of humans as a biological species. In its most extreme form, known as 'sociobiology' (Wilson 1975), all culture is viewed as an evolved biological characteristic and its analysis is reduced to understandings of how culture is determined by the requirement to satisfy basic biological needs such as subsistence and reproduction. This approach is still common among many biologists and ecologists though it has become somewhat more sophisticated in the approach of theorists such as Richard Dawkins (Dawkins 1976) whose concept of 'memes' as a unit of meaningful cultural evolution has given culture a 'life of its own' and drawn the debate away from culture as purely biological adaptation to environment (see also Blackmore 1999; Cullen 1995; Shennan 2002).

While extreme forms of sociobiology were largely rejected by archaeologists[1], its impact on human ecologists was more subtle, and in recent years its influence has filtered back into archaeology through more ecologically oriented studies. Cultural ecology, on the other hand, had a much more direct influence, not least because its emphasis on culture and technology as adaptation to a

---

[1] While extreme sociobiology was clearly difficult for many social-science researchers to accept, its complete rejection was perhaps in part encouraged by strongly cultural-relativist (some might say culturally deterministic) positions widespread in anthropology at the time.

relatively independent and objectively measurable 'environment' was particularly appealing to the positivistic archaeology of the 1960s and 1970s. Indeed, cultural ecology influenced the foundations of modern archaeology and its positive effect, in terms of turning archaeology into a more professionally scientific discipline with a core base focused on the study of technology and (subsistence) economy, cannot be underestimated. Nevertheless, cultural ecology further entrenched the Cartesian view of culture vs nature and built vs natural environment and particularly the idea that environments are to some extent given and can be objectively quantified through scientific study and then applied cross-culturally[2].

As will become apparent below and in the following chapters of this volume, while this basic Cartesian view is now highly outdated in some academic circles, it remains pervasive in popular and less critical approaches to the environment. In particular, it has continued to foster a somewhat problematic yet common notion of humans as either 'adapted' or, conversely, 'maladapted' to their environment; a theme to which I return in the final section of the chapter (see also Davies, Chapter 4 this volume).

Perceptual approaches to environment

In contrast to the positivistic Cartesian view, the now general anthropological approach is to recognize that the environment is in no way a given or objective phenomenon, but rather that all perspectives or views of the environment are social or cultural constructs (see Davies, Chapter 4; Fiore et al., Chapter 5; and Chevalier, Chapter 6 this volume). In this frame of reference the distinction between culture and environment remains core, but human interaction with the environment is recognized to operate not through a given 'natural' environment but rather through culturally constructed perceptions *of* the environment.

At one extreme this perspective reifies the role of culture to such an extent that any sense of the 'physical environment' disappears and attempts to 'objectively' characterize past or present physical environments are seen as inherently flawed. In this view no such thing as environment exists, only ways in which people perceive the world around them; and only in Western thought do these perceptions become anything like the Western scientific concept of environment: such environments are constructed of meanings rather than physical properties. In archaeology the Phenomenological approach of Tilley (1994) and others (Bender et al. 1997) takes this perspective to the extreme and aims to understand how past peoples acted within an environment or

---

[2] Thus all cultures with the same degree of technology should view the same environment in approximately the same way.

landscape inscribed or imbued with cultural meanings. This approach has certainly done much to help archaeologists re-think past environments, particularly in regard to how they may have played into identity and belief, but has come under considerable criticism for neglecting the role of economy or subsistence and for relying heavily upon the highly subjective experiences of the archaeologist; a criticism that echoes broader critiques of the post-processual movement (Barrett and Ko 2009; Fleming 2005a, 2005b).

At the other extreme is the somewhat more pragmatic school which makes a distinction between 'real' and 'perceived' or 'physical' and 'cognitive' environments and which in archaeology is often associated with Karl Butzer (1982)[3]. This approach is particularly attractive within archaeology because it maintains a strong connection with the physical sciences and with archaeology's own broad base of 'environmental' archaeologists (see below), while recognizing the cultural construction of the environment. Butzer points out that humans act not on the objective or 'real' environment but on their own perceptions of it, but nevertheless maintains that we can still 'objectively' reconstruct past environments in part and that such reconstructions are certainly useful heuristic tools. However, this distinction between real and perceived environment emphasizes the dichotomy between environment and culture, which many find problematic. Indeed, this dichotomy has been at the heart of a major debate in anthropology for a number of decades.

Environment as process

This debate is based on the longstanding anthropological distinction between 'emic' and 'etic' accounts, the former being accounts of cultural conceptions of the world and the latter of given, objective, reality. Positions such as that of Lévi-Strauss (1974; cf. Ingold 2000: 15–18), relied on the emic/etic distinction and argued that the mind acts to decode perceptual information through a template or cipher. The perceptual information received by each observer is constant because reality (etic) is given, but the template has subtle cultural differences (although limited to the physical structural properties of the mind) leading to the production of differing emic accounts. In contrast, a variety of *praxis* or social practice based approaches argue that all knowledge about the world is created at the point of practical interaction with the world (Bateson 1973; Gibson 1979). Exact knowledge about the world does not pre-exist, only inherited clues about how it operates, so that the world is not decoded but manifested in an instance of 'revelation' (Ingold 2000: 18). This perspective is important for it implies that all organisms and their environment are mutually

---

[3] Although such thinking in archaeology goes back at least as far as Childe (Trigger 1989: 261).

constituted. It suggests that the organism is created through interaction with the world and also that the world is created through interaction with the organism in a continuous process. In contrast to much thinking in biology, and especially the concept of Darwinian evolution as adaptation to environment, this approach does not set up the organism and its environment as mutually exclusive entities; rather, as Ingold (2000: 19) argues, life is 'active rather than reactive ... [it] is not the realization of pre-specified forms but rather the process whereby forms are generated and held in place'.

This approach further deconstructs the Cartesian view and challenges aspects of Darwinian evolution by arguing that the organism and its mind are themselves part of the environment. The organism cannot adapt to an environment of which it is a part for in its adaptation it would intrinsically alter the environment—cause and effect in this scenario do not act in a linear fashion between one thing or another but rather through the multiple complex pathways of an integrated system. Neither the organism nor the environment is ever given or static but is always part of an ongoing *process* of creation. The 'environment' does not exist, rather 'an environment' is relative to the organism at any one time or in any one context but such perspectives are always fleeting. In terms of human perception, we do not 'live' in a given environment, but rather, to take Ingold's terminology, we *dwell* within it; we are part of a changing environment and it is part of us (Ingold 1993, 2000; see also Balée, Chapter 3 this volume for a similar concept of 'indigeneity'). It also follows from this that human action is conditioned by a mixture of convention and innovative intentionality (social practice) and therefore that human culture is never the sole product of environment but rather that human intentionality acts in part to shape both the physical world and the changing nature of culture (Bourdieu 1977; Giddens 1984; Tilley 1981; see also Davies, Chapter 4 this volume).

Environment as social practice

From a human perspective we might argue that the environment is constructed through 'social practice' as an ongoing process of change, with a history that may be inscribed on the landscape (Ingold 1993), and that present environments are a product of this history, so that explaining the constitution of an environment today requires a historical perspective. Modern British landscape archaeology, although far from homogenous, has strongly embraced this approach of environment as ongoing process, as well as a range of scientific, perceptual and phenomenological approaches. In particular, it has tended to sideline the concept of culture as adaptation to environment and instead focus on human perceptions of, and impacts on, an environment (Darvil 2008; Strang 2008; Tilley 1994). Key to this approach is the term 'landscape', which encompasses environmental history, with a specific focus on its (built) human component. One important development with potential practical applications is the way in which archaeologists and environmental historians are beginning to realize that the landscape does not just have a history of its own, but also a history of perceptions towards it—especially various Western perceptions which have played into the ways in which landscapes have been (mis-)managed through intervention schemes (Anderson 1984; see also Kost, Chapter 7 and Stump, Chapter 10 this volume). Another important dimension is the realization that environmental processes operate over historical (rather than experimental) timescales and that stasis may be uncharacteristic of ecological systems (see Crumley, Chapter 18 this volume). Such approaches draw on 'complexity theory' and have developed in the 'New Ecology' of biologists from where they are influencing archaeology via theoretical positions such as historical ecology (see below).

Perhaps most important, however, is the way in which this concept, of environment as process through social practice, breaks down the Cartesian separation between mind and physical reality. This position strongly challenges the concept of culture as adaptation (or indeed mal-adaptation) and argues for a much more sophisticated historical approach to human environment interactions (Barret and Ko 2009; Tilley 1981). These are themes which I take up in the final part of this chapter; but before doing so I wish to trace the impact of some of these various conceptions of the environment on the history of archaeology.

THE ENVIRONMENT IN EURO-AMERICAN ARCHAEOLOGY

The concept of environment has been invoked in Western archaeological accounts in three primary and often overlapping ways that partially mirror the grand theoretical phases of the discipline itself (Trigger 1989). The first use is purely descriptive and understands that the 'given environment' within which past communities lived is an essential aspect of their character, and that it is therefore a basic task of archaeology to describe environmental context as an aspect of past life. The second takes a synchronic perspective, invoking the environment to partially explain the specific nature or constitution of a society at any given time. This approach is 'functional', in that human cultures are viewed as 'adapting' to the environment in various ways such that the archaeological record is explained, in whole or in part, as a function of the environment at that time. The third approach invokes environment as a prime mover of change in the archaeological record. It often accords 'natural' environmental events, beyond the control of humans, as key factors in major social transformations such as the origins of farming, states, and urbanism as well as societal collapse. The second and third approaches are closely linked, for both see adaptation to environment as a key human relationship; however, in more recent years the third approach has tended to also emphasize the way in which humans significantly alter or modify their environments, particularly with a focus on negative impacts and 'environmental collapse'.

Environment as context

Within the evolutionary perspective of the mid- to late-nineteenth century, history was often seen as a narrative of human struggles with nature; as a battle of the fittest to overcome the limitations of the environment (see Holmberg, Chapter 12 and Leckie, Chapter 13 this volume). Non-Western peoples were considered to be trapped in their environment at early stages of development or, worse, in some anti-evolutionary accounts, to have degenerated from more 'advanced' forms due to the un-fortuitous nature of their surroundings (Trigger 1989: 102). Non-Western peoples were conceived of as exemplars of past evolutionary stages, each of which encompassed the increasing mastery of humans (particularly Europeans) over nature. Such thinking is deeply ingrained into the grand accounts of prehistory of the period, perhaps the best known being those of John Lubbock (1865) in Britain and Lewis Henry Morgan (1877) and Otis Mason (1895) in North America. However, despite this implicit emphasis on the relationship between humans and their environment, past human environments were rarely considered in great detail and specific causal relationships between environmental characteristics and human societies were rarely expounded.

In the mid-nineteenth century it was in Scandinavia that prehistoric archaeology was at the forefront of the scientific perspective of the discipline, and it is here that archaeologists first began to cooperate with geologists and emerging environmental scientists to better understand the environmental context of past societies. The pioneer in this field was Jens J.A. Worsaae (1849), a Dane who worked closely with the biologist Japetus Steenstrup and other specialists to correlate vegetational changes in Denmark with the transition from the Stone Age through the Bronze and Iron Ages. However, it was unclear what effect these environmental changes had had on past communities, and the correlation was used principally as a chronological tool. Nevertheless, Worsaae encouraged the development of a more interdisciplinary archaeology, and began to turn the discipline away from simple typologies towards a more holistic understanding of past communities in all of their aspects, including environmental context.

In Britain and France, the influence of Worsaae's holistic Scandinavian archaeology was felt only slowly, partly because attention was drawn towards Palaeolithic archaeology and the question of the antiquity of humankind (Trigger 1989: 87). However, as this question was gradually settled it encouraged a more detailed focus on the Palaeolithic and the establishment of a relative chronology that subdivided the period into a series of phases. Implicit in this typology was the correlation of cultural phases with environmental conditions, particularly successions of vegetation and fossilized mammalian fauna set against the backdrop of glacial advance and retreat. Perhaps the most influential chronology of the time was that of Edouard Lartet, who subdivided the Palaeolithic into a series of phases correlated with mammalian fauna, such as Auroch and Bison, Reindeer, Mammoth and Woolly Rhinoceros, and Cave Bear (Trigger 1989: 95). While Lartet's sequence was overturned by later writers, there remained an implicit correlation between archaeological phases or epochs on the one hand and geological or environmental sequences on the other (de Mortillet 1897).

By the last decades of the nineteenth century a growing disillusion with enlightenment ideas of human progress and technical advancement (including human mastery over nature) made itself felt in archaeology. Emerging nationalism fed into the idea that cultural and ethnic variations were biologically determined and that the primary human condition was one of stasis and resistance to cultural change. As a consequence, diffusion and migration (as opposed to environmental conditions) acting upon 'cultural' groups became popular as explanations for change and variation in the archaeological record (Ratzel 1896–8). These concepts were taken up by Franz Boas in North America, where, rejecting the idea of cultural evolution, he championed cultural relativism and historical particularism (Trigger 1989: 151). In these new formulations, human societies were no longer seen as in an evolutionary struggle with the environment; rather, each culture, corresponding to a particular ethnic group, was seen as having its own culture-history shaped by chance external influences and, to a lesser extent, local environmental conditions.

The concept of an archaeological culture with its own history shaped by multiple factors (principal among which was diffusion) was most forcefully introduced into European archaeology by V. Gordon Childe in *The Dawn of European Civilisation* (1925). In the United States, Alfred V. Kidder's (1924) culture-historical analysis of the archaeology of the American Southwest, followed by Ford and Willey's (1941) analysis of the Eastern United States, also marked something of a turning point. Childe's concept of culture introduced a new focus to the study of how societies had lived in the past and helped to realign British archaeology with that of Scandinavia.

While Childe's early work is characterized by the idea that human cultural and technological inventions occur only rarely and then diffuse to other regions, his later work is also concerned with explaining how and why those innovations arose in the first place. In this he begins to think of environment as one of the major influences on human development, and in doing so his studies mark the early origins of a much more analytical archaeology which moved beyond description and chronology and towards explanation of specific social characteristics and transitions. Childe's (1942: 49) most notable hypothesis in this respect is the idea, borrowed from Raphael Pumpelly (1908), that desiccation during the early Holocene caused people, plants, and animals to concentrate around fertile oases where close proximity led to domestication. This invocation of environmental factors to explain major transitions in pre-history has remained common up to the present.

This increased emphasis on archaeological cultures and 'how' people had lived in the past went hand in hand with much improved techniques for recording and recovering the archaeological record. In particular, archaeologists began collecting and analysing faunal remains and sampling for botanical remains. Researchers in the Scandinavian tradition had, by the first decades of the twentieth century, developed elaborate chronologies of glacial and sea level changes as well as long climatic and floral and faunal records. The Swede Leenart Von Post conducted the first extensive analysis of vegetation change based on pollen cores, and in the late 1920s pollen analysis was introduced into British archaeology by Harry Godwin (1933). Other pioneers began analysing the relationships between soil and vegetation types and prehistoric settlement patterns (Fox 1922; Willey 1953; cf. Clarke 1977). Work on Swiss lake villages was particularly important with regard to the development of improved biological recovery and analysis, as recounted by Leckie (Chapter 13 this volume).

As analytical techniques improved, so disillusionment grew with the grand diffusion based narratives of the culture-historical approach and there emerged a new emphasis on how societies functioned and changed as social systems. This new paradigm was greatly influenced by the development of British structural-functional social anthropology, which aimed to understand not how cultures existed within an evolutionary or diffusionist paradigm but rather how societies operated synchronically as a series of functionally interdependent social institutions. Although the transition was gradual, the development of social anthropology and the new emphasis on how societies operated marked another turning point in archaeological theorizing. Foremost in this was a move away from descriptive narrative accounts, in which environment was principally conceived as a backdrop or the context of human action, towards explanatory accounts which sought out causal factors, such as the environment, to explain both the constitution of the archaeological record at any one time and processes of change through time.

The development of techniques for environmental reconstruction that began in the early twentieth century progressed with speed such that by the 1960s one could talk of 'environmental archaeology' as a sub-discipline in its own right (David and Thomas 2008b; O'Connor and Evans 2005: 5; see also Evans 1978). This division remains up to the present with environmental archaeology (including palaeoecology, palaeo- and archeo-botany, zooarchaeology, and bioarchaeology) often seen as an objective, scientific, endeavour divorced from more speculative elements of the discipline. Indeed, palaeoenvironmental sampling and reconstruction have become integral and routine aspects of the procedure of archaeological enquiry. However, there has also often been a tendency for palaeoenvironmental data simply to be added into archaeological accounts as background or contextual information, rather than as a critical aspect of archaeological analysis. This division within archaeology itself mirrors that between the humanities and the physical sciences, and tends to reinforce the conceptual division between culture and environment as separate entities for study (Edwards 2001).

Environment as explanation

While V. Gordon Childe's concept of culture gradually introduced functionalism into archaeology, his own brand on functionalism was very heavily influenced by Marxist ideas and allowed only a minor causal role to environmental factors. Grahame Clark (1939), however, was much more explicitly ecological in his approach, arguing that culture was largely influenced by environment. Clark differed greatly from his predecessors in that he explicitly introduced biological concepts into archaeological thinking, most notably the idea of an ecosystem as a self-regulating and self-contained balanced system (Clark 1952). His excavations at the Mesolithic site of Star Carr in Yorkshire, England further introduced new standards for the recovery, analysis and interpretation of environmental indicators. Clark also influenced a new generation who began to study prehistoric economies as a function of the reciprocal interaction between culture and the environment. Most notable was the establishment of concerted research into palaeoeconomics at the University of Cambridge. This work was strongly associated with Eric Higgs and the site catchment analysis (SCA) approach to settlements and their surrounding environment (Vita-Finzi and Higgs 1970).

In North America, the work of Walter Taylor (1948) was also highly influential in bringing about a functionalist approach toward a fuller understanding of human communities. However, Taylor was less influenced than Clark by the concept of human societies as 'organic' self-regulating ecosystems, championed by anthropologists such as Radcliffe-Brown (1922) and Malinowski (1922). Neither Clark nor Taylor was particularly concerned with how processes of change occurred in the archaeological record. Like social anthropologists of the time, their focus was more on how societies operated at a single 'synchronic' moment rather than how they changed 'diachronically'

through time. This particular task was taken up instead by Julian Steward
(1955) whose 'cultural ecology' approach came to be particularly influential as
a theoretical tool for explaining both the nature of prehistoric cultures at any
one time and major processes of cultural change. In general Steward focused
on technology and environment as the two major variables affecting socio-
cultural structure, and placed great emphasis on culture as adaptation to
environment. Apart from punctuated change due to changes in natural environment or to technological advancement, societies were seen to be relatively
static systems.

Although very different, the ecological approaches of Clark and Steward
have remained influential in much archaeological research up to the present.
In the 1950s they fed into a number of large-scale interdisciplinary projects
that aimed to analyse change in the archaeological record and reinterpret the
origins of sedentarization, farming, urbanization, and political centralization
in both the Old and New Worlds. Following Steward, these projects took a
much more expansive approach to the archaeological record. In particular,
they conducted research into prehistoric settlement patterns and analysed
numerous sites in conjunction as aspects of broad-scale adaptive patterns to
regional environments. Such analysis included extensive reconstruction of
changing palaeoenvironments by multidisciplinary specialists and the application of a suite of interdisciplinary techniques. Most notable among these was
Braidwood's research into the Neolithic of the Near East where environmental
factors such as climate, vegetation, and fauna were correlated with archaeological data to produce a deeper understanding of the origins of farming
(Braidwood and Howe 1960). However, while such large-scale archaeological
analyses were often initially conceived as attempts to understand human social
systems in relation to their surrounding environment, the collation of broader
data sets gradually moved understandings of causal change away from purely
ecological 'prime mover' explanations and towards a greater focus on politics,
ideology, and innovation (Flannery 1972).

Nevertheless, despite acknowledging the complexity of causal relationship
apparent in the work of many research projects, North American archaeology
remained very strongly influenced during the 1960s by an emerging 'neo-
evolutionary' perspective with a much narrower focus on causality. This neo-
evolutionism drew very heavily on the ecosytemic approach of Steward and
viewed societies as relatively static and resistant to change except when
external factors beyond their control, most notably the environment and
technological advancement, forced change upon them. Steward advanced a
form of historical particularism of his own termed 'multilinear evolution',
which sought to analyse individual societies as the product of their own
specific evolution within specific environments while at the same time recognizing that at the core of each culture will be a series of features closely related
to subsistence practices and having an environmentally adaptive function.

Steward argued that cultures having similar environments and levels of technology will share core cultural features and that these core features might be formed into a generalized evolutionary sequence.

While Steward's theorizing was more sophisticated than often given credit, the multilinear approach played into a more simplistic unilinear evolutionism popularized by the developmental sequences (band, tribe, chiefdom, state, and so on) of Service (1962), Fried (1967), and Sahlins (1968) (cf. Flannery 1972), which effectively categorized societies based on 'core' social structures. These sequences, supported by the environmental and technological determinism of Steward, were highly attractive to archaeologists and ethnographers alike, since they assumed that social structure or the cultural core could be read from the basic formula of technology plus environment, factors which were readily accessible to archaeology. In addition, the idea that social structure, envisaged as a scheme of increasing socio-political centralization, could be read directly from tiered settlement hierarchies (evident in increasingly sophisticated approaches to settlement patterns) suggested that a combination of the study of technology, settlement, and environment could produce a highly satisfying archaeological account of past societies and past social change with a clear research methodology. Perhaps most importantly, this perspective realigned archaeology into an attractive association with the physical or natural sciences; attention was refocused towards schemes of *human* development characterized by general laws of change that could be explained in potentially quantitative terms, and human societies were conceived of as predominantly the product of natural or non-human (non-cultural) phenomena.

The 'New Archaeology' championed by Lewis Binford (Binford 1962, 1965; Binford and Binford 1968; cf. Calwell 1959) built on this ecological and evolutionary perspective and made explicit the realignment with positivism. Heavily influenced by Leslie White, Binford treated culture principally as a means of adaptation to the environment and re-centred the concept of the ecosystem at the heart of archaeological explanation. In the New Archaeology human economic actions shared a universal rationality and were 'optimized' to a given and relatively static set of environmental conditions (see Fiore et al., Chapter 4 this volume, for a more detailed discussion of concepts of 'optimality' in archaeological thought).

Binford's preoccupation with ecology restricted the explanatory room for internal cultural innovation or social dynamics to effect change within societies, and instead located the cause of change in external and often natural or environmental factors. The New Archaeology further facilitated the introduction into archaeology of systems theory, in which human ecologies were analysed as general systems consisting of interdependent parts. The comparison here with the functional analysis of societies using the 'organic' analogy of Radcliff-Brown is striking (Tilley 1981), with the difference that the new systems analysis introduced the concept of feedback and therefore offered a tool for explaining internal processes of change (Trigger 1989: 303). Initially, the systems analysis approach focused on the relationship between environment, subsistence, and technology but as it increased in sophistication it began to consider a wider range of reciprocally influencing factors such as politics, religion, conflict, and human experimentation (Adams 1966; Flannery 1972). Within later 'multivariate' systems theory, the importance of the environment was gradually downgraded, so that rather than being seen as a primary causal factor it came to be described as a constraint or restriction on the possible forms of social behaviour. More importantly, although multivariate systems analysis tended towards the description of socio-economic systems and failed to deconstruct the neo-evolutionary paradigm (see Flannery 1972), it did draw attention away from narrow ecological approaches and brought a new level of sophistication to the analysis of human societies as both ecological and cultural phenomena.

In the United Kingdom David Clarke (1968) promoted his own brand of the 'New' or 'processual' archaeology, which also came to emphasize the primacy of ecological relationships. However, while the New Archaeology of Binford drew on American traditions of cultural anthropology (with a strongly ecological perspective), Clarke was greatly influenced by the analytical turn in geography during the 1960s, and particularly by the development of quantitative spatial analysis. Nevertheless, in both North America and the United Kingdom, the New Archaeology began to encourage 'regional' and 'off-site' archaeology (Foley 1981) rather than site-based approaches, and began to think of archaeological data as 'continuous' across the landscape (David and Thomas 2008). This further allowed for the cross-referencing of archaeological data with continuous environmental data on, for example, soils or vegetation. Clarke's emphasis on statistical models was further taken up and developed by younger researchers such as Ian Hodder (Hodder 1978; Hodder and Orton 1976), although some of the statistics tended to erase environment from the study of socio-cultural systems and to deal with spatial distributions in highly abstract forms. As in North America, the British processual archaeology gradually drifted away from ecological concerns and into more detailed studies of politics, economy, exchange, and distribution. But British archaeology was not so strongly influenced by the neo-evolutionary paradigm, and further ideas and concepts were borrowed both from human geographers (Hodder 1987; Wagstaff 1987) and social anthropologists (Hodder 1982a, 1982b), including structuralists, leading to deeper concerns over the socially constructed perception of the natural world and the ways in which this plays into identity and meaningful communication and action. Similarly, in continental Europe the 1980s saw a gradual movement away from 'adaptationist' accounts and towards the study of human societies as 'complex systems' (van der Leeuw 1981).

Hodder's early explorations of statistical analyses of distributions led to much more detailed analysis of the spatial patterning of culture and the ways in which such distributions reflected identities, beliefs, and cognitive structures rather than simple ecological relations (Hodder 1978, 1982a, 1982b). Hodder's 'post-processual' or 'contextual' archaeology allowed for factors internal to society—such as underlying structures and cognitive systems, individual agency, class or interest group relations, or kinship—to act causally in processes of social change (see Davies, Chapter 4; Fiore et al. Chapter 5; Chevalier, Chapter 6; and Rudiak-Gould, Chapter 14 this volume for specific examples of how such factors operate). While such 'internal' factors had gradually developed as important within systems theory and developed processualism, they were accorded greater centrality in the approaches of Hodder and others and therefore marked a major break from the processualism of Binford, which sought out primary causal factors external to the human realm. Although a significant theoretical advance, the post-processual movement has also somewhat polarized archaeology between those studies founded on the heritage of processualism, in which ecological and economic relationships are accorded primacy, and those which focus on symbolic and cognitive elements of the archaeological record. This polarization has strongly influenced the development of British landscape archaeology, which, although initially associated with processualism, has grown to be associated with post-processualism, post-structuralism and phenomenology (David and Thomas 2008b; Darvill 2008; Tilley 1994). While incorporating a much wider range of factors and models, North American 'landscape' archaeology has in contrast tended to remain grounded in ecological and settlement pattern studies (Patterson 2008).

Stemming from the systems theory of the 1970s, a somewhat pessimistic turn in archaeological literature is the focus on environmental and social collapse. In contrast to the processualism of Binford, which viewed societies as ecologically adapted, the developed processualism of systems theory, influenced by Malthusian economics and growing popular concerns over anthropogenic environmental damage, noted how conditions of feedback generated by human action may act to irreparably degrade environments and cause societal collapse. Much of this research focused on the collapse of well known societies such as the Classic Maya (Demarest 2004; Webster 2002), Chaco Canyon (Vivian 1990) and Easter Island (Flenley and Bahn 2002) and has continued to the present, playing very strongly into the popular imagination (Diamond 2005; see McAnany and Yoffee 2010 for a critique). The extent to which such events provide clear lessons for the future remains controversial but is an issue treated with due caution by Anderson et al. in Chapter 15 of this volume.

Reconceptualizing human–environment interactions

The diverse body of critiques and perspectives known as post-processualism has shifted the focus of much academic archaeological research away from ecology, even though post-processualism does not inherently discard empiricism or reject the importance of subsistence and economy. It does however argue that the relationships between culture and environment are much more complex than assumed by processualism—that the two are at least mutually constituted and that internally generated cultural traits may have as much of an impact on the environment as the environment has on culture (a theme well discussed in the Soviet tradition: see Smyntyna, Chapter 2 this volume). Indeed it implicitly recognizes that humans actively shape or manipulate their environments, and that they do so not through an objective understanding of the environment but through culturally or historically shaped perceptions of the environment. As noted above, Butzer (1982) is often accredited with such a distinction, though his approach remained grounded in ecology and cultural adaptation. Post-processual landscape archaeology on the other hand strongly recognizes the 'non-environmental' determinants of human behaviour, and points instead to the way in which symbolism and meaning inherent within the landscape interactively shape the way that that landscape is used, both for subsistence or economy and also to re-inscribe meaning (David and Thomas 2008a). For example, Hodder's (1991) *The Domestication of Europe* argued that the process of neolithization in Europe was not only a technical and economic revolution but also a revolution in the way that the environment was perceived, through a process of 'domestication' akin to the taming of nature[4]. Looking at the landscape with respect to both monuments and 'natural places', Bradley (1998, 2000) similarly argues for the creation of a new sense of space and time during the Neolithic.

Many of these new trends in archaeology have been influenced by commensurate trends in social anthropology, and particularly by the development of post-structuralism, which accords deep importance to the agency of individuals both in terms of reproducing and transmitting cultural structures and also in innovatively manipulating them. Consequently, culture itself comes to be seen as an agent of change, including in relation to the environment. Environment and society (nature and culture) must therefore be seen as mutually constituted as an integral whole. While some trends have sought to define landscape as individual or community perception of the physical world, or the interface through which humans interact with the physical world (Hirsch and O'Hanlon 1995) Ingold (2000) and others (such as Gibson

---

[4] Also involving the construction of a concept of the wild as untamed nature. See Kost, Chapter 7 and Stump, Chapter 10 this volume for detailed discussions of changing environmental perceptions in the more recent past.

1979), emphasize the importance of social practice and argue that 'landscape' as a model of the physical world is a misleading reversion to Cartesian duality. They would rather emphasise that all knowledge about the world is generated at the point of interaction with it and the context of that generation is always a mixture of history and improvization.

Unfortunately, despite these critiques, archaeologists brought up in the Western tradition are still often attracted to the Cartesian dialectic between environment and culture. Within archaeology, past environments are still commonly treated as objectively given and as independent causal variables which may be used to explain both the nature of society at any one time and the nature of social change[5]. An obvious example is the way in which the new spatial technologies of Geographical Information Systems (GIS) were quickly incorporated into archaeology and yet initially offered highly deterministic environmental explanations (Lock 2003).

APPLIED ENVIRONMENTAL ARCHAEOLOGY

What then does archaeology have to offer in today's academic and global climate (Fisher and Feinman 2005; Mitchell 2008)? As mentioned above, archaeology has fed into growing popular concerns over global environmental and climatic change in at least two ways. The first and most direct impact is through its concern with societal collapse, which has both publicized the fact that other great civilizations have fallen owing to their misuse of the environment and also made claim to some archaeological predictive power which might be used to inform humanity in the future (Anderson et al. 2007a; Diamond 2005; Tainter 2000). This first impact is misleading both in the way that it reduces the complexity of social collapse to mainly environmental factors[6] and in relation to the predictive power of archaeology, which to date has struggled to produce substantial results.

The second impact is more subtle and stems from the Cartesian view of nature and culture and the way in which archaeology has often portrayed prehistoric societies as either living in harmony with their environment as part of an adaptive system or living out of harmony with their environment as part of a mal-adapted system. Van der Leeuw and Redman (2002) have traced this interplay between 'reactive' and 'proactive' conceptions of human–environment

---

[5] That is, while environmental factors beyond human control (such as a volcanic eruption) may cause socio-cultural change, they do not specify the nature of that change, or even always its scale. See Rudiak-Gould, Chapter 14 for a good example of how environmental disasters have a variable social impact.

[6] It also simplifies the debate concerning whether such 'collapses' really were 'collapses' or actually economic or political shifts/readjustments.

relations and argue for archaeology's role in a more 'recursive' analysis of integrated 'socionatural' systems.

On one hand adaptationist visions of the past play strongly into popular modern environmental narratives that reify traditional or local environmental management practices over external or modern scientific interventions. In contrast, maladaptive images play into modernizing environmental narratives that emphasize humanly induced environmental degradation and advocate Western intervention into local environmental management practices (Anderson 1984; Richards 1993; Sillitoe 1998). Both stances implicitly see human action as external to, and distinct from, the 'environment' rather than a principal constituent part. In both arguments, the environment is conceived of as having a 'natural' static state, which is both timeless and intrinsically 'good'. In the first argument, humans are viewed as living in balance with the environment as custodians, altering it for neither better nor worse. In the second, humans are conversely seen as parasites drawing on the resources of the natural environment and causing degradation of species, soils, and other biophysical components. Balée (1998) has referred to these contrasting perspectives as those of the 'ecologically noble savage' and '*homo devestans*' and pointed out the fallacy of both, noting that humans always alter the composition of biophysical components in their surroundings, but that such action does not always result in the degradation of biodiversity, let alone a reduction in systemic resilience (see also van der Leeuw and Redman 2002). Nevertheless, this second perspective has become particularly influential in archaeology over recent years, such that processual studies of the 1970s framed along lines of the adaptable 'ecologically noble savage' have been replaced by popularist archaeological accounts of the '*homo devestans*' kind which play on environmental concerns of the 1990s–2000s and emphasize humanly induced environmental devastation and societal collapse. As Balée describes in Chapter 3 of this volume, environments are 'indigenous': they are part of the culture of the people who inhabit them and as such we must be wary of attaching universalizing rational (and often moral) judgements to the environmental actions of both past and present communities.

Serious academic archaeology of course offers a counterpoint to both of these positions. The first is to reassert the complexity of ancient societal collapse and to more fully explore the lessons to be learnt from the past without overt simplification (see Anderson this volume; McAnany and Yoffee 2010). This requires much more sophisticated modelling of human–environment relations, in which archaeological data might readily provide a long-term empirical dataset. The second impact requires more fundamental counteraction and involves a strong reassertion and exemplification of the mutually constitutive nature of humans and the environment. Such an approach would demonstrate that humans do not adapt to their environment but rather that they are part of it—that they have always altered the biophysical components of their surroundings (for better and worse) and that human cultural phenomena at all levels do play an essential role in the way in which we as a species interact with the environment. It follows that to understand how humans effect environment change and consequently how we might consciously effect new changes, we must first understand the range of perspective humans have of the environment, and what motivates them to change their actions (see for example Rudiak-Gould, Chapter 14 this volume).

However, archaeology can offer more than this, and examples are outlined in the following chapters and summarized in Table 1.1. In particular, there is a growing recognition that environmental changes operate at temporal and spatial scales which have often lacked consideration and that archaeology

Table 1.1. Summary of possible archaeological contributions to global and local environmental debates

Contribution	Relevant sections of this volume	Discussion
Recursivity in socionatural systems	Sections 2 and 5	Drawing on historical ecology, complexity theory and resilience theory, a more complete discussion of the recursive nature of socio-natural systems. This would involve theoretical critiques and practical demonstrations of the human component of the biophysical world, especially relating to concepts of adaptation/mal-adaptation to environment, environmental sustainability, optimality, 'pristine/natural' environments, environmental stasis/equilibrium, diminishing returns on problem solving, etc.
Long term approaches to the human–environment dynamic	Sections 2 and 5	Empirical analysis of the scales over which human–environment dynamics operate with specific focus on intermediate timescales (decadal to millennial), local to global spatial scales and academic interdisciplinarity. Also a deeper consideration of the nature of environmental change and reciprocal impacts rates of change (—constant, accelerating, decelerating, scalar), types of flux (linear, scalar, cyclical). Archaeology can further extend the short 'experimental' record towards 'historical' (rather than experimental) verification of environmental postulates (sustainability/resilience etc).
Critiques of environmental development narratives	Section 3	Critical reflexive analysis of the historical and political constitution of external and internal approaches to the environment with special focus on shifting development paradigms and their fallibility.

(continued)

Table 1.1. Continued

Contribution	Relevant sections of this volume	Discussion
Rehabilitation and IK	Section 3	Re-establishment of past land management strategies and the recovery of past indigenous knowledge (IK). Archaeological analysis of past environmental practices/technologies and knowledge and their assessment as possible solutions to modern problems. This might also include analysis of indigenous perceptions of the 'environment' and an assessment of their role within local development initiatives (i.e. how to work with rather than against indigenous perceptions).
Memory and risk management	Section 4	Analysis of how people perceived environmental change and reacted (or not) to it. Including analysis of how environmental 'events' become part of people's identity through historical memory and how this re-inscribes risk management practices for the future through processes of heritage making. It might also involve analysis of the psychological and material impacts of disaster and their mitigation as a practical lesson for the future.

might bridge these gaps (see Anderson Chapter 15 and Crumley Chapter 17 this volume). For example, palaeoclimatic records operating over millennia have been collated with empirical observations of real climatic variations over historical timescales. However, the historical data set is short and the palaeo-climatic dataset often too poorly resolved to fully integrate the two and to understand how variations on an annual or decadal scale translate into variations over centuries or millennia—let alone how they impact on human societies. At smaller spatial scales, local environmental degradation often operates over timescales which are beyond the scope of experimental studies of such issues as rates of soil loss or declining yields, but archaeology can produce much more highly resolved data-sets so that such problems may be considered over longer timescales and linked more directly to human action.

This intermediate and interdisciplinary position of archaeology has been noted on a number of occasions, most notably by proponents of the emerging interdisciplinary theoretical and methodological perspective known as histor-ical ecology and by related practitioners of 'resilience theory' (Balée 1998; Balée and Erickson 2006; Crumley 1994; McIntosh et al. 2000; Redman 2005;

van der Leeuw 2008; van der Leeuw and Redman 2002). Historical ecology argues that human–environment systems are integrated complex adaptive systems with unpredictable emergent properties; humans are considered to be both biological and cultural and a keystone species with the ability to significantly alter the biophysical component of their surroundings, resulting in either decreased or increased biodiversity. 'Systemic resilience', that is the ability 'bounce back' and reconstitute the system following the effects of external stimuli (such as climate change), is prioritized over 'sustainability' which suggests continuity and stasis and which may, in the long run, lead to systemic collapse (Davies 2009). In addition, systemic change can be caused by external stimuli but also by internal properties of the system itself, and these changes can be highly unpredictable. Most, if not all, environments worldwide are recognized as at least partially the product of human action and therefore partially a human 'artefact' (section 2 this volume). There is also a strong recognition that, while the aim of historical ecology must be to formulate generalizations that can be worked into projections for future environment change, those predictions must be historically constituted, for human–environment interactions operate over variable timescales.

Although expressed in a relatively different terminology, historical ecology has much in common with post-processual and post-structural landscape archaeology, particularly with regard to the position of individual agency, ideology, belief and cultural perceptions of the environment which are given high degrees of importance in understanding the human–environment dialectic. Historical ecology has not yet fully explored this overlap but the points of intersection are important. In particular, historical ecology recognizes systemic dimensions at a variety of scales, including the individual, family and local community, but these scales have rarely been addressed in global, continental, or even regional environmental narratives, despite the fact that these are scales at which human decision making (especially in the past) commonly occurs. However, post-processual landscape archaeology and the post-structural anthropology on which it draws provide an emergent framework for understanding these dimensions and this may be usefully incorporated into historical ecology and related approaches.

A number of recent and ongoing projects are currently grappling with approaches drawing on both historical ecology and post-processual landscape archaeology as well as engaging with the global scientific community rooted in the physical sciences. Most notable among these is the IHOPE initiative partially hosted at Stockholm's interdisciplinary Resilience Centre (http://www.stockholmresilience.org/ihope), recounted by Crumley in Chapter 17 (see also Costanza et al. 2007a). This involves a number of project clusters united by a holistic approach that fully integrates the humanistic and the biophysical. More importantly these projects aim to engage with policy makers and involve archaeology as a discipline central to understanding

Earth's past and future environmental conditions and their human causes and impacts. Other pioneering archaeology-based projects such as ARCHAEO-MEDES (which focused on the long-term development of the Mediterranean environment) and CAPLTER (on urban ecosystems in arid lands in the United States) have begun the process of placing archaeology at the centre of practical human–environment studies (van der Leeuw and the ARCHAE-OMEDES research team 2000; van der Leeuw and Redman 2002). The Cyrenaica Prehistory Project run by Graeme Barker at the University of Cambridge has looked at the long-term prehistory of North Africa from a variety of perspectives, utilizing a variety of methodological tools (http://www.arch.cam. ac.uk/haua-fteah). Similarly, the Historical Ecologies of East African Landscapes (HEEAL) project run by Paul Lane and based at the University of York, UK has developed a highly sophisticated interdisciplinary approach to the analysis of East African landscapes (Lane 2010; http://www.york.ac.uk/archaeology/research/current-projects/heeal). Such projects are also employing increasingly sophisticated computational simulations integrating multiple variables within complex mathematical models (Kohler and van der Leeuw 2007).

Archaeologists are therefore beginning to recognize the strategically central role of the discipline and to develop sophisticated approaches to the human–environment dynamic as well as interacting with the broader community of environmental scientists and policy makers.

CONCLUSION

Past archaeological approaches to the environment have often implicitly drawn on the Cartesian distinction between nature and culture. While this perspective has formed a cornerstone of Western thought, the last few decades have seen increasing progress towards breaking down the nature–culture divide across the humanities and social sciences. Archaeology has, of course, not been isolated from this phenomenon and post-processual landscape archaeology has particularly embraced humanistic approaches often drawing on post-structural anthropology. As a result, 'environment', once seen as a straightforward key determining factor in the nature of society and as a prime instigator of socio-cultural change, is now being incorporated into archaeological explanation in increasingly sophisticated ways. In particular the concept of an 'objective' and self-contained environment distanced from society and culture is no longer sustainable, and assumed direct unicausal (and often universal) relationships between a society and its physical surroundings are gaining a more nuanced treatment. Nevertheless, current global concerns over anthropogenic environmental degradation and climate change have encouraged somewhat less critical statements from a number of popular archaeological writers, a trend that may act to obscure the real value that archaeology can contribute to such debates.

Fortunately a number of projects are attempting to correct this situation. Central are trends such as the emerging body of theory known as historical ecology and the practical application of archaeology to relationships between humans and the non-human physical world at a variety of scales from the local to the global—many of which are recounted in this volume.

ACKNOWLEDGEMENTS

I am very thankful for comments on early drafts of this chapter from Paul Lane, Peter Mitchell, and Stephanie Wynne-Jones. However, any mistakes, misrepresentations or inconsistencies are entirely my own.

2

Environment in Soviet and Post-Soviet Archaeology

Olena V. Smyntyna

INTRODUCTION

Soviet archaeology, based on a revized Marxist paradigm of historical process, traditionally emphasized the primacy of social and economic processes, while at the same time empirically creating a foundation for palaeoenvironmental studies based on the interdisciplinary reconstruction of a subsistence economy.

The collapse of the Soviet Union caused the break-up of the well-composed strict Soviet methodology of historical reconstruction, provoking intensive searches for new theoretical frameworks for both field and interpretative investigations. This paradigmatic and in some aspects epistemological crisis has created a unique background for the critical revision of a series of approaches and scientific schools which functioned during the second half of the twentieth century. As a result of this difficult, long-lasting, and often ambiguous process of self-reflection only a few concepts applied in Soviet archaeology have demonstrated a vital, cognitive capacity in the post-Soviet period; however, environment is one of these.

The history of environmental thought in Soviet archaeology (as in Soviet social sciences in general) represents a unique genre: officially neglected and even theoretically non-existent, it was nevertheless broadly applied in practical research, and many important theories, concepts, and reconstructions have been developed on the basis of palaeoenvironmental data.

This ambiguity of lack of official status mixed with practical application of an environmental approach in Soviet archaeology explains why a detailed history of Soviet theoretical approaches to the environment is as yet unwritten. However, this contribution tries to begin this process by briefly summing up the history of environmental approach implementation in Soviet and post-Soviet archaeology, outlining the basic stages of this process and examining the main concepts and notions explored in this context.

INTUITIVE ENVIRONMENTALISM: NON-SEGMENTED STUDIES OF NATURE AND PREHISTORIC CULTURES IN PRE-SOVIET ARCHAEOLOGY (1870s TO 1920s)

The specificity of the material remains of hunter-gatherer daily life and subsistence as well as features of their archaeological investigation techniques (including studies of the geological characteristics of cultural layers alongside detailed examination of faunal remains) caused Stone Age archaeology to emerge within the framework of the natural sciences—geology and palaeontology. From the very beginning of Stone Age archaeology the Early Prehistoric population was viewed as an integral part of the natural environment. Classic examples of this genre can be found in works of Charles Lyell, Gabriel de Mortillet, and other 'Great Fathers' of Stone Age archaeology. In such a context the geographical palaeoenvironment was often regarded as the only reasonable explanation of a hunter-gatherer economy and of its household activities and material culture.

Such interpretations were enhanced by the fact that the majority of known sites of this epoch were characterized by an unsatisfactory condition of preservation with few clear ethnographic parallels, so that alternative, non-environmental interpretations were not considered. In such circumstances the attention of scientists was attracted by both the distinctiveness and complexity of hunter-gatherer living conditions (including the severe climate of the glacial epoch and life side by side with large, now extinct animals). Typical examples of such explanations can be found in works of John Lubbock (1865), Hugo Obermaier (Обермайер 1913), Johan Ranke (1895), Karl Ernst von Baer (Бэр 1849) and others.

The Late Palaeolithic and Mesolithic tool kits, houses, and clothes seemed to their first investigators too rough and primitive for such an environment, and interpreters found it hard to believe that such artefacts were adequate to ensure the satisfaction of the Early Prehistoric population's vital needs. These hunter-gatherer communities were therefore often regarded as entities whose daily business was a struggle for survival and basic subsistence. In fact, such an understanding was shared by most archaeologists and prehistorians of that time and was perceived by them as axiomatic, or as an obvious starting point for discussion, and did not require any additional comments or arguments.

The first person in Russian historical thought who did not share this general view was Alexander N. Radischev (1749–1802). Basing his hypothesis on the idea that 'climate and naturalness in general hardly influences the reasonableness of a person', in his philosophical treatise 'About the person, his mortality and immortality' he argued that 'at the initial stage of human history all household activities of a person depend on their natural environment', but contended that the prehistoric population were an active *creative force* who successfully manipulated specific features of their surroundings: 'the mind of the person depends always on his vital needs and was shaped by his location . . . The person who lived near the waters invented a boat and nets, the person who wandered in forests invented bows and arrows, the person who inhabited meadows domesticated peaceful beasts and became a cattle breeder' (Радищев 1941: 64).

So the very beginning of systematic prehistoric field studies was characterized by an unrestrictive theoretical atmosphere which could be called intuitively environmental, having no firm and widely approved (or even consciously shared) theoretical framework. Most illustrative examples of highly skilled early fieldwork artistically combined investigation of prehistoric artifacts with a reconstruction of the palaeogeography. Such studies include the excavations of Konstantin Merezhkovskiy (Мережковский 1880: 106–46) at Crimean Palaeolithic cave sites, highly appreciated by Gabriel de Mortillet who included them in his first manual of European archaeology; the discovery of Late Palaeolithic mammoth-bone dwellings sites in central Ukraine and their first large-scale excavations by Alexey Uvarov (Уваров 1881), Vladimir Antonovich (Антонович 1901) and Vikentiy Khvoiko (Хвойко 1913); the first attempts of Gleb Bonch-Osmolovskiy (Бонч-Осмоловский 1934) to trace the stratigraphic position of cultural layers in Crimean cave sites; and many, many others. This was a brilliant cohort of original researchers, who were not afraid to make experiments and to be 'out of the ordinary'. Even at a first glance it is clear that these researchers contributed to the implementation of an environmental approach in pre-Soviet archaeology by their empiric studies. But one can further see their deeper influence on the development of Soviet archaeology through their historical reconstructions of everyday life, subsistence strategy, mythology and religion, and many other aspects of culture in which environment was regarded as a principal driving force.

FROM THE GEOGRAPHIC NIHILISM OF SOVIET 'PURE MARXIST' ARCHAEOLOGY (1920s–1950s) TO PROFOUND EMPIRICAL INTERDISCIPLINARY PALAEOGEOGRAPHIC STUDIES (1960s–1990s)

The October Revolution of 1917 was not only a *coup d'état* but also led to a theoretical upheaval which covered all spheres of human life and resulted in a total revision of the theoretical background of the social and even the natural sciences. Archaeology at that time was interpreted as a branch of historical science and its paradigm, methodology, and conceptual structure were correlated with the specific, so-called 'Marxist-Leninist-Stalinist' vision of the historical process. A total denial of the role of environment in the history of human society and in cultural evolution was typical for that time; this approach was based on the exaggeration of the role of social and economic agencies in human life.

Simplistic field research with a small audience and little force prevailed in the Soviet archaeology of the 1920s to the 1950s. Tool morphology studies were subject to special attention at that time, and it was from this 'technological' base that the reconstruction of so-called 'cultural' process (a term widely disseminated in Soviet archaeology at that time and referring to reconstruction of 'industries' or tool production techniques) took on special significance as the predominant paradigm of Soviet prehistoric archaeology.

A new phase of environmental approach implementation began in Soviet archaeology after the Second World War when, in the course of restoring the country from ruin, extensive archaeological and geographic fieldwork became the subject of special financial support and management.

'Typically Marxist' (in the peculiar Soviet understanding of Marxism's essence) historiography has had a negative attitude towards any form of 'geographic', 'climatic' or 'environmental' causation; however, the opportunity to overcome this impasse was prepared by Mikhail G. Levin and Nikolay N. Cheboksarov (Левин, Чебоксаров 1955) who took one of the first steps on this road by proposing the concept of cultural and economic phylum. Levin and Cheboksarov regarded phylum as a particular form of social type historically developed in particular natural environments. This concept actually sums up a centuries-old controversy concerning the existence of stages or specific versions in the orientation of population economic activity. Soviet archaeology implicitly held the idea, derived from Dicaearchus in the fourth century BC, that humankind has passed through four stages of exploitation of natural resources: primitive hunting, fishing and gathering; nomadic cattle breeding; agriculture; and finally specialized agriculture. The first doubts about these universal stages were voiced in the second half of the nineteenth century. Results of land management field investigations in different parts of the world, as well as the theoretic reflections of Alexander Humboldt and Friedrich Ratzel, created the context for a revision of this view. The world agricultural systems pattern map developed in 1892 by Edward Hahn was important here because it emphasized the plurality of synchronous ways of land resources exploitation (James, Martin 1981: 256; Kraemer 1967: 79).

The concept of cultural and economic phylum draws on these ideas of plural existence. It is based on the assumption that populations inhabiting the same type of natural environment and at similar stages of social and economic development should inevitably display the same model of behaviour (see Davies, Chapter 1 this volume for discussion of similar and approximately contemporaneous 'multi-linear' evolutionary approaches in Western thought). During the second half of the twentieth century Soviet archaeologists and ethnologists proposed many different variants of a typology of prehistoric societies, based on the cultural and economic phylum concept; the number of these various schemes varies between one and twenty-three, sometimes subdivided into chronological stages (phases) and related groups (see for example, Балакин 1985; Андрианов 1991). Taxonomic imperfections in the phylum concept often resulted in the mis-association of societies with a very different material cultures and ways of adaptation. For example, hunters using the marine resources of the Arctic region were often categorized alongside the savannah hunters of Central Africa in the same phylum of prehistoric hunter-gatherers. In addition, in the framework of the cultural and economic phylum concept, material, social, and normative spheres of culture are separated to some degree: only the first is considered to be connected with the environmental situation while social and normative culture seem to be shaped by other, never clearly explained circumstances. It should be also stressed that in cultural and economic phylum theory, environmental control systems were not considered to have any ethnic peculiarities, nor vice versa: specific features of ethnic culture could not be explained by the influence of a particular environment. Such failures to recognize the environmental implications of certain spheres of human culture could be explained by the fact that economic and cultural phylum theory was a typical child of Soviet Marxism, in terms of which social and cultural phenomena were regarded as a fruit of the conscious behaviour of humans based on their production relations and productive forces—without any influence of external agencies, such as environment.

Nevertheless, despite apparent imperfections, during the middle of the twentieth century the concept of cultural and economic phylum successfully fulfilled an important role in Soviet archaeology. The essence of its attraction was the attention to the pluralism of livelihood systems of different population groups as well as the establishment of a direct connection of this fact with features of the natural geographic environment. As a result, analysis of the geographic components of specific territories inhabited by separate groups of people became the subject of particular attention. From the early 1960s Soviet archaeologists were highly active in the process of creating an extensive database of Late Glacial and Early Holocene fauna, flora, relief, and climate.

The other component necessary for the implementation of an environmental approach in Soviet archaeology was the establishment of fruitful and mutually beneficial cooperation among archaeologists and palaeohistorians on the one hand and representatives of the natural sciences on the other. One can observe the origins of palaeogeography and palaeolandscape studies as independent scientific disciplines at the end of 1950s, when Lev Rukhin (Рухин 1959: 365) stated the principal difference between the understanding of landscape in geography and in palaeogeography. He argued that our ideas about past land-scapes are fragmentary and reflect only the most temporally stable peculiarities of these natural complexes. He stressed that past landscapes are studied only in partial ways and that this fragmentation of our knowledge remains the most striking feature of palaeogeography into the beginning of the twenty-first century (Fisunenko 2000: 38).

In the second half of the twentieth century, large-scale field studies de-veloped by Maxim Veklich (Веклич 1987, 1990) and his colleagues and followers (such as A. Velichko, A. Artyushenko, V. Bibikova, V. Gromov, G. Pashkevich, and many others) resulted in the creation of diversified palaeogeographic databases and palaeolandscape maps containing information about geomorphology, sedimentology, lithology, palaeopedology, palaeoflora, palaeofauna, malacofauna, and palaeoclimate, for a wide number of 'palaeo-landscape sites' (defined as remains of palaeolandscapes in contemporary land-scapes) and 'palaeolandscape indicators' (traces of ancient geographic processes).

Many of these palaeolandscape sites and indicators were located in archaeo-logical sites, and palaeoenvironmentalists and archaeologists were members of the same research teams. Similar close cooperation between 'natural science' and 'social science' in fieldwork was also inherent in the 'geoarchaeology' and 'environmental archaeology' developed at the same time in Western science, but it was stressed particularly strongly in Soviet science. Its proponents saw the principal subject of their specialist studies as the ecological context of individual settlements,with their cooperation resulting in the reconstruction of the natural geographic environment inhabited by specific prehistoric communities.

The first attempt in Soviet archaeology to generalize the results of such interdisciplinary research was made by Sergei N. Bibikov (Бибиков 1969, 1971). In 1969 he proposed the so-called 'method of palaeoeconomic simula-tion', in which he combined the interpretation of the material culture and household activities of a community with reconstruction of its palaeoenviron-ment. With the help of this method it became possible to detect the peculiar-ities of a livelihood system and the economy of a settlement, and to calculate the duration of its occupation by a particular community as well as (tenta-tively) the number of its members based on the result of the excavations of over 90 per cent of the site. Essential conditions for the application of this method are the presence of dwellings (or at least fireplaces) in the cultural layer and of faunal remains suitable for identifying species and estimating the number of individuals, as well as the availability of the results of detailed geomorphological, palynological, and palaeontological studies of the site and its surroundings. Vadim Masson's monograph on Near Eastern prehistoric archaeological sites (Массон 1971) presents a series of interesting results using this method. During the 1970s and 1980s the method was explored further by Bibikov and his numerous apprentices at over one hundred Late Palaeolithic and Mesolithic settlements. As a result it was established that Late Glacial and Early Holocene natural environments significantly influenced the formation and development of separate communities and their respective cultures, and were at the same time subject to many changes caused by collective human activities. These studies are among the earliest in Soviet archaeology of a nature–society feedback which started as early as the Late Palaeolithic. Bibikov has further developed the concept of a palaeoecological and palaeoeconomic crisis as a particular form of non-equilibrium which he regards as an objective and natural result of prehistoric population production activity taking place in a permanently changing environment. According to Bibikov, a crisis starts when a society cannot satisfy its essential subsistence needs by traditional forms of procurement, and to overcome the crisis the society must either change its procurement system or find another living space where traditional procurement forms would remain effective. Bibikov distinguishes several stages of such crisis development from 9000 to 6000 BC which are correlated with phases of geographic change as well as with changes of livelihood activities of hunter-gatherers and the transition to a food production economy (Бибиков 1969; Бібіков 1977). As a result Bibikov's work can be considered to have instigated a new ecological perspective in Soviet archaeological and historical investigation. This ecological perspective can be regarded as the detection and analysis of connections which exist between a cultural object and its natural environment (Герасимов 1979: 19).

From the 1960s to the 1980s representatives of Western European environmental archaeology and proponents of an ecological approach in Soviet archaeology and prehistory (in particular, followers of Bibikov) took a close, if not the same path, looking for specific features to explain Early Prehistoric population, culture, and mode of life. Questions of hunter-gatherer mobility as well as their livelihood activity in particular localities are at the centre of both approaches. At the same time, there is a clear difference in their initial idealized theoretical postulates; in contrast to Western European and American environmentalists, the majority of the Soviet specialists in this field still believed that the *social* sphere of early prehistoric culture was not influenced by environment, although they recognized the importance of the influence of geographic situation on material culture and subsistence strategy (Дмитриев, Белокобыльский 1989: 262, 280).

Another milestone of environmental approach implementation in Soviet archeology is connected with adaptation theory. During the second half of the 1970s the adaptation concept became one of the most popular and fruitful approaches to the interpretation of human–environment interaction. In contrast with Western thought, where one can trace different versions, including social and cultural, of adaptive strategies, in the Soviet science of this period attention was paid mainly to biological aspects of adaptation with an accent on human capacity to fit the environment (that is, to meet its minimal requirements). Adaptation was interpreted in two basic ways: as a specific property (or phenomenon) of a human body and as the evolutionary process taking place within the system that organism enters as a member (Верещагин 1988: 70). It was broadly admitted that the human body reacted to changes in temperature, humidity, sunlight, air quality, and other climatic and geographic factors. This reaction is individual, and could be seen as a mutation as well as a long-lasting evolutionary process. But, at the same time, it was specifically stressed that all the most important physiological constants of human beings (parameters characterizing their condition of health, capacity for work, and ability to resist any external impact, including climatic) were not subject to adaptation (Хлебович, Чуднова, Чупанова 1975: 150).

By the 1980s, it become clear that adaptation in both its basic forms (as a phenomenon and as a process) could not be restricted to the biological sphere. Purposeful productive activity and vitally indispensable subjects ('agents' in Western terminology) were admitted by Soviet science as the basic adaptive mechanism distinguishing human biological adaptation from similar processes in the animal world (Калайков 1984: 46–9). In other words, human culture was for the first time in Soviet science recognized as a specific means of adaptation to external agencies, including the environment. Again this shift mirrors the application of ecological approaches in Western 'New Archaeology' (see Davies, Chapter 1 and Gosden, Chapter 18 this volume) but also emphasizes the fact that Soviet archaeology had previously retained a concept of culture as more dynamic and relatively independent of basic environmental conditions. Moreover, while culture came to be seen as 'adaptive' in Soviet thought, it retained some of the independent causative agency of earlier approaches and avoided the more simplistic environmental determinism of some Western studies.

Interpreting adaptation as a process one should always bear in mind two main aspects of this problem. One of them is external, connected with the analysis of society taken as the collective subject of human activity and interaction with the environment. The second is internal and expresses the relationship existing among the persons and different groups included in the society with their social environment as well as their co-adaptation (Маркарян 1975: 141). In the framework of such an understanding of adaptation, society was regarded as the basic unit which produces and realizes adaptive action in order to bring itself into conformity with environment; society in such a context should be viewed as a particular class of adaptive systems. This re-formulation of the adaptation concept was a sort of compromise between the apparent necessity to legalize the adaptive essence of the non-material sphere of human culture, on the one hand, and the primacy of social agency in human historical progress, which still remained a cornerstone of Soviet prehistory.

In Soviet archaeological science it was Pavel M. Dolukhanov (Долуханов 1985) who at the end of the 1970s referred for the first time to the adaptive character of human society. Using a wide range of natural sciences data he proposed an original concept of prehistoric economy optimization. A little later, on the basis of Australian aboriginal ethnographic studies, Vladimir R. Kabo (Кабо 1986: 5–6) also came to the conclusion that Early Prehistoric communities should be regarded as having an optimal form of social adaptation to their natural and social environment. Such communities, according to him, acted as stabilizing institutions and consisted of several dynamic groups whose interaction potentially created more complicated social structures such as complex kinship systems. Thanks to his investigations the notion of 'social and cultural adaptation' was introduced into the Soviet archaeological literature. Such adaptation was regarded as the active impact of humans on their environment, effected through social organization, tools, housing, religious and magic activities, and so on (Кабо 1979: 87).

These thoughts clearly illustrate a basic difference between Western and Soviet sciences in their understanding of the nature of human adaptation. In very general terms, Soviet archaeologists and prehistorians inferred the presence of a strong creative component in human behaviour, so, in their understanding, human adaptation to climate change or environment was never a passive act; it was always an innovative set of actions to help overcome crises. In the post-Soviet era Vadim M. Masson attempted to continue these ideas, proposing that economic activities, household adaptation, and social adaptation should be considered as three basic facets of social and cultural adaptation of Late Palaeolithic societies (Массон 1996: 16).

The term 'adaptation' is often used in a different context in Soviet compared with English-language archaeological literature. Until about the middle of the 1990s Soviet archaeologists applied it only in frameworks of generalized interpretative studies; at the same time Western archaeologists successfully explored adaptation in the publication of results of separate archaeological site investigations. Papers presented at the Soviet-American workshop 'Problems of Cultural Adaptation in Late Palaeolithic times' (Проблемы 1989) held in Leningrad in July 1989 demonstrated this difference clearly.

ENVIRONMENTAL APPROACH IN POST-SOVIET ARCHAEOLOGY (1990s–2000s): WAVERING BETWEEN EMPIRICISM AND THEORIZATION

The collapse of the Soviet Union and the resulting intensive searches for new methods and theoretical approaches in the social sciences provided wide perspectives for the further implementation of an environmental approach in field and interpretative archaeology, which have tended to become the latest 'top fashions'. Two basic tendencies seem to be typical for this most recent period: on the one hand, one can trace the further development of the most fruitful Soviet concepts and theories that originated a decade before; on the other, the aspiration for a 'Western' experience of environmental theorization has become more and more popular.

With regard to the first tendency, attention should be paid to the evolution of understandings of a palaeoecological approach and the application of the concept of adaptation. Proponents of the palaeoecological approach in post-Soviet archaeology see their main task as interpretation of the results of individual site investigations taking into account natural ambient dynamics. In order to realize this, they try to avoid both broad generalizations and the creation of complicated simulations of nature–society relationships; instead they prefer simple explanations. During the last few years many studies have focused on local palaeoecology, which concentrates its attention on problems of place of residence and visiting territories, ecological reconstruction, and regional palaeoecology. Such studies aim to better understand features of the settlement system and to evaluate the regional resource base (Леонова, Несмеянов, Матюшкин 1993: 8, 10).

During the last few years it has also been possible to observe traces of increasing sophistication in the ecological approach, not only in prehistoric archaeology but also in adjacent fields of knowledge including cultural and social anthropology, ethnology, palaeodemography, palaeosociology, palaeogeography, and within other sciences and humanities (Сминтина 2001; Smyntyna 2004). Attention has mainly been concentrated on the conceptualization of palaeogeographical and palaeoecological impacts on different spheres of life within Late Palaeolithic and Mesolithic societies. In particular, since the 1970s it has repeatedly been underlined that in Pleistocene times the main stages of natural geographic environment changes correlate well with the evolution of human physical morphology as well as with material culture and livelihood systems. The main role in this process, as a rule, was given not so much to living conditions of prehistoric population at any particular time as to their dynamics through time (Величко 1971: 16–17).

Changes in the sphere of application of the adaptation concept are reflected mostly in a new understanding of its scale and subject. During the last several years in Ukrainian and, partly, in Russian Stone Age archaeology one can trace an apparent revival of interest in different models of adaptation of particular human groups. Such models are often characterized by different levels of generalization, beginning from the scale of separate settlements and taking the natural geographic zone as the highest taxonomic unit. In this context special attention should be paid to the understanding of adaptation traced in theoretic reflections of Leonid L. Zaliznyak (Залізняк 1998: 62–3). According to him adaptation is the 'concrete form of human society existence . . . dependent on two factors: on the level of its development and on the natural environment'. On that basis he often explores this term as synonymous with the concept of cultural and economic phylum, but he places more emphasis on 'environment'. Based on the assumption that 'the number of adaptation models in general corresponded to the number of natural landscape zones' (which implies that the inhabitants of every geographic zone demonstrate their own peculiar adaptation) he elaborates a rather complicated classification of economic adaptation models inherent to Early Prehistoric societies. As a result within the framework of four 'lines of development of primitive societies with a hunter-gatherer economy' he elucidates eleven 'adaptation models or cultural and economic phylum of highest hunters'. The majority of these can be sub-divided into several variants, and in development of some of them particular stages can be traced (Залізняк 1998: 62–5). Zaliznyak's approach appears to hold much in common with Steward's (1955) concepts of multi-linear evolution, basing an understanding of the 'cultural core' of a society on the determinants of 'environment' and 'technology'.

Alongside the development of approaches to the adaptive function of society and social life, the post-Soviet period is also marked by a recognition of the adaptive function of culture. Russian ethnologist Sergei A. Arutyunov (Арутюнов 1989: 5, 130) interprets culture as a set of ways in which different kinds of human activity are institutionalized. Its principal functions are the formation and transformation of the environment, on the one hand, and of human beings with their spiritual and physical characteristics on the other. The formation of a cultural system is a process of adaptation to specific niches—natural ones at first, which with the course of time become more social. To be able to realize its adaptive function culture should not only be capable of responding to a minimum of environmental requirements but also have at its disposal the potential necessary for adaptive change in response to new conditions (Арутюнов 1993: 42, 47). Such innovative adaptation seems to have resonance with concepts of 'resilience' now common in Western thought (Costanza et al. 2007), while long-term perspectives of adaptation to natural (non-human) niches through the development and adaptation to distinctly 'human environments' may have much in common with trends in Western biology such as the concept of memes and more dialectical approaches to human–environment relations such as the 'dwelling' perspective (Ingold 2000; see Davies, Chapter 1 this volume for further discussion).

Alternatives to the adaptation concept can be found in co-evolution theory, promoted in post-Soviet science in frameworks of geoecological natural geography. Co-evolution is approached as a 'mutual and guided adaptation of the person and biosphere, which takes place under a continuous search for a stable state as well as under their permanent changes in conformity with the current situation' (Швебс 1993: 29). The essence of the co-evolution geoecological approach is in the substantiation of mutual relationships between nature and society.

This obvious plurality of theoretical backgrounds within environmental approach implementation in post-Soviet archaeology sometimes seems insufficient for determining the essence of human–nature interaction in the remote past. Probably, this is the reason for the simple adoption—without adjustment for the peculiar database and cognitive potential of archaeological studies—of notions and concepts which are widely popular in contemporary Western environmental thought, including theories of sustainability, the concept of resilience, theories of ecological niches, and many others. Another contemporary tendency in this context is connected with the increasingly widespread application of post-modern ideas of human society and understanding of culture (such as the theory of landscape as scene, landscape of habit, and so on) which can be difficult to apply to studies of fossil societies.

The new trends discussed in this section, such as the new vision of a palaeoecological approach, updates in economic and cultural phylum theory, human–culture adaptive theory, geoecology, and others, offer great potential but seem to create a fundamental divide between the requirements of theory application and the possibility of satisfying these on the basis of available empiric evidence; such issues are now at the forefront of the encounter between Western and post-Soviet archaeology.

CONCLUSIONS

A brief outline of the history of environmental approach implementation in Soviet and post-Soviet archaeology allows us to distinguish four stages, characterized by peculiar sets of methods, concepts and notions:

Stage 1: pre-Soviet (1870s–1920s): non-segmented studies of nature and prehistoric cultures;

Stage 2: Soviet 'pure Marxist' (1920s–1950s): geographical nihilism;

Stage 3: Soviet 'interdisciplinary' (1960s–1990s): palaeogeographic studies;

Stage 4: post-Soviet (1990s–2000s): wavering between empiricism and conceptualization.

This brief overview also reveals a series of issues that illustrate the differences in environmental approaches in Soviet and post-Soviet and Western European science.

One of these is connected with differences in disciplinary affiliation of prehistoric landscape studies due to the different historic origins and traditions of national scientific schools. In a broad sense this difference can be formulated as follows: in Eastern Europe palaeolandscape is studied and reconstructed by representatives of natural sciences (physical geography, including palaeogeography) while the Western European tradition conceptualizes palaeolandscape as an integral part of archaeology and cultural anthropology (in the discipline of social sciences and humanities).

This situation is caused by another traditional difference between 'West' and 'East' in the understanding of landscape. In Soviet science landscape is natural in a narrow sense: it is created and contains only elements of nature (flora, fauna, relief, and so on). In Western science human beings and human societies are usually regarded as integral parts of past landscapes, and no palaeolandscape studies are undertaken without reconstructions of human social behaviour and livelihood systems.

In Western prehistoric culture studies, in which no landscapes exist without humans, it becomes easy to assume that it is just human beings who are producing the landscape: this perhaps helps to explain the wide distribution of some 'post-modern' approaches to landscape in Western thought. At the same time, ideas conceptualized along post-modernist lines (belief, symbolism, ritual, and so on) have been largely absent in Soviet environmental science until recently. However, over the last few years one can trace a very slight tendency towards post-modernism, mainly in the interpretative sections of archaeological reports presented as the so-called 'integration into European science' of post-Soviet geography. This does not mean, however, that concepts of 'individual agency' have been absent in Soviet and post-Soviet theorizing: on the contrary they have tended to be present throughout, but have always grappled with the interplay of agency and environment.

One more difference in the conceptualisation of environment in the 'East' and the 'West', also connected with different understandings of human place in the landscape, is displayed in the research methods used for past landscape reconstruction. Soviet and post-Soviet studies based on Marxist positivist methodology have shifted during the last decade towards systems analysis which tends to be quantitative as well as qualitative, trying to describe the temporal and spatial distribution of particular natural elements of the landscape and landscape changes through time. 'Western' landscape reconstructions have moved away from such approaches and are now more deeply integrated with cultural and social anthropology, sociology, behavioural sciences, and ethnography, hence attention is paid not only to landscape reconstruction (which inevitably envisages human culture reconstruction) but also to the means of landscape representation in human society and the mentality of its past inhabitants and their ancestors. In other words attention is paid not only to how people lived in a landscape but also how they 'perceived' it: this is one area which has been lacking in Soviet traditions.

This chapter has attempted to highlight the diversity of spatial and temporal frameworks of prehistoric landscape reconstruction inherent to 'Eastern' and 'Western' science. Soviet and post-Soviet researchers usually explore two versions of localization of the landscape; one of them could be called global and reflects general climatic and geological stages of Earth history, and the other is connected with particular archaeological sites and is used when palaeogeographers are working together with archaeologists. Today the 'Western' approach places human beings (or society) in the centre of the landscape, and its spatial and temporal frameworks are usually determined by the time and place of 'human agency'. However, this has not always been so, and while Soviet and post-Soviet researchers have not always been so explicit about the role of human agency they have consistently considered the human–environment relationship as a two-way process of mutual construction. Western approaches, in contrast, have tended to deterministically polarize this relationship.

So, in 'Eastern' and 'Western' traditions the 'environment' is obviously a different construction which involves the exploration of different methodologies, research techniques and theoretical backgrounds. Such diversity can be connected with the general theoretical discrepancies between national scientific schools which, several centuries ago, were accompanied by different scientific, political, economic, ideological, and cultural implications.

However, these different traditions are gradually coming together through common field studies in multinational interdisciplinary projects. Moreover, the dissemination of the results of such studies at international scientific forums, international professional organizations and societies, and, in particular, international congresses such as the World Archaeological Congress, are creating the necessary background for the establishment of a mutual understanding and the elimination of theoretical and empirical controversies between 'Eastern' and 'Western' archaeology. At the same time such integration will contribute to the integration of post-Soviet archaeologists and their invaluable data-sets and theories into the world archaeological community.

Part II

Environment as Artefact

This section acts to critique widely held beliefs about the nature of human–environment relations. In particular, in its own way each chapter deconstructs notions of past human societies as optimally and somewhat passively adapted to environments. In contrast, the chapters demonstrate how human cultural activities have defined the way in which humans have engaged with the environment and actively shaped the world around them. Each chapter defines the human–environment dialectic as an ongoing creative and dynamic act of artefact making: at their core the chapters challenge modern environmental narratives that view climate change and environmental degradation in terms of concepts of pristine nature and the need to establish some kind of natural balance. A long-term archaeological perspective shows that such pristine nature has never existed and that humans have always interacted with the environment, as much as 'irrational' cultural beings as 'rational' biological organisms. These chapters demonstrate that humans are neither inherently degrading nor inherently in balance with the natural world. Rather they show how humans are *part* of an active environmental dynamic whereby human actions have always altered and modified global environments for better or worse. In chapter three Balée reviews the global evidence of anthropogenic landscape transformations across the tropics. He demonstrates that vast tropical landscapes with high levels of biodiversity, once viewed as pristine environments, are actually the product of human modification. He further argues that human action has often resulted in increased levels of biodiversity and that ongoing human action is required to maintain biodiversity levels. In general Balée argues that all environments are in part human artefacts and as such they deserve protection as cultural artefacts as much as natural wonders.

In Chapter 4 Davies shifts attention to the Pokot agricultural community in Eastern Africa, where he argues that major agricultural landscape transformations, such as hillside terracing and the building of irrigation canals, are not activities 'forced' by the requirements of environment (topography, soils, climate, population) but rather are the product of human choices in a realm of options. Moreover, Davies argues that human environmental decision making is always underdetermined by available knowledge, such that human actions only ever *approach* those which might be most optimal (depending on the scale—whether for example at community, family, or individual level—of such decision making). The decisions of Eastern African farmers are therefore always 'good' choices rather than forced or optimal moves. Such realization has great significance for the way in which modern development planners might engage with these farmers, because simple ecological models do not take into account the complexities of the cultural embeddedness of Pokot environmental perception—particularly the fact that, despite problems, Pokot farmers have 'chosen' a variety of ways to modify the world around them so as to suit their own unique way of life. It follows from this that such choices might include decisions which appear both degrading and conservative from a Western perspective, but which take on a wholly different significance for individual Pokot families.

In Chapter 5 Fiore et al. move away from broader landscape transformations and instead focus on hunter-gatherer interactions with specific animal species in the Tierra del Fuego. Through analysis of ethnographic and historical texts alongside archaeofaunal data, Fiore et al. demonstrate how humans' beliefs cause them to deviate from the optimal exploitation of their surroundings, so that they alter species dynamics in ways which appear irrational to modern eyes. The hunter-gatherer-fishers of the Tierra del Fuego saw their surroundings in highly relative terms; animal species were meaningful symbols as much as sources of food and their environment was a cognitive (if not physical) artefact. Moreover, the undercurrent of this discussion is clear; that humans may not always be expected to act in purely 'rational' ways with regard to their environment. Indeed, such 'rationality' is part of a Western conception of the environment and non-Western peoples look at the world very differently. In Chapter 6 Chevalier takes up a similar theme with regards to pre-Columbian plant exploitation in Peru. He argues that differences in floral assemblages at two otherwise comparable centres points towards the role of food resources in the construction of identity and otherness. The undercurrent is that the environment is co-opted into meaningful cultural expression; that it is a cognitive artefact as much as a physical resource and that people at least partially interact with their surroundings on the basis of cultural preconceptions and the requirements of symbolic communication. Again the underlying message is clear; that tradition and cultural performance often override economic rationality and that peoples engagement with the environment is complex and highly contextualised.

In Chapter 7 Kost returns to the subject of physical anthropogenic landscape transformations demonstrating through a wide range of archaeological, historical, ethnographic, and palaeoecological data that the flora of

Australia's Southwest Botanical Province has been largely shaped by the Noongar anthropogenic fire regime. Moreover, her diachronic perspective demonstrates how the fire regime was changed by the advent of colonialism. She argues that the rationale for this change was based on European misconceptions about the pristine nature of such environments and a lack of understanding of the extent to which these forests were the product of millennia of Noongar activities. Kost's chapter forcefully emphasizes the extent to which global environments are longstanding human artefacts and the problems that can occur when modern interventions attempt to remove traditional practices and re-establish fallacious 'states of nature'. Kost's chapter also brings up the idea of the misleading power of environmental narratives and the ways in which archaeological data may be effectively used to critique them. This is a theme which is taken up more forcefully in the following sections.

3

Indigeneity of Past Landscape Transformations of the Tropics[1]

William Balée

INTRODUCTION

Indigeneity is the living heritage of traditional peoples. It includes not only their languages and cultures but their transformational etchings on landscapes—not just alterations in the form of inanimate structural changes of the substrate, as in the construction of earthworks and edifices, but sometimes changing the composition of the living flora and fauna. Archaeology is crucial to the identification of indigeneity in the past and in the analysis of landscapes and seascapes associated with it[2]. Landscape transformations, from the perspective of historical ecology, refer to the turnover in species of given locales because of human-mediated disturbance. Primary landscape transformation denotes complete species turnover, whereas secondary landscape transformation denotes partial species turnover. In both cases, substrate alterations occur, but in primary landscape transformation these are qualitatively more profound. In order to understand landscape transformations, we might begin with consideration of geographer Carl Sauer's comment (1963 [1925]: 333) that 'We cannot form an idea of landscape except in terms of its time relations as well as of its space relations. It is in continuous process of development or of dissolution and replacement.' Indigeneity is one of the factors involved in dissolution and replacement, which I refer to as 'transformation'.

Landscapes created in the past through mechanisms rooted in indigeneity are often called the 'built environment' by archaeologists. In many tropical

---

[1] Portions of this chapter appeared in Portuguese in an earlier article (Balée 2008). Grateful acknowledgement is made to the *Revista de Arqueologia* (Brazil) for permission to publish those portions here in English.
[2] From here onwards the term landscapes will be taken to mean both landscapes and seascapes.

forests, including those of Greater Amazonia, the Atlantic Coastal Forest, West Africa, Central Africa, Malesia[3], and Micronesia, both primary and secondary landscape transformations have noticeably affected the distribution of plant and animal species. In some cases, with specific reference to primary landscape transformation, entire forests came into existence, such as in the Llanos de Mojos, Bolivia and in Guinea, West Africa (see Fairhead, Chapter 16 this volume for more detailed discussion of anthropogenic forests in West Africa). Secondary landscape transformation occurred in the context of ancient settlements, the alteration of ridge tops, swidden cultivation, and resource management, such as in Pre-Amazonian forests of Eastern Brazil, Central African forests, and various forests of Malesia.

Alpha and beta diversity indices show that human impacts are variable and depend on societal factors, and the variability found in these does not always suggest a decrease in diversity due to human-mediated disturbance (Clement and Junqueira 2010). Alpha diversity is diversity on a local scale; beta diversity represents the diversity between alpha-level sites along an environmental or temporal gradient. The weight of the evidence suggests that cultural forests have existed in various tropical milieus, and blanket categorizations of such areas as pristine and natural cannot be accurate; it is arguably also erroneous to characterize these landscapes as entirely 'built', because in a variety of cases, natural occurrences, such as droughts, floods, volcanism, and river meanders, can account for the rise and fall of forests in particular locales (e.g. Johns 1990). Still, humans have clearly impacted various ancient landscapes that can be studied with tools from archaeology as well as other fields. Primary and secondary landscape transformations are concepts that best explain the formation of anthropogenic forests, as well as certain innovations in the substrate, in various tropical areas worldwide. In addition, they account for the presence of both semi-domesticated and domesticated plant species in these forests. These landscape transformations are the signature of indigeneity of the past, evinced in the living environment of today.

THE CONCEPT OF INDIGENEITY

Indigeneity is the state or quality of being non-exotic. Defining it would almost seem to be a trivial exercise in stating the obvious, except for the fact that considerable political weight is attached to exactly what the term itself means in the world we live in. Like 'race', 'sustainable development', and 'globalization', the term is more than just a buzzword for specific political and economic

---

[3] Malesia is the botanical region that extends in the Asian island tropics from Sumatra in the west to the Bismarck Archipelago in the east (e.g. Baas et al. 1990).

phenomena, groups, and aspirations, at given times and places. It is a bona fide term on the world stage of discourse and debate. The concepts associated with it require careful attention, and their discussion needs to remain clear and effective, since different groups exhibit differences of interest and investment in landscapes and the livelihoods and traditions associated with them.

With clarity and effectiveness in exposition, therefore, let us examine with some exactitude what we mean by 'indigeneity'. For certain purposes, indigeneity is a local phenomenon that labels and assigns distinctive features to human groups; for some political ends, it can be either a local or a global concept with applications, as in the 2007 United Nations Declaration on the Rights of Indigenous Peoples (Merlan 2009), or in pan-indigenous movements that have continental-wide implications, as seen particularly in Australia and Latin America (Merlan 2009; Stavenhagen 1998). Indigeneity can be local and focused, as with the Saami of Scandinavia who must herd reindeer to qualify as indigenous (Beach 2007); the Shoshone of the Great Basin who must have effectively occupied vast territory before it was altered for grazing (Dannenmaeir 2008) in order to gain land title; or the Nuer living in the United States who maintain long-distance connections that impact biota, such as cattle in their Sahelian homeland (Shandy 2007), and it is that homeland that to an extent continues to define their indigeneity.

In my use of the term, indigeneity refers to traditional ways of knowing the world ensconced within small-scale cultural traditions whose adherents have been historically the human targets of European and neo-European colonialism and, more recently, economic globalization. Yet the term indigenous, and by implication, indigeneity, are words most recently subject to debate among social scientists and legal scholars (Beach 2007; Dannenmaier 2008; Merlan 2009—see comments by Alcita Ramos, pp. 325–6).

Indigeneity, in spite of some debate as to its meaning, has acquired currency in various domains and fields, such as the United Nations, international tribunals, the World Bank, public media, emic vantage points from self-designated indigenes, non-governmental organisations, and human sciences, especially anthropology and its related fields. My objective is to describe and determine landscapes that evince indigeneity within a time frame of *la longue durée*, to analyse the value of these both to insiders and outsiders, and to discuss how these landscapes—in reality, archaeological sites contemporaneously occupied by peoples using ancient technologies—and their associated societies might be best conserved, protected, or restored.

Landscapes are the encounter of people and place with given histories etched into and definitive of matter, including living things. The restoration point of landscapes in the field of ecological restoration, or applied historical ecology, appears to be the time when the landscapes can be comprehended within a framework of indigeneity. The bivalent implication is this: if landscapes abundant in species and heterogeneity of environmental gradients bespeak, therefore, the existence within them of indigenous-defining characteristics, those same characteristics are materially referenced by the bioenvironmental richness and diversity of the landscape itself (Niestchman 1992). It is a much more involved issue than a mere dialectic, however, for it engages perforce a specialized notion of time, history, and behaviour of humans in the environment.

The science of the landscape is traced to the Renaissance in painting, polity, and notions of space and place (Olwig 2002). At different times and places, and in different languages, the term undergoes semantic change: in European historiography, *le paysage, Landschaft, landskab, a paisagem, el paisaje,* and *landscape* over time can refer to differentiated political units, landforms, and concepts. Specifically, in some cases, landscape denoted political fragments of states; in others, it represented landforms altered by different facets of feudalism; in still others, it constituted lands that seemingly had yet to be subjected to ownership and cultivation (Olwig 2002). In historical ecology the term is being used in an operational sense (Balée 2006; Clement and Junqueira 2010; Crumley 2007) with roots in past notions that designated given, historical, relationships between certain groups of people and definite environments through time, often with a concept of deep time, or *la longue durée.* Sauer (1963: 333) had offered a distinction between natural landscapes (which preceded the presence of humans) and cultural landscapes (where the 'works of . . . [humanity] express themselves'). Sauer was presciently aware there might be few natural landscapes per se: of the natural landscape, he cogently noted as early as 1925 that 'In its entirety it no longer exists in many parts of the world . . .' (1969: 333). The transformations of landscapes wrought by non-Europeans in the supposed *terra nullius* have been in some cases dramatic, subtle in others.

People and places of tropical landscapes were once thought to constitute nature itself. These were supposedly natural landscapes in Sauer's sense, or *terra nullius* (nobody's land) and *domicilium vacuum* (vacant land) to Renaissance Europeans (Dannenmaier 2008; Thornberry 2002). In fact these lands, resources, and people that were the objects of European expansion and colonialism have been shown in the last twenty-five years often to be final redoubts, not of 'pristine primitives' (Wolf 1982), but rather humanized landscapes made by sophisticated people of the past, and useful in innumerable ways to equally knowledgeable (though in different ways) indigenous people of the present. That is the essence of indigeneity of landscape.

TROPICAL LANDSCAPE TRANSFORMATIONS

Malesia

Around 1800, the Marovo Lagoon on New Georgia in the Solomon Islands had irrigated, terraced taro fields, young slash-and-burn swiddens of taro and yams, and old fallow (or anthropogenic) forest with groves of *Canarium* trees (Bayliss-Smith et al. 2003), of the frankincense or Burseraceae family. These trees have important edible, fatty nuts 'with fleshy fruits that are eaten as olives' (Burkill 1966, vol. 1: 429). *Canarium* trees are considered to be indicator species of human habitation sites (Bayliss-Smith et al. 2003; Lepofsky 1992). At least one of the species, *C. indicum*, is 'never found in the wild' (McClatchey et al. 2006: 214; also see Burkhill 1966, vol. 1: 433–4). As with old fallow and anthropogenic forest islands in Amazonia (Balée 2006; Erickson 2008) as well as tropical forest islands in West Africa (Fairhead and Leach 1996a; Fairhead, Chapter 16 this volume), these Malesian old fallows were orchard-like, and attracted not only people for their edible fruit, but also game animals for the same (Bayliss-Smith 2003: 347). In addition to *Canarium* spp., other species in these cultural forests of Malesia include breadfruit and jackfruit (*Artocarpus* spp.), coconut (*Cocos nucifera* L.), various taro relatives (*Colocasia* spp.), and sago palm relatives (*Metroxylon* spp.) (Burkhill 1966; McClatchey et al. 2006: 224; Puri 2005; Terrell et al. 2003). In other islands in the New Georgia and Russell Island group, there were dense stands of *Camponesia brevipetiolata*, a disturbance indicator. On ridge tops in some of these areas, one finds *Canarium* spp., *Prunus* spp., and *Ixora* spp, all associated with old village sites (Bayliss-Smith 2003: 348).

Indeed, in Malesia, it is precisely on ridges, summits, mountain saddles, and other such high ground that one finds either planted groves of *Canarium* spp. or other areas of 'intensive arboriculture' (McClatchey et al. 2006: 218). Here the summits and ridges were sometimes fortified as well. The Malesians extended their influence eastward. The Bismarck Archipelago, which is the easternmost part of Malesia, was colonized by 35,000 years ago. Much later, in the Holocene, colonization took place in Micronesia and Polynesia to the east and north (Rainbird 2004: 74). The people who moved to these distant islands of Remote Oceania (Latinis 2000) brought with them knowledge of landscape transformation initially acquired in Malesia. Late prehistoric societies had altered the landscapes seen as pristine by the first Europeans in the area, such as Ferdinand Magellan and Captain Cook. Ridge tops and summits in Micronesia, incidentally, are among the most transformed of landscapes and it is not always clear if these transformations occurred primarily for subsistence, defence, or ritual purposes (Rainbird 2004). There is such extensive terracing and transformation of island summits in northern islands of the Palau Archipelago that these are referred to as 'sculpted landscapes' (Rainbird 2004: 138). These landscape transformations went hand in hand with development of complex agricultural and food processing technologies, such as detoxification technology of Cycad nuts in the Marianas, together with advanced nautical technology (Rainbird 2004: 132).

Tropical Africa

The vast forest islands of Guinea in West Africa have been shown to contain evidence of human occupation and formation. Rather than representing relics of the Pleistocene, these are forests that were formed where there were no forests before as a result of traditional (indigenous) human occupation and activity. In the now classic account of Fairhead and Leach (1996a; see also Fairhead, chapter 16 this volume), this involved the deliberate transplanting, planting, and cultivation of a variety of fruit trees and the establishment of firebreaks around nascent plantings to protect these. Savanna soils actually improved with human occupation and cultivation, and the development of shady orchards was favoured. Trees grown in these anthropogenic forest islands include *Ceiba pentandra* (also found in anthropogenic Amazonian forests—*Balée* 1994: 277), *Canarium schweinfurthii* (of the same genus as *C. indicum*, with its edible nuts, found on mountain and ridge tops in Malesia), and *Cola nitida* (Fairhead and Leach 1996a: 208). These are indigenous genera, or signature genera of indigeneity in tropical landscapes.

One also finds in these African forest islands the African oil palm (*Elaeis guineensis*), which produces edible fruits and seeds—this species is especially indicative of forests that bear the mark of human-mediated disturbance (Fairhead and Leach 1996a: 44; Hart and Hart 1985). In the Ituri Forest of equatorial Africa, one finds *Elaeis guineensis* as an unmistakable indicator of former agricultural village sites (Terrell et al. 2003). In these same locales, one also finds *Canarium schweinfurthii*, the edible fruits of which are collected by the hunting-and-gathering Mbuti people (Hart and Hart 1985).

Further south one finds additional support for Fairhead's and Leach's theory against the 'declinist paradigm', wherein it has been shown that the advance of a fruit tree complex was deliberately caused by human propagation, the fruit trees involved being mainly marula and birdplum (Kreike 2003: 40). What these Africanist studies show is that forests before the era of European colonialism in the nineteenth century were actually expanding, not contracting, and expanding because of people's occupation and management strategies, not in spite of the human presence.

Amazonia

The evidence from Amazonia for transformations of landscapes is multifaceted, and both similar to and different from the African and Malesian materials. The principal Amazon transformations occurred before depopulation due to Western diseases, and this appears to be the case in Malesia also.

Marovo (on Georgia Island) experienced a 70 per cent population decline from 1850 to 1930; the Bismarck Archipelago in general underwent major population declines as a result of pathogens (evidently mostly venereal disease) introduced by Europeans that turned epidemic (Bayliss-Smith et al. 2003), a parallel with Amazonia and its massive decreases of population as well as of losses of knowledgeable persons capable of continuing to manage land and resources in the ways of the ancients (Clement 1999a, b).

Amazonianists have spoken of 'domesticated landscapes' (Clement 1999a, Clement et al. 2010; Erickson 2006) in almost precisely the way this term has been used in reference to cultural forests of Malesia (Terrell et al. 2003), and the way the 'making of a landscape' has been used to describe forest islands in West Africa (Fairhead and Leach 1996a: 4). Indigenous people often recognize and linguistically encode human-mediated disturbance in the formation of cultural forests. The Ka'apor people of Amazonia have terms for that distinction (Balée 2010) as do the Nuaulu of Maluku (Ellen 2010) and the Penan of East Kalimantan (Puri 2005). The Kissia language of Guinea distinguishes the current forest island where people reside from abandoned villages now covered in forest (Fairhead and Leach 1996a: 149). In fact, regardless of the origin of the species in question in these widely separated regions—Amazonia, West and Central Africa, and Malesia—the similarities of landscape indigeneity suggest possibilities of similar land management strategies that could contribute to future forest protection.

Whereas one does not find terracing (perhaps if only because there are few if any rocklike structures) as seen in Micronesia and Malesia (e.g. Rainbird 2004) we do find extensive areas of mounds, ditches, ringed-villages, and other manipulations of the earth itself, such as the most recently discovered and spectacular geoglyphs of Acre, western Brazilian Amazonia (Pärssinen et al. 2009; Schaan 2006). The mounds of the Amazon Estuary appear to have been related to exploitation of fish, for in some cases the nature of mound construction affords perennial water sources in the dry season, and without the mounds, such areas would be completely dry (Schaan 2006, 2010). Causeways in the northern Bolivian Amazon appear to have had a similar function (Erickson 2000b, 2008). What cannot be denied in the case of these mounds of the Bolivian Llanos de Mojos in the Upper Amazon and Marajó Island in the Amazon Estuary is intentionality (Erickson and Balée 2006; Schaan 2006). At Ibibate Mound Complex, Llanos de Mojos, before AD 1500 people intentionally dug dirt out of the ground in order to raise a surface at least 18 metres high, and in so doing, they created a barrow pit that has functioned also as a perennial source of drinking water to this day: the area, except next to river courses, is otherwise completely devoid of potable water in the dry season (Erickson and Balée 2006). At Marajó Island, between AD 480 and AD 700, people intentionally built 12 metre mounds, sometimes in the middle of water courses and sometimes next to them, in order to deepen or widen these water courses as well as to form dams to control water and redirect its flow; sophisticated hydraulics are in evidence in these ancient landscape transform- ations (Schaan 2006: 107, 2010). Other mounds on Marajó Island, such as Teso dos Bichos, contain carbonized vestiges of plants such as the tucumã palm (*Astrocaryum vulgare*) (Roosevelt 1991), which in other areas of Ama- zonia is a component of advanced stages of landscape transformation through human-mediated disturbance (Balée 1988, 2006; Corrêa 1985; Wessels Boer 1965); carbonized endocarps of the genus *Astrocaryum* are common in other archaeological sites in the Neotropics (Morcote-Rios and Bernal 2001).

The effects of these manipulations on the biota have been documented at Ibibate mound, Bolivian Amazon (Erickson and Balée 2006). Ibibate and forests like it are what I call primary landscape transformation, which involves a complete or near-complete turnover of species due to humans (Balée 2006, 2009). Such a turnover can increase or decrease the number of species present, but it always changes the distribution. I see this term as superior to 'primary succession' when referring to landscape transformations due to human activity (Balée 2006, 2009; O'Neill 2001). Many sorts of primary landscape transform- ation reduce species diversity: explosions of military ordnance; construction of highways, parking lots, and apartment complexes; flooding of lands to build reservoirs, dikes, and dams. The sort of primary landscape transformation that resulted from Amazon mound building, however, was qualitatively different. There are only about twenty species of vascular plants in the wetland savanna surrounding Ibibate mound; yet there are at least eighty-four species of trees and lianas with diameters of 10 cm at breast height and above atop the mound (Balée 2006; Erickson and Balée 2006). It is likely that mound building of various specific types elsewhere in Amazonia also involved alterations of diver- sity and therefore display indigeneity in the resulting diversity of species (e.g. Balée 2010; Erickson 2010; McKey et al. 2010; Rostain 2010). Many of these species cannot tolerate flooding, seasonal or otherwise. Here we have an indi- genous, if you will, contribution to alpha diversity (diversity in a specific locale, defined by given environmental gradients), as a result of primary landscape transformation.

Living Artefacts, Living Landscapes

Biological diversity atop Ibibate cannot be explained without referencing human and cultural activity. The archaeological signature of greatest signifi- cance here may be not so much the mute ceramic artefacts and the skeletal materials (including human bone) that jut out of the mound, but rather the living components of the mound. The forest and its trees on Ibibate represent living artefacts. The alpha diversity, higher than the natural diversity of the surroundings, is anthropogenic. And so is the quality of biological endemism.

A species of *Sorocea* (a tree in the fig family), which is an important fruit tree used in making a ceremonial beverage of the Sirionó Indians, today only occurs atop mounds like Ibibate. This is a case of primary landscape transformation (by definition, caused by human activity) in which species turn-over and other environmental variables had counterintuitive, positive outcomes. These are lessons from the archaeological past that can be understood from the study of living artefacts that thrive on living landscapes, in which the soil itself is alive, as Amazonian Dark Earths (Woods and McCann 1999), which are always anthropogenic soil horizons. The soil of Ibibate is a kind of Amazonian Dark Earth (Erickson and Balée 2006, Table 7.1, p. 196, 200); 13 per cent of the material is likely also from pure ceramic (Lee 1979), which led one geographer to refer to mounds like Ibibate as 'ceramic forests' (Langstroth 1996). Amazonian Dark Earths account for less than 1 per cent of the surface soils of the Amazon region, but are critical to understanding prehistoric landscape transformations (Woods 2003). Amazonian Dark Earths are sandy loams; they are high in nutrients, low in acidity, and more or less dark to charcoal-black in colour. They exhibit charcoal as well as elevated levels of phosphorus (P) in the form of phosphate, which is perhaps the key indicator of human activity (Woods 2003). Some of the P is coming from bone, but some of it may be coming from ceramics (Lima da Costa et al. 2003). Apart from high P content, Amazonian Dark Earths show high levels of carbon (C), nitrogen (N), calcium (Ca), magnesium, manganese, and zinc (Kern et al. 2003, 2004; Woods 2003). Structurally, also, these soils are appropriate for agriculture. Finally, they are remarkably diverse biologically. These soils, the product of ancient human landscape transformation, contain different microrganisms from those found in recently disturbed sites (Navarette et al. 2010) as well as in undisturbed sites (Tsai et al. 2009). This difference of microbiology of the soils indicates a human-mediated effect on biotic diversity, and it is not a reduction of that diversity, but the opposite. The soil microorganisms unique to Amazonian Dark Earths are, indeed, a microscopic signature of indigeneity of the past.

Indigeneity and Landscape Transformations

Authentic indigenous activity is, by one definition, what created many of the lands that preceded European colonialism. What in postcolonial studies is sometimes referred to as 'hybridity', namely, the mixing of cultural traditions as expressed in individual behaviour, does not disqualify persons from self-identification as indigenes. It merely references an identity that did not exist before the overt success of the enterprise of colonialism. In the pre-European *terra nullius*—that is, the Americas, Africa, Australia, and Oceania—these cultures also were intermingling and influencing one another. This is true even when the initial explorers thought that the people they saw considered themselves to be isolated from the rest of humanity, as the people of Guam thought at the time of Magellan's visit in 1521 (Rainbird 2004: 14). In fact, these seafaring people had vast trading and social contacts throughout Remote Oceania. It is difficult even in prehistory of the *terra nullius* to speak of isolated, essentialized cultures. In the Amazon Estuary, one can arguably speak of pre-Columbian hybridity and even pre-historic globalization of cultures, given the similarity of certain artefacts, such as female statuettes and other symbolically important figurines, over vast areas (Schaan 2006: 105). Indigeneity is therefore an arbitrary concept if one associates it only with what is non-European, for within that world also there were versions of what was indigenous and what was not.

The landscapes discussed above, on the other hand, are inseparable from the cultures—indigenes—that begat them. These are built, living environments that are ultimately anthropogenic in terms of the biota and its diversity, yet anthropogenic of a distinctive sort. They are not industrial or postindustrial artefacts of Western civilization. With but a few exceptions, they are not hybrid landscapes in the sense of their formation having been influenced by neo-European technology. Introduction of steel tools in Malesia did accelerate swidden cultivation, and presumably, therefore, secondary landscape transformation, on some islands (Bayliss-Smith et al. 2003: 347). And the Ka'apor of Amazonia did create old fallow, cultural forests using steel tools; indeed, they claim their ancestors never used the ancient stone axe heads occasionally found in their habitat for swidden agriculture, that such artefacts are *tupā-ra'i* 'thunder-seeds' (Balée 1994: 40). Yet even if intensive agriculture preceded swidden cultivation in the support of large Amazonian populations in late prehistory, which seems increasingly plausible (for a summary, see Denevan 2006), that would not preclude some form of early clearance of forest, on a limited scale, by people using stone axe heads, for limited swidden agriculture. That appears to have been the only kind of secondary landscape transformation utilized in the Atlantic Coastal Forest at the time of the discovery of Brazil by the Portuguese (Dean 1995). Indeed, it seems ingenuous to assume any other reason than that for explaining the existence of stone axe heads in areas lacking Amazonian Dark Earths, yet which were nevertheless arable. In other words, while intensive agriculture seems likely to have supported vast populations, isolated pockets of swidden agriculture could have contributed to long-term forest transformations (secondary landscape transformations), in perhaps ways similar to those effected by contemporary trekking societies, such as the Hoti of Venezuela (Zent and Zent 2004) and the Nukak of Colombia (Politis 2007).

CONCLUSION

Anthropogenic landscapes built long ago abound in what Renaissance European mariners often pretended to be a *terra nullius*. These landscapes in many cases had been *intentionally* planned, engineered, and built in prehistory (Erickson and Balée 2006; Fairhead and Leach 1996a; Rainbird 2004; Schann 2006) and they involved major alterations of the earth's surface, with movement of multitudinous tons of dirt in prearranged patterns, which in turn had effects on the subsequent distributions, diversity, and even endemism of the flora and fauna (Bayliss-Smith et al. 2003; Erickson and Balée 2006; Fairhead and Leach 1996a; Lepofsky 1992; Terrell et al. 2003). Archaeological landscapes in these regions were created by ancestors of people today who are referred to as indigenes, or indigenous people. With globalization, the exact identity and meaning of indigeneity is often assigned to local criteria and values. In any event, the environments that were altered by primary landscape transformation, as discussed in this chapter, constitute prima facie evidence of an indigenous quality that still persists for as long as states and global powers are willing to protect those environments and the indigenous people who occupy them from encroachment, be this gradual (as noted by Dannenmaier 2008) or otherwise.

4

Forced Moves or Just Good Moves? Rethinking Environmental Decision-Making among East African Intensive Cultivators

Matthew I. J. Davies

INTRODUCTION

There has been a tendency in archaeology and in related social sciences and humanities to view human cultures as simply 'adapted' to or 'in tune' with 'nature' (Binford 1962; Butzer 1982; Steward 1955a; White 1959). Nature in this view is difficult to define and is principally considered in opposition to culture; it is not culture, it is external to humans, and it has an active causality of its own. This is often true even when researchers have been considering phenomena with a distinctly 'human' flavour such as population growth or technological development; both have often been seen as 'natural' aspects of human behaviour, as things which 'just happen'. In such thinking, when human societies are impacted by nature (conceived of as a phenomenon emanating from outside of the human realm) their responsive action or behaviour is often considered to be 'forced', in the sense that there is only one way in which society can respond and therefore that the nature of the change is inevitable. The idea that alternative actions might be as appropriate and effective, and equally likely, is given little credence—the specific nature of the response is taken as requisite and the form of the response goes unques-tioned: human agency (choice) is given little opportunity to make its mark. Cause and effect are favoured over choice, opportunism, innovation, and dynamic decision making, while the environment is seen as external to culture and shaped by natural rather than cultural forces. Moreover, this logic is self-fulfilling; things occur as they do because the result was inevitable and only one course of action was possible; ergo the problem is solved!

Of course I am here describing an extreme position and most researchers today would see a much more dynamic interaction between humans and the natural world. However, unicausal thinking does remain pervasive in popular accounts (Diamond 2005, 1997; Fagan 2007: 16–17; Scarre 2005: 35) and in much influential academic work where technology, environment, and ecology remain prime mover explanations, at least partially at the expense of variable responses, individual agency, politics, and ideology (Algaze 2008: 151–4; Demarest 2004: 27–30; Pollock 1999: 22–5; Webster 2002: 327–43). There is, I believe, an under-representation of studies that specifically question the nature or form of socio-natural change. That 'natural' events such as climate change or volcanic eruptions enact change is certain, but such events do not specify the form of that change, let alone its scale and duration. Yet it is exactly such issues that anthropological archaeologists need to address if they are to produce data of relevance to modern environmental debates.

Through a discussion of intensive agriculture in Eastern Africa, my aim in this chapter is to tease out some of the complexities of human decision-making within a given biophysical world and to demonstrate that humans always face multiple choices in relation to the way in which they interact with their surroundings. I argue that the ways in which many people interact with the environment might be conceived of as an interaction between culture and matter, such that the 'environment' or 'nature' is to some extent an artefact (both physically and cognitively), a product of human choices which are historically and culturally grounded, although mediated by a degree of innovation. As with any artefact the raw material places constraints on the ways in which it may be shaped, but it rarely specifies a single course of action and the end result (in this case a socio-natural system) depends on both conscious and unconscious human agency. Moreover, I argue that what we see as archaeologists is only ever the net result of this web of decision-making processes, within which are a whole variety of heterogeneous and often divergent practices.

AGRICULTURAL INTENSIFICATION

The process of agricultural intensification is a good one to address in light of the above discussion, because a variety of unicausal factors have been advanced as explanation and because intensive agriculture itself, particularly irrigation, has been seen as a primary causal factor in the development of civilizations and socio-political hierarchies across the world (Adams 1966; Steward 1955b; Wittfogel 1957). At the same time, intensive agriculture inherently encompasses anthropogenic landscape transformations that attest to the dynamic way in which humans modify and shape the world around them.

Two major 'natural' theories have regularly been advanced as drivers of agricultural intensification[1]. The first might be termed 'ecological' and posits that if the ecological conditions of a given environment are sufficiently challenging then agricultural intensification becomes necessary for survival. In particular, advocates point to regular (but unpredictable) climatic fluctuations and the resulting requirement to buffer farming practices during unfavourable periods through the application of novel technological solutions, especially irrigation. This hypothesis was key to the hydraulic theories of Steward (1955b) and of Wittfogel (1957), who argued that novel ecological conditions encouraged agricultural intensification, with an accompanying need for management structures, leading in turn to increased socioeconomic differentiation and political centralization. Claims for the primary role of ecology (and associated agricultural intensification) on the development of socio-political complexity have continued in a less direct form in a number of studies worldwide (Davies 2009b) and essentially stem from cultural and behavioural ecology perspectives which give priority to environmental conditions and subsistence-based economics as explanation. In Eastern Africa, ecological flux as a driver of intensification has been claimed by Östberg (2004) in relation to the Marakwet of Northwest Kenya and has also been suggested by a number of other researchers (Widgren 2000, 2004; Sutton 2004).

However, an ecological explanation alone invites the question 'Why intensify'? If, as Boserup (1965) argued and others generally agree (Brookfield and Hart 1971), agricultural intensification is at least nominally labour-intensive, then before we conclude that simple ecological factors were the only or even the primary drivers of intensification we must demonstrate that no other possible solutions were open to farmers. In particular we need to show not only that ecological fluctuations were very real and severe but also that there were no other potential courses of action available (such as increasing the area of land under cultivation, moving to new areas, multicropping, or diversification) and importantly that subsistence was the only demand on production. Once other factors such as luxury exchanges, status building, or taxation come to have demands on production then intensification must be seen, in part, as a choice driven by a desire to fulfil social rather than natural or biological requirements, and the environment becomes as much an artefact to be used towards socio-cultural ends as an independent 'natural phenomenon'[2] driving the course of events.

---

[1] Other non-natural mono-causal explanations would include political phenomena such as taxation or tribute. Space and subject matter preclude discussion of these here.

[2] Of course, if we begin to see the 'social' as an element of biology then this distinction breaks down.

It is my contention that people almost always *choose* to intensify and that they do so for a number of interacting reasons, of which ecological concerns are only part of the story. It is this complexity of decision-making which is often missing from archaeological accounts and which makes them of poor use in applied environmental studies because they reduce ecology to subsistence and assume intensification as the only solution to ecological conditions.

The second factor might be termed 'population pressure' and was popularized by the work of Ester Boserup (1965) in her seminal study *On the Conditions of Agricultural Growth*. This hypothesis posits that increasing population results in increased demands on production such that intensification is required to extract more energy per unit of land. The hypothesis relies on the assumption that population growth is inevitable and, owing to physical circumscription of the population, will lead to increasing population density. In application, few studies have clearly demonstrated how populations were physically circumscribed; more normally it has simply been assumed that population growth leads to intensification. More interestingly, population growth itself has often been assumed as a natural characteristic of human communities—a factor beyond culture and in the natural realm of biology. This assumption overlooks multitudinous ways in which communities are able to regulate their own population sizes (Macie-Taylor and Boyce 1988). Studies that have dealt well with the issue of circumscribed populations have tended to rely on island case studies, particularly in the Pacific, where the boundaries of human action are more clearly defined (Brookfield and Hart 1971)[3].

A more novel application of the population pressure hypothesis was devised by Gourou (1991) with reference to Eastern African intensive cultivators. Gourou argued that cultivators in small highland areas were engulfed by a sea of nomadic pastoralists on the surrounding plains and that conflict between pastoralists and farmers confined the farmers to their highland enclaves, where population growth resulted in increased population density and agricultural intensification. Börjeson (2005), however, has eloquently deconstructed this 'siege' hypothesis, demonstrating how exchange between farmers and herders actually stimulated agricultural production, while at the same time arguing that high population density may in fact be the result of high agricultural production rather than vice versa. High levels of intensive production in the highlands may have acted as an attractor to settlement, meaning that the population pressure hypothesis would be turned on its head.

---

[3] The Boserupian model has now been significantly revised and modified by human geographers, although it still remains pervasive. For discussion see Brookfield (2001).

FORCED MOVES OR GOOD MOVES?

Both of these theories view intensification as an inevitable outcome of rational, or even optimal, logic under specific natural circumstances; what I would term a 'forced move'. Neither theory gives credence to alternative solutions to problems of ecology or population. Nor does either theory view intensification as just one of a myriad of socio-economic strategies within a specific set of circumstances. It is my contention, however, that agricultural intensification is not forced but rather a product of agency in a field of choice—a good move rather than a forced move.

We need to better understand the practical options open to individual communities, the variety of possible decisions they face, and the reasons why certain choices are favoured, at certain times, over others. We have to remember that there is nothing inevitable about the ways in which humans make use of the basic resources (such as soils, vegetation, animals, and climate) around them and indeed, that not all members of a community will follow the same strategy. Moreover, broad spatial and temporal patterns in the archaeological record need not be the result of a single resource exploitation strategy, but may arise from numerous different strategies acting at the same time, where variation comes not solely from 'environment' but also from variable sociocultural decision-making (tradition, experience, innovation) (see Rudiak-Gould, Chapter 14 this volume for a similar discussion of diverse decision-making under very different circumstances). It may further be argued that human choices in socio-natural systems are always underdetermined by experience and the complexity of the system such that this leads to variation in response towards heterogeneous but relatively 'good' choices, rather than optimal choices. Practices therefore fluctuate around the 'economically optimal'—but are rarely fully optimal in the sense employed by cultural ecologists. Indeed, as archaeologists, what we often observe as normal practice is actually the net result of a number of diverse practices, some of which leave more material trace than others and some of which may act to obscure the traces of others: we tend, however, to treat this *net* result as a single, normal, optimal practice. Agricultural intensification, for example, is highly misleading in that by modifying the landscape it draws attention away from other less visible practices, such as shifting cultivation or herding, which actually form part of a continuum of practice within the field of choice. Börjeson (2005) calls this the 'tyranny of monuments': it is an issue of which archaeologists must be more conscious. Following this, the question then is not 'What caused people to intensify agricultural production?' but rather 'Why did a certain number of people come to see intensification as a good choice compared to other potential courses of action?' And also, what other less visible choices did other portions of the population make? Why did some people choose to physically modify their environment and others not to do so?

In the following section I will explore such issues further with reference to Pokot farmers in northwest Kenya. In particular I will demonstrate Pokot agriculture to incorporate a variety of heterogeneous acts of decision-making, some of which have greater archaeological visibility than others. The choice to intensify is employed by some Pokot farmers, but made in the presence of alternative choices, many of which are employed by other members of society. Those people who chose to intensify did so because it seemed a 'good' move, but other equally viable choices were also available, and the decision to intensify was not forced. However, other 'choices' may have lower archaeological visibility, meaning that our perception of past practices can be skewed. Most importantly, since the intensification of agriculture is the product of choice within a cultural system it follows that the corresponding landscape transformations were not only the product of 'natural' phenomena but also of human culture, such that the resulting landscape must be viewed as a human artefact.

POKOT AGRICULTURE

The Pokot are a Kalenjin-speaking people who inhabit parts of West Pokot, Baringo and Elgeyo-Marakwet districts of Kenya's Rift Valley province and parts of Karamoja in eastern Uganda (Figure 4.1). They number somewhere in the region of 150,000 to 250,000 (Raymond 2005; Schladt 1997) and are often divided into two groups (Beech 1911: 15; Peristiany 1951: 188). A minority, perhaps one-third, engage in a pastoral lifestyle and inhabit the semi-arid lowlands to the north and east (Dietz 1987: 79). The other two-thirds live higher into the Cherangani and Seker hills and practise intensive agriculture, or a mixture of agriculture and stock keeping.

Pokot intensive cultivators make use of the ecotone between wet forested highlands and semi-arid lowlands. They utilize a variety of intensive agricultural techniques including hillside terracing, inter-cropping, manuring and a large, pre-colonial irrigation network to grow maize, millet, and, today, occasionally sorghum—which would have been the staple crop before the colonial introduction of maize. The farms are surrounded by low-lying plains inhabited by Pokot herders, who practise a specialised form of pastoralism, relying principally on milk and blood derived from their livestock. Around the fringes of the plains, some families mix ephemeral farming with larger numbers of small-stock (sheep and goats). In the highlands extensive rain-fed farming is increasingly common and, unlike farming in the foothills, does not rely upon intensive capital investments such as terracing and irrigation.

The Pokot as they are today are a relatively recent construct stemming from the early to mid-eighteenth century (Bollig 1990; Davies 2008, 2009a,

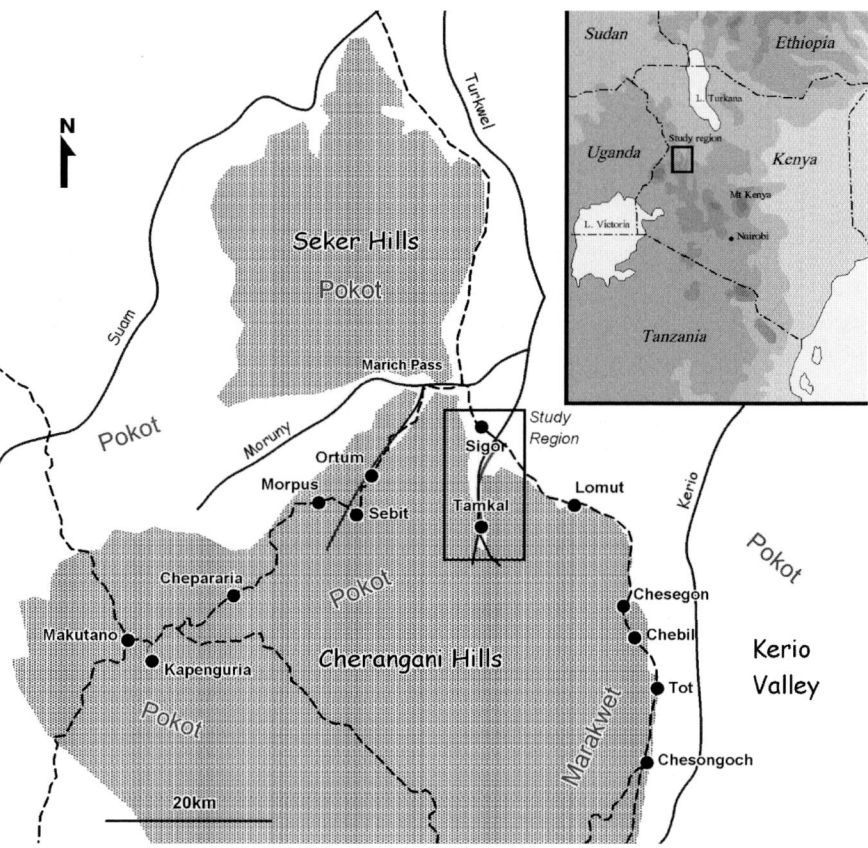

Fig. 4.1. Map showing location of Pokot territory.

2010). The more recent history of the Pokot has largely involved a 200 year pastoral expansion to the west, east, and north and the development of a highly specialized pastoral society (Beech 1911; Bollig 1990). However, this pastoral history has perhaps overshadowed a similar, but less well known, expansion of Pokot agriculturalists who have extended their influence southwards and up into the Cherangani Hills (Davies 2008, 2009a, 2010; Dietz 1987). Recent studies of the history of the Pokot agricultural system have drawn on a wide variety of archaeological and ethnoarchaeological data within a historical ecology framework. Key to these studies has been an approach that looks not at a completely abandoned, purely 'archaeological' landscape, but rather at a living landscape where present-day practices may be compared and contrasted with recent archaeological remains in a direct historical manner (Davies 2008, 2009a, 2010, 2012). This analysis focused on two key areas; changing settlement patterns and changing land-use patterns (as evidenced by abandoned and existing irrigation features), in a single large valley (Figure 4.2).

Fig. 4.2. View of the Pokot Hills, north-west Kenya.

SETTLEMENT PATTERNS AND CHRONOLOGY

A survey of settlement patterns via thirteen transects recorded the location of
both present-day and abandoned house sites and documented the changing
ratio of abandoned and modern homesteads across the landscape (Figure 4.3
and Table 4.1). This data demonstrated a massive abandonment of the northern part of the study region and the concentration of modern-day settlement
to the south. Further analysis of the distribution of changing house styles, and
abandoned house surface features, such as walling, grinding stones, and hearth
stones, led to a number of relative typologies and further suggested that
settlement in the north of the region had a deeper antiquity. This was
confirmed by analysis of the distribution of surface ceramics, which demonstrated that earlier, roulette-decorated wares were confined to the north of the
study region, and was followed up by the test excavation of six abandoned
settlement sites and the selection of material for absolute dating.

    The most southerly of the test excavated sites, EH01, produced material
remains and oral histories dating it to the last fifty years or so, while the second
most southerly, AH29, produced a thermoluminescence (TL) date of 150 years
before AD 2008 (*c.* AD 1860). AH93 produced an uncalibrated radiocarbon
date of 188±23 BP (OxA-18867) giving a preferred calibrated range of AD
1731–1809. The most northerly site S202 (Ortuso Village) gave an uncalibrated
date of 240±24 BP (OxA-18868) providing a preferred calibrated range of

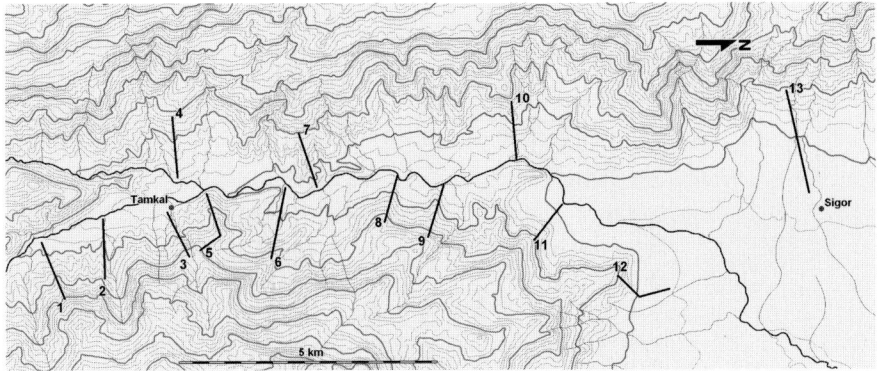

Fig. 4.3. Location of survey transects.

Table 4.1. Numbers of contemporary and abandoned houses by transect

Transect	Modern houses	Abandoned houses	Total houses	Abandoned/modern houses ratio	Abandoned as % of total houses
1	42	13	55	0.31	23.64
2	53	16	69	0.30	23.19
3	24	17	41	0.71	41.46
4	37	12	49	0.32	24.49
5	19	38	57	2.00	66.67
6	25	16	41	0.64	39.02
7	12	20	32	1.67	62.5
8	4	28	32	7.00	87.5
9	9	17	26	1.89	65.38
10	6	31	37	5.17	83.78
11	12	24	36	2.00	66.67
12	3	18	21	6.00	85.71
13	7	17	24	2.43	70.83
Total	253	267	520	1.06	51.35

AD 1630–80. These dates (Table 4.2.) confirm the general impression from relative indicators that settlement began in the south of the region around 350 years ago and then spread further south, up into the valley, with subsequent abandonment of northern regions. Indeed, in the extreme south of the valley today one can observe the new clearance of forest for agriculture and the establishment of new households. Overall the data gives a very strong impression of a community moving across the landscape through time.

In addition to this process of movement, analysis of the density of both past and present settlement demonstrated similar population densities across all transects, showing that settlement is presently abandoned parts of the region had previously existed at densities equivalent to those of modern settlement (Davies 2009a; Table 4.3.). This strongly suggests that the density of settlement

Table 4.2. Summary of radiometric dates from settlement sites and abandoned irrigation channels (★ date before 2008)

Location	Site	Description	Dating technique	Lab no.	Date (BP)★	Cal. 2σ	Preferred date (AD)
South	EH01	Abandoned homestead	Oral histories	N/A	N/A	N/A	**c.1950**
South-Central	AH29	Abandoned homestead	TL on ceramic	Oxford- TL	150	N/A	**c.1860**
North-Central	AH93	Abandoned homestead	C14 on charcoal	OxA-18867	188±23	1658–1686 (20%) 1731–1809 (55%) 1927–1954 (20%)	**1731–1809**
North	S202	Abandoned homestead	C14 on Charcoal	OxA-18868	240±24	1630–1680 (59.6%) 1760–1800 (29.8%) 1940–1960 (5.9%)	**1630–1680**
North	Takow	Irrigation channel	TL on ceramic	Oxford- TL	150	N/A	**c.1860**
North	Takoch	Irrigation channel	OSL	Oxford-X3247	114±33	N/A	**1836±33**

Table 4.3. Absolute (abandoned and modern) house densities per transect. House density is assumed to reflect total population densities

Transect	Total number of houses (abandoned and modern)	Transect Area (km²)	Absolute house density (houses/km²)
1	55	0.41	134.15
2	69	0.38	181.58
3	41	0.29	141.38
4	49	0.46	106.52
5	57	0.49	116.33
6	41	0.38	107.89
7	32	0.34	94.12
8	32	0.26	123.08
9	26	0.25	104.00
10	37	0.33	112.12
11	36	0.34	105.88
12	21	0.23	91.30
13	24	0.22	109.09

has not increased through time, but rather has remained relatively static since the inception of intensive farming in the region some 350 years ago. Moreover, there is very little to suggest that the total population has altered significantly over the last 200 years, only that it has moved steadily across the landscape. This argues against a simple population pressure model of agricultural intensification, and instead asks us to look for other factors involved in both the intensification of agriculture and the movement of farming across the landscape.

LAND USE AND IRRIGATION

A survey of presently used and abandoned irrigation channels identified a complex network of seventy channels throughout the valley (Figure 4.4). These channels varied from 500 m to over 7 km in length with varying degrees of construction technology (Davies 2008, 2009a). A chronology for this system was constructed based on Pokot oral histories relating to the construction of individual channels. This made use of a cyclical age-set system whereby named sets of initiates are established approximately every twelve years, such that one can work backwards from the present to establish the approximate dates during which a new set was formed and active in channel construction (Table 4.4). The oldest abandoned channels are situated in the north of the study region, while channels become progressively younger as one moves southwards. In the extreme south of the region many irrigation channels were constructed as recently as the 1970s and 1980s, while in the north, many large channels have been abandoned for some time.

This chronology was further tested using radiometric thermo-luminescence (TL) and optical luminescence (OSL) dates taken from sections cut through two

Fig. 4.4. Pokot irrigation channel.

Table 4.4. Pokot male circumcision sets, their dates of inception, and the likely period during which that set would have been active in irrigation channel construction

Circumcision set name	Duration of inception	Work period
Kaplelach	–1872	–1880
Murkütwo	1873–1885	1880–1895
Nyonki	1886–1898	1893–1908
Maina	1899–1911	1906–1921
Chumwo	1912–1924	1919–1934
Sowo	1925–1937	1932–1947
Koronkoro (Kapanga)	1938–1950	1945–1960
Kapkoymot	1951–1963	1958–1973
Kaplelach	1964–1977	1972–1987
Murkütwo	1978–1995	1990–2005
Nyonki	1996–present	—

Fig. 4.5. Section through an abandoned irrigation channel.

abandoned channels in the north of the study region (Figure 4.5). A TL date from Takow irrigation channel produced a date of *c.*1860 while an OSL date from Takoch irrigation channel produced a date of 1836±33. Overall these data conform well with the settlement survey, suggesting that large-scale irrigation began in the north of the valley around 200 years ago and then spread southwards into the valley, with subsequent abandonment of the northern parts of the valley over a very similar timescale to that of the settlement patterns.

Again this suggests a fluid pattern of land use with both *in situ* agricultural intensification and expansion across the landscape involving the conversion of former pristine forest to arable. Also, there is little to suggest that Pokot agricultural production was increasingly intensified; rather production appears high from the outset and is maintained through time, but without obvious increases in the intensity or total productivity of the system. However, the spatial patterning of this production certainly varies, with production beginning in the north and gradually spreading southwards, with subsequent abandonment of the north.

CAUSALITY IN POKOT ENVIRONMENTAL DECISION MAKING

This dual pattern of intensification and movement suggests an element of choice in the decision-making of Pokot farmers: the choice to remain in one

location and intensify or to move and exploit new and potentially larger tracts
of land. The factors that impinge upon this decision-making process are
myriad and difficult to ascertain for periods remote in time. However, for
the last few hundred years good ethnographic and ethno-historical data offer
some strong suggestions. In particular, ethnographic research points us towards the social embeddedness of Pokot farming and its connection to
broader concepts of value and exchange.

Increasing population density within a geographically circumscribed population is also not supported in the Pokot data: it therefore seems difficult to
suppose a simple correlation between population density and the process of
agricultural intensification. There is little evidence for increase in the *total*
population and the expansion of farming across the landscape is clearly
evident as an outlet to increasing population density. Like ecological fluctuations, changing population sizes certainly impact on the decision-making of
farmers, but they do so at the household level where they are collated with
multiple other factors which together specify a course of action. We need then
to look towards the other factors that lead both to the intensification of
agriculture and its movement across the landscape.

POKOT FARMING AS EMBEDDED SOCIAL PRACTICE

Elsewhere I have argued that Pokot farming cannot be reduced to a series of
technical procedures and disassociated from its social context (Davies 2009a:
120). Family structure, size, networking, and aspiration are as important to
agricultural success as is mastery of technical cultivation practices. Unravelling
the choice to intensify or move therefore requires detailed understanding of
Pokot family life as a *total social phenomenon*, rather than focus on a single
causal factor such as population pressure or ecological variability.

The first key point is that Pokot production is not geared solely towards
subsistence but aims, where possible, to produce a surplus for the acquisition
of prestige 'goods', such as livestock, increased family size (through marriage),
and the ability to fully participate in extensive social networks through the
selective redistribution of wealth. While the Pokot might be seen as a fully
egalitarian 'segmentary' society, participation in such networks does act to
build social capital or power through the creation of ties of obligation. In
theory all Pokot are equal, but in practice some are more equal than others.

The decision concerning what, when, and how much to produce therefore
relates very strongly not only to nutritional needs but also to the desire to
partake in reciprocal social networks such as *Tilia* or stock-friendships, to build
social credit through the donation of livestock for sacrifice, to undertake various
initiation ceremonies such as *sapana* (the spearing of an ox), to pay bridewealth

for marriage, to have further children, and more recently to pay school fees. Some families will have lower aspirations than others, some will work less hard, or will choose to follow different strategies toward the same goal.

Ecology is, of course, important here but it is impossible to separate from other concerns. Production over and above the needs of current subsistence may be seen as an important security measure, providing a surplus to support the family through times of hardship; and various intensive technical solutions might be employed towards this end. However, given that Pokot production is rarely geared solely to subsistence, and that movement and the cultivation of larger areas of land, in more favourable climatic zones, is also an option available to Pokot farmers, one cannot explain intensification in terms of ecological variability alone. Rather, this is one of many inter-related factors in agricultural decision-making. Participation in social networks may be just as important an ecological strategy as establishing a store of surplus grain; for example, at times of famine the 'storer' may have a store of grain, but the networker may be able to rely on friends or relatives in less affected regions for material support. Both are valid strategies based on sound decision-making relative to the family's broader context. But both networking and storage are also reciprocally motivated by the creation of social capital—which the storer builds through redistribution of surplus at times of need, and the networker through redistribution during times of plenty—and which both may then employ towards ecological (subsistence) aims or to favour their own political ambitions. Although the archaeological signatures (intensification vs expansion) of each strategy are very different, the decision-making behind both strategies is simultaneously ecological and social and the two are inseparable.

LAND TENURE AND ECOLOGY

The motivation to produce sits above more basic, broadly environmental concerns relating to the amount and quality of land available to the family. The primary social institution here is the enactment of Pokot land tenure, the rules of which govern inheritance of, and access to, land. Land is held in parallel strips of varying widths which run down the slope from the highlands to the foothills. These strips of land are first held by patrilineal clan and secondarily split between clan lineages and members of a lineage. In very simplified terms, the land of one man should be divided approximately equally between his sons, so that the amount of 'family' land available to an individual decreases in size each generation. Increasing one's land can only occur through expansion at the expense of one's neighbours—which itself is only possible through a degree of conflict and argument—or through partially abandoning one's inherited land and moving to the fringes of the entire system, often some kilometres away.

In addition, the quality of the land belonging to an individual will vary greatly depending on slope and soil type as well as on previous patterns of exploitation and (mis)management. These fundamental characteristics therefore also greatly affect a family's decision-making with regard to patterns of agricultural intensification or expansion across the landscape. Moving to new areas of land, outside of one's traditional family lands, brings the benefit that one may be able to clear virgin bush and cultivate a much larger area of better quality land. On the other hand, movement takes one away from important kin, exchange, and other social relations. An alternative then would be to remain and invest heavily in the original, smaller plot of family land or to reduce one's aspirations and settle for lower levels of productivity. Different strategies will be followed by different families who weigh or judge the importance of the various factors differently. For example, one family may place greater emphasis on the importance of strong kin ties and networking and opt to remain within their small traditional plot but intensify to increase production. Another family may forgo the safety net of strong kin ties in favour of increased levels of production from larger tracts of land without the need to intensify.

Historically, this pattern of movement and intensification in the system of land tenure is evidenced by the repeated layering of clan lands across the landscape and hints to an explanation of the archaeologically observed patterns in settlement and land use. For example, in Figure 4.6 the Saniak clan seem to have had their first territory in the north; however, as localized pressures on clan land increased through the continual division of land between sons, and as soils became gradually degraded through over-use, some members of the clan intensified production while others moved to a new location on the fringes of the system (now in the central-south of the system). This pattern then repeated itself again in the new location leading to

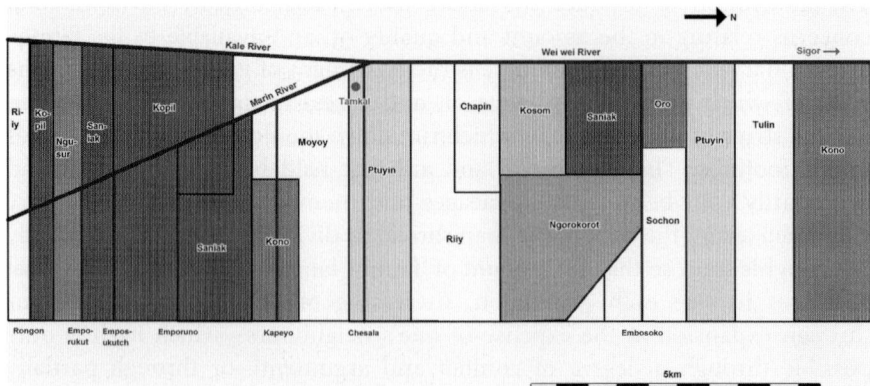

Fig. 4.6. Systematic map of Pokot land tenure by clan.

further intensification and also to the establishment of a third strip of Saniak clan land, now in the south of the system. As the growth of settlement in the new strips of land acted as attractors to younger Saniak clan members, so the disincentive to move away from the original land decreased and gradually the bulk of the Saniak clan shifted southwards, resulting in a de-population of the original northern lands and the abandonment of some of its intensive agricultural features. As one can see from Figure 4.6, this pattern also repeats itself in relation to clans such as Ptuyin, Kono, Kopil, and Riiy; oral histories further support this pattern of movement.

Intensification of agriculture and movement through time thus exist side by side in the Pokot system. Intensification can be partially explained in terms of population pressure, but only at a very localized scale within a constrained system of land tenure. Population pressure only occurs through a socially constructed mechanism to control access to land and the social and the 'natural' are collapsed into one. Moreover, intensification and expansion are clearly both 'good' moves given the specific context of family-based decision-making, but other choices were available and which (if any) strategy might be viewed as 'optimal' is very difficult to assess. For example, a third alternative strategy to both intensification and expansion is to build capital in the form of livestock and then turn away from agriculture completely and become a pastoralist. This is well documented ethnohistorically but space precludes more detailed discussion here.

POKOT PERCEPTION AND CONSTRUCTION OF THE ENVIRONMENT

Consciously or unconsciously, the Pokot view their physical environment as malleable and amenable to modification to suit a variety of household socio-cultural needs. The choices made by Pokot farmers also feed back into the creation of the landscape and condition the nature of potential future changes. Thus while the environment limits the range of possible decisions open to Pokot farmers, in the same way that the raw material limits the actions of an artisan, it does not specify the exact action or end result[4]. Through their choice of 'good' moves, the Pokot are active agents in the construction of their environment rather than passive responders.

---

[4] Culture itself is the same. It provides some limitations, institutions and proscribed structural behaviours, but it is malleable within context. Culture does not specify the exact course of actions in any one situation, only a range of possibilities.

The way in which the Pokot construct their environment is not solely physical but also cognitive in terms of the way in which they (and indeed we) perceive the potential of their world based on a pre-existing template. Such a template may on the one hand limit the ability of Pokot farmers to see alternative potential in their land, but at the same time it empowers them with the belief that the land can and should be altered to suit their purposes. For example, vegetation around water courses has an association with spirits and its use, and that of the land where it grows, is therefore restricted, but mountain-top forest has no such association and so can be legitimately turned to arable. Such environmental beliefs are shared by Pokot farmers and herders despite the difference in their physical environment and economy. While restrictions on vegetation around water courses may make much sense in the lowlands as a means of preventing erosion and rapid run-off, the destruction of mountain forest, unprotected by such prohibition, is likely to be of greater detriment to water catchments. However, the pre-existing cognitive model (likely developed in the differing environmental context of the plains and foothills) trumps all and allows the conceptual space to modify the environment even in ways which may not be economically optimal in the long-term. However, within the context of Pokot perceptions and household ambitions such decisions are normally perceived as 'optimal' or at least 'good' moves by the individuals who make them. Convincing people therefore that their actions are sub-optimal, or indeed in the long term highly detrimental, is thus a difficult and delicate task, but one in which the long-term data of the archaeological record may have an important role.

While space here precludes any more detailed treatment of Pokot environmental perceptions[5], the archaeological record details the application of such perception in broad contexts and provides a long data set through which to detail variability in Pokot environmental decision-making through time. Archaeology's *longue durée* approach may then offer one avenue through which to assess and explain variability in human–environment interactions, both among the Pokot and more widely, and to persuasively encourage the modification of human behaviour in the present.

CONCLUSION

Ultimately, no particular production strategy is a forced move, but rather at the household level, and dependent on individual circumstances, a variety of

---

[5] Save to say that investigations into Pokot perceptions of the socio-natural world, its abstract potential, and an individual's contextual possibilities within this conceptual model, must form the next step in better understanding Pokot interactions with their physical world.

strategies may be seen as potential 'good' moves. Among the Pokot the most significant of these are agricultural intensification and agricultural expansion, both of which are employed contemporaneously. The decision of which strategy to follow relates in part to broadly defined 'environmental' factors, such as soils and climate, but is also as much conditioned by broadly defined 'cultural' factors such as land tenure, personal ambition, individual innovation, and seasonal and life-cycle based family requirements (costs of education, rites of passage, marriage). Moreover, agricultural decision-making feeds back into the broadly defined physical 'environment' by altering soils and vegetation, and changing the value of, access to, and potential of land. Past agricultural decisions therefore condition how farming practices will alter in the future, and turn the environment into an artefact of human action.

The practices of Pokot farmers are thus not an adaptation to the environment. Viewed in the long term they are a constituent part of the environment, which is not static or given but always in flux, and this has important implications for the way in which we approach questions of environmental sustainability[6]. Fundamentally, culture and environment are not independent, but mutually constituted. They cannot force each other for they are one and the same—human decision-making is thus never a 'forced move' but only ever a 'move', for better or worse. This perspective only emerges out of a diachronic approach, and hence I believe that archaeology has a very important role to play, not only in the way that we conceive of human–environment relations in an abstract manner but also in how we create, question, and apply environmental knowledge in a very real and practical sense in the present.

---

[6] Common concepts of sustainability imply a static, unchanging system and development attempts to 'create' sustainability thus involve adaptation to a given environment. However, if humans are rightly acknowledged as part of the environment then any attempt at modifying human behaviour will act to alter the environment itself—by definition this makes the environment 'unstable' and the agricultural system dynamic rather than static, meaning that 'sustainability' only exists in terms of flux and change, not stasis. This problem applies not only to modernizing attempts at development, but also to the application of 'indigenous knowledge' when 'indigenous' populations are wrongly conceived of as 'adapted to' and thus in stasis with—and inherently conservative of—their 'environment'. Such perspectives stem from the fallacy of a synchronic perspective, which cannot appreciate rates of change.

5

Is the 'Environment' Good to Eat or Good to Paint? Faunal Consumption and Avoidance among Hunter-Gatherer-Fishers in the Beagle Channel Region (Tierra del Fuego, South America)

Dánae Fiore, Angélica Tivoli, and Atilio Francisco Zangrando

INTRODUCTION

This chapter discusses some aspects of the multi-dimensional nature of human–environment relationships. It focuses on the interaction established between people and animals in the Beagle Channel region (Tierra del Fuego, South America; Figure 5.1) through an analysis of taxon selection or avoidance in two inter-related spheres: subsistence and ceremonial art.

The selection or avoidance of a particular species can be related to environmental, economic, political, and ideological factors, and our aim is to point out which of these factors influenced the high exploitation of certain taxa and the low representation of others. We achieve this by comparing archaeological data with spatially and temporally contemporaneous ethnographic information about the representation of animal species in ceremonial body paintings. Thus, we seek to explain whether the selection of some species and the avoidance of others in the subsistence sphere was being reinforced by or forbidden according to symbolic values that stemmed from the ceremonial sphere.

Such questions derive from a theoretical premise that dismisses the notion of absolute optimality in human practices. It proposes instead that people's actions and decisions are not guided only by rational principles and cost-minimizing aims: they can also be non-rational and non-optimal, and yet can make a socio-economic system function and reproduce efficiently through

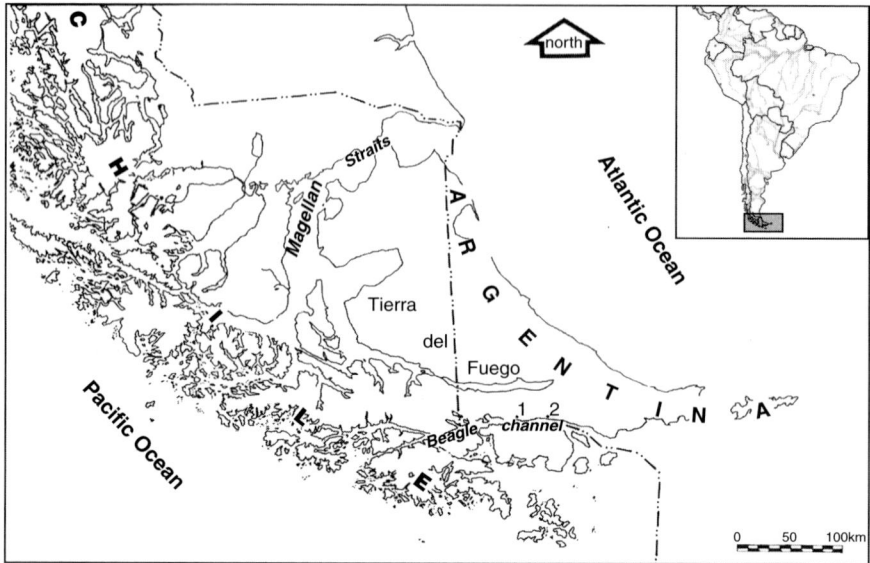

Fig. 5.1. Tierra del Fuego, Southern South America. Archaeological sites: 1, Túnel VII; 2, Imiwaia I and Lanashuaia I.

time and space without collapse. We argue that archaeological techniques and data have much to contribute to an understanding of the complexity of human–environment relations—particularly the ability to critique the overly simplistic economic models that often feed into popular and bureaucratic approaches to human environments.

HUMAN–ANIMAL RELATIONS FROM A MULTI-DIMENSIONAL PERSPECTIVE

During the last fifteen years, one of the most popular approaches to subsistence in prehistoric and non-industrial societies has been the application of optimality models (e.g. Broughton 1994; Grayson and Delpech 1998; Nagaoka 2002, among others). In principle, these models were conceived as methodological tools through which the researcher lays out a hypothetical scenario of how resources should be consumed if people were trying to minimize costs and maximize benefits towards reaching an optimal result. Often optimality was measured according to the greater or lesser consumption of species of higher or lower ranking. Resource ranking could be built taking into account a series of variables: resource size, availability in the environment, technology, loss risk, and so on.[1] The model was then contrasted with the archaeological data to evaluate whether the latter diverged from the optimal state: such possible deviations had to be explained and could shed light on sociocultural preferences which override plainly economic choices (Bettinger 1991; Bird et al. 2009; Gremillion 2002; Politis and Saunders 2002; Shennan 2002).

Yet, in practice, in many cases it has been assumed that human decisions and actions always aim to minimize costs and maximize benefits, thus implying what some authors call a 'formalist' conception of economy (Burling 1962, 1964, 1976; Godelier 1976; Polanyi 1957). Such a perspective assumes that individuals are purely rational, inherently efficient in pursuing individual goals, operate in an ideology-free environment, and always behave competitively. Thus, it not only naturalizes a Western and capitalist economic discourse by applying it to the past (see Armstrong Oma, Chapter 11 this volume for a similar discussion with regard to farming communities) but also disregards the influences of non-rational factors (affection, perception, values), ideology, and symbolism over human actions. From our point of view, the application of optimality models (Bettinger 1991; Shennan 2002; Smith 1983; Winterhalder 1981; Winterhalder and Smith 1981) in such a formalist manner turns a method for the assessment of resource exploitation into a general law of human behaviour (Fiore and Zangrando 2006) and therefore misuses an otherwise useful heuristic tool (Tivoli 2010a, 2010c, 2012; Tivoli and Zangrando 2011; Zangrando 2009a, 2009b).

Optimality models are mainly a means of assessing how much an actual case deviates from its optimal material possibilities: they do not provide an entire framework of conceptual tools to explain why such deviations actually happen. Such conceptual tools need to take into account the multi-dimensional nature of human practice, including the various spheres in which human actions take place and the numerous factors that constitute each of these spheres.

Human practices can be analytically sub-divided into different behavioural spheres, such as subsistence, technology, art, and symbolism; but in practice, these spheres overlap (thus a specific form of subsistence requires the use of a specific technology), and their divisions are presented here solely for analytical purposes (Alvarez and Fiore 1993; Dobres 2000; Fiore 2002; Nielsen 1995) because they are useful to assess how human practices (including human–animal relationships) are often embedded within a complex network of actions. In fact, when tackling the problem of human–animal relationships, it is often necessary to look beyond subsistence: the consumption or avoidance of a certain species can be directly influenced by the technology, art, or

---

[1] Nevertheless, many of these variables are impossible to measure correctly in prehistoric cases: as a result, this ranking is usually based on energetic return, although there are many objections to this (Bettinger 1991; Bird et al. 2009; Madsen and Schmitt 1998; Smith 1983; Winterhalder and Smith 1981).

symbolism spheres. And vice-versa: the artistic representation or avoidance of a certain animal can be influenced by elements from other spheres, such as symbolic values (the species may be a totem symbol and therefore its representation is restricted to a certain clan) or subsistence features (perhaps the species is toxic and therefore should not be represented in any art form, or is dangerous and difficult to hunt and therefore it should be artistically represented as part of a 'hunting magic' ritual). In this chapter we will focus on the interaction of three spheres—subsistence, art, and symbolism—to assess how much they influenced the consumption or avoidance of fish and bird species in the diet and the ceremonial body painting of the Beagle Channel populations. The temporal range includes two archaeofaunal assemblages dated to the nineteenth century AD (Lanashuaia and Tunel VII) and one dated to the fifth or sixth century AD (Imiwaia I, layer B). We will compare these with ethnographic data from the nineteenth and twentieth centuries.

In order to tackle the dynamics of art, symbolism, and subsistence, it is relevant to point out that each of these spheres is constituted by ecological, economic, socio-political, and ideological factors. That is to say, every sphere of action, be it subsistence or art, is constituted by:

a) ecological factors: resource availability, seasonality, ethology of animal species, species visual appearance, etc.;

b) economic factors: labour division, labour investment, etc.;

c) political factors: the rights, duties, and roles of people who carry out each task, the rules that regulate their possibilities to exercise power to do things and power over resources, products, and people, etc.;

d) ideological factors: a discourse of concepts and values which is present in the thoughts, perceptions, and practices of a group, and which allow for society's reproduction.

This theoretical perspective aims to break with the common straightforward association between subsistence, ecology, and economy on the one hand and between art, power, and ideology on the other. Such associations stem from a philosophical split between the material and the symbolic, which lumps the former with economy and the latter with ideology. Such a material/symbolic split treats these two aspects as if they were separate entities, when they are in fact inextricable parts of the same reality (Alvarez and Fiore 1993; Nielsen 1995).

Consequently, our perspective stresses that ecological factors can influence art as much as ideological factors can influence subsistence. Moreover, because art, symbolism, and subsistence spheres in practice have overlapping zones, we have the opportunity to search for the mutual interactions between them in order to shed light on the ecological, economic, socio-political, and ideological factors underlying all these spheres. Optimal and non-optimal choices may be influenced by all these factors, and each one of them should be analysed before asserting that a certain subsistence pattern was originated by ideological values. The same goes for the interaction between spheres: it is not acceptable to assume the influence of symbolism over subsistence to account for the lack of consumption of a certain species. It is first necessary to assess whether such a pattern stems from the technological sphere (perhaps the tool-kit lacked a weapon with which to capture the species) or from ecological factors (such as resource depletion). Thus, subsistence preferences may be guided by a pro-optimality ideology operating within the subsistence sphere, but they may also be influenced by ideological values prescribed or reinforced by the art and symbolism spheres. When these latter values are pro-optimality, it is almost impossible to distinguish in the archaeofaunal record whether patterns come only from a pro-optimality ideology within the subsistence sphere or whether they also respond to the influence of art or symbolism over subsistence, because of their equifinality (that is, if the different spheres end up contributing to the same optimal result, this makes it hard to distinguish their individual inputs in the archaeological record).

Conversely, when these ideological art or symbolism values are non-optimal it can be easier, in the archaeological record, to identify their separate influence on subsistence habits, because the first two generate in the last a pattern that departs from the optimal (Fiore and Zangrando 2006). Yet in order to make this distinction it is necessary to have an archaeological record with good resolution in every sphere of human action, and to complement it as necessary with contemporaneous information from the ethnographic record. This latter strategy is followed in this chapter.

In sum, human–animal relationships are based on rational and non-rational decisions and actions which are developed in different spheres of activity—subsistence, technology, ceremonial art, and symbolism—and are influenced by their intrinsic environmental, economic, and ideological factors. Our analysis aims to shed light on the factors that influenced the consumption and avoidance of animal species of the Beagle Channel region, in order to understand the mutual interactions that occurred between the subsistence, symbolic, and artistic spheres during the nineteenth century and to establish whether the tendencies found can be traced back into an archaeological assemblage dating 1500 years BP.

CONTEXT: HUNTER-GATHERERS AND THE ENVIRONMENT IN THE BEAGLE CHANNEL REGION

The Beagle Channel is located at the southern portion of Isla Grande de Tierra del Fuego, which is the biggest island of the Fueguian archipelago (currently divided between Chile and Argentina). The Channel runs west–east, and is approximately 180 km long and 4 to 7 km wide. The geography of this region is characterized by mountain ranges, several rivers and river valleys which run north–south, and an irregular coast which varies in topography between high-slope rocky and low-slope sandy seashores. The mean annual temperature is 6.5°C. The environment is characterized by woods of Nothofagus (*N. betuloides* and *N. pumilio*) located between sea level and 600 m above sea level, and by a variety of faunal taxa. Coasts and seascapes are inhabited by important populations of cetaceans, pinnipeds (southern sea lions (*Otaria flavescens*)) and fur seals (*Arctocephalus australis*), guanacos (*Lama guanicoe*), and a broad taxonomical diversity of birds, fish, and molluscs.

The inhabitants of the Beagle Channel region were hunter-gatherer-fishers who developed a littoral way of life. Most of the sites are shell middens which show a predominant consumption of maritime resources and a technology of lithic, bone, and shell artefacts (Orquera and Piana 1999a, 2005, 2009). Although the region's archaeological sequence is quite long (dating from 6400 radiocarbon years BP to the nineteenth century), we will focus here on assemblages dated to the nineteenth century, in order to be able to compare them with contemporary ethnographic data, and on another assemblage dated to 1500 years BP in order to assess whether recent trends can be traced back in time.

ARCHAEOLOGICAL DATA AND METHODS

The archaeological sample under study in this chapter comes from the assemblages of three sites from the Beagle Channel region: Túnel VII and Lanashuaia I, which date to the nineteenth century, and Imiwaia I (layer B) dated to 1500 BP. The three assemblages are shell middens, and there are no recorded functional differences among them (Estévez Escalera and Vila Mitjá 1995; Orquera and Piana 1999a, 2009). Within these samples, we have analysed fish and bird taxa: these two groups represent approximately 55 per cent of the animal biodiversity of the Beagle Channel. Other taxa present in the assemblages include southern sea lions, fur seals, guanacos, and mussels.

The archaeofaunal remains studied represent a total of thirty-one species belonging to twenty-one families of birds and fish (Table 5.1). Almost all the bone elements of the fish and bird species are represented and well preserved, which facilitated their exact taxonomic identification (Tivoli 2008; Zangrando 2009a). Previous taphonomic studies on fish remains indicate that there is no correlation between bone density of each bone and its respective anatomical

Table 5.1. Ecological and nutritional information of animal resources from Beagle Channel

RESOURCES	Weight per individual (kg)	Kcal per individual	Gregarious	Seasonality	Potential Dietary Yield (PDY)		
					High	Medium	Low
SEA MAMMALS							
Otaria flavescens (general mean)	232.00	277014	Yes	All year	*Otaria flavescens*		
A. australis (general mean)	53.60	64000	Yes	March–Sept.	*Arctocephalus australis* ↑	puppies	
TERRESTRIAL MAMMALS							
Lama guanicoe (general mean)	77.00	78315	Yes	Winter	*Lama guanicoe* ↓	puppies (chulengos) ↑	Foxs–Nutrias–Rodents
BIRDS							
Spheniscidae	5.00	2880	Yes	Spring–Summer	Colonies ↓	Spheniscidae	
Diomediedae	3.50	2027	No	All year			Diomedeidae
Phalacrocoracidae	2.60	1501	Yes	All year	Colonies ↓	Phalacrocoracidae	
Laridae	1.23	712	Yes	All year			Laridae
Procellariidae	0.68	396	Yes	Autumn–Winter			Procellariidae
Chloephaga	3.00	2461	Yes	Summer		*Chloephaga sp.*	
FISH							
P. magellanica	0.10	80	No	All year			*P. magellanica*
Patagonotothen sp.	0.09	72	No	All year			*Patagonotothen*
M. magellanicus	0.62	470	Yes	Summer	Beachins ↓	Merluccidae–Gempylidae	
Clupeidae	0.01	12	Yes	Summer	Beachins ↓	Clupeidae	
E. maclovinus	0.56	560	No	All year		*Eleginops maclovinus*	
MUSSELS (*Mytilus sp.*)	6.6/1000	1.45	Yes	All year	Colonies ↓	Colonies	Mytilus, Nacella, etc.

Note: The information for pinnipeds and guanacos was obtained in Schiavini (1990). With regard to birds, for Spheniscidae and Phalacrocoracidae the proposed values in Schiavini (1993) were used, whereas those indicated by Tivoli and Perez (2008) were used for Chloephaga. For fish, the values of average weights were calculated from a database generated by one of the authors of this chapter (A. F. Zangrando), while energy yields were provided by Fernandez et al. (2000). Finally, the data for molluscs were presented by Orquera (1999).

representation measured through MAU%[2] in assemblages with diverse chronologies (Zangrando 2003, 2007, 2009a). This lack of a relationship between them suggests that there was not a significant bone loss through time. Analyses of bone fragmentation also show high survival values in all assemblages, and again there are no significant differences between species and assemblages with diverse chronologies (Tivoli 2008, 2010b; Zangrando 2007). Therefore, it can be maintained that the presence, absence, and frequency of bird and fish species in the assemblages under study did not respond to taphonomic factors.

The general aim of this chapter involves finding out whether the patterns of subsistence in the Beagle Channel show a bias towards the selection or avoidance of certain species. In order to achieve this aim, we have used two measurements:

a) the percentage of the number of specimens (NISP%) is used to evaluate the archaeofaunal species in terms of taxonomical abundance;

b) the species' potential dietary yield (PDY) was calculated to analyse whether the selection or avoidance of a species was related to its nutritional importance. The PDY was measured as high or low, and was constructed using the combination of the following variables (as known from current ecological data):

1) body size: average weight and caloric contribution per individual of the species;

2) seasonality of the species: presence of the species in one season or all year round;

3) ethology of the species: presence or absence of gregarious behaviour.

Variable 1 influences the return of prey-capture and thus the choice of hunting-fishing the species; variables 2 and 3 increase or decrease the capturing opportunities of each species according to the available technology handled by the human populations under study. In general terms, the higher value of each variable, the higher PDY the species will have (Table 5.1).

---

[2] MAU (Minimal Animal Unit) as defined by Binford (1984) is a zooarchaeological measurement that allows the archaeologist to assess the consumption of anatomical portions in an archaeofaunal assemblage. Two steps are needed to calculate the MAU: firstly the MNE (Minimum Number of Elements; i.e. skeletal portions of a specific species) represented in such assemblage has to be counted; secondly this number has to be divided by the number of times that a specific skeletal portion is represented in the skeleton of an individual of such species (e.g. if the species is a sea lion and the skeletal portion is a femur, given that sea lions have two femurs the MNE is divided by two). MAU% is a standardization of the values of each skeletal portion under study through its expression in percentages, and it is calculated by considering the highest MAU number of a skeletal portion of the assemblage as 100% and then attributing relative percentages to the rest of the assemblage in comparison.

ETHNOGRAPHIC DATA AND METHODS

The ethnographic information indicates that the native inhabitants of the Beagle Channel during the nineteenth and early twentieth centuries were the Yámana: a hunter-gatherer-fisher society which moved among the islands of the Fueguian archipelago using bark canoes (Orquera and Piana 1995, 1999b). Ethnographic data concerning Yámana art (body painting) is extensive, including fifty-four written records and ninety-eight photographs (Figure 5.2). Written sources about its symbolism are fewer but provide thorough information about Yámana myths and ceremonies. These sources have been analysed to assess their reliability and accuracy. Several variables were taken into account to reveal the texts and photos biases, including the length of stay of each writer (voyager, religious missionary, ethnographer, and so on), the

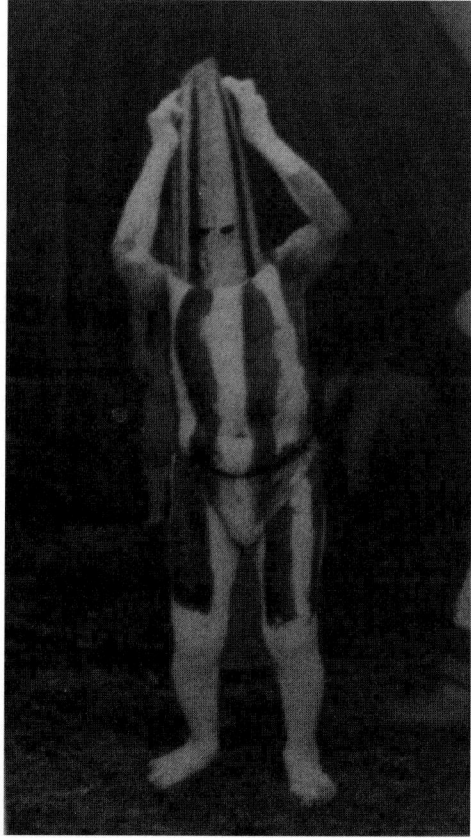

Fig. 5.2. Kina spirit of unknown referent. Photo: published by Gusinde in 1937: plate 34. Copy held in the Museo del Fin del Mundo archives (Ushuaia, Tierra del Fuego).

aims of each voyage or expedition, the language in which they communicated with the Yámana, the terms and concepts used in their texts, and the confirmations and contradictions between texts and between photographs (Fiore 2002, 2006).

Within the Yámana symbolic sphere, the *kina* was an initiation ceremony of young men to adulthood. It was reported by the Anglican missionary Thomas Bridges (1933, 1894), and was later thoroughly described by ethnographers M. Gusinde (1986 [1937],) and W. Koppers (1997 [1924]), who observed the ceremony in 1922. Gusinde and Koppers also took twelve photographs of participants in this ceremony. During the *kina*, young men were initiated to adulthood by men already initiated, who introduced them to mythical and practical knowledge. Some of this knowledge was claimed to be 'secret'. The men and the initiands, who paraded in front of a ceremonial hut, wore body painting and masks to represent more than forty-seven spirits. Although several of these spirits were considered benevolent, they had the general aim of frightening and controlling the women and children. For this reason, the men painted and masked themselves inside the hut, out of the sight of the women. This procedure was carried out in order to keep 'the secret'.

According to the available information about the spirits, which comes mostly from Gusinde (1986) and partly from Bridges (1933), thirty-three of the *kina* spirits represented animals, including maritime mammals, fish, birds, and insects; two represented mythical referents (one of which is a mythical animal); there are no data regarding twelve other spirits (see Table 5.2). In ten cases both authors provide coincidental information about the same animal spirits, augmenting the reliability of the data; in the rest of the cases we can only rely on Gusinde´s information for identification of the species, and therefore the assessment of its reliability is more difficult. Gusinde provides in his 1986 [1937] text both the common name and the scientific name of each identified species. So in order to reduce the potential inaccuracies of his information, we have not taken into consideration a) the cases in which there is no coincidence between the common name and the scientific name provided for the spirit's referent (with the exception of German–Spanish translation mistakes which are quite easily identified), nor b) the cases in which the scientific name provided does not belong to the realm of species known to inhabit the Beagle Channel region.

The *kina* body paintings were made using three colours: black, white, and red. The designs were simple but varied: they basically consisted of a coloured ground that covered the whole body and mask, over which lines, bands, dots, or semi-circles of another colour were painted. Thus, the combination between these elements, their colours, and their position on the body created designs which are different for each spirit and allow its visual identification.

Table 5.2. Kina spirits data: fish and birds

Name of bird spirit	Species documented in ethnographic sources	Current scientific name	Current common name	Ethnographic source	ground lines	short lines	bands	dots	rows of dots	big dots	semi-circles
Haimus-yaka	Patagonian blennie (*Eleginus maclovinus*)	*Eleginops maclovinus*	Patagonian blennie	G 1986: 1349 B 1933	WB						
Suna-yaka UI	Diodon (*Diodontidae*)	Unidentified	Unidentified	G 1986: 1349	W						R
Ilésci-yaka UI	Herring (*Clupea pectinatal*)	*Sprattus fueguensis?*	Sardine?	G 1986: 1349	W		B				
Imakai-yaka UI	Sea trout (*Atherinichthys*)	*Austroatherina nigricans?*	Silverside?	G 1986: 1349		W					
Lepalus-yaka UI	Small salmon	Unidentified	Unidentified	G 1986: 1349	W	R					
Kalampasa-yaka MA	Kalampasa	Mythical referent	Mythical referent	G 1986: 1349 B 1933: 178	W						R
Name of bird spirit	**Species documented in ethnographic source**	**Current scientific name**	**Current common name**	**Ethnographic source**	**ground lines**	**short lines**	**bands**	**dots**	**rows of dots**	**big dots**	**semi-circles**
Kixinteka-yaka	Grey Gerifalte (*Circus cinereus*)	*Circus cinereus*	Cinereus harrier	G 1986: 1347	W			B			
Akimagaia-yaka	Falcon (*Ibycter australis*)	*Daptrius americanus?*	Red-throated caracara?	G 1986: 1347	W		R				
Kilaxila-yaka	Eagle (*Buteo poliosomus*)	*Buteo polyosoma?*	Red-backed hawk	G 1986: 1347	R			B			
Lurux-yaka	Grey head goose (*Chloëphaga poliocephala*)	*Chloepaga poliocephala*	Ashy-headed goose	G 1986: 1347	RW						
Kimoa-yaka	Magellan goose (*Chloëphaga picta*)	*Chloepaga picta*	Upland goose	G 1986: 1347	R					W	
Alakus-yaka	Duck (*Tachyeres brachypterus*)	*Tachyeres brachypterus*	Falkland steamer-duck	G 1986: 1347	W		B	R			
Wemar-kipa-yaka	Small gull (*Larus glaucodes*)	*Larus scoresbii? Larus maculipennis?*	Dolphin gull or Brown-hooded gull?	G 1986: 1347	W	R					

(continued)

Table 5.2. Continued

Name of bird spirit	Species documented in ethnographic sources	Current scientific name	Current common name	Ethnographic source	ground	lines	short lines	bands	dots	rows of dots	big dots	semi-circles
Touwisiwa-yaka	Pufino (*Puffinus griseus*)	*Puffinus griseus*	Sooty shearwater	G 1986: 1347	B							
Wilauileaka	Skua gull (*Magalestris skua chilensis*)	*Catharacta chilensis*	Chilean skua	G 1986: 1347	W	RW	R					
Gёrapu-yaka	White albatross (*Diomedea exulans*)	*Diomedea exulans*	Wandering albatross	G 1986: 1347 / B 1933: 246	W	R						
Katanux-yaka	Maritime dove (*Daption capensis*)	*Daption capense*	Cape petrel	G 1986: 1348	W				B			
Taperola-yaka	Small dun diver (*Podiceps calipareus*)	*Podiceps gallardoi*	Hooded grebe	G 1986: 1348	B			W				
Yesex-yaka	Black cormorant (*Phalacrocorax atriceps*)	*Phalacrocorax atriceps*	Imperial shag	G 1986: 1348 / B 1933: 274	WB							
Wasenim-yaka	Bow cormorant (*Phalacrocorax gaimardi*)	*Phalacrocorax gaimardi*	Red-legged shag	G 1986: 1348	WB			W				
Sursa-yaka	Magellan penguin (*Spheniscus magellanicus*)	*Spheniscus magellanicus*	Magellanic penguin	G 1986: 1349	RW			x				
Kiwaguiaka	Sea gull (*Larus dominicanus*)	*Larus dominicanus*	Kelp gull	G 1986: 1351 / B 1933: 170	ind	ind	ind	ind	ind	ind	ind	ind
Takasaiaka	(*Larus belcheri*)	*Larus atlanticus*?	Olrog's gull?	G 1986: 1351 / B 1933: 413	ind	ind	ind	ind	ind	ind	ind	ind
Uswiler-yaka	(*Haematopus ater*)	*Haematopus ater*	Blackish oystercatcher	G 1986: 1349 / B 1933: 117	W			RB			ind	ind

Note: The ethnographic information refers to the existence of 47 spirits, including maritime mammals, maritime fish, other maritime fauna, birds, insects, mythical referents, and unknown referents. Only fish and bird spirits are represented here; mythical animals are marked 'A' in the table, while species of uncertain identification are marked 'UI' in the table. The names of the spirits are usually constituted by the common Yamana term used to designate a species, plus the term 'yaka' which means 'game' (Gusinde 1986) or 'imitation of resembling' (Bridges 1933).

Table key: W = white; B = black, R = red; ind = not determined; x = presence of a design with no known colour.

Many animal features can be taken into account by a human group for their artistic representation[3]:

a) visual features: size, shape, colour, presence or absence of fur, feathers, claws, teeth;
b) non-visual features: sound, smell, texture;
c) ethological features: whether the animal is gregarious, non-gregarious, aggressive, passive, fast, slow, aquatic, aerial, terrestrial;
d) symbolic features: values attached to the animal by a myth, legend, a shared belief etc. which makes them sacred, totemic, cursed, good omens, bad omens, etc.

Several approaches from the anthropology and the archaeology of art have taken into account some of these features when analysing the visual ways in which a species is depicted in various art forms (Leroi Gourhan 1968; Morphy 1989; Ucko and Rosenfeld 1967). In our case study, the animals that serve as referents for the *kina* spirits body paintings are maritime, terrestrial, and aerial, are of different sizes, colours, and shapes, and include those with feathers, with fur, and with scales (Fiore 2002). But besides these features, the PDY is relevant not only for the analysis of the dietary consumption of a particular taxon but also for the analysis of which species is—or is not—represented within the artistic repertoire of a society (see next section).

EXPECTATIONS

By applying the theoretical framework presented above to the data of our case study through the methods outlined here, it is possible to develop a series of expectations to contrast with the archaeological record. Taking into account that subsistence and ceremonial art are two different but interacting spheres, the assessment of the archaeological and ethnographic record can show that each species of fish and birds may have been represented only in the archaeo-faunal record, only in the body painting record, or in both. Moreover, each of these species may have a high or low PDY. All possible combinations of these categorizations are expressed in Figure 5.3.

Species that are represented only in the archaeofaunal record may have (a) all a high PDY, (b) all a low PDY or (ab) some a high and some a low PDY. Species that are represented only in the body painting record may have the same possibilities: (c) all a high PDY, (d) all a low PDY, or (cd) some a high and some a low PDY. Species that are represented both in the

---

[3] These features can also influence faunal consumption, although they will not be assessed in this chapter.

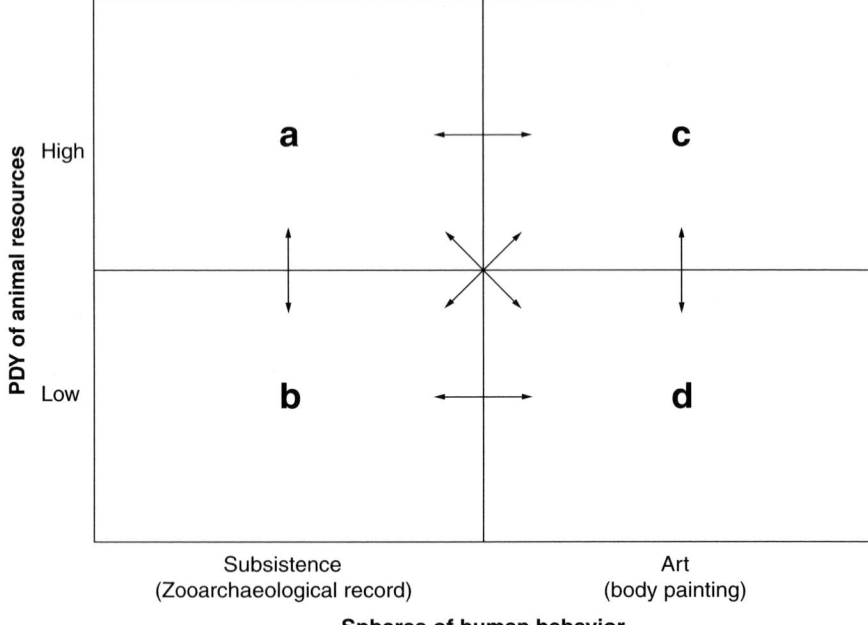

Fig. 5.3. Expectations for archaeofaunal and body painting records.

archaeofaunal and body painting record may have (ac) all a high PDY, (bd) all a low PDY, or some a high and some a low PDY with two possible combinations: (ad) high PDY in the archaeofaunal record and low PDY in the body painting record or (cb) low PDY in the archaeofaunal record and high PDY in the body painting record.

This set of expectations will be used to interpret the results obtained from the data analysis. Given that these expectations are only qualitative, their application to the actual cases will also include the assessment of the taxonomical abundance indexes, measurements, and rates mentioned above in order to provide complementary quantitative data.

RESULTS

Birds

The analysis of bird species shows that fourteen taxa[4] were represented in the ceremonial body painting and fifteen families are found in the archaeofaunal

---

[4] This concept involves any category between order and species, since different types of birds are represented by different taxonomical categories in the ethnographic data.

record. When considering the overlaps between the artistic and subsistence spheres, results show that six species are represented in both, while nine appear only in the archaeofaunal record and eight only in the artistic record.

The total avifaunal[5] sample comprises 2770 remains that come from Lanashuaia I (NISP = 228), Túnel VII (NISP = 2159), and Imiwaia I, layer B (NISP = 383) (see Table 5.3). The assemblage of Lanashuaia I is dominated by Kelp Gull, *Larus dominicanus*, with 67 per cent of the NISP. In Túnel VII, *Phalacrocorax* sp. has the highest percentage (39%); second are the penguins (27.5%); and the group of Diomedeidae and big Procellariidae is in third place (18.5%). Meanwhile, this last group of birds is the most abundant in layer B of Imiwaia I with 85 per cent, and with a much smaller percentage are the *Phalacrocorax* sp. (12%). Other families are represented with very small percentages: Accipitridae, Anatidae, Ardeidae, Emberizidae, Falconidae, Furnariidae, Psittacidae, small Procellariidae, Stercorariidae, and Tytonidae.

The assessment of the species which are represented only in the body painting record indicates that they all have a low PDY (Falconidae, Stercorariidae, *Daption capensis*, *Podiceps calipareus*, *Larus belcheri*, *Haematopus ater*). This situation fits expectation (d), and indicates that if a prescription to avoid eating these species had stemmed from the ceremonial sphere, it would not in practice have influenced the dietary intake of the Yámana.

Regarding the six species which are both represented in the archaeofaunal and body painting records, it is interesting to note that this group includes the only three cases of medium/high PDY in the whole sample (*Chloephaga* sp./ *Tachyeres* sp., *Phalacrocorax* sp., and Spheniscidae), while the rest are of low PDY (Accipitridae and Stercorariidae, which are represented only by one specimen each). Out of these high PDY taxa, *Chloephaga* sp. and *Tachyeres* sp. have a very low, and *Phalacrocorax* sp. and Spheniscidae, an intermediate archaeofaunal representation (see Table 5.3). Therefore, this situation seems to be a special case of expectations (ad), indicating that species of both high and low PDY were both consumed and painted. It implies that there was no open avoidance of their consumption, but at the same time indicates that consumption was not intense, therefore suggesting that some kind of restriction may have applied to these PDY taxa due to their ceremonial involvement and symbolic status.

Conversely, the taxa which only appear in the archaeofaunal record include the Diomedeidae and Procellariidae and *Larus dominicanus,* which are of medium/low PDY and have a high quantitative representation in the sites (see Table 5.3). These cases fit with expectation (b) and reflect subsistence choices that have not emphasized PDY as a central aspect of dietary habits when consuming birds.

---

[5] Bird species found in a particular geographic region.

Table 5.3. NISP and NISP% of bird and fish species per site

Resources	Family	Species	Túnel VII NISP	Túnel VII NISP %	Lanashuaia I NISP	Lanashuaia I NISP %	Imiwaia I (layer B) NISP	Imiwaia I (layer B) NISP %
BIRDS	ACCIPITRIDAE	Buteo sp.	1	0.05	0	0.00	0	0.00
	ANATIDAE	Tachyeres sp./Chloephaga sp	9	0.42	6	2.63	7	1.83
	ARDEIDAE	Nycticorax nycticorax	4	0.18	0	0.00	0	0.00
	DIOMEDEIDAE and large PROCELLARIIDAE	Diomedea chysostoma/ Macronectes giganteus	400	18.53	29	12.72	326	85.12
	EMBERIZIDAE	Zonotrichia capensis	3	0.14	6	2.63	0	0.00
	FALCONIDAE	Milvago chimango	22	1.02	3	1.31	0	0.00
	FURNARIIDAE	Cinclodes sp.	6	0.28	2	0.88	0	0.00
	ARIDAE	Larus dominicanus		0.00	153	67.1	0	0.00
	LARIDAE/ STERNIDAE	Larus dominicanus/ Sterna hirundinacea	63	2.92	0	0.00	1	0.26
	PHALACROCORACIDAE	Phalacrocorax sp.	843	39.04	18	7.89	46	12.01
	PSITTACIDAE	Enicognathus ferrugineus	74	3.43	0	0.00	0	0.00
	PROCELLARIIDAE	Fulmarus glacialoides or Thalassoica Antarctica	139	6.44	5	2.19	3	0.78
	SPHENISCIDAE	Aptenodytes patagonicus/ Spheniscus magellanicus/ Eudyptes chrysocome	594	27.51	5	2.19	0	0.00
	SPERCORARIIDAE	Catharacta chilensis		0.00	1	0.44	0	0.00
	TYTONIDAE	Tyto alba	1	0.05	0	0.00	0	0.00
FISH	ATHERINOPSIDAE	Odontesthes sp.	0	0.00	0	0.00	1	0.04
	ZOARCIDAE	Austrolycus sp.	0	0.00	0	0.00	8	0.34
	CLUPEIDAE	Clupeidae sp.	32	2.32	29	5.02	65	2.75
	NOTOTHENIIDAE	Eleginops maclovinus	0	0.00	1	0.17	1	0.04
	MERLUCCIIDAE	Macruronus magellanicus	70	5.08	95	16.44	27	1.14
	MERLUCCIIDAE	Merluciidae sp.	65	4.72	0	0.00	17	0.72
	MERLUCCIIDAE	Merluccius sp.	1	0.02	0	0.00	48	2.03
	NOTOTHENIIDAE	Nototheniidae sp.	69	5.02	39	6.75	6	0.25
	NOTOTHENIIDAE	Paranothenia magellanica	842	61.02	32	5.54	149	6.30
	NOTOTHENIIDAE	Patagonotothen sp.	301	21.82	4	0.69	25	1.06
	GEMPYLIDAE	Thyrsites atun	0	0.00	378	65.40	2019	85.33

Note: The values of bird remains from Túnel VII and Lanashuaia I were taken from Mameli and Estévez Escalera (2004). The values of fish remains from Túnel VII were taken from Piana et al. 2000.

faunal and ceremonial representation = 6

only faunal representation = 9

only ceremonial representation = 8

In sum, the analysis of bird species consumption and artistic representation shows three patterns according to the expectations defined above: (b) in the archaeofaunal record, (ad) in the archaeofaunal and body painting record, and (d) in the body painting record. These patterns point towards a trend which did not prioritize the consumption of high PDY bird species, since species of middle to high PDY were represented in ceremonial body paintings and only consumed in low quantities, while the species consumed in high quantities are of low PDY. This trend suggests an overall non-optimal attitude towards the consumption of bird taxa, and a certain partial restriction of middle to high PDY species due to their symbolic implications in ceremonial body paintings.

It must be pointed out that there were no technological restrictions on the hunting of penguins or shags and cormorants; there are records of their capture in earlier layers of other sites of the Beagle Channel region (Tivoli 2008, 2010b). Therefore, it could be the case that populations of those species decreased because of human over-exploitation in the past: in earlier assemblages of several archaeological sites of the region these avifaunal resources were very abundant.

Fish

The same analysis carried out on fish species shows that six taxa were represented in ceremonial body paintings and nine in the archaeofaunal record. Only one species is found in both, while eight appear only in the archaeofaunal record and five only in the ceremonial body painting record.

In historical times, the ichthyoarchaeological assemblages were dominated by two kinds of fish resources: two small and littoral species of the Nototheniidae family (*Paranotohenia magellanica* and *Patagonotothen* sp.), which represent 82.2 per cent of the identified specimens in Túnel VII; and *Thyrsites atun* in Lanashuaia and in layer B of Imiwaia I, with 65.4 per cent and 85.3 per cent respectively (Table 5.3). Other species are represented by low frequencies in the three assemblages.

The five species which appear only in the ceremonial body painting have an uncertain ethnographic identification or correspond to mythical fish referents (Table 5.2; Fiore 2002). We have therefore excluded these from the analysis.

The single species represented in both the archaeofaunal and body painting records is *E. maclovinus*, which has a medium PDY but a low quantitative archaeofaunal representation (Table 5.3). This corresponds to expectation (ad), and indicates that because *E. maclovinus* was represented as a spirit in the *kina*, its consumption was very much restricted (to the point of being almost non-existent): hence its extremely low archaeofaunal representation (see details in Fiore and Zangrando 2006).

The nine species represented only in the archaeofaunal record include cases of different PDYs. Among these are *P. magellanica* and *Patagonotothen* sp., which have a low PDY and the highest archaeofaunal representation in Túnel VII, and *Thyrsites atun* which has a high PDY and the highest archaeofaunal representation in Lanashuaia and Imiwaia I. This situation fits expectation (ac), since it includes cases of high and of low PDY. The fact that precisely those of high PDY are represented more than those with low PDY indicates an optimal behaviour underlying their consumption. Besides this, the fact that such high PDY species were not represented in the *kina* ceremony suggests that they were not symbolically meaningful for the Yámana, and perhaps for this reason there were no obstacles to their consumption.

In synthesis, the analysis of fish species consumption and artistic representation shows two patterns according to the expectations defined above: (ab) for the archaeofaunal record and (ad) for the archaeofaunal and body painting record. These patterns point to a trend which consumed high and low PDY taxa, but in proportion prioritized the consumption of high PDY species. Yet, although with less frequency, low PDY taxa were also exploited for dietary purposes, while a medium PDY species (the *E. maclovinus*) was practically not consumed. This last species is the only one which was both included in the artistic sphere and the subsistence sphere (with an extremely low frequency): its near-omission from the dietary repertoire seems to have stemmed from the symbolic value that the species had as a result of its involvement in the *kina* ceremony.

DISCUSSION AND CONCLUSIONS

The perspective outlined in this chapter stresses the importance of analysing the mutual interaction of subsistence and artistic symbolism in the assessment of human–animal relationships. The results of our case study have helped outline a series of trends that underlie the relationships of the Yámana people with fish and with birds during the late occupations of the archaeological sequence:

1) some fish species of high PDY are represented in the subsistence sphere in high amounts, but not in the ceremonial art (e.g. *Thyrsites atun*), which suggests an optimal dietary choice;

2) fish and bird species of low PDY are represented in the subsistence sphere in high amounts, but not in the ceremonial art (e.g. fish: *Paranotothenia magellanica*, *Patagonotothen* sp; birds: *Laridae/Sternidae*), which suggests a non-optimal dietary choice;

3) some fish and bird species of medium to high PDY which are represented in the ceremonial art sphere are represented in the subsistence
   sphere in intermediate to low amounts (e.g. fish: *E. maclovinus*; birds:
   Phalacrocoracidae, Spheniscidae), which suggests that the two spheres
   interacted and that the symbolic contents of the ceremonial sphere
   influenced the subsistence sphere with different intensities. In the case
   of the birds the consumption of *kina* species was not openly avoided, but
   some kind of restriction seems to have operated, given the medium
   quantities of these taxa in the archaeofaunal record. However, there
   seems to have existed a stronger aversion to the consumption of one
   kina fish species, given the extremely low quantities of this species in the
   archaeofaunal record.

Using the expectations developed above, in spite of the fact that there are no
(c) cases (in which a high PDY species would only be painted and not
consumed), these (ad) cases, combined with the low archaeofaunal representations of the high PDY species, suggest that certain restrictions may have
applied to these high PDY fish and bird taxa due to their symbolic value and
ceremonial involvement.

As noted above, even though the ideological factor is always present in every
human action, and even though the symbolic sphere can interact with the
other spheres of production, it is easier to recognize the influences of ideology
and symbolism when the actions under study depart from the optimal. It may
well be that ideological factors were reinforcing the exploitation of high PDY
species such as *Thyrsites atun*, but because of their low archaeological visibility
we cannot identify them. It may well also be that ideological values were
involved in the consumption of low PDY species such as the *Paranotothenia
magellanica*, but in spite of this non-optimal archaeological trend the ethnographic data indicate that they did not have special symbolic value within the
kina ceremony.

Conversely, given the degree of resolution of the available archaeological
and ethnographic data, the patterns that we have been able to pinpoint do
include, as predicted, some non-optimal choices which were indeed influenced
by ceremonial symbolism (*E. maclovinus,* Phalacrocoracidae, Spheniscidae).
This happens because people do not always proceed by an exclusively rational
protocol but are also deeply influenced by their symbolic practices and
ideological values, which are both rational and affective. In the case under
study, the development of these non-optimal choices seems to have been
stimulated through the *kina*: this male-centred ceremony seems to have
empowered men to prescribe certain dietary choices over the whole society.
Its symbolic values and the male adults' power emanating from its celebration
seem to have had simultaneous ideological and political effects over the
subsistence of the whole society.

The theoretical perspective that underlies this chapter maintains that human–environment relations are not exclusively based on optimal choices oriented by rational decisions: rather, such relations also involve social and ideological values which are expressed through symbolic means via artistic activities which in turn dialectically influence patterns of consumption. This is due to the fact that people do not just operate in a 'neutral' environment conceived merely as a source of material resources. Rather, they bring their own values, perceptions, and technical possibilities, which are thus reflected in their selection, consumption, avoidance, production, and reproduction of faunal species. This perspective is not only applicable to hunter-gatherers but also to the study of farming communities, where the assessment of consumption–avoidance attitudes towards a species would not only involve its PDY, its ethology and seasonality, its physical features, and the availability of the technology to capture, domesticate, or process it, but also the anatomical transformations undergone by the species once it has been domesticated. Such transformations may have been a new focus of ideological beliefs or symbolic values, and these may have re-oriented the community's dietary and artistic consumption or avoidance. In sum, the environment is not conceived here as a neutral context in which humans develop their daily activities, but rather as a value-laden scenario which clearly influences human actions, and which is also shaped and re-shaped by human agency.

ACKNOWLEDGEMENTS

We are grateful to Luis Orquera and Ernesto Piana for their general support during this project. To Federico Degrange for his help with the identification of the early taxonomic scientific names cited in the ethnographic sources.

Sites Túnel VII and Lanashuaia I have been jointly excavated by Luis Orquera and Ernesto Piana (Argentina) and Jordi Estévez Escalera and Asunción Vila Mitjá (Spain).

We are also grateful to Matthew Davies and Freda Nkirote M'Mbogori for inviting us to contribute to this volume.

This project has been funded with grants PIP 6186 (CONICET, Argentina) and PICT 2071 (ANPCYT-MINCYT, Argentina).

6

From Ecological Constraints to Cultural Identities: Pre-Columbian Attitudes toward Food

Alexandre Chevalier

In Huánuco, the Potato National Day will be celebrated with a food tasting. The goal of the fourth festival is to promote the use of this highly nutritional tuber and to create regional identities. (*El Comercio*, Peru, May 26th 2010, translated from Spanish by the author)

INTRODUCTION

In archaeology, differences of plant remains between contexts, regions or periods are usually interpreted in terms of social inequality (Bender 1978; van der Veen 2003), political power (Hastorf 1993; Quilter and Stocker 1983), territory exploitation (Rosenberg 1990) and, lately, feasting activities (Dietler and Hayden 2001; Duncan et al. 2009; Hastorf 2003), but rarely in terms of group identification, despite the fact that anthropology has highlighted more than once that food expresses one's identity better than any material culture (Counihan and Kaplan 1998; Fischler 1985; MacClancy 2004; Montanari 2000; Scholliers 2001). In a comparable way to the faunal exploitation strategies discussed by Fiore et al. in the previous chapter, we propose here that plant exploitation strategies relate not only to factors such as optimality or expediency but also to group identity. Based on models drawn from the anthropology of food (Counihan and Van Esterik 1997; Douglas 1971; Fischler 1988; Goody 1982; Lévi-Strauss 1964, 1997; Mead 1997; Mennell et al. 1992; Mintz 1996) and social psychology of intergroup relations (Tajfel and Turner 1979, 1986), as well as on ethnobotanical examples (Pieroni and Price

2006a), we argue that cultural groups produce, select, and eat different food, and therefore exploit different territories, in order to differentiate themselves from other groups and to build strong group identities. In addition to economic rationality, ecological constraints, or technical limitations, social group alimentary choices may also reflect the need to express positive differentiation from an external group and similarity with those from the same group. Appealing to psychological theories of social identification that explain how individuals' behaviours are affected by their relationships within their groups, we seek to explain how food choices as an expression of group identity may have shaped environments, created long-distance trade, and in some cases led to environmental overexploitation. In this way social identity concepts (Tajfel and Turner 1979, 1986) can help us to understand the link between trade, exotic products, prestige, and identity and the pivotal role plants may have played in the creation of group identity and in defining intergroup relations. Indeed, social identity is defined as one's cognitive awareness of being part of a group together with the emotional significance attached to this membership. When the group's interests are at stake, a person's cognitive representation of their own group (ingroup), as well as of the other group (outgroup), are modified in order to strictly stick to the ingroup stereotypes in terms of beliefs, attitudes, and behaviours (Turner 1982). In that way the social cohesion of the group can be maintained and individuals may ensure the protection of other ingroup members. Individuals have a basic need to enhance and maintain a positive social identity, which is satisfied through ingroup identification. In the case of intergroup conflict, self-esteem enhancement can be achieved through a whole range of psychological and behavioural strategies that ensure the positive differentiation between the ingroup and the outgroup. Analyses carried out on botanical remains from two contemporaneous pre-Columbian sites, Cardal and Mina Perdida on the Central Peruvian coast, support our interpretations of the relationship between food choices and identity.

THE CULTURAL AND ENVIRONMENTAL SETTINGS

Mina Perdida and Cardal are ceremonial complexes in the Lurín valley, located just south of the Peruvian capital Lima (Figure 6.1). The sites are 8 km distant from the shoreline, and 3.5 km from each other. Mina Perdida's extension is estimated as around 30 ha, though most of the standing architecture has been destroyed by homeowners and road infrastructure. Cardal is somewhat smaller and its structures cover only 20 ha (Figure 6.2). Each site comprises a central pyramidal body with two wings enclosing a U-shaped patio (Figure 6.3). It is generally assumed that these structures would have functioned both as ceremonial and administrative centres; however very few

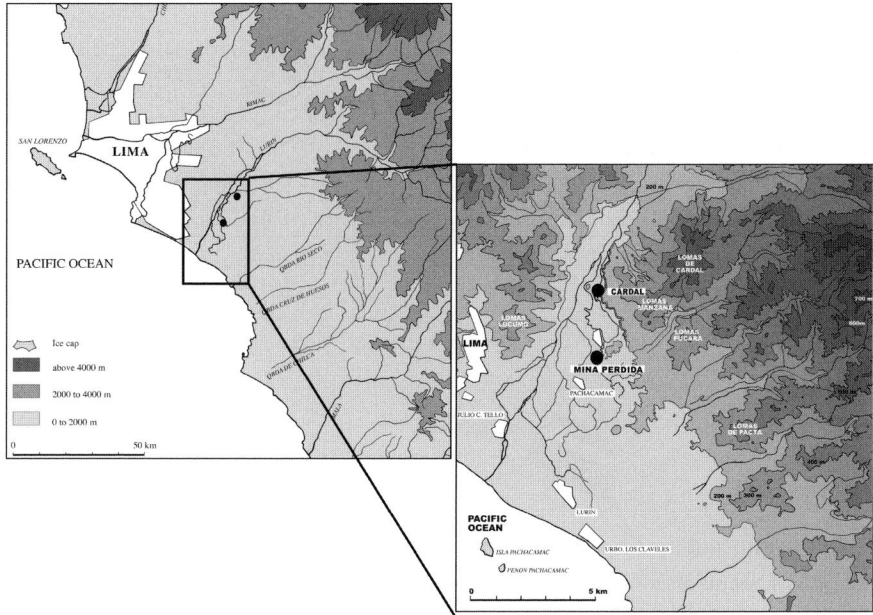

Fig. 6.1. Map of the Lurín Valley, Peru.

Fig. 6.2. Cardal ceremonial complex.

Central pyramid

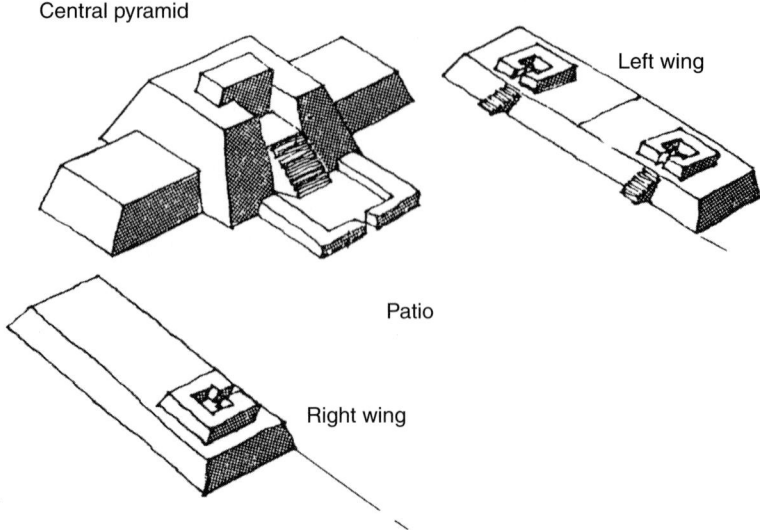

Left wing

Patio

Right wing

Fig. 6.3. Layout of a typical pre-Columbian ceremonial complex. Adapted from Williams León (1985).

excavations have shed light on their specific function and meaning (Burger 1987, 1991). Eighteen radiocarbon dates give an occupation period for Mina Perdida between 1600 BC and 950 BC and for Cardal twenty-five radiocarbon dates give a slightly younger range between 1400 BC and 800 BC, so the settlements are broadly contemporaneous (Chevalier 2002).

The South American Pacific desert is one of the driest in the world, and the only vegetation grows on the shoreline, in the *lomas,* and in the river valleys. *Lomas* are specific ecosystems on the South American Pacific coast with seasonal vegetation and scattered perennial trees on the hill slopes facing the ocean, between an elevation of 400 m and 800 m. They are 'irrigated' during the austral winter by a deep fog created by a local temperature inversion due to the cold Humboldt current. The Lurín valley is narrow (2 km wide at Cardal), with a very steep altitudinal gradient starting from the shoreline up to 5,000 m, some 106 km away, ending at the Surococha glacier. A high number of different ecological and vegetation communities coexist in the valley: seashore, marshes, sandy dunes, gallery forest, thalweg, floodplain, arid rocky piedmont, and *lomas.* As a result, the plant diversity is relatively low in each ecological zone, but the diversity across the valley is high.

The lack of palaeoclimatic data for the Lurín valley makes any past vegetation reconstruction hypothetical. However, according to data from other coastal valleys, as well as from the Andes, we know that past coastal climatic conditions have not changed since 5000 BC, with an almost complete lack of rainfall since then, except for occasional catastrophic downpours due to ENSO

(El Niño–Southern Oscillation) conditions. If the present climate prevailed in the Lurín valley by 1600 BC, then it seems likely that the same kind of ecosystems coexisted, although their relative extents were probably different. For instance, we know through ethnohistoric sources that marshes were more extensive than today, and that a now extinct forest was growing at around 2,700 m above sea level until the 1930s (Rostworowski 1989); finally, thanks to the presence of former tree cover (Moutarde 2006) we also know that the *lomas* were more extensive until the Spanish conquest. Food resources were, however, limited by the size of the valley itself, since the coastal desert does not provide any biological resources except for some lichen and invertebrates. This small, confined, arable territory would have obliged past settlers to carefully manage its exploitation, intensively and extensively through irrigation, or to resort to exchanges to overcome food shortage (particularly under population pressure), and to obtain products that cannot grow in the valley. The strategies developed by past groups, as well as the reasons that led them to choose one solution over another, are at the core of this discussion.

Temporally, Mina Perdida and Cardal fall in the Initial Period (2200–1200 BC) and Early Horizon (1200–100 BC) phases. On the coast, the Initial Period has been defined by a number of cultural features (Burger 1992) including territorial exploitation, food production, the arrival of ceramics, the development of inland monumental sites, and the building and maintenance of irrigation canals: indeed these 'innovations' are interpreted as a switch from exploitation of marine resources to a production economy based on agriculture. The impact of these cultural innovations on food production and territory exploitation is, however, controversial (Chevalier 2002). First, until recently, archaeological methods applied in Peru largely neglected the recovery of both macro and microbotanical plant remains; as a result, the impact of marine resources was overestimated while plant importance was undervalued. We now know that Preceramic groups relied as much on plants as on marine resources, and therefore that agriculture was practised at a large scale before the Initial Period in the same territorial limits. Secondly, no new cultivated crops appear in the Initial Period archaeological contexts that were not already known previously, except maybe for the coca (*Erythroxylum coca*). Thirdly, agriculture does not require ceramics, as proven by groups such as the agricultural Anasaszi who used only basketry. Finally, the existence of irrigation canals has never been proven as built and managed by Initial Period groups, and we lack any direct radiometric or relative date for the origins of these canals.

None of these new cultural features, such as increased food production, monumental structures, or irrigation can therefore be proven to be new to the Initial Period; rather we argue below that they stem from the increasing diversification and intensification of new social identities at this time. These new cultural features are not new economic orientations, driven by food shortages due to population growth in a limited territory or climatic disruption, or induced by the rise of a new social class, but rather grow from the development of new social identities expressed by an emphasis on agriculture over marine exploitation. Based on the theory of social identity described in the introduction we posit that the new inland settlements reflect the new social identities that the populations of Cardal and Mina Perdida wanted to express.

THEOCRACIES VS EGALITARIAN CHIEFDOMS

Two different and mutually exclusive socio-political models have been proposed for the Initial Period: a coercive model in which the key elements of the social organization are centralization, hierarchy, and accumulation of goods; and an *ayllu* model in which the key elements are decentralization, competition, and redistribution. The coercive model assumes that the monumental architecture of the ceremonial centres, their internal organization (with restricted access and large storage rooms), and the localization of graves, as well as the rich material they contained, reflect a complex and hierarchical society, dominated by a bureaucratic elite who controlled the accumulation and the distribution of a centralized surplus (Moseley 1989; Pozorski 1976, 1987; Pozorski and Pozorski 1992). Notions of hereditary chiefdoms, royal status, theocracy, and even statehood are usually employed in this model. The monumental centres are thus thought to reflect independent socio-political entities, each federating a number of smaller sites located in different ecological settings and specialized in the exploitation of their own ecosystems. Larger centres would have controlled networks of complementary exchanges, overcoming in this way the ecological constraints of the coastal valleys by obtaining products from various ecological settings under a subordination relationship with the smaller sites. Leaders would have exercised power in three domains: economic, by control of the means of production and unequal wealth redistribution; ideological, via the elaboration and control of an ad hoc iconography and of ritual activity; and militarily, by the creation of specialized armed forces. Each site would then have its own social identity, but they would refer to the same overall cultural identity and system of values since they would be part of the same society. Plant consumption in this model would not reflect site group choices, but rather a selection made by leaders or the dominant social class. As a consequence, archaeobotanical assemblages should be very different between sites of different sizes, and between the contexts within sites, in order to reflect this social hierarchy. But sites of the same rank or size within the same culture should have similar overall assemblages reflecting the similar status of their inhabitants.

In contrast, the *ayllu* is usually referred to as 'the traditional' organization of Andean communities, though major variations in social organization of indigenous communities across time and space are documented (Rivière 1983). The *ayllu* is both a social and geographical unit, defined spatially as composed of extended families who share the same mythical ancestors and revere their own minor god, or *huaca*, usually a natural landmark within the space or at the limits of the *ayllu* territory. *Ayllus* are divided in two symbolic parts or moieties; the upper (*hanan*) and lower (*hurin*), which may also have their own shrine or *huaca*. In this socio-political organization, the means of production are private, but the land is common property. Whenever possible, *ayllus* try to exploit agricultural fields in different ecologies to secure their food sources, otherwise they may develop their own economic solution to overcome ecological constraints, whether through exchanges or by setting up colonies in other ecological zones. *Ayllus* are not hereditary chiefdoms: leaders, or *curacas*, are elected according both to their ability to lead the group and to their social network of reciprocity; their role is to lead common works such as irrigation canal cleaning or path maintenance, as well as to act as community judge. *Ayllus* are said to have the power to create and transform reality by competing with others toward the same goal (Bastien 1978). This competition, expressed symbolically in the *huacas*, economically through material culture such as plant products or group skills in agriculture, and culturally through music, dances, or oral expression, corresponds to a unique stimulus: to distinguish one's own group from others through the pride of positive achievements, and thus create a strong ingroup identity (Tajfel and Turner 1979, 1986; Turner 1982) that will reinforce the social cohesion of the group in order to protect every member against any external challenge. The competition needs to be constant in order to nurture this identity.

According to Burger, the presence of several ceremonial complexes of the same size in the Lurín valley suggests there were several cultural groups of the *ayllu* kind, each associated with its own social and ideological emblem, represented in these monumental ceremonial centres, the *huacas* (Burger 1991, 1992; Burger and Salazar-Burger 1993). These centres would play an integrative role for small residential units of families and lineages scattered in the valley, in other words the *ayllus*, via an ideology expressed by religious rituals performed in a common ceremonial structure, and non-religious rituals carried out in the construction and the maintenance of a common infrastructure.

The differences in size between Cardal and Mina Perdida are related to the number of accretions as a function of the duration of their occupation, and would not reflect a subordination relationship as is the case in a coercive model. Each ceremonial centre should thus reflect the particular expression of the *ayllu*'s competition, and therefore its identity. Even if inequalities due to social status existed, it would not imply the existence of a coercive elite, nor an advanced chiefdom. In this case, archaeobotanical assemblages should differ between each site, but not within a site, to reflect this equalitarian society.

PLANT PRESENCE IN CARDAL AND MINA PERDIDA

Our analyses carried out in Cardal and Mina Perdida are based on more than 100,000 macroremains from *in situ* sampling as well as from sediment flotation. Because many different contexts have been sampled in many different ways (1987–8 for Cardal and 1991, 1992, and 1994 for Mina Perdida) we considered only plant presence–absence occurrences in order to avoid potential interpretation biases. Results indicate strong divergences of plant presence between the two sites (Table 6.1). In fact, certain taxa were present only at Mina Perdida: these included the lupine (*Lupinus mutabilis*), avocado (*Persea americana*), palillo (*Campomanesia lineatifolia*), Lima bean (*Phaseolus lunatus*), soursop (*Annona muricata*), a species of Flame tree (*Erythrina edulis*), the thorn apple (*Datura stramonium*), and the soapberry (*Sapindus saponaria*). Other taxa are exclusive to Cardal: prickly pear (*Opuntia* sp.), as well as other Cactacae, the wild tomato (*Lycopersicon peruvianum* var. *peruvianum*), Peruvian ragweed (*Ambrosia peruviana*), wild begonia bulb (*Begonia geraniifolia*), mito (*Vasconcellea candicans*), and taxa from the herbaceous stratum (*Cleome* sp., *Geranium* sp., *Commelina* sp., *Sisyrinchium* sp., *Ranunculus* sp.). If we analyse these data in conjunction with plant distribution (Table 6.2), it is clear that the assemblages are drawn from different ecologies. Mina Perdida has plants from the Amazonian and Andean, while Cardal has plants from the surrounding desert and *lomas*. Both sites have plants that grow in the thalweg or the floodplain.

If we turn to the number of contexts in which a plant is present, or plant frequency (Table 6.3), we see that some taxa in Mina Perdida have very high frequencies—more than four times greater—in comparison with Cardal. These taxa are the achira (*Canna indica*), the chile (*Capsicum* spp.), the Peruvian prune (*Bunchosia armeniaca*), onions of Liliaceae, rhizome of Cyperaceae, the jiquima (*Pachyrrhizus tuberosus*), and the passion fruit genus (*Passiflora* sp.), as well as Solanaceae (*Browallia* and *Solanum* genus) and the common purslane (*Portulaca oleracea*). Other taxa also have a high frequency—between two and four times greater—such as the Cape Gooseberry genus (*Physalis* sp.), the pacay (*Inga feuilli*), the goosefoot genus (*Chenopodium* spp.), the sweet potato (*Ipomoea batatas*), the maca (*Lepidium meyenii*), the maize (*Zea mays*), the peanut (*Arachis hypogaea*), the guava (*Psidium guajava*), the lucuma (*Pouteria lucuma*), the cotton (*Gossypium barbadense*), and a tobacco-related plant (*Nicotiana* sp.). All plants found in Mina Perdida with high to very high frequencies grow in the thalweg and valley floodplain

Table 6.1. Synthesis of the taxa from in situ macroremains and flotations sampling in Mina Perdida and Cardal

	Presence–absence		Ubiquities	
	Mina Perdida	Cardal	Mina Perdida	Cardal
Food plants			2.21	1.30
Annona cherimolia Mill.	x	x	0.74	
Annona muricata L.	x		62.29	32.18
Arachis hypogaea L.	x	x	27.20	0.8
Bunchosia armeniaca (Cav.) DC	x	x	9.56	3.2
Canavalia ensiformis (L.) DC	x	x	56.12	2.22
Canna indica L., rhizome	x	x	40.35	8.62
Capsicum sp	x	x	64.52	25.6
Chenopodium sp.	x	x	18.38	0.8
Cucurbita ficifolia Bouché,	x	x	24.24	17.96
Cucurbita maxima Duch.	x	x	33.21	18.93
Cucurbita moschata Duch.	x	x	40.91	40
Cucurbita sp.	x	x	6.45	0.8
Cyperaceae rhizome ch	x	x	11.16	
Erythrina edulis Triana	x		40.70	14.67
Inga feuilli DC	x	x	7.19	4
cf *Ipomoea batatas* (L.) Lam.	x	x	7.19	3.82
cf *Lepidium meyenii* Walp	x	x	12.50	0.8
Liliaceae, bulb	x	x	1.61	
Lupinus cf, *mutabilis* Sweet var *mutabilis*	x		4.70	4.44
cf. *Manihot esculenta* Crantz.	x	x		0.8
Opuntia sp.		x	33.21	0.8
Pachyrrhizus tuberosus (Lam.) Spreng.	x	x	3.23	0.8
Passiflora sp.	x	x	20.56	
Persea americana L.	x		5.58	5.6
Phaseolus vulgaris L.	x	x	12.19	
Phaseolus lunatus L.	x		8.06	3.02
Physalis sp.	x	x	88.76	44.262
Psidium guajava L.	x	x	96.84	54.21
Pouteria lucuma (R&P) Kuntze	x	x	6.45	4.44
cf *Solanum tuberosum* L.	x	x	25.15	12.22
Zea mays L.	x	x	2.21	1.30
Industrial plants				
Acacia sp. wood	x			2.22
Cyperus sp. ch	x	x	42.35	31.4
Gossypium barbadense L.	x	x	100	55.02
Gynerium sagittatum (Aubl.) Beauv.	x		29.37	
Juncus sp.	x	x	4.70	5.6
Lagenaria siceraria (Mol.) Standl.	x	x	25.29	32.4
Scirpus sp.	x	x	31.57	30.22
Medicinal/hallucinogenic plants				
Campomanesia lineatifolia R&P	x		18.78	
Datura stramonium L.	x		5.58	
cf *Lycopersicon peruvianum* var. peruvianum (L.) Miller		x		0.8
Nicotiana sp.	x	x	51.61	32

(*continued*)

Table 6.1. Continued

	Presence–absence		Ubiquities	
	Mina Perdida	Cardal	Mina Perdida	Cardal
Sapindus saponaria L.	x		29.34	
Wild plants (some may be edible)				
Aizoaceae		x		4
Amaranthaceae	x	x	33.87	24.8
Amaranthus sp.	x			2.22
Ambrosia peruviana Willd.		x		1.6
Apiaceae	x	x	8.06	8.8
Argemone subfusiformis Ownbee subsp.	x	x	3.23	0.8
subfusiformis				
Armatocereus sp.	x	x	19.35	12.8
Asteraceae	x	x	3.23	42.4
Asteraceae #1	x	x	14.52	1.6
Asteraceae #2		x		0.8
Asteraceae #3	x	x	25.81	28.8
Asteraceae #4	x	x	3.23	2.4
Asteraceae #5		x		0.8
Asteraceae #6	x	x	4.84	1.6
Asteraceae #7	x	x	4.84	2.4
Asteraceae #9	x		1.61	
Asteraceae #10	x		1.61	
Asteraceae #13	x		1.61	
Asteraceae #14	x		1.61	
Asteraceae #15	x		1.61	
Asteraceae #16	x		1.61	
Atriplex sp.	x	x	1.61	6.4
cf. *Begonia geraniifolia* Hooker. bulb		x		2.22
Boraginaceae		x		2.4
Brassicaceae#1	x	x	19.35	8.8
Brassicaceae#2	x		14.52	
Browallia americana L.	x	x	37.10	0.8
Cactaceae		x		9.6
Cactaceae #2		x		1.6
Cactaceae #3	x	x	3.23	4
Cactaceae #4		x		1.6
Cactaceae #5		x		2.4
Cactaceae #6		x		0.8
Calandrinia sp.	x	x	6.45	15.2
Caryophyllaceae, ch	x		1.61	
cf *Distichlis spicata* (L.) Greene	x	x	4.84	3.2
Carex sp.	x	x	6.45	0.8
Cheno-Am	x	x	6.45	26.4
Chenopodiaceae		x	3.23	0.8
Cleome sp.		x	16.13	8
Commelina sp.		x	19.35	17.6
Convolvulaceae	x	x	4.84	10.4
Diodia sp.	x	x	4.84	3.2
Echinocactus sp.	x	x	6.45	0.8
Eleocharis sp.	x	x	6.45	26.4

Euphorbiaceae	x	x	33.87	24.8
Fabaceae	x	x	37.84	22.04
Festuceae	x	x	11.29	6.4
Festuceae cf *Bromus catharticus* M. Vahl.	x	x	1.61	3.2
Festuceae cf *Poa annua* L.	x	x	4.84	2.4
Haageocereus sp.	x	x	25.81	42.4
Heliotropium sp.	x	x	9.68	5.6
Jacquemontia sp.	x	x	9.68	2.4
Lamiaceae	x	x	14.52	7.2
Luzula sp.		x	1.61	0
Malvaceae#1	x	x		2.4
Malvastrum cf. *coromandelianum* (L.) Garcke	x	x	25.81	25.6
Melochia lupulina Swartz	x	x	11.29	0.8
Nolana sp.	x	x	32.26	46.4
cf *Oxalis* sp.	x	x	1.61	0.8
Paniceae	x	x	11.29	4.8
Paniceae cf. *Panicum* sp.	x	x	3.23	4
Paniceae cf. *Setaria* sp.	x	x	3.23	0.8
Paniceae cf. *Paspalum* sp.	x	x	3.23	1.6
Phytolacca dioica L.	x		1.61	
Plantago sp.		x		4.8
Poaceae cf. Eragrostoideae	x	x	6.45	2.4
Polygonum sp.	x	x	8.06	6.4
Portulaca oleracea L.	x	x	66.13	16
cf *Ranunculus* sp.		x		0.8
Rubiaceae	x	x	1.61	1.6
Scrophulariacea	x	x	20.97	0.8
Sesuvium portulacastrum (L.) L.	x	x	12.90	40.8
Sida cf. *rhombifolia* L.	x	x	4.84	6.4
cf *Sisyrinchium* sp.		x		1.6
Solanaceae	x	x	3.23	17.6
Solanum americanum Mill.	x		40.32	
Solanum cf *multifidum* Lam.	x	x	1.61	27.2
Solanum montanum L.	x	x	14.52	9.6
Solanum sp.	x	x	17.74	38.4
Stellaria cf *cuspidata* Willd.	x		3.23	
Tillandsia sp.	x		14.52	9.6
Trianthema portulacastrum L.	x	x	16.13	3.2
Valeriana sp.	x	x	11.29	3.2
Vasconcellea candicans L.	x	x		1.6
Verbena sp.	x	x	24.19	21.6
Urocarpidium sp.	x	x	1.61	1.6

Others

Algae	x		25.77	

Table 6.2. Ecological distribution of single presence taxa from Cardal and Mina Perdida

		Amazonian	Andean	Coastal valley	Coastal desert	Coastal lomas
Cardal	Food plant				Cactacae Opuntia sp.	Begonia geraniifolia
	Medicinal			Lycopersicon peruvianum		
	Wild plant			Ambrosia peruviana		Cleome sp. Geranium sp. Commelina sp. Sisyrinchium sp. Ranunculus sp.
Mina Perdida	Food plant	Erythrina edulis	Lupinus mutabilis	Annona muricata Phaseolus lunatus Persea americana		
	Medicinal	Campomanesia lineatifolia		Datura stramonium Sapindus saponaria		

Table 6.3. Ecological distribution of highest frequencies taxa from Cardal and Mina Perdida

			Andean	Coastal valley	Coastal lomas
Very high frequency	Mina Perdida	Food plant		Canna indica Bunchosia armeniaca Capsicum	
					Liliaceae onion
				Cyperaceae rhizome Pachyrrhizus tuberosus	
High frequency	Cardal	Wild food plant		Sesuvium portulacastrum	
	Mina Perdida	Food plant	Chenopodium	Zea mays Arachis hypogaea Psidium guajava Pouteria lucuma Ipomoea batatas Inga feuilli	
		Medicinal Industrial	Lepidium meyenii	Physalis Nicotiana Gossypium barbadense	

except for the maca, which comes from the highlands. Curiously enough, Cardal does not show such high frequencies for any taxon except the sea purslane (*Sesuvium portulacastrum*), which may be a contamination.

Mina Perdida does have exogenous plants from the high Amazon with the flame tree fruit and from the Amazonian lowlands with the palillo, as well as from the Andean highlands with the lupine and the maca, while Cardal has remains reflecting plants mostly from the *lomas* (the coastal desert) as well as from the Lurín thalweg. In the same way Mina Perdida shows higher plant diversity than Cardal. The differences pointed out in both presence and ubiquity seem to relate more to food and pharmaceutical plants than to annual wild plants. However, within both archaeological sites, the functional attribution of some of these plants remains unclear. First of all, the identified medicinal plants (the tobacco-related plant, the palillo, the maca and the datura) are wild, and a lot of other wild plants may have been used for their medicinal properties (Girault 1984); these are the so-called functional foods (Pieroni et al. 2006b), such as the *lomas* annuals uncovered in the Cardal assemblage. For instance, the maca is edible but is currently used for its attributed medicinal properties; the palillo is used as a condiment in Peruvian cuisine, but also has antiseptic and antioxydant properties, and has a further use as a yellow dye; the seeds of the flame tree are edible but the pods and bark are medicinal. Another related difference between Mina Perdida and Cardal is in the choice of fuel. On the Mina Perdida central pyramid mostly this was wood, while in the central pyramid of Cardal coproliths were mainly used. The opposite is the case in the residential areas, where in Mina Perdida mostly coproliths were used, while in Cardal there was a preference for wood and cotton seeds.

SOCIO-POLITICAL ORGANIZATION

The botanical remains from Cardal and Mina Perdida support the hypothesis of the existence of small independent groups of the *ayllu* type: even if plant distribution varies according to the kind of archaeological context in every site (domestic area, public courtyard, central pyramid altar area, lateral wing ceremonial structures), the plant composition is stable among samples of the same context: Cardal domestic area contexts, as well as in Mina Perdida, various cesspits and accretion levels do not show drastic variations, as indeed would be the case in a non-hierarchical society. Thus the differences in archaeobotanical assemblages between Cardal and Mina Pedida should probably be understood in the light of the *ayllu*'s competition for ingroup positive identity reinforcement, which can also be expressed in agricultural products, by providing an exceptional quality and quantity of crops such as cotton or maize, by obtaining new products such as the avocado, soursop or Lima bean, by importing exotic plants such as the palillo, maca, or flametree fruit, and by using different kinds of fuel such as cotton seeds, coproliths, or wood.

The only notable intra-site variability is found in Cardal between three sunken circular courts (EC-1, EC-2 and EC-3) built on the right wing after 800 BC. They probably functioned as complementary ceremonial structures. These three structures have broadly the same size, although they have two different types of internal structure and the composition of the plant remains is different in every structure (Chevalier 2002). With similar internal structures but different plant compositions, EC-1 and EC-3 may have been used for the same purpose but by two sub-groups, such as the moities of the *ayllu*-like groups, while the middle structure (EC-2) would correspond either to a third sub-group or to another ceremonial use by the whole group. In either case this would fit with the existence of small independent entities of the *ayllu* type.

Other archaeological data further support the existence of *ayllu*-like groups. First, the monumental architecture, the internal organization (such as a double central altar in Cardal), and the very similar material culture un-covered in all contexts suggest an egalitarian lifestyle, in which power was achieved through one's personal capacity and was directed towards communal rather than personal aims (Burger and Salazar-Burger 1993). Second, the regional density of monumental sites of a similar size built according the same formal and architectural characteristics (Mesía Montenegro 2000; Scheele 1970) supports the proposition of the existence of independent groups of the same size with an *ayllu*-like organization. There is also no evidence of warfare, such as weapons or skeletal traumatism on human remains (Vraden-burg 1992) that could support the hypothesis of the existence of a coercive society according to the Pozorskis' definition, or that Mina Perdida and Cardal were at war for territorial reasons. Both ceremonial centres should be therefore considered as particular religious expressions (*huacas*) of two different groups not in a subordination relationship, nor in territorial dispute for the control of the resources, but competing toward the same goal according to the definition of the *ayllu*.

OVERCOMING THE ECOLOGICAL CONSTRAINTS

But was it just ingroup identity reinforcement that prompted the Mina Perdida population to get food plant from extra-local ecologies, or were there other reasons such as economic necessity or social power? In a closed environment such as the Lurín valley, surrounded by desert and blocked on one side by the Pacific Ocean and on the other side by the arid Andean slopes, the need to obtain products from 'outside' seems to be obvious. In this 'terrestrial island' environmental carrying capacity can be quickly reached, and it seems reasonable to consider managing the economic risks by expanding and diversifying the exploited territory outside of the valley.

As already mentioned, the diversification of resources through a multiplicity of exploited ecological zones is one of the principal aspects of the traditional Andean agricultural strategy (Brush 1976; Golte 1980; Murra 1985). Indeed, several systems of economic complementarity have been described for the Andes (Chevalier 2002: 240) that offer good examples of the exploitation of discontinuous environments to obtain plants from the supra-regional and continental scales. Direct vertical complementarity implies the creation of colonies in other ecologies in order to exploit them for the sole profit of the community of origin; this system involves a stronger leadership than assumed under the social organization of the *ayllus*, and would therefore correspond more to the coercive model. Indirect vertical complementarity with direct exchanges between elites living in different ecologies would also correspond more to the coercive model. In turn, indirect complementarity with generalized indirect exchanges between entities or communities having the same kind of social organization correspond more to the *ayllu* model. Finally, horizontal complementarity could correspond to either the coercive or the *ayllu* model, since it merely implies exchanges on the same 'altitude'— coast to coast, or valley to valley. Curiously enough, no system of direct complementarity with generalized direct exchanges—in other words, direct commercial ties between two *ayllus*—has been ever described or proposed.

Most of the plants in Mina Perdida are found at a local scale, which comprises only one or two ecological niches (a one-hour walk, or 3 km), and at a regional scale (the river basin or up to a one-day walk). Additional fruits and vegetables, such as sweet potatoes, maize, or chilies, may have been imported to the Lurín valley from other coastal valleys, through horizontal complementarity, such as with the northern Rímac valley which is less than a day's walk (Figure 6.1). However, the maca and the lupine could have been obtained only at the supra-regional scale that includes all of the ecosystems and territories exploited in the course of a year (requiring many days' walk). In the hypothesis of the presence of *ayllu*-like groups in the Lurín valley, indirect complementarity with generalized indirect exchanges would be the most probable economic system allowing such importation of products from the highlands, though the existence of colonies cannot be excluded. A permanent colony would imply, however, a more coercive power than an *ayllu*-like society is able to offer, but a seasonal occupation would fit this kind of social organization. In this perspective, certain members of the *ayllu* would be asked to participate in seasonal works in the highlands. Finally the palillo and the flame tree are found only at the continental scale (many thousands of kilometres) and they can be obtained only through an indirect exploitation of resources.

CULTURAL IDENTITIES

Nonetheless, the choice of the exchange system and of the plants to be exchanged are not determined by energetic or environmental constraints but are driven by social and cultural stimulus. If we look closely at the Mina Perdida plants from other ecologies, the maca and the lupine from the Andes and the flame tree fruit from the High Amazon, we realize that they are starchy food plants that are an addition to the already existing numerous coastal starchy food plants, such as the sweet potato, the achira, the manioc, or the bean. There was therefore no vital energetic need to obtain these products from other ecologies. Furthermore, if we consider the presence of plants in terms of the energy used to get them, utilizing techniques such as site catchment analysis (Higgs and Vita-Finzi 1972), it is clear that some of the plants in Mina Perdida required more energy to obtain than they provided, and therefore that other reasons for their presence than energetic optimization have to be considered. Also, the presence of a non-food plant from another ecology, the palillo from the Amazon Lowlands, indicates clearly a sociocultural stimulus behind its acquisition, given that, on the basis of the Cardal assemblage, it would have been possible to live in the Lurín valley without relying on other ecologies, the range of products grown on the coast being enough to sustain this site.

Prestige and identity

How should we understand the differences of plant assemblage observed between Cardal, which shows a limited catalogue of local plants, and Mina Perdida where there is a greater diversity of plants, including exogenous ones? I have argued that control over a specific portion of the valley is quite unlikely and would not have an impact on the plant assemblages in any event, since both sites have nearly identical local ecosystems. But the existence of control over exogenous resources through some economic exchange system would fit with the plant assemblages in Mina Perdida. We do not suggest here that Cardal was self-sufficient while Mina Perdida had to resort to importations to sustain its activities, since both sites may have developed a trade network with other coastal valleys according to the 'horizontal complementarity' model, and in such a case it would not be possible to distinguish the imported products from local ones. Rather, access to 'exotic' plants can be considered as a sign of prestige, requiring either complex economic complementarity networks or direct access to the plants—in other words, a huge economic input that should be balanced, if not exceeded, by its 'symbolic' return. Production or exploitation monopolies can greatly empower those who control the access to them.

We have seen from the lack of differentiation within sites that it is unlikely that social elites existed in the Lurín valley who would have organized access to these exotic plants and benefited from them. It seems more likely that the responsible entities were small independent groups, the *ayllus*. Social control over production is extremely strong in the Andean world, and is exercised at virtually every level of economic organization: even if the workforce is private, the land is common property. Therefore its production and exploitation is also common property up to its division in 'equal parts', corresponding to the social status and needs of every household (Isbell 1978; Orlove and Godoy 1986). Anthropology has highlighted the influence of social position on food, and therefore on crop choices, and has brought to light some of the mechanisms for gaining and keeping socio-political power through food and by extension through plant products (Goody 1982; Mintz 1996). Prestige plants can therefore not only represent the socio-political status of a group but also help to define its identity and provide the means to achieve it and maintain it. Above all, Andean group identity is nurtured through participation in communal production (Bastien 1978). Therefore, exploiting directly or indirectly a very distant territory would contribute directly to the group prestige, improve their self-esteem and reinforce the group identity against others, such as the inhabitants of Cardal (Tajfel and Turner 1979, 1986; Turner 1982).

Tradition and social identity

In his study of wild plant use in Lucania, Southern Italy, Pieroni points out that two groups, who live in the same ecological conditions, have the same overall economic bases, and are thus obviously in competition, gather and use different wild plants: of fifty-six identified wild plants, only twenty-two are common to both groups. Their different cultural origins are invoked by the groups themselves to explain these differences. However, the 'foreigners' had been settled in the same region as the 'locals' for up to six hundred years (Pieroni and Quave 2006b). The permanence of a specific identity across centuries through plant choices relates to ingroup identification and the necessity of ingroup positive differentiation, enhanced by the fact that both groups are 'of similar status' and in competition. Human alimentation is determined by a complex ensemble of factors, which makes it relatively insensitive to change. It is in fact one of the most stable cultural elements. Whenever changes in the domain of alimentation become perceptible, they are certain to reflect profound socio-economic, symbolic, and political changes (Gumerman 1997; Hastorf 1990; Lévi-Strauss 1964, 1997; Mead 1997; Mennell 1985). We suggest that the same kind of social identification process is at stake in the Lurín valley during the Initial Period. The need for positive social identity, expressed according to Burger in the ceremonial structures, is also expressed in plant choices. The plant composition differences may be due to older 'traditions' at Mina Perdida that would have been kept alive for identity reasons, as we have seen in the Lucanian example. And indeed, the already mentioned avocados, lima beans, and soursops suggest that some tradition was at stake in Mina Perdida, since all these plants grow on the coast: it would be very surprising if their existence was ignored in Cardal while they were being eaten in Mina Perdida. Since the same archaeological contexts have been excavated in both sites, it is difficult to invoke research issues to explain these differences. It is also difficult to suggest that Mina Perdida had a monopoly on these products, because it would imply a subordination relationship between the two sites. Cultural identity reasons based on traditions constitute in this case the best explanation. It would be, however, inexact to interpret the Cardal site plant composition as a negative choice, in which the only plants culturally available for the Cardal group were those that the Mina Perdida group had not used as a source of identity. Even if this were objectively true at some point of the historical process, social identity issues would transform this forced choice into a positive ingroup representation of free and deliberate choice.

The very high density of the sites within the Lurín valley, as well as the geographical proximity of the two sites, may have boosted competition between groups, intensifying this identity process and thus giving rise to important differences in plant choices, since according to social psychology the more frequent are the intergroup interactions, the more pronounced will be the positive differentiation (Tajfel and Turner 1979, 1986; Turner 1982). This would have been at the economic expense of Mina Perdida which would have had to maintain a complex and costly exchange network through which to bring in the exogenous products that defined its identity—'the need for positive social identity motivates a search for, and the creation and enhancement of, positive distinctiveness for one's own group in comparison to other groups' (Turner 1982: 34). Paraphrasing Douglas (1977) we could say that plant choice is both symbolic and functional in the sense that it plays a central role in a society, and each kind of plant conveys a social attitude, if not a strong sense of membership.

CONCLUSIONS

'Tell me what you eat, and I will tell you what you are' wrote Brillat-Savarin, the French nineteenth century 'physiologist' of taste (Brillat-Savarin 2009). If we cannot say who the Mina Perdida and Cardal inhabitants were, we can at least try to explain the differences we have pointed out in the plant assemblages of their two contemporaneous sites. The socio-economic models proposed for this specific pre-Columbian period in Peru are unsatisfactory because they address only power relationships and means of production, without taking into consideration the complexity of human behaviour. Other interpretive models are needed to address these plant assemblage differences.

Specialization of production based on ecological constraints can lead to specific redistribution of goods according to the exchange systems and the ways these systems are controlled. This can be applied perfectly to the case of Mina Perdida and Cardal to explain differences of archaeobotanical composition: one site would have had access to specific ecologies, the other not, because of the history and social organization of their respective populations. Today, structures of current Andean groups are crucial in the organization of production and in the determination of economic choices. Whether these organizational structures might have applied to groups living between the seventeenth and ninth centuries BC is quite uncertain, but our plant assemblages may support the hypothesis of the existence of *ayllu*-like groups. However, the anthropological and historical literature on food has shown the influence of social position on crop choices, and brought to light some of the mechanisms for obtaining and keeping socio-political power through plant products. Plant choices can therefore represent the social identity of a given group and at the same time the means to achieve and maintain it. As suggested by the anthropology of food, the plant component of meals, of rituals, and so on is tightly linked to one's identity. We argue that the main agent behind plant choices, and therefore the archaeobotanical data, is a search for a positive identity. We believe that people from Mina Perdida and Cardal selected different food products in order to differentiate themselves from 'others' and to build strong and positive group identities.

7

Burning the Bush: The Development of Australia's Southwest Botanical Province

Fiona Kost

INTRODUCTION

Though early historical records frequently mention Aboriginal, or *Noongar*, firing in south-western Australia, little is known about how the Noongar people managed the vegetation with fire, or the impact this has had on the environment. This study uses interdisciplinary archaeology, with information from ethnographic data, historical records, and pollen records from the last 6,000 years to determine the actions of the Noongar people and demonstrate how the Southwest Botanical Province can be viewed as an artefact of Noongar land management.

It is widely accepted that Aboriginal people have had an effect on some of Australia's vegetation types through fire (Bowman 1998; Hallam 1975; Kershaw et al. 2002) although the extent of the influence of Aboriginal firing is debated (Mooney et al. 2007). However, pollen data and the study of fire indicators in *Xanthorrhoea* and *Eucalyptus* trunks have been used to demonstrate that the frequency of fire events in the south-west has decreased since European colonization (Atahan et al. 2004; Ward et al. 2001), resulting in the loss of fire-dependent vegetation species and changes in vegetation distribution patterns. This disruption of the vegetation communities has been compounded by the extensive clearing of land for farming and the displacement of the Noongar people (Dodson 2001). The impact that European colonization had on vegetation becomes more apparent as an understanding of the Noongar fire management practices is gained.

There is increasing acknowledgement by researchers of the need to understand the influence of the past fire regime on vegetation patterns and to acknowledge traditional land management practices (Hopper and Gioia

2004), as well as the changes caused by European attempts to create a 'natural' regime, so that land management groups can take them into account when determining modern-day prescribed burning timetables. Archaeological studies such as this one can provide a unique insight into the past actions of people such as the Noongar, allowing us to determine how they shaped the landscape prior to European colonization (see Balée, Chapter 3 this volume for a more direct discussion of the 'indigenous' nature of pre-colonial landscapes; see Stump, Chapter 10 this volume for similar discussions of colonial and post-colonial environmental narratives).

THE CURRENT VEGETATION OF THE SOUTHWEST BOTANICAL PROVINCE

The Southwest Botanical Province of Western Australia (Figure 7.1) has one of the most biodiverse vegetation assemblages in the world (Beard 1979). It has been suggested that the relatively high diversity in south-western Australia

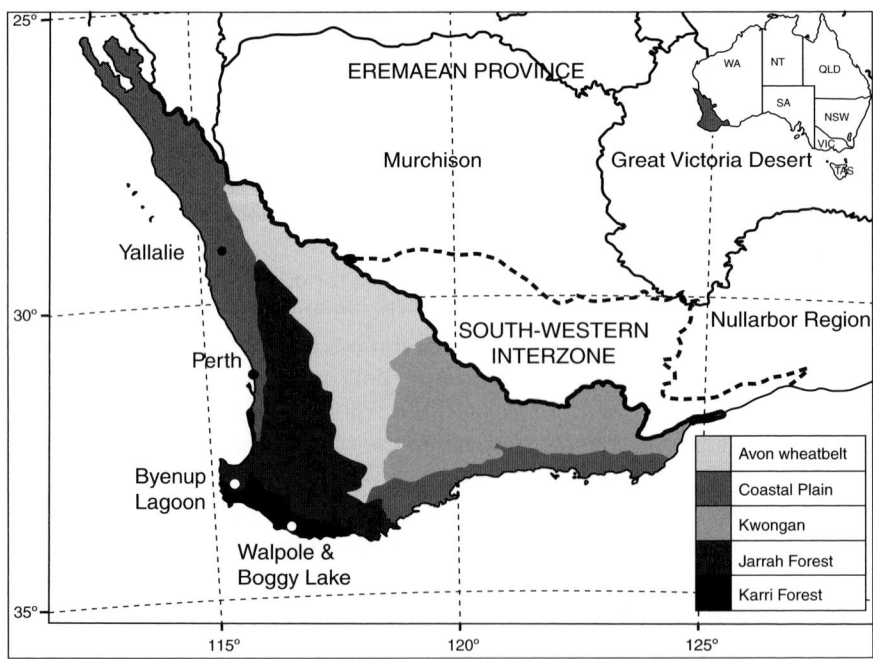

Fig. 7.1. The location of the Southwest Botanical Province within Australia indicating the approximate boundaries of the four main vegetation types, the Avon Wheatbelt, and the positions of the pollen coring locations of Walpole (Walpole River Swamp), Boggy Lake, Byenup Lagoon, and Yallalie.

may be because it was subject to less disturbance than south-eastern Australia at the Last Glacial Maximum (LGM; *c*.18,000 BP), when Australia's climate became colder and more arid (Dodson 2001). If this is the case, and the vegetation types of the south-west were established before the Holocene, the main factors driving vegetation change in the last 6,000 years are likely to have been rainfall, natural bushfires, and the anthropogenic fire regime.

The Southwest Botanical Province is part of the Darling Plateau, which still has some early Tertiary landscapes due to tectonic stability and slow erosion (Hopper 1979). The plateau is generally less than 500 m in height, with the exception of the Darling Scarp and Stirling Ranges, and is mostly weathered lateritic gravels from the Oligocene and Miocene and nutrient-poor sand plains (Hopper 1979). Along the coast sea level fluctuations have resulted in coastal plains and limestone (Hopper 1979). Despite the poor soils there are four main vegetation types: Karri dominant forest, Jarrah dominant forest, mixed shrub/heathland known as Kwongan (Beard et al. 2000) and coastal plains vegetation. The region has a Mediterranean climate with high winter rainfall and dry summers, with rainfall decreasing in a south–north direction as well as inland.

For the purpose of this study, the vegetation of the coastal plains can be characterized as low heath with root systems that are either widespread to take advantage of rainfall or adapted to exploit the groundwater system (Semeniuk 1986). Areas inland from the coastal plains, with gravel or sandy soil low in nutrients and annual rainfall of between 800 and 300 mm, are usually characterized by Kwongan interspersed with smaller eucalypts (Brown and Hopkins 1983). Kwongan generally has a high level of species richness, with little homogeneity between Kwongan patches (Brown and Hopkins 1983), which contributes to the status of the Southwest Botanical Province as a biodiversity hotspot. Rangeland environments in the south-west (the Stirling Ranges and Darling Scarp) generally have a combination of vegetation types.

FIRE AND THE SOUTHWEST BOTANICAL PROVINCE IN THE HISTORICAL RECORD

Historical archaeology is invaluable in a study such as this. The Swan River Colony of Western Australia was established in 1829 and there are numerous historical documents from the settlers in the colony as well as the records of sailors and explorers prior to this (Hallam 1975). There are a variety of historical sources that contain observations of when and where fires occurred, as well as the condition of the vegetation at the time of burning. A survey of historical references collected by Hallam (1975) and of other primary documents revealed many references to Noongar firing. These fire events were occasionally recorded in the context of potential damage to European property (such as by Friend 1931), or more often in terms of the effects seen by settlers and explorers on the vegetation they encountered.

The historical record indicates that all four vegetation types were fired, but there are differences in the firing patterns recorded for each. On the coastal plains there are several recordings of frequent firing in various locations described as dry grass and 'bush' in the months between November and February (Collie and Preston 1833; Friend 1931; Hasluck 1965). The majority of historical recordings in Kwongan areas come from the diary of Captain Collet Barker, who recorded the activities of the local Aboriginal people and their intent to burn the bush in early April (autumn), among other information, including times that it was dangerous to light fires (Mulvaney and Green 1992).

The 'rangeland environments' of south-western Australia, the Stirling Ranges and Darling Scarp, are more frequently noted in historical documents. In these areas there is some recording of fire-hollowed trees and 'fresh' vegetation thought to indicate burning (Bannister 1833; Preston 1833) as well as densely vegetated areas with no evidence of firing or occupation by Aboriginal people (Grey 1841).

In historical records Jarrah forests were often recorded as burnt 'lately' or 'recently' (Anon. 1833a; Bussell 1833), likely indicating regular firing, though the timing differs from that of the coastal areas with a more seasonal pattern. The recorded frequency of burning ranges from yearly to every three years (Bunbury 1930; Stokes 1846) and seems to be dependent on how frequently areas were used. The effect of the burning on the vegetation is still evident, however, with areas recorded as grassland with occasional trees, rather than the dense Jarrah forest vegetation that may be expected (Anon. 1833a; Bunbury 1930; Bussell 1833).

The clear division between burnt and unburnt areas seems to be best defined in the Karri forests. Some records from the inland edges of the Karri forest mention fire-hollowed trees and summer firing (Bussell 1833; Nind 1831), indicating that the fringes of the Karri forest were occasionally burnt. But generally records from the coastal side and interior of the Karri forest speak of impassable vegetation and thick scrub (Bannister 1833; Irwin 1835).

Whatever the reason, some areas, such as the interior of the Karri forest, were not burnt. These records are perhaps the most telling as they show that the open grassy forest lands that the European settlers appreciated were only open and free of undergrowth because of the land management of those who had lived on the land for the centuries before colonization (Hallam 1975). Table 7.1 summarizes some of the historical records relating to fire, showing the season or timing, what was written about fire or lack of firing in different areas, and specific records of vegetation.

Table 7.1. Summary of some of the historical documents available, listed by vegetation type, illustrating the way fire was used differently for each vegetation type. Note that different vegetation types were recorded to have been burnt at different times of year and some vegetation types were noted to have not been visibly fired at all

Season	Fire	Vegetation	Reference
Coastal Plain			
Early Summer	Raging fires	–	Hasluck 1965: 157
Late Summer	Fire to drive kangaroos	Dry grass	Friend 1931: 8
Late Summer	Many parts burnt	Bush	Friend 1931: 7
Late Summer	–	Open, flat, sandy	Mulvaney and Green 1992: 264
Late Summer	–	Sandhills and thick brush	Mulvaney and Green 1992: 266
Autumn	Smokes and fire		Mulvaney and Green 1992: 275
Kwongan			
Autumn	(Aboriginals) intended firing the bush	–	Mulvaney and Green 1992: 280
Autumn	It is their fire we see . . . near the top of a hill	–	Mulvaney and Green 1992: 280
Autumn	Mokare said that was it not for the present state of affairs [very dry], which made it unsafe, he should . . . (make) a fire on the beach	–	Mulvaney and Green 1992: 284
Autumn	Blacks prepared a bundle of a kind of torches made of the grass tree for fishing	Grass, trees	Mulvaney and Green 1992: 294
Winter	(Fire) They are unable to kindle it at this time of year and if their fire goes out, must go without	–	Mulvaney and Green 1992: 321
Rangelands			
Probably burnt last year	–	Green and fresh vegetation; 'mahogany' trees	Bannister 1833: 101–2
Fire sighted to coast	–	Patches of grass, dense forest, open country Stream in a valley	Dale 1833: 162–5
Late Summer	Blacks burn for wallabi		Mulvaney and Green 1992: 262
–	Fire hollowed trees	Almost no low vegetation; large trees	Preston 1833: 10

(continued)

Table 7.1. Continued

Season	Fire	Vegetation	Reference
–	No natives	Dense forest/thick scrub	Grey 1841: 321–2
–	Extensively burnt	Grassy forestland	Roe 1852: 55
Jarrah Forest			
Frequent burnt look	Distant view several fires	Trees	Collie and Preston 1833: 49
Lately	Burnt	Grass cleared of timber	Anon. 1833a: 111
Recently	Burnt	Free from woody bush	Bussell 1833: 187
Recently	Burnt	Tall shrubs—open grassy forest to the North	Collie 1833
Do sections yearly	Burning the bush	–	Stokes 1846: 228
Every 2–3 years	–	Scattered red gums—lots of 'cattle food'	Bunbury 1930: 95–6, 105
Late summer	Burnt	–	Bunbury 1930: 179
Late Summer	Very good ground burnt	–	Mulvaney and Green 1992: 260
–	Unsullied by burnt sticks	Grass; occasional trees—gum and peppermint	Bussell 1833: 185, 192
Karri Forest			
Late Summer	–	Considerable annoyance in walking through thick brush	Mulvaney and Green 1992: 255
Late Summer	–	Bad walking for an hour through unburnt wood	Mulvaney and Green 1992: 255
Late Summer	–	Good and thick grass	Mulvaney and Green 1992: 259
–	–	Large trees injured by fire	Bussell 1833: 185
–	Not burnt	Thick underwood—cut with hatchet	Bannister 1833: 105
–	Not burnt	Thickly wooded	Irwin 1835: 67

THE SOUTHWEST BOTANICAL PROVINCE BEFORE EUROPEAN COLONIZATION

Firing information from Ethnographic sources

Prior to European settlement the south-west of Australia was occupied by several Aboriginal groups who are now collectively known as the Noongar people. These people exploited a wide range of environments for their subsistence, with food sourced from the sea, rivers, and freshwater lakes as well as the Jarrah and Karri forests and Kwongan (Dortch 2002). There were extensive trade networks between the family groups who occupied distinct areas of the landscape (Dortch 2002). Today the Noongar culture is clearly identifiable and the people take an active interest in local archaeological studies.

Interviews with a number of Noongar Elders have been conducted. Topics covered in these interviews included what people remember or have been told about the purpose, season, and intensity of lit fires and which plants were used for food crops, medicinal purposes, and to attract game. The preliminary ethnographic information from these interviews shows a consistency of recollections between the Noongar Elders, indicating that their recollections are credible and that they are still very knowledgeable about past fire management.

The interviews also suggest that the use of fire to drive animals out of the scrub for hunting was not as well supported in the ethnographic recollections as it appears to be in the historical record. Though there was some recollection of using fire to 'burn out roos' (Ivor Woods, personal communication) many of the Elders who mentioned driving out game for hunting spoke of young people flushing the animals out by walking and making noise. One of the Elders did recall that fire had been used to drive animals but it was unclear when or how often fire was used in this way. Some of the Elders also recalled fire being used on small patches of the vegetation, to encourage the new shoots which would later attract animals for grazing. There were a small number of recollections of fire use for clearing dense undergrowth to make access easier and perhaps to aid plant ecology. A more common recollection of fire use was in land clearing for farms. This illustrates that though fire use has decreased since European settlement it was still used for some purposes where Europeans approved.

The ethnographic and historical records both agree that fires were lit in summer, though some of the ethnographic information describes late summer (Treasy and Ivor Woods, personal communication) whereas the historical record mentions the start of the fire lighting season at Christmas (Nind 1831), which is in the middle of the Australian summer. This difference may be a result of the different geographical locations of the Noongar groups and the vegetation types in each area. Noongar accounts of burning the bush also suggest that autumn was a good time for burning as fires were easier to control after the first rains of the season. The recollection of firing the bush in autumn correlates with Captain Barker's historical recording of fires being set in Kwongan at this time of year (Mulvaney and Green 1992). This practice may have become more pronounced after European settlement, since protection of farmland was also important to the Noongar people as the environment was altered. All of the Elders interviewed had worked on farms in their youth.

There was consensus among the Elders concerning the control of fire, with several methods mentioned. These included patch burning, back burning, extinguishing flames with greenery, and close observation of fires. Other methods involved the prediction of weather and wind conditions to control fire; the wind was used as a tool to direct the fire back against previously burnt areas. Fires to promote the growth of new vegetation would also be lit at the end of summer, at a time when the first rains of autumn could be used as fire control.

There were also recollections of fire specifically not being used. Some Elders identified types of vegetation which would not recover from fire, such as thickets inhabited by the Tammar Wallaby (*Macropus eugenii*), and explained that these areas were not burnt (Treasy and Ivor Woods, personal communication). Burning around areas to protect certain vegetation types from fire has also been supported by historical evidence regarding the preservation of berry patches (Hammond 1933), and more recent studies (Kelly 1999) suggest that 'spear thickets' were preserved in much the same way so the trees could reach the size needed for making spears. An interdisciplinary approach to archaeology, with the historical and ethnographic records viewed together, makes clear that fire was used for a variety of reasons (Figure 7.2) and used differently for different vegetation regimes.

Palaeo-vegetation information from palynology

Palynological studies can give us insight into the past vegetation profile and firing regimes of an area. This is a technique used by many disciplines, including geography, biology, and botany, but when viewed in an archaeological framework we can use it to answer questions about the past actions of social groups. This section discusses three key sites—Boggy Lake, Byenup Lagoon, and Yallalie—in terms of what cores from them have shown through the pollen and charcoal records.

The Boggy Lake site (Figure 7.1), was investigated by Churchill (1968) and later by Newsome and Pickett (1993). The present-day vegetation at the site is consistent with coastal plains and heathland vegetation with Agonis and Melaleuca thickets around the lake (Newsome and Pickett 1993). Two cores have been taken from Boggy Lake, one dating to *c.*7000 BP taken by Churchill

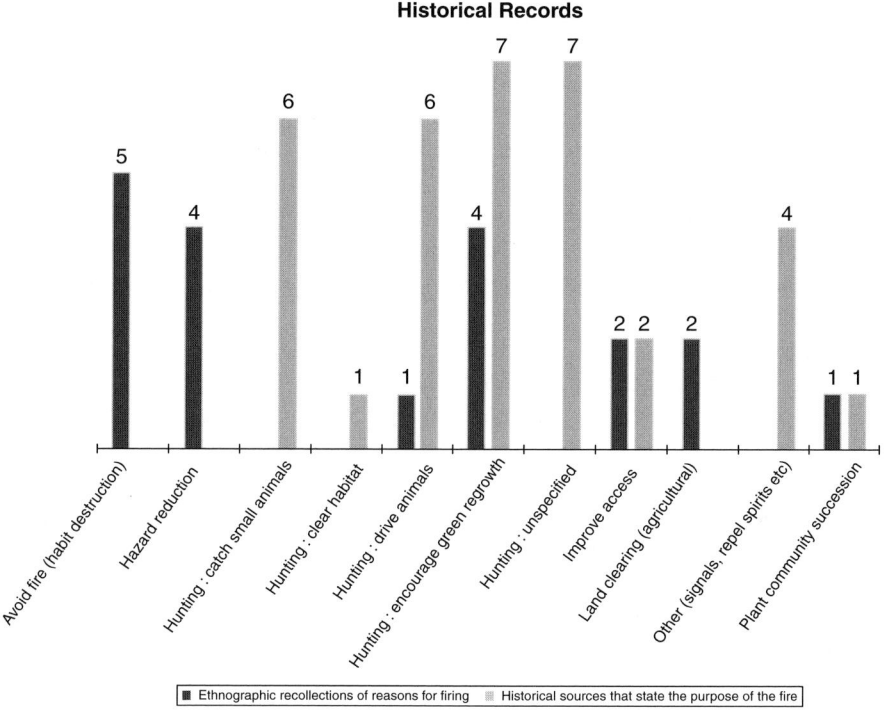

Fig. 7.2. Summary of ethnographic recollections and historical documents where the reason for lighting fires is clearly stated.

(1968) and the other with a basal date of *c.*4380 BP taken by Newsome and Pickett (1993).

Churchill's (1968) analysis of the Boggy Lake data assumed that relative changes in pollen frequencies were directly related to rainfall patterns and water availability. Using this assumption Churchill created a climatic sequence that hypothesized a wet period between 6950 and 4550 BP, linked to abundant Karri (*Eucalyptus diversicolor*), followed by a dry period shown initially by increased Marri (*Corymbia calophylla*), which peaked at 3150 BP when Jarrah (*Eucalyptus marginata*) levels peaked. An increase in Yate (*Eucalyptus cornuta*) around 2450 BP demonstrated a second wet period, which ended around 1550 BP as Jarrah became the dominant species again. The present-day vegetation was established *c.*550 BP.

Churchill (1968) also stated that charcoal was common in the cores he took, indicating a high frequency of fires over the past five thousand years. These common fires were judged to be unrelated to the substantial changes in pollen frequencies and therefore to rainfall, and so were hypothesized to be anthropogenic.

The climatic sequence of a wet Mid-Holocene followed by a dry period has since been rejected by Newsome and Pickett (1993), whose data indicated that, as a whole, Eucalyptus had remained constant over the past four thousand years, though there did appear to be changes in frequency. Their data has been used to hypothesize a change from forest to heathland, suggested to be the result of rising sea levels in the Mid-Holocene, with sand replacing the lateritic soils at the site (Newsome and Pickett 1993).

To the west of the Boggy Lake is Byenup Lagoon (Figure 7.1), a fresh water lagoon situated amongst Jarrah-Marri forest. Two cores have been taken from Byenup Lagoon that together give a combined record of *c.*4800 BP (Dodson and Lu 2000).

Dodson and Lu (2000) have stated that the pollen data indicates an early Holocene vegetation profile dominated by Marri and Jarrah with a heath understory. By *c.*3500 BP Jarrah is the dominant tree species with a small component of Blackbutt (*Eucalyptus patens*) until about three hundred years ago when Marri becomes more prominent (Dodson and Lu 2000). Though the composition of the heath understory remains relatively constant, periods of Marri dominance are related to a decrease in understory density (Dodson and Lu 2000).

The charcoal record of Byenup Lagoon indicates a sporadic fire regime in the early Holocene. Around 4200 BP and again between 2000 and 3000 BP there are dramatic peaks in the charcoal levels that are thought to represent major local fires. The increased density of the heath understory occurs be-tween these two major fire events and the increase of Marri follows the second fire event. It is hypothesized by Dodson and Lu (2000) that fire was used as a control on the ratio of Jarrah and Marri, selecting against Marri and leading to a sparser understory and easier access.

On the coastal plains north of Perth is the Yallalie site (Figure 7.1), which was a lake in the Upper Pliocene (Dodson et al. 2005). The site is currently surrounded by heath and woodland dominated by Eucalyptus and Banksia species (Dodson et al. 2005). The Yallalie site is highly significant in the fine resolution of the sediment cores, which allow us to look at fire return intervals on a yearly scale. The evidence from Yallalie allows us to determine the natural fire regime and compare it to the Aboriginal fire regime as well as the post-colonial regime. The Yallalie core shows an average fire return interval of six to ten years in the Upper and Mid-Pliocene, which Dodson et al. state to be 'longer than for the historical period' (2005: 592). Dodson et al. (2005) use the Yallalie data to support the hypothesis that the vegetation of the south-west evolved under a longer fire return interval than the anthropogenic fire regime.

The pollen cores used in this study were taken from swampy areas and the core discussed in this chapter was taken from a channel of the Walpole River (Figure 7.1), hereafter referred to as the WRS core. The total core depth was

138 cm and has yielded a basal date of 9310±60 BP. The primary vegetation at the site is currently Karri Forest with Marri trees also present.

In the upper levels the WRS core shows introduced species including dandelions (*Taraxacum officinale*), pine (*Pinus* sp.), and cereal grasses. The intermediate levels appear to be Jarrah-dominant but include Karri and also Swamp Mallet (*Eucalyptus spathulata*). Marri, *Melaleuca*, and *Casuarina* species are also relatively frequent as are understory species including *Banksia*, *Acacia*, and Asteraceae.

The Jarrah-dominant levels of the WRS core indicate an open-forest vegetation profile with low trees and tall shrubs. Open forest tends to have an intermediate level of vegetation, including small trees such as *Banksia* and *Acacia* forming the understory, which appears to be consistent with the identification carried out to date. Open forest correlates with the historical records that mention open grassy forest (Collie, 1833), gum, and peppermint (Bussell, 1833).

Some of the lower levels show similar species to the Jarrah-dominant levels, but with a much higher frequency of Karri and Marri. This Karri/Marri dominant vegetation profile indicates tall open forest. In a tall open-forest profile from the south-west we would expect to see a dense understory consistent with that cited in the historical records as causing 'considerable annoyance' to travellers (Mulvaney and Green 1992: 255).

The palynological data from the WRS core appears similar to that of Byenup Lagoon, showing that a Karri/Marri-dominant forest became a Jarrah-dominant forest due to fire selecting against Karri and Marri. The Jarrah-dominant profile would have benefited the Noongar people as the less dense understory would have provided easier access. This supports the hypothesis that the forests and grasslands of the south-west were largely anthropogenic, at least in areas that were frequented by Noongar groups. Therefore the 'virgin bushland' discovered by the European settlers was actually a result of Noongar land management.

Palaeo-vegetation information from grasstree studies

The fire return interval has also been shown by studies of species like grasstrees (*Xanthorrhoea* sp.), which grow in layers and preserve fire history in the rings of their trunks. Ward et al. (2001) sampled 150 grasstrees at fifty sites in the south-west, dating back to approximately AD 1750. The validity of using grasstree rings to determine fire history was verified using recent and documented fire events (Ward et al. 2001).

Ward et al. (2001) state that analysis of *Xanthorrhoea* trunks shows a defined change in the fire regime of the south-west after 1869, with the fire return interval decreasing to between one and four fires per decade, with increased variability in the regime. Prior to European settlement the fire return interval was between two and four fires per decade, and it remained at this level for forty years after the Swan River Colony was established (Ward et al. 2001).

SO WHAT ACCOUNTS FOR THE CHANGES IN THE VEGETATION OF THE SOUTHWEST BOTANICAL PROVINCE?

Taking the data as a whole, the first evidence of vegetation change related to a fire regime can be identified at the Yallalie site (Dodson et al. 2005), where the fire return interval in the Upper and Mid-Pliocene was longer than that of the anthropogenic fire regime established with Noongar colonization of the south-west. We can see that the natural fire return interval of between 6 and 10 years in the upper and Mid-Pliocene and the Noongar fire regime of between two and four fires per decade were different, at least on the coastal plains and the surrounding heath and woodland vegetation.

After the initial change to the fire regime, the main factors driving vegetation change seem to be changes in the Noongar fire regime itself (Churchill 1968; Dodson and Lu 2000), fluctuating sea levels (Newsome and Pickett 1993), and, perhaps, rainfall (Churchill 1968). Changes in sea levels would have caused changes in the sediments due to wave action depositing sand along the coastline, and would have been visible in the cores as sandy layers. Increased rainfall would have had an effect on species that reacted to fire in similar ways but had different rainfall requirements. As demonstrated by the grasstree data (Ward et al. 2001), for at least the eighty years prior to European settlement the Noongar fire regime was reasonably constant, with the major changes occurring forty years after European colonisation.

The two major changes that occurred with European settlement of the south-west are the clearing of land for agriculture and the change in fire return interval. The latter is hypothesized by Ward et al. (2001) to be a result of decreased Noongar firing due to the 1847 Bushfires Ordinance, which made lighting fires illegal, and of the devastation of the Noongar population by viruses such as measles. The decrease in fire return interval also corresponds with extensive logging by European settlers (Ward et al. 2001) which may have altered Noongar land use patterns.

Though the early restrictions on lighting fires were intended primarily to protect property, it was a common European misconception by the late 1800s that the Australian bush was virgin forest, and that by defending forests from fire they would revert to their pre-European state. This 'protection' of the forests led to the accumulation of undergrowth resulting in intense bushfires and loss of life, particularly while logging was in the early stages and largely unregulated.

DISCUSSION

By using interdisciplinary archaeology we can demonstrate that the vegetation communities of the south-west today are a relic of generations of Noongar land management. Since European colonization the fire regime has changed dramatically from that recorded by the early settlers and recalled by the Noongar people.

In 1997 Western Australia's Department of Environment and Conservation carried out controlled burns in the Jarrah forest at intervals of five to seven years and in the Karri forest at intervals of six to eight years (Conservation Council of Western Australia 1997). Though this is closer to the Noongar fire regime of burning every one to three years than one fire per decade, which was the regime between 1920 and 1960 (Ward et al. 2001), it is still enough of a difference to have had an effect on the vegetation communities, which can be extremely sensitive to the intensity and frequency of fires. This is particularly true for vegetation such as Kwongan, where increased time since firing has been shown to correlate with a marked decrease in species diversity (Brown and Hopkins 1983). A counter-argument is that the increase in fire return interval promotes the growth of species adversely affected by fire: however, these communities are often not endemic to the areas where they are now being found, and their presence is often harmful to the endemic species that rely on fire. If we are aiming to reverse the negative impact European colonization has had on the vegetation communities of the south-west, and prevent the loss of rare and fire-dependent plant species, a fire regime closer to that of the Noongar people is a step in the right direction.

More frequent controlled burning will also reduce the fuel load, the dry debris, and undergrowth in forest areas. In some extreme cases it has been argued that the fuel load of an area has little to do with the severity of bushfires, such as the Victorian bushfires in early 2009. But in this case there was a combination of strong winds, record temperatures, very low humidity, and extremely dry conditions after a relentless drought. It may be true that in situations such as this, the fuel load of an area has little effect once above a certain threshold, but the reduction of the fuel load through controlled burning certainly would not have made conditions any worse. Furthermore, the reduction of fuel load will be advantageous in less extreme conditions, reducing the severity of fires and therefore the amount of damage these fires cause.

It is inevitable that Australia will have bush fires and that the longer the period without a fire, the more severe and devastating the next one will be. Apart from extreme cases where there is a combination of the worst possible conditions, such as in Victoria in 2009, reduction of fuel load in order to reduce fire intensity is a good hazard reduction strategy as well as being a good management strategy for maintaining the balance of species in areas that have become fire-dependent. In the aftermath of the Victorian bushfires, Western Australia was held up as an example to the rest of the country for carrying out controlled burning.

The most effective controlled burning schedule for the south-west will be one that takes past fire regimes into account and integrates traditional knowledge with that of the current land managers. This is not a new approach in management of Australia's environment, though it is still far from being widespread. A notable example of the integration of knowledge has been established in Kakadu National Park in Australia's Northern Territory, where the control of the fire regime has been returned to the traditional owners, who work with park rangers to manage the park (Russell-Smith et al. 1997) (see Isendahl et al., Chapter 8 and Kendall, Chapter 9 this volume for discussions of the re-establishment of pre-colonial environment management practices among agricultural communities).

Prior to European settlement the vegetation of the south-west evolved over time with consistent and thoughtful management through fire. The Noongar people used their connection with the land and their knowledge of the environment to promote and control the vegetation in the majority of vegetation types. The disruption to this regime following European settlement has resulted in a radical change in the vegetation and a gradual loss of species diversity for both flora and fauna.

While it is impractical to think of returning to the pre-European colonization fire regime of the south-west, much can be gained from the long-term study of these past regimes that can help us to manage the present-day ecology and ensure the maintenance of biodiversity. Such studies also allow us to counteract simplistic development narratives that aim to restore 'natural' or 'pristine' environments, but which may actually damage biodiversity and make the landscape much more difficult to manage.

CONCLUSIONS

The use of interdisciplinary archaeology has demonstrated that the vegetation of the Southwest Botanical Province was an artefact of Noongar firing at the time of European colonization. What the European colonists regarded as virgin bushland was the result of years of frequent low-intensity controlled burns. This misconception has promoted ill-informed land management strategies.

This study uses a suite of techniques from various disciplines to determine the past actions of the Noongar people and how these actions have altered the landscape of the Southwest Botanical Province. It shows that the knowledge of local indigenous groups can and should be used as a resource when managing the landscape, an integration of knowledge familiar to archaeologists but not necessarily to land managers. The use of interdisciplinary archaeology allows us to view the landscape as the artefact it is and to tailor our management strategies accordingly.

ACKNOWLEDGEMENTS

I thank the Noongar people for their assistance with this project, particularly through sharing their knowledge. The manuscript has benefited from comments by Jane Balme, John Dodson, Joe Dortch, and Damien Kost. Lorraine and Bill Wilson are thanked for providing technical palynological assistance. This research is being carried out at the University of Western Australia. Funding for this research is provided by an ARC grant for the Linkage Project *Aboriginal landscape use and management in south-western Australia during the recent past* in conjunction with the following Industry Partners: South Coast Regional Information Planning Team (SCRIPT), The South West Catchments Council (SWCC), and the Western Australian Department of Environment and Conservation.

Part III

Environmental Narratives and Applied Archaeology

This section aims to introduce practical means by which archaeology can contribute to modern environmental debates and initiatives. Two primary areas of contribution are established; in Chapters 8 and 9 Isendahl et al. and Kendall respectively consider the role of archaeology in reviving past indigenous knowledge and re-establishing past systems of land management; in Chapters 10 and 11 Stump and Armstrong Oma take a different tack and point to archaeology's potential to critique longstanding but ultimately misleading environmental narratives. Isendahl et al. consider the concept of applied archaeology in detail and then outline ongoing work in the Bolivian Yungas which aims to recover past practices of land management so as to make their consideration available to modern farmers. In particular the project aims to foster a dialogue between the past and the present towards more effective environmental management, doing so through community participation and education. Kendall outlines an even more direct route towards applied environmental archaeology via the widespread rehabilitation of Inca and Huari terrace and irrigation systems in Peru. Here archaeological data was used to analyse the subtle complexities of pre-Columbian agricultural works particularly with regard to seemingly innocuous technical characteristics, such as the use of specific soils and construction materials. This information was then used to test rehabilitate a number of terrace systems and develop a rehabilitation model which has been replicated on a larger scale across the region. The result is an applied archaeology success story.

In Chapter 10 Stump analyses the ways in which pre-conceived narratives of environmental change, often employing unfounded pseudo-historical narratives, have been used to justify colonial and post-colonial land management policies across Eastern Africa. With reference to a number of archaeology-based case studies, Stump demonstrates how commonly assumed narratives of both sustainability and degradation are historically unfounded. Stump argues that in Eastern Africa, where environmental intervention schemes are commonplace, archaeology may serve a very important role with regard to challenging assumed environmental narratives and highlighting gaps in current environmental knowledge as revealed by long term diachronic study. In Chapter 11 Armstrong Oma takes the concept of environmental narratives a step further and points to the role of archaeology in actively reinforcing environmental narratives. In particular, she argues that archaeological narratives of the origins of European farming have long been misused to justify the practices of modern 'factory' farming. She points to the moment of domestication of cattle as one which has been presented as the mastery of humans over animals. As a counterpoint she emphasizes various changes in terms of 'engagement' between humans and animals through time, with special focus on the development of the three-aisled Bronze Age longhouse and the new relationship it established between humans and animals. She further points to the major landscape transformations initiated at this time and argues that the Early Bronze Age of Scandinavia was a period in which the landscape itself became domesticated as part of a partnership between humans and livestock. The undercurrent to her argument is that modern notions of animals as simple resources to be used and exploited has no universal basis in the past. Armstrong Oma further points us towards the often forgotten role of archaeology in the development of modern environmental narratives and challenges us to critically reassess aspects of our discipline.

8

Archaeology's Potential to Contribute to Pools of Agronomic Knowledge: A Case of Applied Agro-Archaeology in the Bolivian Yungas

Christian Isendahl, Walter Sánchez, Sergio Calla, Marco Irahola, Dagner Salvatierra, and Marcelo Ticona

INTRODUCTION

Over the last two decades the concept of applied archaeology has been used increasingly to refer to how archaeology can contribute more broadly to society at large. Depending on the intellectual and geographical context there are many different ways that applied archaeology is understood. One important set of approaches builds on the standard definition of applied science as the application of scientific knowledge in creative problem-solving. Many archaeologists find that evidence which sheds light on resource exploitation strategies in the past is particularly rewarding in this regard, arguing that the insights gained from archaeological research can guide land use planning and resource management and make a positive impact on local livelihoods for people today and in the future (Costanza et al. 2007a; Hayashida 2005). This kind of applied archaeology is usually associated with rural livelihood development, but there is also an emerging applied archaeology of land use planning in predominantly urban sectors (Smith 2010). Some of the most prolific projects of applied agro-archaeology for rural development are those engaging in rejuvenating prehistoric agricultural features that have fallen into disuse or are being mismanaged. Groundbreaking applied agro-archaeology in the Andean region demonstrates considerable advances in this field, reconstructing abandoned raised fields, irrigation canals, and cultivation terraces in order to understand pre-Hispanic agricultural systems and long-term land-use dynamics and to re-apply ancient technologies for contemporary use

(Chepstow-Lusty and Winfield 2000; Erickson 1985, 1994, 1998; Kendall 1997b, 2005, Chapter 9 this volume). The Andes are exceptionally rich in archaeological remains of pre-Hispanic agriculture and demonstrate considerable diversity in peoples' approaches in the past in addressing the many different managerial issues associated with sustaining a farming livelihood in these environments (Denevan 2001; Donkin 1979).

Linking the broad scope of applied agro-archaeology to the theoretical framework of historical ecology (Balée 1998, 2006; Balée and Erickson 2006; Crumley 1994, 2000, 2007), the motive of this contribution is to discuss some of the problems and opportunities facing an on-going applied agro-archaeological project in the Yungas of the Bolivian Andes (Isendahl 2008). We report on a Swedish-Bolivian research partnership that has been investigating a complex pre-Hispanic agro-archaeological landscape at Rasupampa in Bolivia's Department of Cochabamba that includes several solutions to slope, soil, and water management that have not been reported in a similar configuration from elsewhere in the Andes (Isendahl 2008; Isendahl et al. 2008; Sánchez 2008). The goal of ongoing research is to understand in detail the forms, functions, distribution, and chronology of the agricultural system, ultimately to inform land use management in the Yungas.

We consider the suitability of archaeological reconstructions as a model for agricultural land management in local context but argue that archaeological narratives of past agronomies cannot form a priori models for current agriculture. Rather, the main advantage is to complement other land use narratives and contribute to composite pools of agronomic knowledge for local land management decisions that include a long-term perspective (see also Stump, Chapter 10 this volume for further discussion of applied archaeologies).

APPLIED ARCHAEOLOGY AND HISTORICAL ECOLOGY

Applied archaeology is broad in scope, a point well reflected in the definition of the concept that the Society for American Archaeology's (SAA) Committee on Curriculum proposes:

> applied archaeology refers to the application of archaeological research and its results to address contemporary human problems, including (but not limited to) issues that involve cultural resource management, heritage tourism and development, long-term modeling of human/environment dynamics, and public education aimed at awareness and stewardship of archaeological remains (Neusius 2009: 19).

This definition integrates several aspects of applied archaeology that are emphasized differently in different regions and archaeological traditions. In the United States, applied archaeology is often used as synonymous to contract archaeology, and essentially distinguishes Cultural Resource Management (CRM) from academic research archaeology (Neusius 2009). In Sweden, the expression (*tillämpad arkeologi*) is less common but is normally associated with public education and outreach. The social and political roles of archaeology in contemporary society—for instance in the social construction of identities, in territorial claims, and in resource disputes—form other understandings of applied archaeology; of how knowledge of the past is used in contemporary society for different ends.

Over the last twenty-five years archaeology has become a self-reflexive discipline, and archaeologists are increasingly concerned with how they and the discipline can contribute to society at large. Asked provocatively if archaeology is useful, archaeologists at an SAA meeting session in Atlanta 2009 responded generally affirmatively but differed as to how, to what extent, and to what ends archaeology has been and should be used (Dawdy 2009). Pointing out the important distinction between value and utility, Holtorf emphasizes that many ideological uses of archaeology are questionable, but that 'some uses of archaeology, such as those improving contemporary agricultural practices, are, of course, not dubious or problematic at all' (2009: 182). But the idea that archaeology should be an applied science or that its usefulness and value to society needs to be transparent to motivate its *raison d'être* certainly does not permeate the discipline, and does not reflect how the majority of its practitioners, or many other people, regard archaeology and its public role. For instance, discussing sociology as an applied social science, Bourdieu notes that:

> One only has to think of the archaeologists, ... who are never asked what use they are, what their work is for, who they work for or who needs it. No one calls them into question and they consequently feel completely justified in doing what they do (1993: 27).

Perceptions of archaeological knowledge and the long-term perspective as gratuitous are unfortunate but influential outside the field, and run contrary to an internal critical discourse that finds the discipline in the present looking as much towards the future as into the past. One broad area of investigation where archaeologists are finding a particularly important applied role to play is in addressing issues in human–environment relations, with the overall objective to provide insights that are potentially valuable for designing sustainable or resilient resource management principles. Reconstructing and rejuvenating past agronomies and agrosystems generates insights of local resource management practices valuable in rural development projects. Approaches to applied archaeology concerned with the relationship between humans and the environment are closely aligned with the interdisciplinary research programme of historical ecology, which integrates historical perspectives in the humanities, the social sciences, and the natural sciences in the study of the relationship between people and environment (see in particular Balée 1998, 2006; Balée and Erickson 2006; Crumley 1994, 2000, 2007, this volume). Balée (2006: 76) defines historical ecology as a 'research program concerned with the interactions through time between societies and environments and the consequences of these interactions for understanding the formation of contemporary and past cultures and landscapes'. In this sense it is an applied research programme. Historical ecologists question the validity of a number of widespread, often markedly normative, assumptions on the interaction between people and the environment in the past. Some of the main postulates, perspectives, and points made in historical ecological research with particular relevance for applied archaeology include the following:

1. The present is contingent with the past.
2. Societies transform landscape, they do not simply adapt to environments.
3. Landscapes form primary sources for understanding the interaction of humans and the environment over the long term.
4. Landscape-scale management and exploitation strategies are governed by interacting social and environmental processes and systems at multiple scales, from the local to the global.
5. Humans have had an impact on practically all environments, but different societies and land-use strategies impact different landscapes in dissimilar ways.
6. Human impacts on environments *may* increase landscape biodiversity.
7. Low-technological indigenous systems of resource exploitation are not merely by definition ecologically sustainable. The sustainability of any resource strategy over different time-periods needs to be detailed, contextualized, and evaluated rather than simply assumed.

RASUPAMPA IN THE BOLIVIAN YUNGAS

A recent addition to the list of Central Andean projects in applied agro-archaeology for rural development is currently unfolding at Rasupampa, a slightly sloping platform plain at an altitude of *c.*1850–1900 m above sea level, near the village of Tablas Monte in Bolivia's Department of Cochabamba (Figure 8.1). Rasupampa is located in the Yungas of the Eastern Andean *Cordillera montaña*—the eastern face of the eastern mountain range of the Central Andes. This entire macro-region of the Central Andes from the Eastern Cordillera to the lowlands forms a complex and heterogeneous environment with great biogeophysical diversity. The pronounced, vertically-based ecological zonation of the composite mountainous environment is mirrored in a mosaic-like geographical distribution of current and past resource

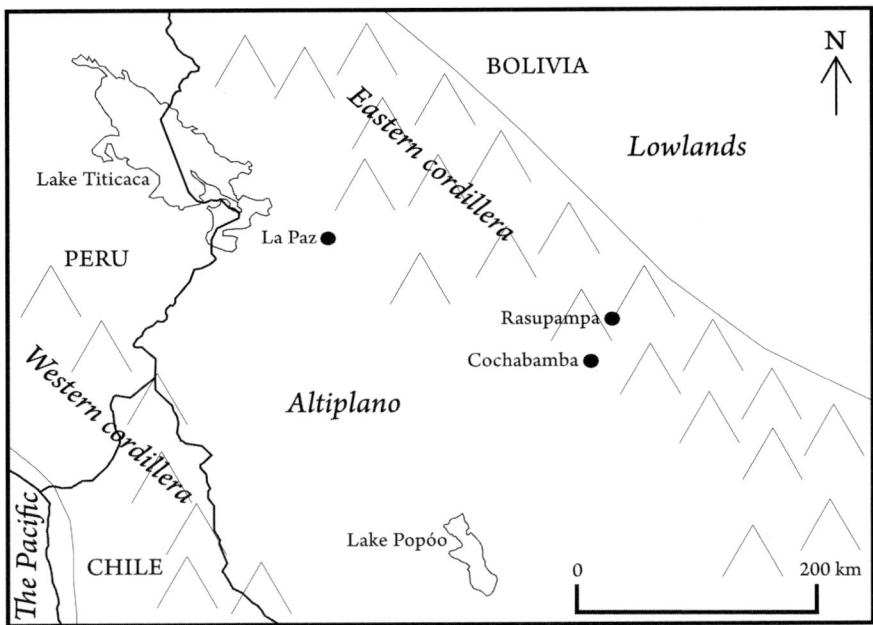

Fig. 8.1. The location of Rasupampa in the eastern cordillera of the Andes.

exploitation strategies and forms the basis for economic complementarity (Murra 2002; see also Goldstein 2005; Hastorf 1993). Forming part of the greater Amazonian hydrological system, the *montaña* plays a decisive ecological role at continental and global scales: it forces the moist easterly air masses of the South Atlantic anticyclone to ascend and release heavy precipitation that ultimately feeds the Amazon with nutrient-rich, sediment-laden water. Average rainfall is in the range of 3000 mm. There is no distinct dry season, but precipitation is heavier during the southern hemisphere summer.

The environmental variation of the *montaña* is principally based on differences in altitude, precipitation levels, and slope gradient. 'Yungas' is a word used in Quechua and Aymara—the two main Central Andean languages—for 'hot valleys' (Bertonio 2005 [1612]: 751) and refers to land surfaces in the mid- to low-altitude humid meso-tropics at elevations between 400 and 3,000 m, commonly covering flanked colluvial terraces of long, often intermittent and complex slopes that are partly covered with rain forests (Sánchez 2008: 47–57). The Yungas do not comprise a continuous section of the *montaña*; these are composite and broken landscapes, circumscribed by mountain ranges and river floodplains. Soil characteristics, hydrological patterns, and moderate slope gradients of the Yungas offer good and varied conditions for agricultural production. At different altitudes, distinct Yungas correspond to the growing ranges of different sets of domesticated plants, thus producing a series of broadly vertically defined agro-ecological zones with different crop suitability.

The mosaic distribution of agro-ecological zones, high humidity, and the location between the Neotropical lowlands and the Andean region in all their complexity and variation contribute to make the Yungas among the world's richest biodiversity hotspot regions (Myers et al. 2000). At the margin of high elevation Andes and the lowland Neotropics, the Yungas might have provided species refugia during climate change at the Pleistocene–Holocene boundary and earlier (Pennington et al. 2010; Prance 1982), but there is a need for historical ecological research to provide long-term perspectives on the dynamics between resource exploitation and species biodiversity at different spatial scales and time intervals. Despite exceptional and endangered biodiversity, resource abundance, and the agricultural potential of the Yungas it has until recently remained an archaeological terra incognita, partly reflecting a common idea of the *montaña* as a culture historically peripheral zone. Even though archaeologists at the Universidad Mayor de San Simón (UMSS) in Cochabamba have conducted important investigations in the Yungas since the 1970s (for a research summary see Sánchez 2008: 21–5), much archaeological field research is still needed to understand the long-term dynamics of this complex and logistically difficult region in any detail.

RECENT ARCHAEOLOGICAL RESEARCH IN THE YUNGAS OF COCHABAMBA

The archaeological and ethnohistorical research recently initiated in the Department of Cochabamba is an important step towards a better understanding of the later prehistory and early history of the Central Andean Yungas. Archaeological field investigations, in particular at Tablas Monte and Rasupampa (Figure 8.2), demonstrate continuous human occupation and inter-regional interaction networks since at least the Middle Horizon of the mid-first millennium AD and until the Inca Horizon of the 15th century (Sánchez 2008). Throughout the sequence local wares dominate the ceramic assemblage, indicating local continuity. Ceramics of the Middle Horizon also include Tiwanaku-style pottery of the Illataco (350–725) and Piñami (725–1100) phases as well as ceramics from the Chapare of the Neotropical lowlands, demonstrating interactions between the Yungas and the Altiplano, the mid-altitude valleys of Cochabamba, and the lowland plains by at least the second half of the first millennium AD (Sánchez 2008: 212). The integration of the Yungas into interregional interaction networks is further evidenced from sections of the extensive pre-Hispanic Andean road system reaching

Fig. 8.2. Panorama towards the southeast of the Rasupampa plain with the community at Tablas Monte in the background *c*.1 kilometre uphill (photograph author's own).

Rasupampa and other areas of the Yungas (Hyslop 1984; Sánchez 2008). Following the demise of the Tiwanaku state, relations between the Altiplano and the Yungas is less clear during the Late Intermediate (*c*.1100–*c*.1400) while there is clear contact with the mid-altitude valleys and the lowlands. The same pattern of regional interactions is maintained in the Late Horizon (15th century AD), with only minor occurrences of Inca pottery in the assemblages.

The most significant result from the investigations is the discovery of a complex pre-Hispanic agrosystem at Rasupampa that includes a range of land-tenure, slope, and water management solutions that have not been reported in a similar configuration from elsewhere in the Andes. Located on slightly sloping plains at Rasupampa, the agro-archaeological remains are characterized by a system of walled field or garden plots (Figure 8.3). In the interior of these plots there are parallel rows of stone that form a series of channels or furrows. Sánchez (2008: 213) suggests that these furrows had a number of functions: controlling erosion, retaining soil moisture, redistributing excess water in the soil profile, raising soil temperature, and facilitating weed control. Water canals were also documented at Rasupampa and—in more steeply sloping terrain at the limits of the plain towards the river gorge to the west—stepped terraces of a kind common to pre-Hispanic terracing in other parts of the Andes (Denevan 2001; Donkin 1979). Sánchez (2008: 213) argues that several components of the agrosystem in the Rasupampa plain do not resemble Inca-style construction forms or techniques, and suggests that

Fig. 8.3. The agro-archaeological landscape at Rasupampa. Note the canal in the centre of the photograph. View towards the south (photograph author's own).

the agrosystem pre-dates the Late Horizon and represents a locally developed resource exploitation strategy. This agricultural system appears to be endemic to the Yungas and the findings significantly supplement previous understandings of the diversity of pre-Hispanic agriculture in the Andes and Neotropics. The research results further underline that the prehistory of the Yungas is rich and complex, and does not support orthodox conceptualizations of the Yungas as simply a boundary, a frontier, or a periphery (Sánchez 2008: 248–9).

APPLIED AGRO-ARCHAEOLOGY AT RASUPAMPA AND TABLAS MONTE

A second phase of field investigations at Rasupampa was initiated in 2007 with the formation of the archaeological research collaboration project 'Cultivating the Past: Applied Agro-Archaeology for Rural Development in the Bolivian Yungas', supported by a research grant from the Swedish International Development Cooperation Agency (Sida). Rasupampa is an elongated plain platform stretching and slightly sloping towards the north, measuring some 2,000 m by 400 m and covering about 40 hectares. The plain is topographically well defined by higher terrain to the north, east, and south and by the steep slope of the Jatun Mayu river gorge to the west. Large sections of the steep slope towards the west, known as Rasufalda, are covered with pre-Hispanic agricultural terraces, partly mapped by Sánchez (2008: 150–3). The entire Rasupampa plain might once have been covered with pre-Hispanic agricultural features, but only a part of the maximum extension remains today. We know that many walls have been dismantled and the materials carried off to be used in the renovation of a road and because they occasionally obstructed smallholder cultivation. Current farming at Rasupampa is dominated by long-fallow swidden agriculture, with a fallow period of up to 25 years, but with wide variation. Some plots are under semi-permanent cultivation while others have been taken out of production owing to the increasing emigration of farmers from Tablas Monte to work in Argentina and Spain over the last decade. Several farmers cultivate at the locations of the pre-Hispanic farming system and enjoy some of the functional benefits of the interior furrows (for instance, top-soil erosion control, surface drainage, and soil infiltration), but the agro-technology is currently not operated in the way that it was designed: the agro-archaeological features essentially represent lost agronomic knowledge.

The research process necessarily involves a long-term engagement and close cooperation with the local community at different levels and stages, and fundamentally engages archaeology in the broader social context throughout the course of the work. The challenge and the opportunity is to provide insight into past land uses that can be added to the pool of knowledge accessible to local farmers and land managers. If applied archaeology seriously aspires to something different from a purely academic discourse, research insights resulting from the approach must, by definition, be disseminated to those that are the potential users of these insights. There cannot be an applied archaeology without an associated plan for public outreach, however that public is defined. In the case from the Bolivian Yungas discussed here, significant emphasis has been placed on community engagement through organizing a village museum as a venue for disseminating research results and increasing community awareness of heritage issues and landscape history.

The research strategies involved (1) mapping agro-archaeological features, (2) excavating and reconstructing a small sample of the main agro-archaeological features, (3) implementing a test-cultivation programme, (4) documenting current agronomic knowledge and practices among Tablas Monte farmers, and (5) organizing a community museum at Tablas Monte. Some preliminary characteristics of the agro-archaeological landscape are presented here.

An eight hectare-sample in the southern section of the plain has been mapped (Figure 8.4). This represents an estimated 20 per cent of Rasupampa, but a much larger share of the area where agro-archaeological features still remain today. Mapping the sample area hectare by hectare, we are collecting an extensive database of the agro-archaeological landscape, which currently includes information on nearly 600 features (Figure 8.2). Most of these features are walled plots that vary greatly in size, from about 2 by 5 metres to 20 by 40 metres. The shapes of the plots similarly vary significantly, from nearly perfect rectangles to amorphous polygons. The density of walled plots also changes over the mapped section of the landscape owing to differences in micro-topography, the sizes of the plots, and the degree of preservation, from about fifty to over one hundred defined plots per hectare. The walls are usually between half a metre and a metre high and similarly wide. They are constructed from rocks appearing naturally in the plain, with larger boulders at the base and fist-sized rocks in the upper levels. Most walled plots have parallel rows of stone in the interior, spaced at intervals of about 65 to 80 cm and perpendicular to the direction of the very slight slope (Figure 8.3). The rows of stone and the furrows created between them potentially served a variety of different functions according to the season of the agricultural calendar: horizontal drainage of excess water, topsoil erosion control, vertical distribution and levelling of soil moisture content, raising soil temperature, reducing high solar radiation, and facilitating tending. These features have not been documented in agro-archaeological research from elsewhere, but are unique to the Yungas landscape. Hence, the emerging evidence adds significantly to our understanding of long-term agro-ecological diversity in the Andes. Other agro-archaeological features in the landscape include larger inter-plot networks of canals draining and distributing water, slope terracing, circular

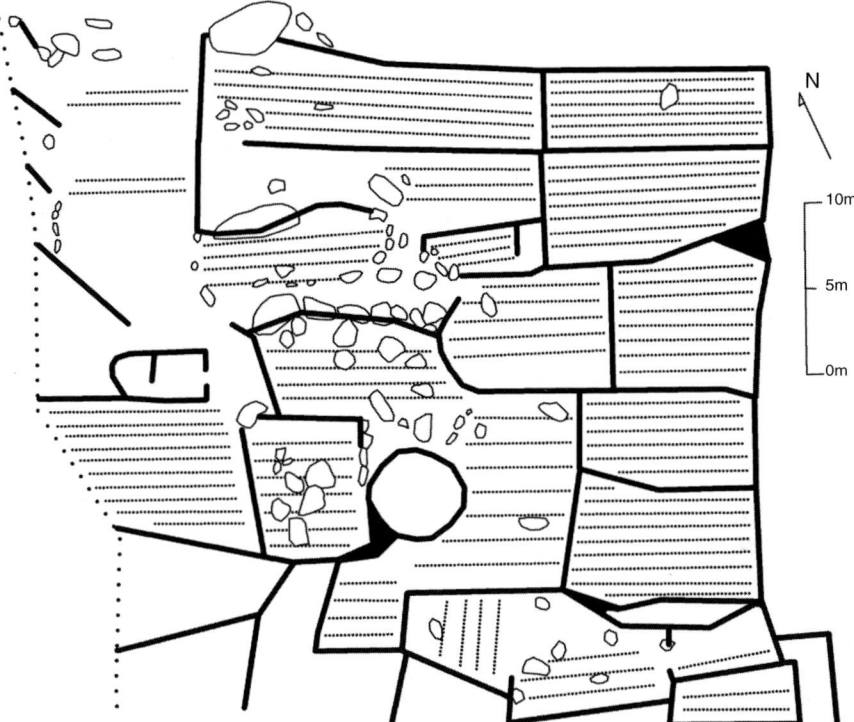

Fig. 8.4. A section of the Rasupampa field system. Full lines indicate stone walls and the dotted lines the interior furrows of a Rasupampa garden plot.

walled features lacking interior furrows (probably the remains of storage structures), and rectangular and apsidal field houses. The general pattern of the agro-archaeological remains currently sampled quite clearly suggests overall planning. These are not ad hoc gardens: they form part of a large planned agrosystem of soil, slope, and water management designed to increase the productivity of the land.

There are currently no unambiguous chronological indicators available that can be directly associated with the agro-archaeological features. Problems of dating are issues of compulsory concern in archaeological approaches to large and complex landscapes and our work at Rasupampa is no exception. Until datable excavated data is recorded from Rasupampa itself, ceramic evidence from Sánchez's excavations at Tablas Monte about a kilometre away offers a rough indication of the temporal dimension of the agrosystem, and suggests that it dates from the period between the Middle Horizon of the mid-first millennium AD until the Late Horizon of the 15th century.

To further determine the function of the agricultural system in general— and of the intra-plot furrows in particular—necessitates excavation, reconstruction, and test cultivation. A representative field plot will be selected for more detailed investigation and reconstruction, and we are initiating an experimental cultivation programme to test the functions and productivity of the agrosystem with various Andean cultivars and cropping and tending strategies, which will be determined in dialogue with the community conducting the test cultivation. Important indigenous plants include tubers such as arracacha (*Arracacia xanthorrhiza*) and yacon (*Smallanthus sonchifolius*), which we suspect both originate as domesticated crops from Yungas environments. It is evident that substantial results from the test programme and the evaluation of the reconstructed Yungas agrosystem will take time to achieve, and so we are looking forward to engaging in applied archaeology at Rasupampa with the community at Tablas Monte on a long-term basis.

HISTORICAL ECOLOGY, APPLIED ARCHAEOLOGY, AND NARRATIVES AND KNOWLEDGE SYSTEMS AT RASUPAMPA

The ongoing investigations at Rasupampa demonstrate well that applied archaeology—'the application of archaeological research and its results to address contemporary human problems' (Neusius 2009: 19)—in actual practice often involves several interlocked aspects: community interaction and different kinds of public archaeology, cultural resource and heritage management concerns, historical ecological perspectives on long-term human–environmental dynamics, and rejuvenation of pre-Hispanic resource exploitation and land use strategies. The community is engaged in the research in several different ways. First of all, as proprietors and land managers they are generously granting us permission to do archaeological investigations at Rasupampa. As research has progressed, first with Sánchez's initial work and then with the current cooperative project, local interest in archaeology, the culture history of the Yungas, and in particular the agro-archaeological remains at Rasupampa has increased (Isendahl et al. 2009), and we have long shared the vision with key members of the community to organize a community museum at Tablas Monte (Figure 8.5). A central idea is that the museum will communicate the updated research results from the investigations at Rasupampa, but exhibitions should not be confined to archaeology. In order to stay relevant it must be managed to accommodate the needs of the community and we are encouraging village authorities to invite relevant nongovernmental organizations (NGOs) to present their work. One such example is Fundación Promoción e Investigación de Productos Andinos (PROINPA), an NGO that works with research and promotion of indigenous Andean crops

Fig. 8.5. Tablas Monteros studying a reconstruction of pre-Hispanic farming at Rasupampa on the opening day of the *Museo Comunitario Tablas Monte*, 22 November 2009 (photograph author's own).

and has field experimental plots near Tablas Monte (see www.proinpa.org). Many community members are actively participating in actual fieldwork at Rasupampa, and we are making sure that the different objectives, tools, and phases of research are meticulously explained and understood in outline by everyone working with us. Furthermore, we are participating in capacity-building programmes initiated by local authorities, providing guided visits to other archaeological sites and museums in Cochabamba. From our point of view as archaeologists and cultural heritage specialists, we are particularly concerned with the protection and sustainable management of the agro-archaeological remains at Rasupampa, as well as in other regions of the Yungas where similar agro-archaeological remains may occur but have not yet been recorded. We think that the museum—in particular through the dissemination of research results from Rasupampa—has a very important role to play in promoting local and regional awareness of the value of the cultural heritage among land managers, in that this may ultimately have protective effects against further destruction of the little-known agro-archaeological heritage of the Yungas. In other words, the emphasis on long-term landscape dynamics in historical ecology has the added benefit that the knowledge generated in applied research can first and foremost be used in the landscape in which it is generated, supplementing the available pool of knowledge on land use and resource exploitation strategies.

Ethical aspects of archaeological research come to the fore in the kind of applied work being attempted at Rasupampa and with the community at Tablas Monte. With a pronounced focus on community interaction and partnership, involving the application of archaeology in rural livelihood development through the local dissemination of research results, we are addressing several of the main ethical issues raised. For instance, the *Principles of Archaeological Ethics* adopted by the SAA include concerns for the stewardship of the archaeological record, community accountability, discouraging commercialization, promoting public education and outreach, providing open access to archaeological knowledge, and public reporting (Lynott and Wylie 2000). But the need for transparency of archaeological research is all the more central when there are claims of commercial value or perceived potential application of research results. It is a mistake to assume that the ethical aspects of archaeological research are by definition simply resolved in applied work— on the contrary, owing to the potential use-value of research results, the ethical issues are potentially more complicated. Do we, for instance, need to address issues of intellectual property rights in respect of useful resource management strategies and technologies that archaeologists may be exploring? This is a perspective of research that archaeologists normally need not ponder, but which parallels ethical issues in ethnobiology regarding plant genetic property rights (e.g. International Society of Ethnobiology 2006).

Community interaction in research and the different aspects of public archaeology is not a matter of one-way communication in which academics and specialists simply educate the general public—far from it. We are working with people that have life-long experiences of making a livelihood from farming in these Yungas landscapes. While it is clear from observation and talking to farmers that much knowledge about how to optimize the use of the pre-Hispanic field systems has been lost, farmers still have a practical experience of these systems which it is useful for us to learn about, and so we are conducting formal questionnaire-based interviews to record local narratives of resource management and agronomy. Although we are recording current land use practices partly to gain insights that can be used to interpret those of the past, the historical ecological approach is different from ethnoarchaeological approaches that use present analogies to model the past (Gosden 2005). Understanding landscapes as archaeological artefacts, as palimpsests of the long-term interaction between humans and environments (Balée and Erickson 2006), historical ecologists view the past as directly conditioning the present. This is in stark contrast to much previous ethnoarchaeological research which tends to stretch analogies across time thus collapsing history and decontextualizing the past and the present. This distinction epitomizes well the ontological and epistemological bases that set historical ecological approaches in applied archaeology apart from much of the broader mainstream archaeological discourse. Whereas the ontological foundation and *raison d'être* of mainstream archaeology is in some sense based on an objective separation of the past from the present (the traditional view reflected in Bourdieu's comment cited above), historical ecology takes a different approach in emphasizing that the present is contingent upon the past. The approach taken here acknowledges the key epistemological contradiction of interpreting past land uses on the basis of contemporary observation and charters a dialectic modelling process with two parallel goals: (1) to understand agricultural practices in the past from archaeological sources, local agronomies, and test cultivation, and (2) to use the insights gained of land use practices in the past to inform current resource management. There is a reflexive relationship between these two goals that together form a composite long-term applied historical ecology of resource management at Rasupampa.

Over the past twenty years or so there has been an increased interest worldwide in rural livelihood development and in conservation projects that attempt to learn from local resource exploitation strategies and land management practices, with the objective of protecting biodiversity. Although allusions to the past are frequently made in ethnobiology, conservation ecology, and rural development, historical arguments routinely yield to recentism (that is, they focus on recent periods (Sluyter 2010)) and claims about the more distant past are based on stereotyped—and often normative—assumptions, rather than referencing the kind of long-term anthropological data that archaeological research provides. At the same time, there is often an assumed time-depth to applications of 'local', 'indigenous', 'traditional', or 'situated' knowledge in the broader biodiversity discourse that seems to inadequately address significant pre-industrial agricultural change, as has been discussed from a number of critical viewpoints (Berkes 1999; Ingold 2000; Nazarea 1999, 2006; Nygren 1999; Stump 2010, Chapter 10 this volume).

In the investigation of the Rasupampa field system we are avoiding these ambiguous and problematic terms to focus on the distinction between the more specific terms 'agronomies' and 'narratives of agronomies'. For the purposes of our research, a particular 'agronomy' refers to the core cultivation practices and knowledge about farming and related subsistence activities shared by a social group, such as the current farming population at Tablas Monte. From in-depth interviews with the farmers and from observing their work in the Yungas landscape it is clear that there is a shared agronomy and that these skills—how to treat the soil, which crops to cultivate, when to plant and when to harvest, crop rotation, fallow periods, and so on—are in the main passed on from one generation to the next. Ingold's dwelling perspective to learning and practice 'in the context of an ongoing engagement with the land and with the beings—human and non-human—that dwell therein' (2000: 133) makes much sense here, and so practice varies to some extent between different farmers on the basis of social and economic differences and individual choice and preference. Some report that farming has changed and that current agriculture is different from that of their ancestors and elders (sometimes using the word '*machitos*' or 'old-timers'), but indicate that this has a basis in individual variation rather than representing a pronounced agronomic break.

There are several factors that complicate this image of a largely coherent agronomy with a long landscape tradition. There is, for instance, considerable demographic mobility in the Yungas and at Tablas Monte today (pre-Hispanic and early historic population movements in the Andes have been well addressed in Andean scholarship and offer time depth to regional diaspora phenomena and demographic mobility (e.g. Goldstein 2005; Sánchez 2008)). Over the last decade in particular many community households have left Tablas Monte to earn a better living working in low-wage agricultural labour in Spain or Argentina. There is a simultaneous stream of alleged climate refugees from the dry Altiplano that bring the farming skills and experiences from an entirely different landscape to the humid and warm Yungas. Some of these skills are certainly useful for smallholder farming in the new social and environmental context but many practices will also have to be modified to suit the new conditions. There will also be a whole new set of agronomic knowledge to experience in order to make the most out of farming under radically different environmental circumstances and in stressful, 'disengaged', social situations. Hence, demographic mobility makes the interaction and cross-fertilization of different landscape agronomies not only possible but a frequently occurring aspect of the dynamics of agricultural knowledge and practice. The increased use of insecticides and the fertilizers compulsory in contemporary agriculture is singled out as the most important difference in recent years marking a process of change from 'old-timer' agronomy. Local agriculture is receiving input from other sources and by a range of other processes, producing both for domestic consumption and for vending at the farmers' market in the city of Cochabamba. Although some seeds for planting are drawn from previous years' harvests or exchanged between relatives or provided by PROINPA, most are purchased in Cochabamba.

It is important to first keep in mind that locally managed agrosystems with low external input are not static and are linked into larger interaction networks and, second, to maintain an analytical distinction between past and contemporary agronomies that keeps track on how different kinds of knowledge-systems relate to each other. These are key epistemological issues which need to be addressed in order for historical ecology to inform current land use management strategies. The interesting thing is that the insights we are gaining on current agronomies from interviews, observation, and interaction with local farmers (in particular regarding different aspects of planting, tending, and cropping strategies) are instrumental in interpreting past land use on the basis of the agro-archaeological features. The narrative of past agronomies we are advancing on the basis of archaeological data (in particular the use of parallel stone furrows to control both topsoil erosion and vertical and horizontal water movement) is thus cross-pollinated with our understanding of current agronomies and emerges in the intersection between our competencies as archaeologists with current local agronomies. This mode of reflexive and communicative interpretation highlights the complex interrelationship between current local agronomies and the archaeological narrative of past agronomies that we bring to the table. In other words, the reconstruction of pre-Hispanic cultivation techniques in this local context is a binary process that simultaneously informs and is informed by local farmer knowledge. To be successful, field projects in applied archaeology—perhaps more than in any other subfield of archaeology—must be firmly anchored locally, and to a significant extent must build on the exchange of knowledge between the specialist competencies of the archaeologist and the knowledge systems based in long-term engagement in a landscape. These narratives and agronomies are complementary rather than competing.

CONCLUSION

As outlined briefly here, the research currently carried out at Rasupampa and Tablas Monte is multi-spectral and integrates several different aspects of applied archaeology: cultural heritage management, community capacity building, public education and outreach, and, above all, the application of archaeological knowledge of land use to provide insights on resource exploitation and landscape dynamics. That said, there is also a very strong component of descriptive science, aiming to contribute to an emerging archaeology of the Yungas. Applied agro-archaeology of the kind we are undertaking in the Yungas can contribute insights on land management to a composite pool of agronomic knowledge that local farmers can test and apply as they see fit. The data emerging on the pre-Hispanic use of micro-terracing and parallel stone canals in the field plots at Rasupampa provides new and previously unconsidered information of potential use for current land managers. The important job for us as archaeologists is to generate archaeological data on past land use, to interpret the information, and to present those conclusions to the scientific and local communities for transparency and consideration.

ACKNOWLEDGEMENTS

None of the work discussed here could have been realized without the cooperation with the community at Tablas Monte. We are very grateful to community members for their hospitality, their interest in sharing their knowledge with us, their work, and for permitting us to do field research at Rasupampa. We are also grateful for permission to conduct archaeological fieldwork in Cochabamba granted by the directors of the Instituto de Investigaciones Arqeológicas in Cochabamba, David Pereira and Maria de los Angeles Muñoz. Financial support was provided by a research grant from the Swedish International Development Cooperation Agency to Christian Isendahl. This chapter has benefited greatly from several insightful comments and useful suggestions offered by Matthew Davies and Freda Nkirote M'Mbogori.

9

Applied Archaeology in the Andes: The Contribution of Pre-Hispanic Agricultural Terracing to Environmental and Rural Development Strategies

Ann Kendall

INTRODUCTION

Patterns of civilization in the Central Andes can be seen to have fluctuated over the last 5,000 years in relation to climate changes (Table 9.1). Starting with the first American civilization at Caral, on the Peruvian coast, other impressive coastal centres and cultural areas followed and subsequently the highland cultural areas and civilizations took over in what now seems to have been at least partly a response to periods of climate changes.

While the early coastal environment offered economic advantages of maritime resources and made it easy to adapt and benefit from the early arrival of imported cultigens, greater effort was required to develop agriculture from wild local species at high altitudes in rugged terrains. However, by the first millennium BC, following adverse effects of droughts in coastal areas, the highland religious centre at Chavin de Huantar developed an influential impact in the Early Horizon Period (*c.*500–*c.*200 BC), expanding through trade networks to adjacent regions and southwards towards Paracas on the southern coast. Following the centre's demise around 200 BC (due to the increasing impoverishment of the highland environment) impetus returned to a new surge of coastal developments, notably the emergence of the Mochica and Nazca cultures on the northern and southern coasts respectively, and at Pucara in the *altiplano*.

Here Rowe's chronological system of Intermediate Periods characterized by regional states and Horizon Periods characterized by broader dominating cultures can be seen to be influenced by the swings of past climate. Temperature and precipitation have been shown to be prime influences underlying the

Table 9.1. Climate change events showing their impact on cultural developments between AD 500 and 1500

Date (AD)	Climate/ Evento	Humidity	Temper-ature	Environmental Impact	Social impact	Period/Culture
1490– 1700/1900	Little Ice Age	Increased rains 25% in the highlands, 50% on the coast	Colder	Improved pasture	Increased European animals	Arrival of Spanish Colonial Period 1532 –
1250–1500	'Warm Medieval Period'	Increased precipitation: 25%	Warmer	General improvement of natural resources	Unification under the Inca + irrigated terraces Increased population. Expansión of irrigated terracing	Inca Empire Late Horizon Period Inca to Inca Empire Late Intermediate Period to Late Horizon
1250	• Prolonged drought	Continued drought with sporadic precipitation	Colder, by 6°C	70 m descent of ecological zones.	Regionalizatión	Early Inca Late Intermediate Period
1050/1100	• Extreme drought followed by	(10–15% reduction) Extreme drought for decades		Drastic degradation of environment in the *altiplano*: 12m reduction in depth of Lago Titicaca. 50,000 ha of dried-out and abandoned camellones	General increase in irrigation works and terracing in the southern highlands Abrupt end of Tiahuanaco and breakup of Huari	Intermediate Period Chimu culture on N. coast End of the Middle Horizon Tiahuanaco—Huari
900–1000	Period of increased precipitation	Increased humidity	Warmer	General increase in natural resources in the *altiplano*	Cultures continue	Middle Horizon Period Continuation of Huari and Tiahuanaco
750–800/ 900	Drier Period	Dry	Colder	Degradation	Decline of Huari. Start of decline and conflicts in the highlands	Middle Horizon Period Huari and Tiahuanaco
600, 610, 612, 650 681 etc.	El Niño events	High, increased precipitation, with humidity	Extreme climates	Erosive floods and landslides principally in coastal valleys	Social changes on the coast.	Middle Horizon Period Huari and Tiahuanaco
594–600	Severe drought	Dry—reduction of precipitation by 25–30%	Warmer	Desertification	Expansion of irrigated terraces in the highlands. Formation of Huari State	Emergence of Huari and Middle Horizon from Huarpa/Huari
511–512, 546, 562– 594, 576	Earthquakes and El Niño events	Intensification of precipitation inconsistencies, short droughts	Extremes, inconsistencies	Erosive floods principally affecting the coast	Settlement changes, population movements	Huari appears. Tiahuanaco in *altiplano*. Abrupt end to Early Intermediate Period

sustainability of cultural developments, driven by agricultural developments, at key centres of Andean power (Kendall and Rodríguez 2009), (see Table 9.1).

Early economic and cultural developments centred on Lake Titicaca (Figure 9.1) in the southern *altiplano* were supported by agricultural systems, including *cocha* (ponds) networks developed for specialized cultivation (Flores Ochoa and Paz 1986) and *camellones* or *wayru wayru* (raised fields) around wetland shores (Erickson 1985). These systems became more significant in the area *c.*1200 BC following an increase in rainfall from *c.*1600 BC. They endured, with some periods of abandonment due to droughts (for instance at the time of the demise of Pucara), to become highly specialized agricultural systems underpinning the luxury food supply for the capital of the Tiahuanaco civilization (Mohr Chávez 1989). However, their dependence on precipitation and lake levels proved them to be unsustainable in the drastic decade of drought between AD 1050 and 1100 (Thompson and Mosley-Thompson 1987). Their demise accelerated the abandonment of the capital of Tiahuanaco (Kolata 1996) and the subsequent end of this civilization, with continuing intermittent droughts until *c.*1250. Ultimately this agricultural system was not permanently sustainable in the face of drought.

It is evident from the archaeological record that the eventual emergence of highland dominance in the Central Andes began after about AD 200 during periods of El Niño activity and unstable temperatures and precipitation. New developments were supported by experimentation with terracing in the

Fig. 9.1. Inca area location map.

region of Ayacucho, initially by the Huarpa culture, subsequently built on by the locally emerging Huari culture in the same region (Figure 9.1). The development of increasingly sophisticated sustainable terrace systems was later to reach its highest achievement under the Inca: the food security that this provided supported the development of elaborate administrative centres and the success of a thousand years of highland civilizations. The Spanish Conquest in AD 1532 brought social changes which drastically undermined Andean culture and the knowledge systems that had underpinned its success. More recent conflicts and poverty have also led to the disintegration of highland cultural systems and knowledge as populations have left rural for urban areas. Particularly damaging was the recent decade of conflict from 1983 to 1993, when highland populations migrated to coastal areas.

Today, archaeological investigations have begun to contribute to the re-establishment of key areas of knowledge, which can lead to the successful rehabilitation of pre-colonial agricultural systems and reinforce the rural highland districts and their agricultural communities. Destroyed or abandoned Andean terrace systems can be revitalized through well-prepared rural development organizations working with traditional communities. Such interventions provide the necessary support for the reacquisition of skills in rehabilitation projects. Today this approach is also key in informing and supporting the mitigation of current climate changes.

The author's reconnaissance and archaeological investigations supported by the Cusichaca Trust (CT) and its personnel since 1977 in the regions of Cuzco, Apurimac, and Ayacucho have led to the identification of three main types of pre-Hispanic terrace systems (*andenerías*) spanning the Huarpa to Inca periods (Keeley 1984; Kendall 1991, 2005; Kendall et al. 2005/6; Kendall et al. 2008; Kendall and Rodríguez 2009). These systems have been documented and studied by archaeological excavations to elucidate their development, technical characteristics, and future rehabilitation value. In addition, ethnographic investigations have contributed to the identification of past maintenance processes and production strategies. The institutional focus has been on integrated rural development projects with applied rehabilitation in key areas of abandoned or underused terrace systems and their associated irrigation systems. It was found that where these still existed they could be reconstructed following similar technological and engineering concepts, even where many specific local details had been lost. The accumulated evidence provides a wealth of information towards the future of terracing and its potential for wide rehabilitation with the re-establishment of traditional agro-ecological Andean agricultural practices (see Isendahl et al., Chapter 8 this volume for similar discussions of archaeology and the creation of 'pools' of agronomic knowledge).

HIGHLAND ANDEAN TERRACE SYSTEMS

Highland Peru is rugged with high soil erosion as well as risks from landslides, extreme temperature, and altitudinal and weather variability enhanced by current climatic changes (Figure 9.2). Key to the Central Andes and its terracing development are the Atlantic rains brought by westerly winds to the cold mountain chains and their warm valleys. These valleys extend through eight agro-ecological niches (Pulgar Vidal 1962) with a diversity of autochthonous, wild, and domesticated species. This richly varied biodiversity of plant species underlines the emergence of the Central Andes as one of the great nuclear areas for the early development of civilization. However, the human effort required in the rugged highlands for the development and strategic cultivation of these plant species was underpinned by detailed local ecoclimatological, meteorological, topographic, and environmental knowledge (Earls 2006), informed through social and climatic changes experienced by the community over many thousands of years.

The Andean grains of *quinua, kiwicha,* and *canihua* were key in underpinning the expansions of the long-lived Tiahuanaco and Huari states. In the case of Huari and particularly in the later Inca expansion, maize became the priority staple, supported by the development of increasingly sophisticated terrace platforms and systems for irrigation (Kendall and Rodríguez 2009), irrigated by extensive irrigation networks (Ardiles 1986).

The development of the highland terraces

The first step in agricultural terracing—the soil terrace (Figure 9.3, type 4)—must have been in early pre-ceramic times. No formal archaeological studies have been undertaken into this form of terracing (Treacy 1994) of which there are varied examples formed slowly during the cultivation process through the

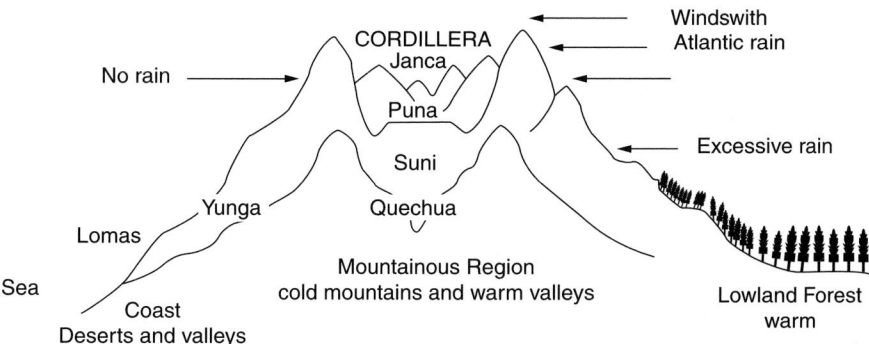

Fig. 9.2. Altitudinal profile of the Central Andes.

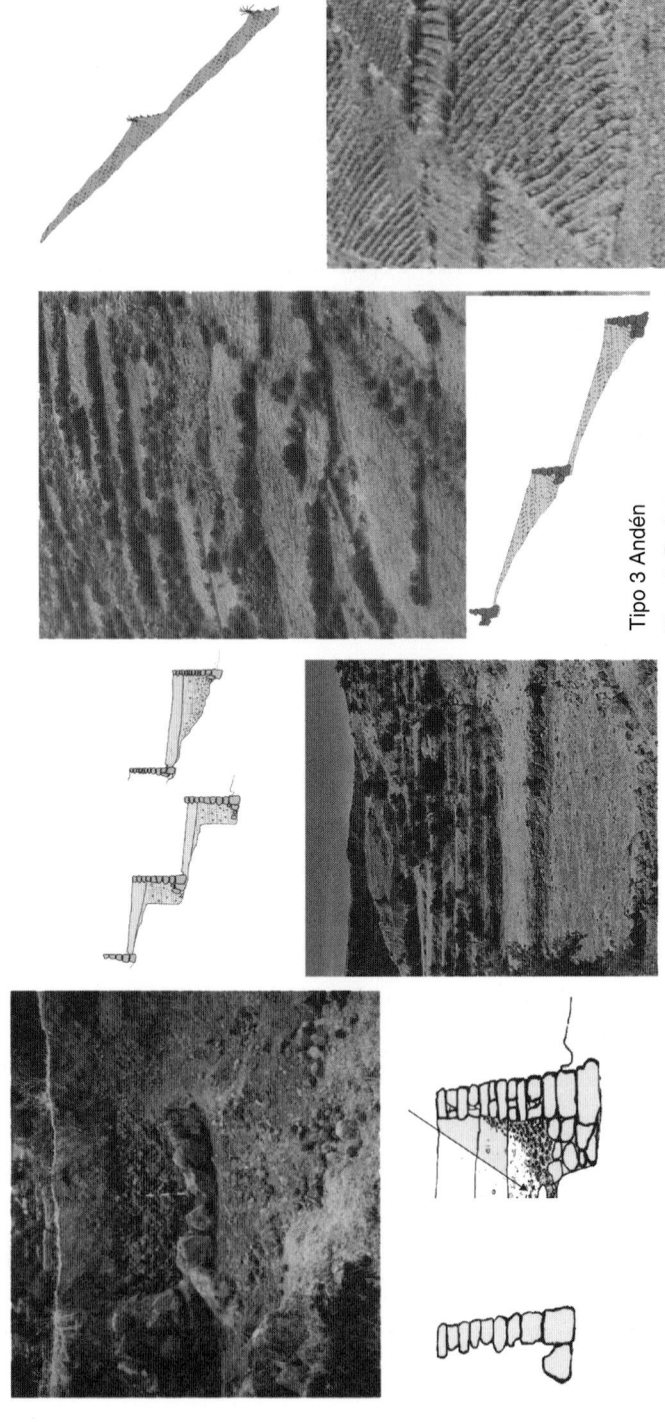

Type 1: Inca platform terrace

Type 2: Huari platform terraces

Tipo 3 Andén
Type 3: Early terrace with inclined profile

Type 4: Soil terrace

Fig. 9.3. Stone-faced Andean terrace types 1 to 3 and soil terrace type 4.

accumulation of soil, secured by vegetation, on the lower bank. They provide some control of erosion and add to moisture retention by deepening the soil. Occasional stones are added for retention of sediments and water. Low, small stone-faced agricultural terraces in the highlands occur widely at least by the mid first millennium BC, but possibly much earlier.

The development of more substantial, stone-walled terraces (*andenes*) is now confirmed in a threefold typology (Figure 9.3, types 1–3), supported by excavations at Cusichaca in Cuzco, Chicha-Soras valley, Ayacucho, Apurimac and in the District of Andamarca, Ayacucho (Kendall 2005, 2008; Kendall and Rodríguez 2009). Possibly the earliest formal agricultural terrace design, the widely found type 3 has a reduced but pronounced inclined profile on the slope and an inclined, stone-built wall. It appears as an early type in the Ayacucho region in the Huarpa culture, and is known as far south as the Colca Valley, Arequipa (Treacy 1994). However, the potential of this terrace type is limited by the fact that it is not suitable for irrigation.

Type 3 terracing appears to have led to type 2, through experimentation with irrigation by the Huarpa culture in the sandy, semi-arid highland terrain of Ayacucho. After further droughts and El Niño events (Table 9.1), the expansion of the type 2 terrace systems by the Huari state followed in c. AD 600. Platform terraces to which irrigation water can be brought for distribution ideally should have only a subtle inclination: this technological advantage is recognized for the first time in the type 2 Huarpa and Huari terraces. This innovation, and its later Chanca culture edition (*c.*1100–*c.*1450), were excavated and studied as part of the Chicha-Soras Valley excavations carried out in 1999 and 2001 by Royal Holloway College, London with CT (Branch et al. 2007; Kemp et al, 2006; Silva 2005) and later by CT in the Sondondo Valley in 2004–5 (Kendall et al. 2005/6).

The Huari state's major achievement was to develop this terrace system together with an integrative organizational structure that provided a broadly inclusive ideology and substantial administrative facilities for the exploitation of agricultural potential (Kendall and Rodríguez 2009). The local communities living in the Sondondo Valley were dramatically changed under Huari rule from High Puna pastoralism and the cultivation of tubers to intensive grain production on lower slopes (Schreiber 1987, 1991). Terracing was part of the Huari state infrastructure and the form of labour tribute used was later copied by the Chimu and the Inca. Extensive Huari systems were built at least as far as Moquegua in the south and to the Cajamarca region in the northern highlands. Elaborate administrative centres were built at key locations including Cuzco at Piquillacta, which was later to influence Inca development. Although the Huari built many irrigation systems they did not do so systematically, and many of their terrace systems were at 3,300 m altitude or higher.

Table 9.2. Description of Andean terrace types (see Kendall 1991, 2009).

TERRACE TYPOLOGY	Platform profile	Support wall	Irrigation	Distinctive features and ecological levels
Andean Type 1	Horizontal	Inclined	Generally	Stratified fills of stones and soils, *quechua-lower suni* level
Andean Type 2	Horizontal	Vertical	With and without	Fill with some stones behind the wall foundations, *quechua-suni* levels
Andean Type 3	Inclined	Rustic	Generally no	Fill with some stones behind the support wall, *suni* level
Soil Terrace Type 4	Inclined	None	None	Formed by erosion and walking across the base of the steep-slope, *suni-puna* level

Following the experience of climate extremes with devastating *huaicos* (landslides) which covered substantial Huari towns in the region of Ayacucho, the disbanding of this state later as well as the abrupt fall of the Tiahuanaco empire by about AD 1100 was due to droughts. From AD 1250 there followed an increase in rainfall and warming of the environment. This latter change was particularly evident in Cuzco with the melting of glaciers (Chepstow-Lusty et al. 2009). The resulting expansion of irrigation systems in the archaeological record is clearly associated with Late Intermediate Period settlements and the rise of the Inca (Ardiles 1986; Kendall 1991; Kendall and Rodríguez 2009).

Inca terracing

The Inca experimented with irrigated terracing primarily for the cultivation of maize, *quinua*, *kiwicha*, and *poroto* beans. Their more sophisticated terrace (type 1) brought improved construction including superior detailing for drainage as a response to the clay-rich local soils found around Cuzco. Its features include a canal for irrigation and water distribution features, a metre of agricultural soil, and gravel behind the support walls and at the base with stones for improved drainage. This terrace type brought increased agricultural productivity and a new interest in the eastern slopes of the Andes for terrace systems and coca leaf plantations.

Following the Inca dominance over neighbouring ethnic groups in Cuzco, their expansion during the Late Horizon period led to the establishment of extensive improved terrace systems adjacent to their centres. Hundreds of storehouses were built next to administrative centres in major towns, such as Vilcashuaman, Xauxa, and Huanacopampa, for the security of their armies and administrators and for redistribution of goods in times of shortfall. At Hatun Xauxa, the provincial Huanca capital, the capacity of the storehouses is estimated at over 30,000 tons productive output from a surrounding area 10 km in radius (D'Altroy 1992).

Recognized terrace systems were represented and celebrated in the landscape. In the Sondondo and Chicha-Soras valleys in Ayacucho the form of specific terrace systems and other landscape features were carved into nearby rocks where they may have been the focus of water and agricultural rituals. The Inca irrigation canals and terracing works have regularly lasted over five hundred years and are relatively easy to rehabilitate. No other local culture had developed such an integrated design approach in their engineering detail, and late hydraulic and terracing works show a continued evolution of sophisticated refinements across all aspects of rural infrastructure (Kendall and Rodriguez 2009). Key to this achievement would also have been the lessons learnt on the importance of maintenance supported through well developed social and administrative systems. Cooperative manual work in the organization of building works had been crucial since Pre-ceramic times at Caral but the sheer scale of Inca works emphasizes the unprecedented organization and effectiveness of the Inca communal workforce (*mit'a*).

While the Inca method of water and soil management through terracing was highly sophisticated, water management is all the more important today with Peru among the three most vulnerable countries in the world facing a severe loss of water resources as a result of climate change (IPCC 2001). Traditional management of surface water has been lost or severely reduced due to lack of maintenance of *amuna* (also called *milpo*) mountain-top collection systems and its improper distribution through highland landscapes and their dilapidated terrace systems (Figure 9.2). There is, therefore, a premium importance on learning from and rehabilitating the pre-Hispanic water and terrace systems, not least because their technologies were developed and refined over millennia as adaptations to this highland ecology, but also because each type was perfectly adjusted for optimum production in its specific niche zone[1].

---

[1] The distribution of the terrace types in the three recognized Central Andean highland ecological zones is part of the essential conditions for successful cultivation of crops at appropriate altitudes and weather conditions. Traditional knowledge of the distribution of the different terrace types associated with these agro-ecological niches is key to successful agricultural production: the soil terraces (type 4) are found mainly at over 3,800 m altitude on the upper slopes and in the Puna (tundra) ecological zone where root crops are a priority, but some introduced crops such as barley and oats may be grown. Beneath them the Suni ecological zone, centred at about 3,600 m, has a concentration of types 2 and 3 terraces on which are grown a wide variety of crops including some varieties of potatoes and other root crops, traditional grains such as canihua and quinoa, and some beans and maize strains within its lower limit. Today some appropriate horticultural crops and fruits are also grown. The Quechua zone, where type 1 terracing and irrigation predominates, is highly productive and is ideal for the production of maize, kiwicha, beans, horticultural crops, and fruit. The tuna fruit is also cultivated in the lower parts and cochineal may be collected from cacti.

ARCHAEOLOGICAL INVESTIGATIONS
OF TERRACE SYSTEMS

Selected excavations of stone-walled terracing have been undertaken by CT in a number of regions. The first step in CT terrace investigations was initiated in 1978 by Dr Helen Keeley, who investigated the profiles and characteristics of rural Inca terracing of a local 'provincial' use at Cusichaca, District of Machu Picchu in the Cusichaca Archaeological Project. These terraces, estimated to date to between AD 1400 and 1450 did not vary significantly from the general run of agricultural terraces throughout the late Inca empire, having a sloped retaining wall, some stratification of internal soils, and stone drainage facilities (Keeley 1984). In special cases, mainly in Cuzco, support walls may have two faces (Kendall and Rodriguez 2009, figure 3.3).

Archaeological excavations of terraces rehabilitated by the Inca in pre-colonial times at Andamarca, Sondondo valley, revealed earlier terraces buried in or even under areas of Huari intervention. At Huaylla, evidence was found of *huaicos* (alluvial landslides due to excessive rain) caused by El Niño events. These had cut across and demolished the upper part of early terrace support walls, which were then replaced by a wider terrace rebuilt by the Huari. This latter construction had in turn been incorporated into the rebuilding of a much higher, more substantial Inca terrace that contained the destroyed parts of the earlier terraces (Kendall et al. 2005/6).

Two terraces excavated at Chimpa, opposite Andamarca, included a well maintained standard Huari terrace with its original stone-built drainage canal and a substantial, apparently Inca, terrace in the Sillutu sector of Chimpa. The standard Huari terrace revealed a vertical support wall without interior gravel for drainage and a base with a step and cut posterior profile. Its internal contents consisted simply of 50 cm depth of agricultural soil over a stone-built drainage canal which crossed the terrace to the front, and a level of purposefully selected or sorted soil lacking stone inclusions, underlain by a natural soil deposit. The Inca terrace revealed some exterior and interior details of an earlier Huari-style drainage canal under the level of the one metre depth of Inca agricultural soil. The construction of this Inca terrace had modified the height, inclination, and general interior of the original smaller Huari terrace, demonstrating the Inca practice of renovating and upgrading older agricultural technologies.

In the regions of Ayacucho, Apurimac, Colca, and Moquegua (and else-where) creation of new terrace systems and rehabilitation of Huari terraces were widely undertaken by the Inca. At the time these Huari terraces were already seven hundred to a thousand years old. Late pre-Inca terraces in the Cuzco homeland were also improved or modernized with irrigation systems (Farrington 1980; Kendall 1997a). New irrigation systems were also developed by the Inca in many regions because early Huari terrace systems were situated at relatively high altitudes where precipitation was greater and where water appears to have been collected on site or, if necessary, distributed in open ditches. Although Huari stone-built irrigation systems had become more frequent toward the later years of the Middle Horizon, they did not normally endure over hundreds of years—none survived in use in the Chicha-Soras valley, where the Inca introduced new canals. Elsewhere the Inca also replaced or remodelled Late Intermediate Period systems. One example is of a canal at Quishuarpata, Cusichaca Project, Cuzco, which was remodelled because of changes in settlement patterns and the redevelopment of the area (Farrington 1980; Kendall 2005).

Abandonment of terraces systems and the loss of related social organization and knowledge management

The impact of the Spanish Conquest in AD 1532 was immediate and drastic: the changes in socio-political orientation underlined by the dramatic move of focus from the highlands to the coast with the establishment of a capital in Lima. With a decade's worth of food in the highland Inca storehouses, such as those of Xauxa (Espinoza Soriano 1971), the Spanish apparently had little immediate concern for agriculture or its continuity. Following decimation of the population, the priority was to send the remaining population to work in the mines or for large property owners. New laws enforcing resettlement separated many communities from their agricultural lands and more importantly from the infrastructure of the terrace systems, with a consequent loss of local knowledge.

The best known exceptions to loss of knowledge were in Cuzco, where maize markets existed until the end of the eighteenth century (Glave and Remy 1983) and to some extent in Colca, where compromise between terrace and cattle interests came to be coordinated (Benavides 2004). In marginalized areas such as the Sondondo valley some remaining populations were evidently also able to maintain their terraces for subsistence purposes (Kendall et al. 2008): the Andamarca community is a well known but rare example of the maintenance of continuing traditions.

Elsewhere, newly imposed Spanish colonial rule caused the break up and abandonment of successful past terrace systems. Removal of the native agriculturalists from the terraces opened the way to colonial approaches such as cattle-grazing and to the introduction of Old World domesticated animals and crops more generally (Stern 1982). The colonialists' ignorance of the importance of complex local ecoclimatological knowledge, on which each micro-region depended for annual productive success, led to the loss of this valuable environmental knowledge (Earls 2006). Abandoned terraces were eroded by cattle and vegetation, or were destroyed by mining activities or by the salvaging of

Fig. 9.4. View of Huari terraces rehabilitated by the Inca, Huaylla, Andamarca.

materials for other building works. Of the estimated original half-million to one million ha of terraces, regional abandonment varies between 25 and 75 per cent.

The rehabilitation of terrace systems

The first stage of the challenge for the rehabilitation of terrace systems—or, more rarely, for the construction of new ones—has been to focus on the recovery of their technical details and to better understand the importance of these so as to explain the underlying rationale (Figures 9.4, 9.5 and 9.6). The physical qualities of the terraces have important agricultural advantages. The stone walls have the capacity to absorb and store the sun's heat and radiate it during the night, deflecting and modifying the effects of winds and frosts. This stimulates a more rapid germination and improved growth and results in increased production. The walls also act to retain water and facilitate drainage, maintaining optimum soil moistures and preventing down-slope erosion. Today the terraces can also play an important role in mitigating the effects of climatic changes, including extreme events such as storms with increased run-off resulting in landslides and flash flooding. More generally, by retaining moisture the terraces combat reductions in precipitation and increases in evaporation, resulting from increased temperatures, thus improving hydrology for agricultural production and sometimes for domestic water sources. Terraces therefore have a range of infrastructural, subsistence, and

Fig. 9.5. Archaeological excavation at Silluto. Chimpa, Andamarca: interior of a terrace of Huari origin enlarged and rehabilitated by the Inca and subsequently generations of local farmers who also tried to repair the interior drainage canal.

commercial benefits. Moreover, if more extensively rehabilitated they could provide an agroecological diet that is potentially carbon and chemical free, eliminating the need for chemical fertilizers and for machinery such as the tractors used in 'modern' agriculture.

The development and implementation of CT's main terrace rehabilitation projects can be seen as a series of demonstration projects tackling different challenges over more than three decades from 1977 to 2010. Over 30 km of varied canals and irrigation works have been restored to use with some 700 ha of terracing systems rehabilitated. The importance of these works lies in their impact on the tens of thousands of people who have materially benefited

Fig. 9.6. Community farmers undertake the building of a new terrace (*Pomacocha*).

directly and indirectly from these examples in over thirty-five highland districts and fifteen provinces. CT's main projects in the southern Andes are summarized in the next part of this chapter.

THE CUSICHACA PROJECT

In 1978, the CT team and Ian Farrington investigated the different sections, gradients, and variability of materials of the pre-Hispanic Quishuarpata canal at Huillca Raccay in the Cusichaca Valley, identifying its Inca re-build and its association with Late Intermediate Period sites. This investigation and that of its engineering details, provided by Binnie and Partners engineers, contributed key information on engineering and the selection of different materials and treatments employed. This information was then used to inform the successful re-establishment of the canal, completed in 1983. As a result, 45 ha of terracing were brought back into full production by the community, with CT support, working with an Instituto Nacional de Cultura (INC) master mason. The establishment of a maintenance committee along traditional lines guaranteed its continued use.

THE PATACANCHA VALLEY PROJECT

As part of a wider, integrated rural development project, a major rehabilitation and restoration work was carried out on the Upper Pumamarca Canal to irrigate 160 ha of local terracing. Detailed surveys were carried out to inform the regional Cuzco INC and identify areas and materials required for rehabilitation, including specific qualities of clays, soils, gravels, sands, and stones required for the measured areas of intervention. Twenty-three Valley farmers contributed every week to the onsite rehabilitation works over a period of 30 months. Subsequently, the prime Inca terraces of Choquebamba were cleared and rehabilitated once their special characteristics had been identified. Community members made new access routes to the site and over three-quarters of the terraces came into productive full use.

APURIMAC AND AYACUCHO REGIONS

Following the completion of the 'demonstration' projects in Cuzco, CT was called in 1997 to move to the areas of extreme poverty in the Ayacucho and Apurimac regions. The effects of the conflict years had been so dire that there were virtually no agriculturalists to work within the Chicha-Soras valley (an area which once boasted of well over 14,000 ha of terracing identified and mapped). CT had to begin with social, domestic, and small capacity projects for family support. It took several years to build up to a viable rehabilitation proposal for increased food production in the area. In Chicha Soras the Huari irrigation canals had disappeared and Inca ones were not operative while in the case of Ayapampa the canal had left only a few traces, presenting considerable technical challenges. Since rehabilitation of terracing without irrigation is rarely an option, the former canal at Ayapampa in Pampachiri was selected for a complete reconstruction of its original Inca route, with typical Inca solutions to solve the engineering problems of its course. This was completed successfully in 2003. This was followed by further rehabilitation of irrigation features, including three traditional reservoirs at Laymecocha, Larcay. These works and many smaller canal rehabilitations in further districts fuelled widespread interest in the rehabilitation of terracing in the Chicha-Soras and Sondondo valleys. Farmers became trained as masons and master masons and in quick succession numerous families were identified and trained to rehabilitate their terraces. Today there is a wide drive in the valley to achieve commercialization of key crops such as *quinua* and *kiwicha* and to connect the farmers with markets. A grain processing plant installed in Pomacocha district in 2009 supports this drive to increased food production and improved livelihoods. Already other local districts are showing an increased interest in commercialization by forming associations of producers.

The formation of a new entirely Peruvian NGO—the Asociación Andina Cusichaca—as an independent partner has also been part of the final phase of the development process. This NGO is currently implementing with CT a new project covering the eight districts of the Chicha-Soras valley. This involves extending the rehabilitation of terracing and supporting the communities in their formation of associations of producers. It is hoped such projects can be widely replicated in the future, working to mitigate the effects of climate change and improve rural livelihoods via the practical application of the past technology recuperated through archaeological and ethnographic research.

CONCLUSION

In Peru the drastic events of the past have seen the rise and fall of civilizations on the coast, but the highland civilizations with terrace systems were, until the Spanish Conquest, more resilient. Renewed climate changes herald possible damage to livelihoods, agricultural and domestic resources (food production, water), reduction of population, and damage to infrastructure and communication systems (through earthquakes, landslides, and flooding). Terrace platforms and their integrated systems in the landscape can make many contributions to the mitigation of the often drastic effects of these events as well as to improved livelihoods in highland landscapes. Abandonment, initially through social change brought about by the colonial separation of families from their lands, was the cause of the deterioration of the highland strategies essential to the management of terrace systems and their varied environments. Great civilizations supporting large populations were founded on these strategies, which were abandoned for political and historic rather than ecological reasons. In this new period of ecological stress their rehabilitation may therefore be highly desirable. However, harvesting water, maintaining irrigation systems, and managing the reduction of this resource will require renewed organization and commitment. Using archaeologically derived knowledge, an increasing number of rural development organizations have made, and are making, contributions to the future of terracing and the benefits it confers. In the highlands 'Andean Culture' might again make a major contribution to the future of Peru and its neighbouring countries.

ACKNOWLEDGEMENTS

I would like to thank the Cusichaca Trust staff and volunteers and the Asociación Andina Cusichaca, our partner in Peru since 2003, who have all directed their energy to our projects and to the communities who have trusted us and shared experiences with us; also, organizations and colleagues in Peru and elsewhere, including those cited and especially Gerard den Ouden, Abelardo Rodríguez, Ismael Peréz, and Cirílo Vivanco. I am particularly indebted to the Institute of Archaeology, UCL for academic support and the Instituto Nacional de Cultura in Lima, Cuzco, and Ayacucho for research permits. Funding for the Trust's rural development work and investigations included major grants from ODA/DFID for UK overseas development funding. Community Fund and EU grants following early funding from the Leverhulme Trust, the Royal Geographical Society, the British Museum, the British Academy, BP, Tarmac, and many commercial and individual donors and small Trusts were key in setting us on our way. A World Bank Development Marketplace Prize 2009, the Baring Foundation, the Bertucci-Lynch family, through the King Baudouin Foundation, and the Burguera family are supporting current work and its dissemination.

10

The Role of Agricultural and Environmental History in East African Developmental Discourse

Daryl Stump

INTRODUCTION

The past, or the perception of the past, plays a pivotal role in the formation of modern policies on land-use, since the rhetoric of conservation favours the protection of 'ancient' or 'pristine' landscapes, whilst the focus on economic or environmental sustainability has led to the endorsement of apparently long-lived 'indigenous' practices, especially where these appear to have permitted extended periods of cultivation whilst conserving local soil, water, and forest resources. Focusing on examples of locally developed intensive agriculture from Kenya and northern Tanzania, this chapter aims to highlight how the history of landscape management in these areas—although still poorly understood—continues to be cited within developmental and conservationist debates. It will outline how a combination of archaeological, historical, and palaeoenvironmental research might be employed to produce a more complete understanding of these agronomies, and argues that work of this kind is essential to qualify the historical assumptions that have been used to justify external intervention.

The invocation of historical arguments in support of either economic intervention or wildlife conservation is not a recent phenomenon, but the critical appraisal of such arguments has gained momentum over the last two to three decades. It is by no means a coincidence that this is also the period that has seen a rise in interest in the precepts of 'historical ecology' (e.g. Balée 2006; Crumley 1994) and in resilience theory (e.g. Walker et al. 2004), both of which emphasize the need to study social, economic, and environmental factors from a long-term historical perspective in order to fully understand the relationships between them in any given place or time, and both stress the importance of seeing modern landscapes and resource exploitation strategies as legacies of former periods of land-use. More recently, a resurgence in interest in world systems theory—itself formerly influential on developmental thinking via dependency theory (e.g. Frank 1969)—raises similar themes through the notion that most if not all local economies have been influenced by their interaction with broader webs of trade relations at regional and global scales for several centuries (e.g. Hornberg and Crumley 2007). However, in terms of the African case-studies outlined here, these interdisciplinary approaches have been little referenced until recently. Of far greater influence has been the increase over the last twenty to thirty years in developmental and conservationist studies that reject the imposition of Western technologies or techniques in favour of exploring the potential economic and environmental benefits of local approaches to resource exploitation; an approach often referred to as studies of 'indigenous knowledge' or IK. Ignoring for now that the term 'indigenous' itself contains inherent historical connotations, studies and initiatives that advocate the adoption of IK frequently include an historical dimension, at least in part because its proponents tend to stress the durability and longevity of local techniques (Dove 2006: 195; Nazarea 2006: 322–3; Sillitoe 1998: 224; see Isendahl et al., Chapter 8 and Kendall, Chapter 9 this volume for specific examples of archaeology and the recovery of 'IK'; see Balée, Chapter 2 this volume for a novel approach to 'indigeneity'). The historical arguments within these debates have taken other forms, however, and include outlines of the histories and perceived failures of large-scale modernization schemes (e.g. Adams and Grove 1984) as well as critiques of the historical narratives used to justify such modernization projects, especially where these relied on assertions as to the absence, inadequacy, or destructiveness of local practices (e.g. Lambin et al. 2001; Leach and Mearns 1996; see Armstrong Oma, Chapter 11 this volume, for a more general discussion of historical narratives relating to modern farming practice). The inclusion of this historical dimension has led to the suggestion that archaeologists, historians, and palaeoecologists should take a more active role in these developmental and conservationist debates (e.g. Costanza et al. 2007b; Niemeijer 1996) and, indeed, some have suggested that archaeology is well placed to act as the lead discipline on the grounds that it bridges the sciences and humanities and provides a greater time depth than documentary or oral history (e.g. van der Leeuw and Redman 2002; Minnis 2006). It would thus seem timely to review the ways in which historical arguments have been marshalled and critiqued within developmental and conservationist discourses, and to ask what role archaeologists might hope to play in this process.

In order to do so this chapter focuses on a series of east African agronomies that have a long history of employing soil and water conservation techniques in the form of agricultural terraces or irrigation features, and in some cases incorporate labour-intensive practices such as the stall-feeding of cattle to accumulate manure as fertilizer (for a gazetteer and examples of these areas see Adams and Anderson 1988; Widgren and Sutton 2004; as well as Davies, Chapter 4 this volume). Many of these agronomies were well established prior to European colonial expansion into the east African interior in the late nineteenth century AD, with a number of examples known to have had their origins several centuries earlier (Widgren and Sutton 2004). The histories of these communities have thus excited the interest of historians and archae-ologists, the latter no doubt partly attracted by the high archaeological visibility of major landscape modifications, especially in those areas where terraces and irrigation structures are built in stone. However, these same properties of apparent durability and longevity also make them attractive as potential precedents of sustainable agriculture (e.g. Critchley et al. 1994 and references therein) or as examples of local community-based biodiversity conservation (e.g. Stocking and Perkin 1992). The use of stone-revetted agricultural terraces alongside water conservation features in the Konso high-lands of south-western Ethiopia, for example (Figure 10.1), has been described as one of a limited number of African 'lessons from the past' by the Food and Agriculture Organization of the United Nations (FAO 1990), whilst the local management of the indigenous irrigation system in the Marakwet area of Kenya

Fig. 10.1. Dry-stone agricultural terraces in Konso, Ethiopia. Oral historical data suggests that terraces of this sort have been part of the Konso economy since at least the 16th century AD (Amborn 1989: 73).

has been cited as a possible paradigm for similar systems elsewhere (Ssennyonga 1983: 96).

A review of the literature and previous research pertaining to east African intensive agronomies thus offers an opportunity to examine the position of socio-economic and environmental history within these broader debates, and to explore how archaeological enquiries can directly engage with these developmental discourses in eastern Africa.

HISTORICAL CRITIQUES OF DEVELOPMENTAL NARRATIVES IN EASTERN AFRICA

> Indigenous technologies are not perpetual; they change, evolve, expand, contract, and even die out. Identifying the dynamics behind these shifts should be of relevance to the planning of modern development in sub-Saharan Africa (Adams and Anderson 1988: 531).

The significance of historical arguments to development planning or policy formation has been highlighted by what are in effect critiques of earlier or existing historical narratives and their use within agricultural, developmental, or conservationist discourses. In essence, these critiques can be divided into three main strands: (1) examinations of the veracity of historical narratives employed as the motivation or justification for intervention; (2) discourse analyses which explore changing attitudes to local or introduced technologies; and (3) studies which assess the applicability or indeed validity of generalized models of social, economic, or technical change. These approaches are not mutually exclusive, with many historical critiques combining aspects of all three, as indeed is the case with what are perhaps the most frequently cited of examples concerning slash-and-burn shifting agriculture and the rejection of the view that such practices are necessarily destructive and unsustainable (Fairhead and Leach 1996b; Sillitoe 1998: 224). By demonstrating that areas of 'virgin' forest had formerly been employed for shifting cultivation, research of this kind provides a striking example of how a short-term perspective can present a radically different picture to one that is based on an examination of historical context and change, and is paralleled by work which questions the conclusion that long-term pastoralist use of savannah areas in Africa has led to environmental degradation through overgrazing (e.g. Brockington and Homewood 2001; Gillson et al. 2003: 376–8). Such studies stem from a variety of disciplinary standpoints but share an emphasis on an historical perspective, with methodologies ranging from the comparison of current land-use surveys with documentary, pictorial, and oral historical sources (e.g. Börjeson 2007;

Carswell 2007), to the examination of palaeoenvironmental proxies (e.g. Eshetu and Högberg 2000) and soil erosion histories (e.g. French et al. 2009; Lane 2010).

In the words of Leach and Mearns (1996) this case-study based approach aims to challenge 'received wisdom' by questioning the historical accuracy of assumptions regarding environments and the communities that inhabit them; a methodology that correlates well with examinations of the discourses that produce, perpetuate, or manipulate these assumptions. Such studies not only explore the political motivations behind the denigration or promotion of particular resource-use strategies, therefore, but also chart the history of paradigm shifts between periods of respect for indigenous techniques and periods in which these same practices have been viewed as inefficient or destructive (e.g. Rocheleau et al. 1995; Warren 1989). The locally developed irrigation systems on Kilimanjaro, Tanzania, and in the Kerio Valley of Kenya, for example, were both described as technically impressive but antiquated and wasteful of resources by successive colonial observers throughout the early twentieth century (Adams 1996; Stump and Tagseth 2009). However, further well documented examples attest to attempts by colonial governments to learn from 'tried and tested' local techniques, and include Richards' (1985) and Anderson's (1984) studies of how agricultural policy during the 1930s and 1940s explored the utility of indigenous soil conservation measures following the 'dust bowl' environmental crisis in the USA, whilst Beinart (1984) notes a further political twist in such narratives since white settlers in South Africa lobbied for similar policies in the hope that better soil conservation on black-owned lands would free more territory for commercial farming.

To paraphrase Mackenzie (1992: 1), the history of intervention in local agronomies could thus be characterized as being as much a matter of 'politics' as it is of 'policies'; obvious examples of which are the Marxist stance at the heart of dependency theory (Frank 1969), or the advocacy of development through Modernization as a means to prevent the spread of communism (Rostow 1960). Discourse analyses that highlight these political motivations (and in particular their more subtle variants) thus form one type of historical critique, but such analyses may also question both the political manipulation of historical data and the veracity of that data itself. It is interesting to note, for example, that subtly different forms of neo-Malthusianism are cited by environmentalists, advocates of Modernization, and by proponents of the genetic modification of crops (Stone 2005), but there are also numerous studies that challenge the validity of the Malthusian premise of landscape carrying capacities. Indeed, in a recent overview Nazarea (2006: 322) notes that the use of historical case-studies to challenge neo-Malthusian degradation narratives was a common feature of what she calls 'first generation IK' studies (e.g. Rocheleau et al. 1995). Similarly, Boserup's (1965) belief that technological innovations have historically always been developed to avoid the degradation described by Malthus has also been challenged in individual cases, and it is noteworthy too that this thesis was much cited by advocates of Modernization and employed to promote the adoption of individual land rights in the developing world (Tiffen 1996 citing Boserup 1970; see also Patterson 1994).

Several of the east African economies discussed here have been the subjects of analyses of this sort, with Boserup's thesis a particular focus of historical critiques. Davies (2008; Chapter 4 this volume), for example, notes that surveys and excavations of used and abandoned house platforms and irrigation channels in the Pokot area of Kenya do not support Boserup's assertion that agricultural intensification is prompted by population pressure, since the Pokot data indicates that population remained relatively stable over the last 200 years. Moreover, combining this archaeological evidence with oral historical interviews and observations of modern practices challenges the assertion that the Pokot irrigation system required centralized control for its construction and management (Davies 2009b citing Wittfogel 1957). In a further example, Östberg (2004) considers population rises to be a consequence rather than a cause of intensive agriculture in Marakwet, while several east African communities now employ less labour-intensive agricultural practices than those reported in the nineteenth century despite since experiencing population growth (e.g. Conelly 1994 in reference to Rusinga, Kenya; Håkansson 1995 regarding Usambara; Börjeson 2007 in reference to Iraqw, Tanzania). Historically informed studies from the region have also questioned (neo-) Malthusian assessments of on-going or impending environmental degradation, and include Watson's (e.g. 2009: 217–24) use of oral history and modern observations in Konso, Ethiopia, and Carswell's (2007) re-examination of survey transects undertaken by colonial Agricultural Officers during the 1940s in Kigezi, Uganda.

Although it is unnecessary to discuss in any great detail what is known of the histories of these systems here, it is clear that a range of social and economic stimuli have prompted the adoption of soil and water conservation techniques within these agronomies, and that such structures can be built and maintained within communities operating very different systems of political and social organization. This recognition thus emphasizes the dangers of applying single-cause models in predicting agricultural change both retrospectively and in terms of future developments. Loiske's (2004) research at Iraqw, Tanzania, for example, demonstrates that the relationship between agricultural intensification and proximity to markets may be the inverse of that expected, whilst studies in other east African intensive agronomies draw attention to the fact that modern markets and improved mobility have increased out-migration and opportunities for non-farm incomes over the course of the twentieth century (e.g. Carswell 2007: 138; Conelly 1994). In doing so, however, these case-studies also point to a central problem with the promotion of IK as a developmental model, in that drawing a link between apparent systemic longevity and economic or environmental sustainability is to risk comparing very different social, economic, and ecological environments. Such arguments might be regarded as nostalgic where it is implied or assumed that prior to some historical event or process local communities and ecosystems existed in harmonious equilibrium, and thus that intervention can restore this pre-disturbance baseline (Gillson et al. 2003; Niemeijer 1996; Stahl 2001). In consequence, modern African agricultural communities clearly cannot be regarded as pristine survivals from a precolonial past, but neither can it be assumed that the colonial encounter or 'incorporation into the world economic system' necessarily marked a sudden shift in social and economic institutions in all societies (for a discussion of which see Koponen 1988, particularly chapter 1). In other words, it is not enough to assert that a long-lived system is necessarily sustainable or resilient without details regarding the environmental, economic, and demographic conditions during the lifetime of that system.

On a more methodological note, this impression that the period prior to European incursion was characterized by stability may in part be a consequence of a disparity in the quantity and quality of data: the view that the colonial and post-independence periods represent unprecedented change and crisis is perhaps fuelled by a lack of detailed historical information pertaining to the precolonial period (Stahl 2001). If archaeological enquiries are to move beyond critiques of existing developmental narratives to provide details of relevance to policy makers, as envisioned by historical ecologists, it will be necessary to demonstrate the archaeological visibility of 'indigenous knowledge' in the past. Indeed, if the various historical critiques demonstrate the role of historical arguments within the models and narratives employed by developmental or conservationist discourses, they also highlight the range of pertinent factors that may be overlooked by purely archaeological or palaeoenvironmental studies.

APPLIED ARCHAEOLOGY AND THE ARCHAEOLOGICAL VISIBILITY OF 'INDIGENOUS KNOWLEDGE'

In many cases, archaeological and traditional systems may be more sophisticated, more environmentally sound, more culturally appropriate, and more productive than those introduced from outside.... An approach that combines basic archaeological techniques with agricultural experimentation not only can yield many insights on now-abandoned agricultural features, but may also provide models for present day rural

development in landscapes where archaeological remains of cultivation
systems are found (Erikson 1994: 147).

By focusing on material remains archaeology has access to communities that
are not recorded by either documentary or oral historical sources, including
not only non-literate or prehistoric societies but also those individuals and
groups whose lives are not the subject of historical record. If this temporal
depth and ability to study the lives of all sections of a community represent
archaeology's principal strength, then its major weakness is its frequent
inability to gain direct access to local conceptions and institutions. In terms
of the current discussion, therefore, the problem is less a question of whether
archaeological techniques can retrieve information about the resource-use
strategies of communities in the past, and is instead a question of whether
this evidence is likely to be of sufficient detail to allow the reconstruction of the
practical knowledge employed. In consequence, lack of data pertaining to local
conceptions and institutions necessitates the extrapolation of this information
from analogous or related communities either by studying these groups
directly (ethnoarchaeology or historical archaeology) or by referring to the
work of historians and ethnographers. Either way, this introduction of an
additional subjective step in archaeological interpretation must be seen as
a limitation in terms of archaeology's ability to reconstruct indigenous
knowledge.

Although this limitation is perhaps most obvious in terms of social
institutions, even relatively mundane considerations such as the definition of
crop repertoires are potentially problematic since both oral historical
and archaeological approaches may lack pertinent details regarding varieties
cultivated and techniques of cultivation. The indigenous African grain crop
sorghum, for example, includes at least 31 African sub-species, 157 varieties,
and 571 cultivated forms (BOSTID 1996: 142). These variations are the result
of local adaptation and reflect a wide range of selective pressures including
taste, storage characteristics, ease of processing, early root or tiller development
(to maximize use of available water following rains), plant height (lowering the
crop ratio but maximizing stalk length for use as fodder, building material, or
fuel), short growing cycle (to maximize number of crops per season), long
growing cycles (to make best use of low soil fertility), and resistance to pest and
parasites (BOSTID 1996; Harlan 1993). This level of variation is impossible to
distinguish on the basis of archaeological evidence such as charred grains
(Harlan 1993); an issue that is complicated further by the prevalence of
intercropping in African agronomies (e.g. Conelly 1994: 162), and by the
cultivation of 'weeds' to provide fodder, green manure, pest breaks, and shade
for other crops (e.g. Amborn 1989: 78–9). Accurate modelling of even relatively
simple agronomies therefore requires information regarding the particular

characteristics of the specific crop varieties employed as well as knowledge of the water requirements and yields of specific cultivars; the range and proportions of crop species grown; the area under cultivation; the area under fallow; an understanding of past environmental conditions; and, in the case of many of the agronomies discussed here, an indication of the quantities of water available to irrigation systems and an appreciation of how that water was allocated within furrow networks.

Thus, although archaeological surveys and excavations have proved very capable of mapping the development of irrigation systems (Davies 2008; Stump 2006; Sutton 1998), the physical attributes of such structures do not permit reconstructions of yields or assessments of systemic sustainability without knowledge of local methods of water allocation. Indeed the importance of archaeologically invisible social institutions was demonstrated by an attempt to simplify the locally developed irrigation system at Marakwet between 1959 and 1963; an intervention that failed in part because it did not appreciate that rights to water were conferred by participation in furrow construction and maintenance (Adams 1996: 162–3). This integration of water rights, labour organization and structural maintenance can therefore be seen as a significant contribution to the sustainability of the agronomy as a whole and, indeed, this 'non-bureaucratic management' at Marakwet has been cited as a potential paradigm worthy of replication in other irrigation systems or developmental interventions (Ssennyonga 1983: 96).

This recognition that knowledge is socially embedded and that several local institutions may be inextricably interlinked could be seen as forming an aspect of critiques of developmental interventions where the failure of these schemes can be blamed on an inability to foresee how imposed changes would be perceived locally. The compulsory construction of *matuta* anti-erosion ridges as enforced by the Usambara Scheme in Tanzania between 1950 and 1957, for example, disrupted a local institution where landless individuals were lent plots for subsistence cultivation, since the raising of ridges was seen locally as constituting an enhancement that would confer rights of ownership (Feierman 1990: 169–85; see also Gillson et al. 2003: 375–6 for a similar point in reference to tree planting schemes in Pare). Interestingly, this same example also highlights the potential influence of cosmological conceptions, since local protests against the imposition of ridges were often directed towards rainmakers who were perceived as having lost this supernatural ability through association with foreigners (Feierman 1990: 171–2).

Such examples thus illustrate the range of interconnected factors that contribute to the sustainability or resilience of an economy—factors including systems of land tenure and inheritance (Morrison 1994; Davies, Chapter 4 this volume), communal labour organizations (e.g. Watson 2009), divisions of labour (Widgren 2004), and systems of figuring the value of commodities or social status (e.g. Håkansson 2003; Sheridan 2002). To this list could be added other processes with limited archaeological visibility such as the movement of individuals between different 'ethnic' groups (e.g. Niemeijer 1996: 99–100, on adoption by the Chamus of irrigated agriculture in Baringo, Kenya) and the degree to which communities may maintain long-term reciprocal relationships through trade, stock loans, or as refuges in times of stress (e.g. Hodder 1982b on the Njemps [Chamus], Pokot and Tugen of Kenya). It is for this reason that 'second-generation IK studies' (Nazarea 2006: 322) have focused on supporting indigenous practices *in situ* rather than within central 'knowledge banks', since the creation of such archives risks abstracting local knowledge from the environments it was developed to exploit, and from the institutions that produce, maintain, and continuously adapt it (Agrawal 1995; Dove 2006: 195; Sillitoe 1998: 223, 228; Isendahl et al., Chapter 8 this volume). This is also no doubt partly why the few projects that have attempted to reinstate agricultural features defined through archaeological investigation have done so by re-establishing these *in situ* (e.g. Erickson 1994; Kendall 2005, Chapter 9 this volume).

These rare examples of 'applied archaeology' therefore employ archaeological data in a very different fashion to that envisioned by proponents of historical ecology or resilience theory, since the applied projects incorporate data derived from modern observations and experimentation with the primary intention of producing functional models that provide benefits for modern communities. Advocates of resilience theory and of historical ecology, in contrast, aim to integrate data from human and environmental history in the hope of informing future management practices (e.g. Crumley 1994), perhaps by providing information necessary to restore landscapes to their former conditions (termed restoration ecology by Hayashida 2005, and 'applied historical ecology' by Balée 2006: 76); or by modelling the likely future resilience or sustainability of a given system (e.g. Dearing 2007). Note, by way of distinction, that a project to rehabilitate pre-Hispanic raised fields in Andean Peru examined the utility of cultivating local crops alongside old world cultigens (Erickson 1994: 143), and in doing so combined enquiries into the original function of these structures with an assessment of their potential future contribution to local livelihoods. Applied projects of this sort may therefore show some parallels with less historically informed initiatives that seek to re-use aspects of local technologies, such as the attempts by a series of international and national NGOs from the early 1990s onwards to build concrete irrigation reservoirs on the sites of locally built earthen irrigation in-takes in the Pare Mountains of Tanzania (Sheridan 2002). However, quite aside from the fact that the applied archaeology projects outlined by Erickson (1994) and Kendall (2005, Chapter 9 this volume) generally stuck closely to the designs of features as revealed through archaeological excavations, the combination of archaeological and palaeoenvironmental enquiries employed by both these projects means they avoid the historical critiques summarized above in reference to former interventions in eastern Africa.

CONCLUSION

Even from the brief summary presented here it should be clear that there are several points of crossover between debates conducted from the standpoints of development, conservation, history, archaeology, and palaeoecology, and that these areas of mutual interest have been recognized for some time. For example, whilst many of the early proponents of IK were writing from a developmental background and made reference to historical critiques of earlier interventions (e.g. Brokensha et al. 1980), historians were quick to note the potential relevance of their work to this subject area (e.g. Anderson 1984; Beinart 1984), prompting some historians and historically informed geographers and anthropologists to write pieces specifically aimed at developmental and conservationist audiences (e.g. Adams and Anderson 1988; Anderson and Grove 1987; Sutton 1991). At their simplest these discussions highlight incidences where external intervention had been justified via deliberate misrepresentations or overt simplifications of an area's ecological and economic history (e.g. Ferguson 1990), but this same broad approach includes what are effectively discourse analyses examining how perceptions of land-use history were marshalled within changing developmental paradigms from the early colonial period onwards (e.g. Warren 1989). It needs to be stressed, however, that variants of this position persist in the form of conservation narratives which present even currently occupied environments as 'pristine' or 'natural'; where perceived environmental crises are attributed to incremental damage or to recent changes in local conditions, practices, or demography; or where development schemes employ models of socio-economic change which are themselves extrapolated from specific historical case studies.

There are thus a series of spatial and temporal scales at which archaeological enquires might contribute to developmental narratives at this discourse level either by demonstrating that past communities have shaped contemporary environments, by questioning the applicability of the historical models employed to justify intervention, or by emphasizing the dynamic nature of human communities and ecosystems in the past and thereby challenging interventionist assumptions concerning the existence of ecological baselines and equilibrial ecosystems. However, as Hayashida (2005) points out, the level of detail required to inform specific policies at a community scale is far higher than that required to challenge assumptions or generalized models of ecological or technological change. For example, although the presumption that modern rainforests represent previously unexploited wildernesses may be questioned by evidence of previous occupation (Willis et al. 2004), 'the discovery of artefacts or ancient settlements deep in the forest tells us nothing about the extent and kinds of human impacts nor about forest resilience and recovery' (Hayashida 2005: 56). Consequently, any project that aimed to replicate local strategies or to model their future resilience would require in-depth data concerning the full suite of interrelated practices that collectively form indigenous knowledge. Archaeological enquires are unlikely to produce this level of detail since this will include not just the physical aspects of a particular technology or resource exploitation strategy but also the social institutions that continuously produce, maintain, and adapt that knowledge.

The possibility of initiating east African applied archaeology projects of the type previously attempted in South America is worthy of examination, therefore, not least because by prioritizing modern benefits over historical authenticity such projects may be able to employ data drawn from analogous communities despite the archaeological invisibility of social or management institutions on any given site. This having been said, large areas of formerly productive, abandoned agricultural structures like those investigated by the South America projects are largely absent within Africa, where communities have either adapted to changing conditions through successive periods of intensification and disintensification, or where areas vacated by one intensive agricultural community have been subsequently re-occupied by another, as with the use of irrigation structures by Maasai communities in what were probably former Sonjo areas of irrigated cultivation at Pagasi, Kenya (Adams et al. 1994: 21).

Archaeological studies in east Africa may therefore be destined to remain primarily critiques of the historical perceptions employed within developmental narratives rather than as integral components of developmental project design, but the ubiquity of historical arguments within wider discourses demonstrates the need for an interdisciplinary approach that includes targeted historical and archaeological research. At this discourse level, therefore, an archaeological contribution to development might simply involve an awareness of the potential relevance of project data, coupled with an effort to advertise the nature and limitations of this material in a form accessible to a wider audience. Participation at this level need not require an in-depth knowledge of the debates involved, and is simply a recognition that archaeological investigations routinely produce an array of evidence that might be employed to address questions asked from within other disciplines. In the meantime this ability to point to existing knowledge gaps and to highlight the complexity and dynamism displayed within historic and contemporary agricultural communities can itself act as a contribution to these wider debates, and can serve to act as a check on the deliberate or inadvertent misuse of historical narratives.

11

Past and Present Farming: Changes in Terms of Engagement

Kristin Armstrong Oma

INTRODUCTION

In archaeology, changes in human–animal relationships are rarely considered beyond the moment of domestication. This is influenced by Ingold's idea that domestication led to a shift in the human engagement with animals (Ingold 2000: 61–76; see Armstrong Oma 2007: 62–4, 2010 for critique). I do not question the validity of such a claim; however, I argue that changes in terms of engagement also happened beyond domestication, and that various configurations of human–animal relationships have existed throughout history. Further, I argue that such changes also have consequences for the environment, by choice of land use strategies and husbandry regimes. A twofold purpose is pursued: first, to investigate how changes in social systems, in my case changes in terms of engagement between humans and animals, affect land use in such a way as to impinge upon natural systems and ecosystems. Second, I wish to grasp the political underpinnings of the models that are employed by archaeologists and, by doing so, to deconstruct the political use of the past (see also Stump, Chapter 10 this volume). Alternative models regarding economic strategies are sought, and the implications of these are discussed.

Human–environment studies frequently deal with the impact of human intrusive land use strategies on ecosystems. Awareness has been created around these processes regarding land use techniques and practices (for example Denham and White 2007; Mazoyer and Roudart 2006). However, in European archaeology the impact of husbandry practices upon ecosystems has received considerably less, if any, attention. People in past societies from the Neolithic onwards made the conscious decision to live with animals as herders or as farmers, blending together social and economic choices that had repercussions for landscape developments and ecosystems. Investigations into the relationship between environmental changes caused by husbandry practices and the social systems that instigated those changes are an important contribution to research on past environmental development. These changes are identifiable in the archaeological record.

A particularly significant example is associated with the architectural development from two-aisled to three-aisled longhouses in Scandinavia in the early Bronze Age, around 1800–1600 BC (Montelius period I–II) (Ethelberg et al. 2000; Rasmussen 1999; Rasmussen and Adamsen 1993; Tesch 1993), coinciding with changes in land use and also environmental changes (Høgestøl and Prøsch-Danielsen 2006; Prøsch-Danielsen and Simonsen 2000a, 2000b). The architectural change is believed to reflect indoor stalling of animals, representing a shift—from products to producers—in how animals were perceived (Årlin 1999). Simultaneously, extensive deforestation is traceable in pollen diagrams (Høgestøl and Prøsch-Danielsen 2006) which may indicate that forest clearance took place to aid the grazing of domestic animals. A case study from south-western Norway is explored in depth to examine the validity of this hypothesis.

On a more philosophical note, I also investigate the ontological status upon which human–environment relationships rest. Human–animal relationships are at the core of the connection between natural and cultural systems, since domestic animals are in themselves simultaneously culture and nature (e.g. Franklin 2002; Haraway 2003, 2008; Macnaghten and Urry 1998). This investigation into the ontological status of human–environment relationships strives for a novel direction in human–animal studies, as it seeks to focus in a new way on the role of domesticated animals within the wider ecosystems, beyond the household arena. My position springs from a personal ethical concern with the philosophical underpinnings of modern farming, which informs my study.

I will start with my second tenet and critically evaluate models used to think about husbandry practices. Following this, economic strategies that had significant impacts upon Bronze Age settlement and land use are discussed as an essential starting point to investigate changes in the relationship between natural and social systems. The discussion of Bronze Age husbandry practices and their social implications is informed by a more reflective view whereby the participation of animals is brought into a wider social and economic arena.

DECONSTRUCTING MODELS: ECONOMIC STRATEGIES AND THEIR PHILOSOPHICAL UNDERPINNINGS

There are a number of areas in which archaeology unwittingly contributes to legitimize present-day ideologies. In this respect we need to critically evaluate and deconstruct the models we are using to talk about past societies. One example is past husbandry practices that frequently are understood through presentist models based upon a priori assumptions. Modern farming constitutes one of the most common models, and I wish to identify and deconstruct the foundation of this narrative.

Modern farming has had an impact upon the epistemology of archaeology, stemming from the days of functionally-minded positivist processualism (e.g. Binford 1981a; Higgs 1972; for critique see Grant 2002: 17). It has a bias towards cost-efficiency and maximization strategies with a single-minded focus on economic gains (see Fiore et al., Chapter 5 this volume for a more general critique of optimality models in archaeology). The rationale of the model rests upon a short-term perspective, underlying most farming strategies in the Western world (Dabbert et al. 2004; Lund 2002; Lund et al. 2004a; Lund and Röcklinsberg 2001). The model lends support to a form of intensified agriculture that is not inherently sustainable and where high yields rely upon pesticides and fertilizers. This is a considerable source of pollution and ultimately is a threat to biodiversity while depleting the soil of its nutrients (Dabbert et al. 2004; Lovelock 1992 [1991]: 156–9; Mazoyer and Roudart 2006: 435–7).

In archaeology, similar ambitions for the outcome of farming practices are frequently projected on past societies, which are portrayed as being driven by maximization strategies very like today's agricultural aims (Zimmermann 1999). For example, very little consideration for animals is recognized, nor any affinity with them: they are assumed to have been regarded merely as meat and calories (Albarella 2001; Grant 2002; Hamilakis 2001). The study of animals in the past, and subsequently of human–animal relationships, is normally done by zooarchaeologists, or even zoologists. The sub-discipline of zooarchaeology has been instrumental in developing ways of studying animals in relation to issues such as nutrition, disease, traction, and taphonomy. Zooarchaeology focuses on identifying faunal remains that give information about the economic uses of animals, as described by Whittle (2003: 82) '[i]nnumerable specialist animal bone reports (to which no disrespect is intended) principally establish species present, and patterns of age and sex, with some detailed attention also to taphonomical processes'. These studies are valuable as they have shown that there are several economic strategies which past societies might viably have pursued. However, zooarchaeology is obsessed with one factor above all others: animals as outcome, which is seen as a one-sided focus on economy that frequently fails to take social factors into account. This mindset is inherited from Binford's (1978) position that without exception, all the documented variability in faunal assemblages is directly referable to functional variability. The zooarchaeological economic model falls under the general critique formulated by Knight (2005: 5) that 'we should be wary of collapsing the two separate dimensions of the human relationship to domestic animals—outcome and process. The preoccupation with the outcome of the relationship (e.g. slaughter for meat) is apt to conceal the protracted relationship of nurturance and care that precedes it'.

Rather than seeing past and present farming practices as embodying the same understanding, we should consider changes in terms of engagement throughout history. The historian Keith Thomas (1984 [1983]) illustrates, by his study of the English countryside, that human–environment relationships have been subject to changes in terms of engagement, expectations, and attitudes throughout history. The sixteenth century Tudor drive to break new land and cultivation was challenged by the nineteenth century Romantics' idea of the conservation of the wild.

Still, in archaeology changes in terms of engagement are rarely considered beyond the moment of domestication. For example, Ingold's postulated shift from a relationship of trust between hunter and prey to one of the farmer's domination over domestic animals (Ingold 2000: 61–76; Armstrong Oma 2010), is often taken at face value (Denham and White 2007: 9–11; Wengrow 2006: 81). However, greater complexity in the domestication process is increasingly claimed (see Dransart 2002: 5–7; Jones and Richards 2003: 50; Whittle 2003: 80).

A useful point of departure when investigating alternative models is to take a closer look at social economic theory in order to understand these changes in terms of engagement. The importance of deconstructing economic models is related not only to how choices are made, but also to how they are justified. In neo-liberal economics, the model used by traditional archaeologists and zooarchaeologists is known as the 'shareholder value model'. This model aims at enhancing profit for the owners from a short-term perspective (Almond et al. 2003). For example, it justifies a perspective upon the environment as a limitless resource that can be exploited with no consideration for the consequences of endangering species or even entire ecosystems.

An alternative model is the 'stakeholder value model' (Donaldson and Preston 1995; Freeman 1983). In place of short-term outcomes for individuals this model takes a longer perspective and, based on trust and commitment, aims at achieving a gain for all members of society—including, at its broadest, both human and animal members and even the environment (Hosmer 1995; Jones 1995). As such, it is analogous to what in organic farming is known as an eco-contract—a contract between humans, domestic animals, and the local environment (Alrøe et al. 2001; Dabbert et al. 2004; Lund 2005; Lund et al. 2004a; Lund and Röcklinsberg 2001). Further, it is comparable to a social contract (see Armstrong Oma 2007: 69–71, 2010), and could grow out of emotion; Milton (2002) argues that people are motivated by a deeply felt love and respect for the environment and nature in which they live and which they thus perceive directly. From this point of view, the shareholder perspective advocated by zooarchaeology lacks an understanding of the complexities that can govern human–animal relationships in a stakeholder model.

CHANGES IN TERMS OF ENGAGEMENT: BRONZE AGE FARMING IN NORTHERN EUROPE

Bronze Age societies in northern Europe, particularly in Norway from about 1800 BC to about 500 BC, were farming communities and lived a sedentary life (Barker 1999; Løken 1998; Rasmussen 1999). However, land use extended beyond the farm, since transhumance and pastoralism were probably also practised (Prescott 1991, 1995). Animals form part of the life strategies that are embedded within farming practices, therefore joining together various farming practices in space and time, such as milking, grazing, haymaking, and stalling. Although there is a limited number of domesticated species to be found in Bronze Age societies, a plethora of economic strategies could be chosen when living with these species. The choice of strategy has a profound effect on both social human–animal relationships and on ecosystems and landscape development.

Economic herd management strategies are assumed from the composition of faunal assemblage in terms of species, age, and sex, which vary according to the different flock or herd management strategies (Legge 1981a, 1981b; Payne 1973; Serjeantson 2007; for discussion see Halstead 1998: 4–5). Cattle generally comprise as much as 40–60 per cent of the total amount of the domesticates in central and northern parts of Europe, and are therefore the most intensely exploited domestic animal in most regions (Benecke 1994: 131–4). The agricultural strategy of the early and middle Bronze Age in southern Scandinavia seems to have been founded on extensive cultivation and the breaking of new ground, requiring draught animals. The symbolic presentation of the relationship between humans and cattle on rock art almost always shows arding (ploughing), but hardly ever pastoral activities such as herding (Rasmussen 1999). Arding with draught animals joined together economic and social aspects in creating a new way of living for humans and animals, implying that husbandry was a very important task in the lives of farmers (Rasmussen 1999: 286–8). The management of livestock had become pervasive in the everyday life of people. In some places, unintended consequences of the intensified land use led to environmental changes such as deforestation, land erosion, and the development of heathlands that still remain today (Prøsch-Danielsen and Simonsen 2000a, 2000b). Thus, Bronze Age environmental changes are a complex interplay between social, economic, and ecological factors.

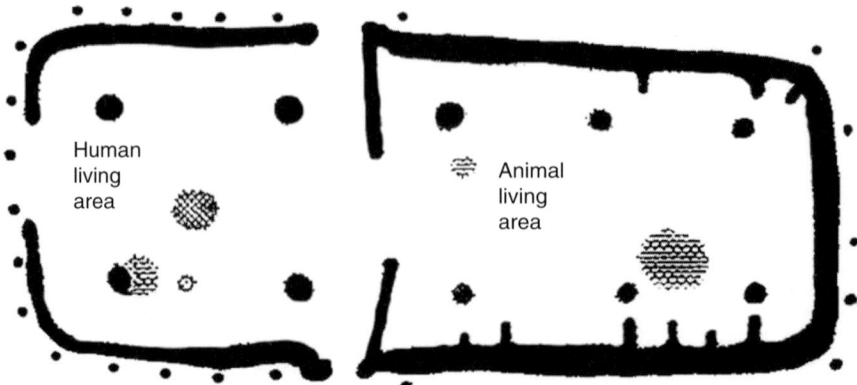

Fig. 11.1. Example of a three-aisled longhouse (late Bronze Age house Köpinge B14: VIII) with a byre section: animals are presumed to have lived in the eastern part, and humans in the western. Redrawn after Tesch (1993: 166).

The focus of husbandry strategies and aspects of human–animal relationship in Bronze Age archaeology has traditionally been on economy (Earle 2002; Tesch 1992), but has lately been broadened to include a greater emphasis upon social processes. For example, several authors (Årlin 1999; Fokkens 1999; Rasmussen 1999; Roymans 1999; Zimmermann 1999) argue that in Bronze Age northern Europe factors other than economy were crucial in the choice of animal husbandry practices. Here, a particular architecture developed whereby humans and animals both lived inside the house; in other words, humans chose to open and share their house with their animals. The longhouse changed in construction; from being built with three rows of posts it now had four, and thus three aisles. One section of the building was devoted to the habitation of humans and another—termed the byre—to stalling animals (Årlin 1999; Lagerås and Regnell 1999; Rasmussen 1999: 281; Rasmussen and Adamsen 1993: 138; Tesch 1992: 290). The three-aisled longhouse was probably designed for the specific purpose of stalling animals indoors (Ethelberg et al. 2000: 203), suggesting that a concern for the animals governed this architectural change (Figure 11.1).

Rasmussen (1999: 287) suggests that a unique *human to animal relationship* developed in the early Bronze Age, and advocates a point of view, simultaneously social and economic, in which taking animals into the house was an expression of 'relations of affiliation or ownership' of livestock. She continues by arguing that the reason for stalling the animals indoors was because they became members of the household, belonging and relating to somebody, ownership being defined by the building that houses them. Following Rasmussen, a stakeholder perspective is an appropriate model to discuss in relation to the archaeology of Bronze Age northern Europe, since bringing animals into houses suggest that they were also held to be stakeholders.

THE BRONZE AGE SETTLEMENT AT KVÅLE, SOUTH-WESTERN NORWAY

Environmental changes from the Neolithic to the Iron Age caused by human agents by way of farming practices have been studied rigorously in south-western Norway, particularly in the fertile Jæren region (Høgestøl and Prøsch-Danielsen 2006; Lillehammer 2007; Prøsch-Danielsen and Simonsen 2000a, 2000b; Soltvedt et al. 2007). Høgestøl and Prøsch-Danielsen (2006) observe two distinct environmental trends that are noticeable in all pollen diagrams from Jæren from the late Neolithic until the early Bronze Age: deforestation and the development of pasture. These indicate an expansion in pastoralism and permanent fields. The environment was formed in a particular way by farming practices and the increasing importance of animal husbandry—demonstrating that animal agents, by way of farming practices, were crucial to environmental changes (Argent 2010; Armstrong Oma 2010).

The site of Kvåle on Jæren, South-western Norway, is unique in its continued settlement from the late Neolithic until Medieval times combined with an extensive study of the well-preserved fossil landscape in the immediate vicinity (Soltvedt et al. 2007). A permanent farm represented by a sequence of houses was established on one of the lower hills around 1900–1800 BC, and remained for 400–500 years (Soltvedt et al. 2007: 45, 196; Figure 11.2). The oldest house (House 1) was a two-aisled longhouse, a type common in Northern Europe from the onset of the Neolithic. Lacking internal divisions, two-aisled longhouses are interpreted as having been for human habitation only (Ethelberg et al. 2000; Tesch 1993). House 1 was replaced by a second two-aisled longhouse (House 2) dated to 1820–1720 BC (Soltvedt et al. 2007: 39) built above House 1; this was a larger building with a slightly different orientation. It in turn was replaced by a three-aisled longhouse (House 3) dated to 1750–1665 BC, following the orientation of House 2 and slightly overlapping it. This uniquely captures the transition from one type of architectural choice and building technique to another.

House 3 also differs from the two earlier houses in its architectural layout, in which clearly marked opposite entrances are situated at the middle of the house. This trait is associated with a functionally specific practice, that of indoor stalling of animals. The architectural differences indicate that House 3 had different practical and/or symbolic functions compared to the other, earlier, houses. It has been suggested that the break in the conservative

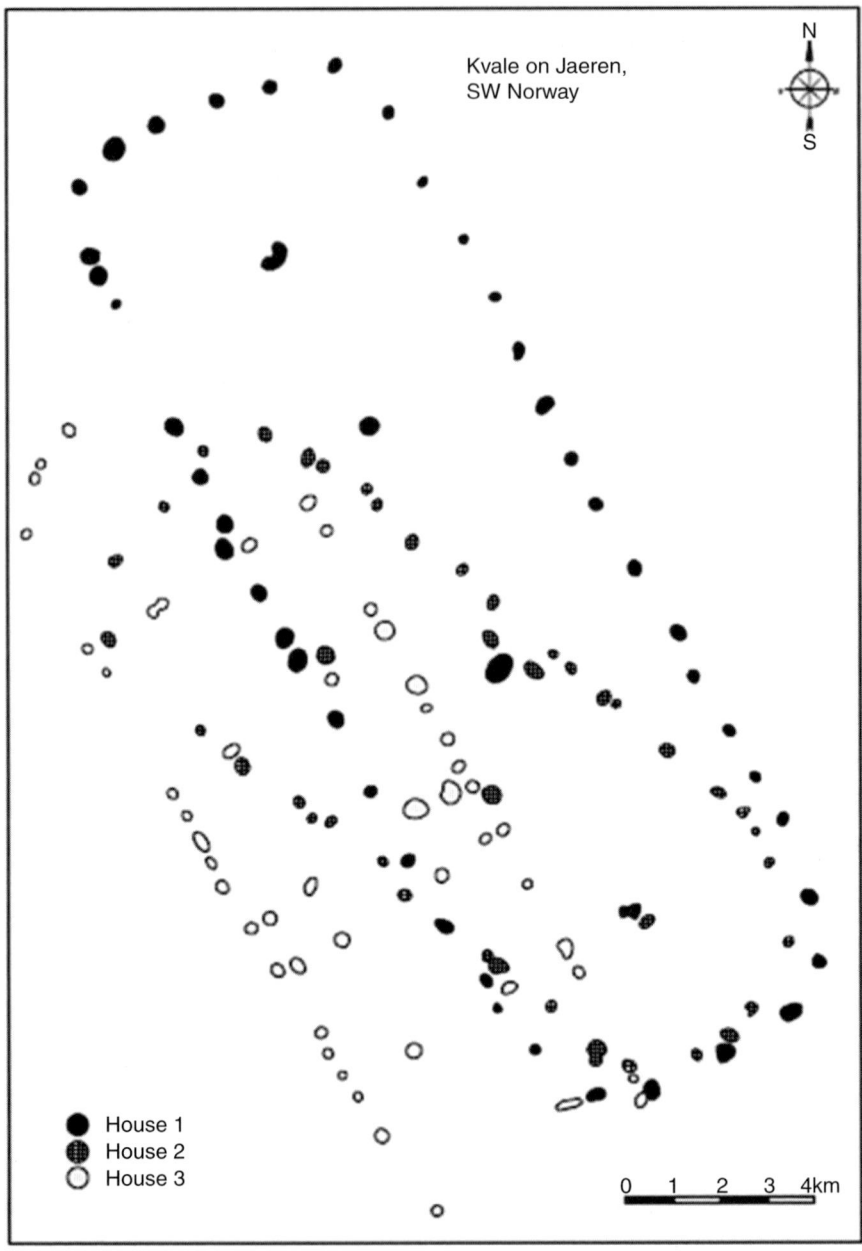

Fig. 11.2. Houses 1, 2, and 3 from Kvåle. Houses 1 and 2 are two-aisled; House 3 is three-aisled. Figure by Ragnar Børsheim, AmS.

building tradition of two-aisled longhouses represents 'radical or gradual changes in society' presumably of economic, social, and political character (Tesch 1993: 145). Following Rasmussen (1999) and Årlin (1999) I argue that this shift is also, at core, a change in human–animal relationships.

The transition from two-aisled to three-aisled longhouses is traditionally connected to moving livestock into one part of the house, believed to represent a new order in terms of living arrangements, enabling people and animals to live together under the same roof (Ethelberg et al. 2000; Rasmussen 1999; Rasmussen and Adamsen 1993; Tesch 1993). The introduction of the long-house with byre in northern Europe is interpreted as a result of the increased engagement with livestock management, as well as of the developing personal relations between humans and cattle—also signified by the use of cow hide to wrap dead bodies, and by rock art panels that depict ploughing scenes with cattle and men (Rasmussen 1999: 287–8). The architectural innovation of shared living space is significant because it marks the onset of a period, stretching from the Bronze Age until the end of the Viking period in about AD 1000, during which humans and animals cohabited.

Expanding upon this case study, the wider environment on Kvåle has been studied rigorously by both archaeological and scientific methods. Two trends are clearly discernible between 2000 and 1500 BC: first, there is extensive deforestation of the original deciduous birch, elm, and hazel forest by burning. This was visible as a preserved layer of charcoal in soil profiles. Dating of the charcoal demonstrated that this was a recurrent event that took place intermittently throughout this period. Additionally, pollen taken from preserved soil layers under clearance cairns show grasses and weeds that are consistent with grazing, particularly *Plantago lanceolata, Rumex acetosa, Asteraceae,* and *Succisa* (Soltvedt et al. 2007: 151, 174, 198). Deforestation and intensified land use correspond with Høgestøl and Prøsch-Danielsen's (2006: 23, 32) 'clearance phase 3', identified for the region of Jæren in the period 1900–1400 BC, and are interpreted as a direct reflection of the introduction, intensification of, and also preference for, the practising of animal husbandry. Together, these factors demonstrate that Bronze Age people altered the face of their land to improve the conditions for their cattle and sheep. Beyond economic considerations, this process has implications for shared human–animal practice. By altering the landscape, humans and animals were, in a sense, domesticating the environment to their mutual benefit, thus deepening their joint life-world and reciprocal reliance on each other. It seems very likely that people could not imagine their lives without their animals, nor could the animals survive without humans.

During the second phase, clearance of forest continued, and the altering of the landscape became further intensified. Stones were piled into clearance cairns, creating smaller patches of more manageable fields. Pollen samples from buried land surfaces under clearance cairns show further increase in grasses and weeds such as *Cichorioideae, Campanula, Lychnis, Trifolium repens* and *pratense,* and *Ranunculus acris* that are consistent with grazing and field mowing (Soltvedt et al. 2007: 113). Production of hay is consistent with indoor stalling of domestic animals and with the necessity of feeding the animals through the hard northern European winters. Worth noting is that in both phases there are no traces of fences or pens—seemingly the grazing herds roamed free in the landscape. Control over animals seems of less importance, and perhaps the bringing of animals indoors is not merely a tool for herd management: rather, the people are there for the animals, and a practice of seamless giving-and-taking establishes both humans and animals as stakeholders.

Further north-west on Jæren is a remarkable Bronze Age rock art panel, Valhaug 1 (Figure 11.3). It depicts an uncommon scene: a shepherd with his arms open drives a flock of four-horned animals. A smaller animal, probably a dog, seems to aid the shepherd in rounding up the animals (see Armstrong Oma 2010; Høgestøl and Prøsch-Danielsen 2006: 31–2). This panel demonstrates the practice of grazing in this region during the Bronze Age and its importance is testified by its commemoration in stone.

What implications can be drawn from this case study about human–animal relationships and their impact upon the environment? The change in architectural choice from two-aisled to three-aisled longhouses coincides with land

Fig. 11.3. Rock art scene from Valhaug, Rogaland, depicting a human and four horned animals, and a smaller animal that is possibly a dog (photograph author's own).

use that facilitated the presence of animals, through both grazing and hay production. On this basis I argue that the novel architectural choice embedded in three-aisled house construction represents a change in terms of engagement between the Bronze Age people of Jæren and their animals. This change had consequences for the ontological perception of domestic animals. It has been suggested that the advent of the three-aisled longhouse could have led to a transformation of the animals' status from product to producer (Årlin 1999), and eventually to a social practice in which humans and animals were both embedded, leading to a development of mutual affinity and trust (Armstrong Oma 2007, 2010). I further argue that this is also a change in economic terms, into a stakeholder economy in which the number of stakeholders had been expanded to include domestic animals. As such, a new husbandry practice was developed. Further, this brought about large-scale environmental transformation, and thus had unintended consequences for both landscape and ecosystems.

Such changed strategies led to domestic animals living in greater proximity with people (Serjeantson 2007). In order to make a relationship between humans and animals happen, space must be created for it to develop. Today we have technology that allows farmers to only partake in that space to a minimum degree. Because of this, we believe that we have a choice regarding whether or not we need to make a relationship happen. Not so in the past: tangible interactions were inevitable and would invariably lead to relationships. Humans and animals were embedded and interacted in a mutually inclusive shared space. I have previously termed such spaces meeting points (Armstrong Oma 2007). In the three-aisled longhouses the meeting points, the space to make the relationship happen, were pre-planned. The houses were built with this particular purpose in mind, and facilitated points of interaction between humans and animals.

CONCLUSION

The situation in early Bronze Age northern Europe suggests that economic models other than modern farming may have a greater relevance to our understanding of these societies. Rather than employing a shareholder value perspective, in which maximization and cost-efficiency are core principles, a stakeholder value perspective presents a model that might hold greater validity. The latter includes a concern for a living society and its members and their social relationships. Such an outlook might be deduced from the changing engagement between humans and animals that is found in the transition to the three-aisled longhouse found at Kvåle. These houses facilitated living together with animals, and I argue that this suggests that Bronze Age farming might have worked according to the stakeholder perspective, with both people and domestic animals felt to be stakeholders.

The functionalist economic models discussed can be applied to situations and institutions where they are not suitable. For example, cost-benefit analyses are very simplistic tools that cannot account for the complexity of prehistoric societies. Likewise, studying cull patterns of domestic animal populations only considers the death of the animal and not its social relationships and agency. In order to redress this imbalance, it is necessary to explore the political economics which underpin the models employed in archaeology, in particular by zooarchaeologists. By analysing past societies with such models we assume an exclusionary evolutionistic drive towards ever greater yields (Trigger 2006: 207; Olsen 1997: 31; Prescott 1994: 89) whereby archaeological studies of human–animal relationships keep reproducing a fallacy, which might in fact be an historical anomaly, thus also circularly creating a false time-depth and continuity to justify modern farming. As a consequence, in advocating industrial farming as a model for past farming practices, we are in fact legitimizing the use of such present day agricultural strategies.

In today's political climate counter-movements are emerging and winning ground. For example, modern-day organic farming posits a number of alternative models with strongly articulated philosophical bases (Alrøe et al. 2001; Dabbert et al. 2004; Lund 2005; Lund et al. 2004a; Lund and Röcklinsberg 2001). Buzzwords are soil protection, sustainability, biodiversity, and ethical treatment of animals. Such ideas have not yet penetrated into the archaeological discourse but bringing such perspectives into archaeology is necessary to counter any tendency by archaeologists to project the shareholder ambitions of modern-day farming practices into the past. By use of alternative models archaeology can become a positive tool to counter the damage done by earlier misconceptions.

ACKNOWLEDGEMENTS

I am grateful to Niall John Oma Armstrong and Erica Gittens for constructive comments and ongoing support, and also to the editors of this volume for giving me valuable feedback. Thanks to Lisbeth Prøsch-Danielsen and Eli-Christine Soltvedt for discussing the case studies from Jæren with me. Thanks also to Helene Johansen for introducing me to neo-liberal economic theory.

Part IV

Environment, Disaster and Memory

This section focuses on a certain form of environmental event—that of the 'disaster', with the aim of highlighting a number of issues relative to broader human-environment relations. In particular, disastrous events, or their threat, emphasize how humans live with and manage environmental risks. This section further emphasizes how environmental disasters become active aspects of community memory and identity; how they become inscribed and how this inscription can act to prepare communities but also to 'numb' them to future risks and suppress positive action (see especially Rudiak-Gould's account of sea level changes on the Marshall Islands). Humans live with environmental risk, they manage it and adapt to it, but they can also at times fail to see disasters of unprecedented magnitude—this point is as true for both rapid fast-acting 'disasters' as it is for gradual slow acting phenomena such as desertification or climate change. The focus on 'disasters' here therefore merely acts as a muse to lay bare broader contradictions inherent in human–environment relations. The archaeological analysis of past disasters (both slow and fast) usefully directs us towards the ways in which people coped with disaster and also towards the instances in which impending disasters were disastrously overlooked.

This section also emphasizes archaeology's own contribution to the collective memory-making surrounding the nature of disasters and the relationship between humans and environmental risks. In particular, a number of the chapters deconstruct the archaeological 'Pompeiian' myth of disaster as an instant single event which preserves the past *in situ*. Disasters are shown to be processes in themselves (Holmberg) or sequences of processes (Leckie; Rudiak-Gould). Disasters do not always come in the singular: often communities experience sequences of disasters over decades or centuries and each of these events acts to condition responses to the subsequent event. Disaster (like all human environment interaction) is an ongoing process through time and should be studied historically and archaeologically as appropriate. Anderson et al. make this point forcefully in Chapter 15 by demonstrating the usefulness to our own society of analysing past environmental and climatic disasters and inscribing these into the present popular consciousness.

In Chapter 12 Holmberg explores the role of Pompeii both in the development of archaeology as a discipline and in popular consciousness as the
quintessential archaeological disaster. She deconstructs the notion of Pompeii
as a single event and rather points towards the lived experience of the
eruptions of Vesuvius over seventeen years. She further contrasts the powerful
Pompeiian metaphor of 'humans at the mercy of an unpredictable nature' with
more recent metaphors of humans as enactors of environmental damage.
From this dialogue comes a critique of concepts of nature in balance or
equilibrium and the conclusion that nature is always in flux—that it is always
a process of change that can be best understood through historical and
archaeological narratives. In Chapter 13 Leckie draws on the contradictory
metaphors of life in Swiss Lake dwellings to emphasize the recursive interaction between life around the Swiss Lakes and the risks that it involved.
Leckie's paper again emphasizes the lived experience of environmental disasters, the re-inscription of risk as an aspect of community identity and cohesion, and the notion of environment in constant flux. The underlying message
of this chapter is that human communities will not always value risk equally
and thus dealing with future risks will require sensitive analysis of a community's environmental perceptions. In Chapter 14 Rudiak-Gould analyses
the perception of environmental disaster on the Marshall Islands and explains
why the islanders seem relatively impervious to current predictions of
impending climatic disaster. In particular, Rudiak-Gould emphasizes the
long-term environmental challenges to colonization and habitation of the
Marshall Islands and effectively describes a culture built on living with risk.
However, he also leaves us with the chilling conclusion that one of the most
common responses to disaster is death. Nevertheless, Rudiak-Gould emphasizes the way in which the present and past act in dialogue to inform current
perceptions of disaster and act to develop future environmental practices. This
points us to ways through which the calamities of future events may be better
conveyed to the public by emphasizing their historical irregularities—in the
case of the Marshall Islands—by making it clear that the threat of modern
climate change is much greater that the disasters of the past. Archaeological
case studies of situations where communities clearly failed to recognize the
difference of magnitude of impending disasters may serve to emphasize this
point.

Finally, in Chapter 15, Anderson et al. take a much broader view of the
dramatic effects of climate change on past human societies. They show how
many past civilizations have dealt with climatic conditions similar to those
predicted for the coming century and cautiously emphasize flexibility and
resilience, as opposed to ignorance and collapse. They further suggest that
climate change can lead not only to reductions in social complexity (collapse)
but also increases in complexity (state formation). The archaeological record
shows us that climate change offers opportunity as well as danger and that this

may act as a cause for hope. However, Anderson et al. are particularly aware of the power of archaeological accounts to create popular narratives—archaeological memories—which play into our perceptions of the future and they stress the need for caution and detailed demonstration of causal relationships between climate and social change. In particular they argue that the fine-grained analysis of archaeologists at local scales offers a significant addition to analysis of climatic changes at global or continental scales. Archaeological projects have generated vast amounts of 'micro-ecological' data which may be usefully used to supplement broader climatic predictions and translate global trends into localized affects.

12

An Inheritance of Loss: Archaeology's Imagination of Disaster

Karen Holmberg

Disasters often *de-scribe* (Blanchot 1995: 7); they evade written description or complete encapsulation in the narratives we try to create about them. In this chapter, I explore the inveterate metaphor that Pompeii and the AD 79 eruption of Vesuvius have provided in both archaeological literature and larger Western culture. I suggest that this metaphor is not only incomplete, which per Blanchot's admonition is inherent to accounts of disaster, but is also erroneous and needs to be significantly revised in terms of how it frames environmental perceptions of the past and present and the temporality of the archaeological record. While much of the entrenched allegorical role of Pompeii should be jettisoned, the metonymy of the site remains exceptionally important in that it reveals how integral archaeological fieldwork can be in larger societal conceptions of how humans and their environment intersect in the promiscuous nature and culture of disaster.

INHERITING LOSS

Kiran Desai's Man Booker Prize winning work, *The Inheritance of Loss* (2006: 305), includes a passage that describes a 1980s riot scene in north-east India at the foot of the Himalayas:

> The cook could see the fires burning below him and the men scattering. As they crossed the heat vapours of the flames, they seemed to ripple and blow like mirages. Above was Kanchenjunga, solid, extraordinary, a sight that for centuries had delivered men their freedom and thinned clogged human hearts to joy. But of course the cook couldn't feel this now and he didn't know if the sight of the mountain could ever be the same to him. . . . How could anything be the same? The red of blood lay over the market in slick pools mingled with a yellow spread of dal

someone must have brought in anticipation of a picnic after the parade, and there
were flies on it, left behind old slippers, a sad pair of broken spectacles, even a tooth.

This literary example of a disaster scene collocates some key archaeological
research topics: landscape, memory, monumentality, material culture, the
interface of nature and culture, and the passage of time.

If we were to attempt an archaeological excavation of the disaster scene
described by Desai, we would interpret how and why the tooth and the broken
spectacles and the slippers are associated. Without chemical analyses of soil
samples (and the wherewithal to collect them and funding to analyse them),
we would most certainly miss the dal and blood, though they were important
in the scene and experience. We would likely ignore the mountain while trying
to photograph the spectacles *in situ*. It would likely never occur to us to call
them 'sad' in our field notes. Instead we would focus on Munsell colours and
stratigraphy, with perhaps a passing glance at the mountains at lunch break.
What would be lost is a great deal of the human experience for which the
material culture leaves a shadow residue. It is neither possible nor desirable for
archaeologists to provide as emotively detailed an account of past disasters as a
fictionalized or literary account can provide. Material culture does, however,
permit us to construct plausible and influential narratives that can provide
more nuanced conceptions—which would otherwise be lost—of how nature
and culture intersected in the past.

Pompeii: lost and found

The AD 79 eruption of Vesuvius that destroyed and preserved Pompeii and
Herculaneum had a direct and continuing impact on the development of
archaeology as an academic discipline. The way in which the two sites were
excavated became a polarizing topic for intellectuals interested in ethical and
practical elements of archaeology in the later eighteenth century (Ramage 1992);
for the purposes of this discussion I will use Pompeii as synecdochical for
both sites. German art historian J. J. Winckelmann, in particular, critiqued the
destructive practices favoured by antiquaries in his *Open Letter on the Discoveries of Herculaneum* (1762). The influence of Winckelmann's argument led to the
first systematic archaeological field methods, which were implemented by Swiss
army engineer Karl Weber and his successor, Spanish engineer Francesco La
Vega. This eighteenth-century debate and fieldwork helped transform antiquarian studies into classical archaeology (Trigger 2006: 60).

The allusion to Pompeii as a benchmark of arrested civilization is clearly
attractive even if the perception that any site can represent a static snapshot of
a particular event—as I will discuss in more depth later in the chapter—is
problematic. The unusualness of Pompeii is invoked in the description of

other archaeological sites, both volcanic and non-volcanic, that are referenced to the Roman city to highlight their exceptional level of preservation. Some recent examples of such references include Ceren, El Salvador ('the Pompeii of the Americas'), Tambora, Indonesia ('the Pompeii of the East'), Biskupin, Poland ('the Polish Pompeii'), Santorini, Greece ('the Pompeii of the prehistoric Aegean'), Nola-Croce del Papa, Italy ('the first Pompeii'), and Thorjsardalur ('the Pompeii of Iceland').

In modern archaeology, the focus upon what is left behind—what is lost—is key; as James Deetz (1996) phrased it, the small things forgotten often provide an intimate window into elements of past life and the experiences of past people. A sense of loss is also, of course, built into the amount of material culture and immaterial practice that eludes excavation as well as the destructive nature of excavation. It is the absence of this loss—that is, the presence of myriad items normally lost—that provides one of the main sources of modern fascination with the site of Pompeii since excavation began at the site in the mid-eighteenth century. The site is uncanny and exceptional due to what Charles Dickens (1846: 231) termed the 'fresh traces of remote antiquity' it provides. At Pompeii, 'the passage of time should take its toll on objects and yet, here it is, complete and almost as if it was made yesterday' (Lucas 2005: 128).

Small things that should be lost were not, including quotidian objects and the forms of long-dead people and animals. The presence of well-preserved shops, houses, and graffiti-filled public spaces easily prompts speculation on the daily existence of residents two millennia ago while the plaster casts created from voids left by some of those who died in the disaster permit evocative narratives of personal relationships or social values depending on who or what a person chose to hold in their final moment. Blanchot (1995) is most certainly correct in stating that disasters are difficult to describe, yet Pompeii provides an exceptionally rich source of numerous and varied descriptions ranging from the early volcanological bent of Pliny (see Gilman 2007) to a broad literary swath (e.g. Bulwer-Lytton 2003 [1834]; de Stael 1998 [1805]; Dickens 1846; Dickenson 1924; Fairfield 1832; Harris 2003; Jensen 2001 [1903]; Lowry 1961; Twain 2007 [1869]).

While it was undeniably catastrophic for its victims, the AD 79 eruption of Vesuvius and destruction of Pompeii arguably is more important in its modern societal impact than it was in its ancient Roman societal context (Allison 2002). The 'age of archaeology' began in the nineteenth century as a direct result of Pompeii's rediscovery and its incorporation into western European consciousness (Blix 2009: 1). The archaeological excavation of Pompeii was the first large-scale excavation to take place in the public eye and, through its role as a Grand Tour destination, became an important component of overall Western thought. It compelled a personal identification with its victims and became symbolic of what the influential Paris *salonnière* and author Madame de Stael termed 'death's abrupt invasion' (de Stael 1998

[1805]: 198). Pompeii became an imaginative location of sudden and unpredictable disaster from a threat that loomed over the city. The excavation of Pompeii prompted the growth of an array of Western literature invoking natural calamity and universal extinction (Goldstein 1979). Pompeii became—along with other 'lost' worlds such as Atlantis, El Dorado, and Troy—an emblematic warning of civilization's fragility. Pompeii, however, was the only one of these lost places which was easily accessible to visitors and hence became far more intimately linked to people's personal experience.

This experiential resonance helped prompt the implementation of archaeological excavation as an important metaphor for a wide array of practices. Novelist Honoré de Balzac used archaeology as the source for his cultural observations, proposing that 'archeology is to social nature what comparative anatomy is to organised nature' (Balzac 1896: 2); it could lay bare—or excavate—the hidden or lost histories of people, objects, and structures. Sigmund Freud (1917) drew on a novel—*Gradiva: A Pompeiian Fantasy* (Jensen 2001 [1903])—that featured an archaeologist who visits Pompeii. Freud used the city and archaeological practice as an analogy for repression; the psyche, like the buried city, could be revealed through careful excavation.

During the Age of Revolutions, Pompeii became an important social phenomenon and metaphor (Goldstein 1979: 229). The French Revolution, in particular, became heavily associated with the volcanic destruction of Pompeii (Blix 2009). Artistic renditions of the revolution portray liberty as a physical substance that erupts violently from a volcano (e.g. Desperret 1833). Walter Benjamin (1983: 1056; see Blix 2009: 233; Buck-Morss 1999: 66), reiterated the symbolic linkage of Paris and Pompeii at the time of the revolution by stating that 'Paris is in the social order the counterpart of what Vesuvius is in the geographical order. A dangerous, threatening mass . . . ' The purportedly 'cultural' disaster of social upheaval was symbolically referenced to the prior 'natural' disaster of volcanic eruption in an encoding that invoked not only a destructive disruption but also a healing release of pressure.

The Pompeiian metaphor continued to be employed in varied twentieth century examples. Marcel Proust (1990 [1927]: 34, 113, 114), for example, drew upon the destruction of Pompeii in *Le Temps Retrouvé* to describe the rupture that World War I represented in Parisian life and Vesuvius as a metaphor for the threat that Germany offered the French. Feminist artist Eleanor Antin (2001) plays upon the title of the book by Bulwer-Lytton (2003 [1834]), *The Last Days of Pompeii*, in a series of photographs by the same name. Antin's work, like that of literary examples such as *Pompeii* by Robert Harris (2003) parallels life on the brink of the AD 79 eruption to contemporary life to indicate that disaster is an always present threat. In the short story 'The present state of Pompeii', Canadian author Malcolm Lowry (1961) describes the site as a material emblem of the fact that 'man no longer belongs to or understands the world he has created. Man had become a raven

Fig. 12.1. *The Dog From Pompei*, 1991, by Allan McCollum. Cast glass-fibre-reinforced Hydrocal. Approximately 21 x 21 x 21 inches each. Produced in collaboration with the Museo Vesuviano and the Pompei Tourist Board, Pompei, Italy, and Studio Trisorio, Naples, Italy. Installation: Sprengel Museum, Hannover, Germany, 1995.

staring at a ruined heronry. Well, let him deduce his own ravenhood from it if he could.' Pompeii, in sum, shaped a particular vantage of how people relate to the environment that embraced a palpable sense of personal loss.

A lucid and evocative physical manifestation of this metaphor of loss and its lived relationship to the environment is provided by contemporary artist Allan McCollum. For the work, *The Dog from Pompei* (1991), McCollum made moulds and numerous casts of a dog killed by the AD 79 eruption (see Figure 12.1).[1] The first cast of the dog, left chained by a bronze-studded collar

---

[1] McCollum deliberately chose to use the modern spelling of the city to connote the passage of time.

in front of the house of Vesonius Primus, was made in 1874 when archaeologists filled the empty space left by its body with plaster. The helplessness of a chained animal in the face of a volcanic eruption prompts a strongly empathetic response for many people who view McCollum's dog casts displayed together in gallery contexts (Bartman 1995: 13–14).

McCollum's work and the vast amount of literary, artistic, and cultural reference to Pompeii that precede and follow it are a testament to the cultural relevance that archaeology can have. Given its great resonance, I suggest that the use of Pompeii as a conceptual metaphor merits archaeological reconsideration in order to provide the seminal and iconic site of disaster more accurate contemporary valence in our own environmental discussions.

RE-THINKING THE NATURE AND CULTURE OF POMPEII

If the human experience of the world dissolves boundaries between nature, humans, and expression (Merleau-Ponty 1964: 163), then the highly experiential phenomena of disasters can provide amplified examples of this merging. Disasters, or sudden and adverse changes, defy categorization into 'natural' or 'technological' forms (Casimir 2008; Hoffman and Oliver-Smith 2002) and can be seen as hybrids of varying nature–culture components.[2] This more recent understanding of disaster is in direct contraposition to the way in which Pompeii has long been utilized as a metaphor for how humans intersect with the natural world.

Archaeological and popular culture interpretations of Pompeii beginning in the eighteenth century were largely framed by the interpretation of an unpredictably threatening environment that suddenly destroyed an unprepared civilization. Nature acted disastrously on culture; the binaries of nature and culture were firmly divided from one another. This reading of Pompeii is anachronistic in the contemporary context. Nature, as we enter the twenty-first century, is no longer seen as something to be separated from or appropriated by culture (U. Beck 2006; Haraway 1991; Hulme 2010; Latour 2007; Strathern 1992). Contemporary concerns reframe the planet as vulnerable to deleterious anthropogenic changes and confound any easy dichotomy between nature and culture, humans and environments, or any other myriad

---

[2] A more complete definition of a disaster is offered by Hoffman and Oliver-Smith (2002: 4): 'a process/event combining a potentially destructive agent/force from the natural, modified, or built environment and a population in a socially and economically produced condition of vulnerability, resulting in a perceived disruption of the customary relative satisfactions of individual and social needs for physical survival, social order, and meaning.'

binaries that can be used; these terms are too narrow when used in isolation from each other (Shellenberger and Nordhaus 2005).

While environmental change has been noted and discussed throughout the post-Enlightenment period (Glacken 1967: 658–63), there is a growing consensus that equilibrium cannot be assumed in nature–culture intersections and that disturbances—or disasters—can importantly reveal relationships between societies and environments (Dove and Carpenter 2008: 21–4, 60; Dove 2010; Hoffman 2005; Jasanoff 2010). Mutual dynamics are entailed in human–environment interactions (Casimir 2008). Unlike the nineteenth-century period during which Pompeii first provided an emblematic metaphor of culture at the mercy of nature, current conceptions of the natural world place it as both a font and recipient of harm.

The envisioning of a nature-in-balance prior to human intrusion exists simultaneously in the human mind with an idea of nature as currently lacking equilibrium (Massey 2006; Žižek 2008: 435). One problematic issue with conceptions of nature as out-of-balance is the implicit assumption that balance once existed; this implies a 'First Nature' or harmonious balance prior to human intervention (Demeritt 1994; Hinchliffe 2003: 207; Massey 2006: 37–9). The opposite view, however, that nature is always 'turbulent, troubled, indeed destructive as well as creative' prevents easy evaluation of the role of human intervention and impact on the planet and hence is problematic in an era of anthropogenic global climate change debates that require political and ethical stances (Massey 2006: 39).

Slavoj Žižek (2008: 435) proposes that the contemporary period is leading humans into a time when 'it is simply *nature itself* which melts into air'[3] and goes on to suggest that scientific breakthroughs are leading to the 'end of nature'. This invokes influential discussions of the contemporary period as one that is 'after' nature (McKibben 1989; Sebald 1988; Strathern 1992). Rather than the end of physical nature itself, the implication is that an essentialized view of a pristine nature is increasingly eroded by the human ability to create, sustain, and alter life (Haraway 1991; Strathern 1992; see Crumley, Chapter 17 this volume for discussion of the extent to which humans have altered the entire globe). In such a context, what is the role of archaeology? My answer to that question would be that it is uniquely capable of 'experiencing' the environment; that is, of demonstrating the different ways in which people in the past have intersected with their environments, thus providing context to how we understand the present. Pompeii offered an exaggerated and potent example of this from its rediscovery in the seventeenth century to the present.

---

[3] Žižek's phrasing draws upon the lyrically poetic statement by Karl Marx that, 'All fixed, fast-frozen relations, with their train of ancient and venerable prejudices and opinions, are swept away, all new-formed ones become antiquated before they can ossify. All that is solid melts into air.' (Marx and Engels 1969 [1848]: 98).

Like the vantage of nature–culture derived from the site, however, the concept of temporality in the context of the Pompeii metaphor merits reanalysis.

RE-THINKING THE TEMPORALITY OF POMPEII

The assumption of material loss over time and the story of Pompeii were conjoined in a late twentieth-century theory debate over site formation processes. Michael Schiffer (1972, 1976) made a distinction between archaeological sites and the past cultural system that created them and highlighted that the archaeological context does not offer a direct representation of the past systemic context. In response to the 'transforms' that Schiffer proposed as being important to consider when examining archaeological material, Louis Binford (1981b) borrowed a phrase from an earlier article by Robert Ascher (1962) to accuse Schiffer of invoking a 'Pompeii premise' by proposing that the archaeological record is potentially pristine and frozen in place but inevitably distorted.

While Binford's point that the archaeological record does not reflect any particular past moment is well taken, he still saw the archaeological record as a fixed accumulation of events and deemphasized the roles of contemporary social process and the archaeologist in the interpretation of the past (Lucas 2005: 33–4; see also Trigger 2006: 426–7). Both the archaeological record and our perceptions of material culture, contra Binford, are dynamic and constantly changing; neglecting this constant flow and change artificially divorces past events from present events. Temporality is more intimately embedded in events and human life than Binford's events-based conception allows (Lucas 2005: 36). The underlying assumption of the 'Pompeii premise'—that the ancient city was destroyed in a singular transformative juncture—additionally also requires reconsideration in terms of its temporality.

The volcanic eruption of Vesuvius is generally portrayed as a single, catastrophic event that froze the city at a precise moment. This conception was utilised by Binford (1981b) when he invoked the 'Pompeii premise'; even at Pompeii, however, the Pompeii premise is problematic. Rather than occurring in one unexpected event that defined a concise 'before' and 'after', the final eruption sequence took place over a series of three days—24, 25, and 26 August AD 79—during which vast numbers of people and objects were removed from the city. While some of those who chose to or were forced to stay in the city were surprised by *nuée ardente* (or 'glowing clouds') of fast-moving, superheated gases, many others simply walked away from the ash as it fell as one walks on the surface of a snowfall. Technically, the early stages of the eruption that buried Pompeii actually began seventeen years earlier on 5 February AD 62 when a large earthquake destroyed many buildings in

Pompeii and aftershocks occurred for several days following. Two years later, in AD 64, earthquakes destroyed buildings in Naples as magma and pressure began to build under Vesuvius. The final stages of the eruption were part of a long period of volcanic activity that prevented the local landscape from seeming entirely placid or stable; the eruption should not be properly viewed as a single or easily delineated event. This problem is not inherent only to natural occurrences like volcanic eruptions.

The same problem of defining a concise time frame occurs with ostensibly cultural events. The term 'event' is applied archaeologically to varied durations: the agricultural revolution, the Maya collapse, or the act of burial can all be seen as single events, but can also be broken into smaller stages (Lucas 2008: 60). Each of these past actions spanned time periods and ranges of actions that can be collapsed or expanded and are not easily defined or linked as a single unit. The 'event' does not provide a comfortable fit in trying to describe the geophysical world, human actions, or the intersection of humans and environments, and requires careful denotation.

One recent suggestion of how to approach an 'eventful archaeology' proposes that an event is a 'relatively rare subclass of happenings that significantly transforms structures' of society (R. Beck et al. 2007, drawing on Sewell 2005: 100). In this conceptualization, was the historically influential eruption of AD 79 even an event? Cultural change in response to volcanic eruptions is relatively rare (Grattan and Torrence 2007). While the individuals and families of first century AD Pompeii and Herculaneum clearly were catastrophically impacted by the AD 79 eruption, Roman life continued without major change (Allison 2002). Per the definition offered by Beck et al. (2007), then, the eruption of Vesuvius was a non-event. Following this line of reasoning, the transformative impact that the excavation of Pompeii had both in the discipline of archaeology and wider Western culture makes the archaeological excavation—rather than the natural disaster that led to its burial in the first century—denotatively the real event.

Though I see the utility of the definition of an event proposed by Beck et al. (2007) and fully support their intended purpose of interdisciplinary engagement, the heavy emphasis upon change or stasis is not neutral when applied to nature–culture intersections. In general, studies that link environmental events and cultural changes approach those changes 'negatively, as a kind of entropy' in the social order (per Demian and Wastell 2007: 124; Wagner 1981: 29). Stability and continuity, conversely, are seen as ideals. This is a tendency of processual-based archaeology, which values 'equilibrium and changelessness' in social structures (Thomas 2004: 120). For archaeologists working with the role of environmental changes in human life, it is appropriate to heed the opinion of Demian and Wastell (2007: 120), who point out that 'the phrase [social change] once popular in anthropology, has now fallen somewhat from favor, if only because of a growing recognition that if it describes anything, it describes a tautology: change is a categorical constituent of sociality'.

Change and mutability are quite 'natural' elements of the planet and human life. An overemphasis on 'impacts' or responses to a natural event 'positions humans as *outside* the system under analysis' and 'assumes a stable natural baseline and experimental method in which only one variable is changed' (Head 2008: 374). Focusing upon the singularity of the 'event' of a disaster provides an assumption of a 'before' and 'after' or baseline of normality that is disrupted (Dove and Carpenter 2008: 21). This conception, which is critiqued in disaster studies, is prevalent in processual archaeological studies that emphasize concepts of resilience or culture change in response to disasters. More recent archaeological discussions note that all components of a disaster are important research foci and do not centre only on the identification or absence of culture change (Torrence 2002: 11). The elucidation of the fuller story of a disaster is key to understanding how the environment is perceived.

THE IMPORTANCE OF EXPERIENCING ENVIRONMENTS

Ethnographic contexts provide richly evocative examples of human narratives of the environment (Basso 1996; Cruikshank 2005). Archaeology is no less capable of providing narratives and is, additionally, the only way to query contexts not recorded in written or oral history. To return to the literary example cited at the beginning of this chapter, as archaeologists we will never be able to recreate the full scene of the riot that Kiran Desai described through evocation of the spilled dal and the 'sad' spectacles; much detail of the overall disaster experience will be lost. This is not to say that excavating the spectacles and tooth that remained could not provide useful information. The examination of past narratives—or rather present narratives of the past—do not require the graphic preservation that made Pompeii iconic but simply require the archaeological imagination to envision what the data can and cannot say regarding past environments.

The perception of the environment and the performance of nature–human relations provide the focus of a number of intriguing new approaches in social science literature (e.g. Ingold 2000; Szerszynski et al. 2003). I do not propose that there is one particular way that archaeologists could or should highlight narratives of past environments, but I suggest that one example of how it can be done is provided by the emphasis on experience adopted by Chris Tilley (2004) and the discussion he provides of strikingly changing climates in

Mesolithic western Europe. People watched as old landmarks, resources, and favourite places of settlement were erased by sixteen metres of post-glacial sea level rise. Fresh water was polluted, grasslands became rivers, and social relationships and memories that were linked to the places were lost along with them. The megalithic stones erected after this period served as new landmarks and were possibly intended to act as guardians of fresh water and the overall sense of place. Tilley (2008) describes images of moving deer and human skeletons found in Vingen, Norway that were created in a context of a very harsh and highly mutable microclimate; Irish Neolithic peoples used glacial erratics transported from distant places as kerbstones and orthostats for temples; imagery of bronze objects from Östergötland, Sweden was created at a time when land uplift and the formation of rapids changed river flows. All of these contexts entail unstable climates and changing local environments and hint at the way people perceived and experienced their environments.

Enigmatic remains such as Neolithic megalith sites certainly cannot provide as fine-scaled a 'peopling' of the past experience of disastrous environmental change as one associates with Pompeii. As discussed by Tilley (2004), however, they can hint at lived experiences of environmental change that were dramatically important on a personal and community scale, even in contexts where large-scale cultural change was not prompted. Sociologist Maurice Halbwachs (1980 [1950]) proposed that memories and stories survive when they accrue to material objects to which they are linked; for archaeologists, however, only the material objects will survive. Even at Pompeii—with its remarkable preservation and historical accounts—the memories and stories originally attached to the objects are not attainable. We have instead created new narratives from those objects through archaeological interpretation. It is this creation of narratives of human experience that makes the past vivid for non-archaeologists and can provide broader perspectives of how humans and environments intersected in the past in order to contextualize the present.

Archaeology as a discipline, via the eighteenth-century commencement of formal excavation at Pompeii, has an acute heritage of deep-seated cultural relevance to environmental perception and legitimately has a voice to contribute to current debates of disaster and environment. While not negating the importance of quantitative data regarding past disasters, I suggest that the cultural resonance of Pompeii highlights the importance of memorable qualitative narratives in communicating archaeological insights into human experience outside of the academic discipline in ways that are culturally relevant. Archaeology lends itself to narrative as a medium for making the past meaningful to the present (Schofield 2010: 327; Spector 1996). The meta-stories of archaeology—or ways in which narratives of the past contribute to what Holtorf (2010) terms the 'experience society' of the present—form the most significant contribution that archaeologists can uniquely provide.

This is not to imply that archaeologists can fully encompass disasters, but simply to state that we should try to explore qualitative and not just quantitative data in order to flesh out the human experience of the past and its role to the present.

NARRATIVES OF LOSS AND ENVIRONMENTAL ANXIETY

How everything turns away quite leisurely from the disaster

W.H. Auden, 1940

Disasters are difficult to encapsulate in narrative form. Auden's famous line on how everything 'turns away' from the disaster can be interpreted in this light; disasters are evasive in human conception. It is easier to 'turn away' than to attempt to mentally grapple with disastrous events. In this chapter, I suggest that Pompeii became vivid in the Western imagination because of the way that the site successfully invoked the lived experience of the past; the site prevented the viewer from turning away from the disaster.

Through the excavation of Pompeii, archaeology became widely perceived by the nineteenth century as a means by which to attain knowledge about the past that also had pragmatic applications for modern social, political, and artistic practices (Blix 2009: 200). This is a cogent example of how archaeology and the unique vantage it can provide of the past can clearly have far-reaching influence outside of the academic discipline. The iconicity of Pompeii, however, is a potentially misleading component of archaeological heritage; the twenty-first century has brought a growing realization that a reciprocal relationship exists between humans and environment. No disaster is easily defined as a single event and the environment cannot be viewed in terms of equilibrium or stasis in which a violent nature acts upon a vulnerable culture.

In this chapter, I have touched upon the concept of loss in archaeology which is generally framed as a negative aspect through elements of contextual and material destruction. Loss can also be re-characterized in a positive light; the loss of a perceived existence of a nature–culture binary and the loss of rigid disciplinary separations are highly productive in the study of people and environments. Narrative, nature, and culture—*poesis* in its most inclusive form—is a cross-disciplinary, cross-cultural topic of great contemporary importance (McLean 2009). Quantitative data may provide the backbone by which we are able to create narratives, but I propose that it is the qualitative component of the past that sparks the imagination of other academic practitioners and those outside of academia.

Geographer Mike Hulme (2008: 5) notes that we currently live in a climate of fear about our future environment in which

> public discourse around global warming routinely uses a repertoire which includes words such as 'catastrophe', 'terror', 'danger', 'extinction', and 'collapse'. To help make sense of this phenomenon the story of the complex relationships between climates and cultures in different times and in different places is in urgent need of telling.

The examination of different times and places that Hulme calls for in order to provide such stories or narratives is precisely what we as archaeologists do best, and it allows our work to provide unique contributions to such discussions through our ability to incorporate deep time and material culture (Mitchell 2008). As interdisciplinarity slowly becomes an implemented reality rather than a catchword it will be crucial for archaeologists to speak to researchers in other fields who are similarly interested in how we perceive the worlds around us.

The excavation of Pompeii was formative in morphing antiquarianism into modern archaeology; the site, however, was important on a far wider scale. Starting in nineteenth-century Europe, the recovery of the past at Pompeii became, a way to assuage the 'tangible anxiety of loss' brought by a period of rapid cultural changes and prompted 'an urgent archival impulse' in which Pompeii and the excavation of its material culture was enveloped (Blix 2009: 1). Archaeologists were, through their role in 'taming' this anxiety (per Hacking 1990), portrayed with a near 'heroic bearing . . . and almost mythical aura' (Blix 2009: 34).

I shy from any suggestion that archaeologists can or should aspire to return to that status or should mimic the scientist-as-hero genre described by Susan Sontag (2001) in her essay 'The imagination of disaster'. Nor do I propose that we can create detailed accounts of disasters similar to the one cited from Kiran Desai's *An Inheritance of Loss* at the beginning of this chapter. What we can do, however, is carefully query the material of the past for elements of experience that help us to flesh out how we as humans relate to our environments over time and to convey what we learn outside of our disciplinary boundaries. The stories that we tell about the environment change the way that we relate to and interact with it, and it in turn is changed (Cronon 1992: 1375). Archaeologists do have legitimate and valuable insights into the broad spectrum of relationships that people and the planet can have; until we share our stories, however, we have little impact outside of the very bounded confines of conference halls and classrooms. Our disciplinary heritage is something greater.

13

Nature, Identity, and Disaster: Prehistoric Lake Dwelling in Central Europe

Katherine Leckie

INTRODUCTION

Exploring human–environment relations has been an area of great interest to archaeologists, especially for the purpose of reconstructing past environments and investigating methods of human adaptation in the face of changing climates. However, despite the great fruitfulness of such research, particularly in raising awareness of the diversity of human practices, archaeologists often do not account for the influence that preconceived notions of human–environment relationships have in such reconstructions. In fact, archaeology can play a part in constructing or reinforcing Western perceptions of the environment, and as such, sometimes tell us more about our own associations with the natural world rather than informing us about those in the past (see Stump, Chapter 10 and Armstrong Oma, Chapter 11 this volume for similar statements). Using the example of the prehistoric Swiss lake dwellings, this chapter argues that preconceived notions of human–environment relations affect how we interpret and present the archaeological record and past communities. As a consequence, these presentist preconceptions can influence interpretations of the past, creating research trajectories that are monopolized by influential historic debates and obscure the potential subtleties to human interactions with the natural world.

This chapter maintains that the environment often shapes cultural and community identities, both now and in the past, with implications for how such communities deal with environmental change or disaster. In fact, environmental change and risk can itself become inscribed into the cultural identities of the communities that inhabit such landscapes (see Fiore et al., Chapter 4 and Chevalier, Chapter 5 this volume for further discussion of environment and identity). Archaeologists must therefore approach the question of past human–environment relations by considering the place of the environment in the construction of community identities through the daily process of 'living with nature'. Cogent arguments have been made for the inextricable relationship between culture and the environment and particularly for the way in which the environment is perceived through the process of 'dwelling' within it (Ingold 2000). Such work has opened up new avenues of investigation particularly in relation to the mutually constituting association between an environment and its inhabitants.

Reviewing the research trajectory and representations of Swiss lake dwelling sites in the late nineteenth and twentieth centuries, it will be shown how preconceived notions of 'prehistory' (particularly in the nineteenth century) affected the research trajectory of these sites. By assessing the dichotomous approaches used to represent these sites over the past 150 years, and understanding the motives behind their conflicting representations, we might be able to navigate between such one-sided representations and raise questions that reflect on the dynamic interactions between the social world and the environment, and the role the environment may have in the construction of local identities and community cohesion—a theme relevant to human communities both past and present.

ACCESSING AND PRESENTING THE PAST

Our attempts to access the past are often informed by contemporary agendas and assumptions when interpreting the archaeological record. It is thus through a process of mediation that we access aspects of prehistoric communities, partly through the methods and goals we employ to interpret the record and partly through the representations we create. 'Scientifically' based narratives or interpretations of human–environment relations are also representations of sorts, for the methods and approaches to the past—whether 'scientific', 'archaeological', or 'imaginative'—are historically contingent and often mutually constituting. Representations of the archaeological record, whether in 'scientific' publications or in popular representations (textual or visual), convey and explain that material record through narratives, and drawing on physical evidences, that have knowledge-creating efficacy. Historically contingent archaeological methods and objectives used to access the archaeological record can therefore be said deeply to inform the results of such endeavours.

The historical contingencies behind visualizations of early human ancestors and the place of the image in creating ideas about the past, and ways of seeing it, have also been highlighted (Moser 1998, 2001). Instead of simply being the product of archaeological research, archaeological representations feed back into the way we formulate our research questions. Non-academic images in particular can end up becoming central to our theories and are a strong force in constructing knowledge about past societies (Moser 2001: 264–5, 2009: 1048). This is very true for the way we popularly perceive the human–environment dynamic both in the past and today.

Such processes can be observed by considering research that was driven by popular and archaeological illustrations of the Swiss lake dwellings. The major debate, termed the *pfahlbauproblem* earlier in the twentieth century (Menotti 2001), was a long-running controversy that aimed to determine the exact form and location of these settlement sites in relation to the water's edge. Of extreme importance at the time was whether these houses were suspended on stilts over the water or on the littoral zone next to the lakes, which would at times be flooded. The debate was initiated primarily by an early, controversial illustration that had depicted these dwellings planted on stilts (or piles) *above* the water, an image which gained a certain authority as it was reproduced and published widely. The illustration was later challenged by further archaeo-logical evidence, which suggested the houses were in fact built on the lake*side*, a zone which flooded intermittently, the houses built on stilts in preparation for this eventuality. It was only with the development of microscopic analytical techniques (Harding 1980; Pétrequin and Bailly 2004; Schlichtherle 1997, 2004) that the question of whether the villages stood on stilts in the water, or were constructed directly on the land, lost its appeal. What is particularly interesting in this regard is the influence that an early illustration had on determining the course of archaeological research.

PRECONCEIVED PREHISTORY

Preconceptions or received ideas about the nature of prehistoric humans and their environment have at times been hugely influential in how the archaeo-logical record was approached and the sorts of images of prehistory that were produced. Anthropologist and historian Wiktor Stoczkowski's approach to the historiography of human origin myths, set out in his book *Explaining Human Origins: Myth, Imagination and Conjecture* (Stoczkowski 2002), is an informa-tive way of thinking through the place of preconceived ideas—both visual and intellectual—in the construction of prehistory. He suggests that narratives of prehistoric human life and development appear to conform to a sort of standard set of images and explanatory schemes—such as 'man's upward struggle against nature'—suggesting that these accounts are not based entirely on empirical evidence, but that evidence is integrated into pre-existing con-ceptions of human history. That representations and visual narratives were so foundational to the study of Swiss lake dwellings compels a recognition of the 'power by which a conceptual tradition conditions the observation of new phenomena' (Stoczkowski 2002: 3). Making the case for historically parallel but contradictory representations of prehistoric communities and their environment, Stoczkowski demonstrates that views of nature and prehistory between the eighteenth and twentieth centuries tended to emphasize the animosity of nature as key to the creation of culture, whereas by contrast 'in our [Western, Classical] culture, a substantial number of transitional narratives situate the beginnings of humankind in a paradisiacal world' (Stoczkowski 2002: 19). Despite the influential Rousseauian trope of the noble savage that partially influenced the mindset of the eighteenth and nineteenth centuries, we are reminded that the 'educated European…remained an optimist…and would have felt no great enthusiasm for a return to an original state of "pure nature"' (Stoczkowski 2002: 11). Instead, as Stoczkowski demonstrates, the view that pervaded the eighteenth century, and triumphed in the following century, can be exemplified by Boulanger:

> 'So it [prehistory] was a time when the wretched inhabitants of the earth had to look with disgust on their dwelling place, which was the scene of the most terrible catastrophes' and when man had 'so many legitimate reasons to hate a nature that denied him everything, that destroyed even his hut, that constantly alarmed him and satisfied hardly any of his needs.' (Stoczkowski 2002: 12, quoting Boulanger 1766)

Evolutionary archaeology of the nineteenth and early twentieth centuries played into these preconceptions by interpreting cultural change as a progressive development in technology and modes of settlement, each having reached a certain 'grade' of civilization (Keller 1866). Furthermore, such preconceptions played into representation of the prehistoric past, creating as Moser and Gamble have suggested, different visual traditions whose visual language 'depends on the repeated association of icons to form interpretative images of its subject matter' (1997: 184–6). In their analysis of an early twentieth century image of Palaeolithic life, Moser and Gamble explore the 'repertoire of icons and scenarios' used to portray a view of prehistoric life. They note that 'one of the most striking characteristics of these pictures is that ancient humans tend to be identified in terms of their ecological settings. The prevailing story is one of perpetual struggle, where our prehistoric relatives were constantly challenged by the environment and the beasts that inhabited it' (1997: 190). Preconceived ideas about such a human–environment relationship can become embedded in imagery, reinforcing and propagating such ideas.

SWISS LAKE DWELLINGS

In the course of research into Neolithic and Bronze Age Swiss lake settlements these prehistoric communities have been closely identified by their inhabitance of a wetland environment, and thus pose a particularly interesting case study when considering the interplay between archaeology and the representation of human–environment relationships in the past. Located in the littoral zones of the lakes of Switzerland, southern Germany, and northern Italy, the sites variously date from the mid-Neolithic to the end of the Bronze Age (*c.*4300 BC to *c.*800 BC). Because of the degree of organic preservation they have become enormously important in the development of wetland archaeological techniques and practices and fundamental to the development of an increasingly 'scientific' archaeology throughout the twentieth century. The dramatic context of their discovery—the wooden piles or stilts that originally held platforms and houses above the wetland areas literally rose out of the water of the Swiss lakes in 1854 after an unusually dry winter—resulted in prolific visualizations and descriptions of these structures and their imagined inhabitants.[1]

KELLER'S RECONSTRUCTION

When the dwellings were first noticed in the 1850s, word of these discoveries rapidly spread throughout the European antiquarian and natural sciences community. In his first publication, the prominent Swiss antiquarian Ferdinand Keller (1854) recounted the nature of the discoveries and provided a hand-drawn sketch, an 'ideal reconstruction', of the sites, which was in fact, a hybrid of archaeological, anthropological, and inspired features. This 'exciting icon that suddenly succeeded in unveiling the primordial aspect of Switzerland' (Vogt 1998: 227) was printed and disseminated across Europe. Notably, Keller presented the structures as being on platforms over the water rather than on the shores of the lakes. This was the image that stuck in both the popular and archaeological imagination—and the image that partly fuelled the *pfahlbauproblem*—and although there was some debate, the picturesque image of houses carefully balanced on long stilts on the Swiss lakes very quickly solidified.

Keller's illustration was almost entirely based on a late eighteenth century image by Louis-Antoine de Sainson, from a voyage with Dumont d'Urville to Dorei, of houses on stilts from the Pacific Island culture. Although Keller was

---

[1] Recent publications regarding visual representations of Swiss lake dwellings in Switzerland include Flüeler-Grauwiler and Gisler (2004) and Kaeser (2008).

aware that 'the analogy to Polynesia was retrograde ethnological inference', he argued 'that it aimed to supplant "mythological approximation" of first origins with "a pragmatic approximation"' (cited in Vogt 1998: 232). From the outset comparisons were made between the lake settlements in the Alpine region and similar forms of habitation across the world, such as ethnographic examples of 'lake dwelling' from Lake Moyhrga or Bealmah, in Central Africa, as well as archaeological discoveries of crannogs in Ireland and Scotland and the historical records of Herodotus about the communities that lived on Lake Prasias (Keller 1866). Although there were clear structural differences to the houses, most markedly between the Swiss lake sites and the Crannogs, the discussion centered on how these communities, as a result of sharing such a similar environment, might in some way be culturally comparable. Keller's reconstruction inspired further representations including dioramas, models, reconstructions, and paintings as well as illustrations in popular publications at the Great Exhibitions of 1867, 1878, and 1889. The conception of lake dwellings also solidified more locally in Swiss farmers' almanacs, schoolbooks, and antiquarian collections. Placed in their historical context, the discoveries and first visual interpretations of these remains emerged at a time when Europe was acutely conscious of emerging antiquity and many were attempting to realize it in minute detail through visualizations and museum exhibits.

IMAGERY AND NATIONALISM

Descriptions and visualizations of the past further fed into a concurrent discourse on the ethnicity and nationality of past peoples, and lake dwellings became very much entangled in this process. The practice of identifying past ethnic communities is just one example of the wider late nineteenth century zeal for naming and categorizing prehistoric peoples—for example, the Lake Dwellers, the Cave Dwellers and the Mound Dwellers—by their manner of inhabiting the natural world, as well as by their material culture. Some of these ideas, like equating architectural structures with cultural—and often national—characteristics, had roots in the work of writers like John Ruskin who wrote on the architecture of the nations of Europe 'as considered in its association with natural scenery and national character' (Ruskin 1893). In the Swiss context, interpreting the lake sites in this way paved the way for their use in the affirmation of Swiss national identity (Kaeser 2001, 2004, forthcoming). The lake dwellings were conceived of as a distinct and unique way of living. As Marc-Antoine Kaeser has shown, nineteenth century archaeologists drew upon the archaeological record as evidence of the characteristics of Swiss lake-dwellers, which corresponded with the ideological requirements of the mid-nineteenth century and 'virtues that were valued in the democratic and liberal Swiss Confederation of 1848' (Kaeser forthcoming). Though similar forms of settlement could be found elsewhere in the world, the apparent homogeneity of these sites in Switzerland, and their similarity of structure and location, resulted in descriptions in some of the earliest publications showing groups of houses that were built upon huge communal platforms supporting all the houses in the village. Ferdinand Keller was fascinated by the idea of community life above water and, based on the idea of 'communal platforms', he concluded that the builders of the pile-dwellings constituted an ethnic community, a 'lake-dwelling people', expressed by the relationship between 'one platform—one village—one community' (Vogt 1998: 237).

THE SWISS LAKE DWELLING RESEARCH TRAJECTORY

Conceiving of lake dwelling as a means of inhabiting a landscape motivated numerous but often conflicting representations. Immediately after the Swiss discovery the idea of lake dwelling had seized the public imagination: 'perhaps the single most extended exercise in the imaginative re-creation of Neolithic communities anywhere in the world' (Sherratt 2004: 268). The sites were internationally agreed to be of central importance to the debates about the 'antiquity of man'. Parallel to such concerns were enthusiastic reconstructions of these 'lake villages' in the form of models, romanticized paintings, and construction of life-sized settlements, for example at Unteruhldingen on Lake Constance (Bodensee). During the nineteenth and twentieth centuries private individuals and museums eagerly collected artifacts that came from these sites, collections that became the basis of many foundational prehistoric collections across Europe and as far as the United States (Leckie 2011).

CONFLICTING REPRESENTATIONS

The contrasting representations of the Swiss lake dwelling sites in the nine-teenth and twentieth centuries have drawn archaeological investigations along often contradictory lines of enquiry, providing distraction from what might be seen as more fundamental aspects of a 'lake dwelling way of life' such as the risks intrinsic to living in such a way. Popular portrayals of prehistoric communities have promoted ideas of living in harmony with nature, or conversely in battle against it. But they have failed to consider how people actually lived in dialogue with the natural world, with environmental risks (such as flooding and fire) an integral part of their culture and identity. By looking at the representations of lake-dwelling life that were created over the last 150 years, and understanding the motives behind them, we might be able to move beyond one-sided, dichotomous representations of the past and raise questions that reflect on the dynamic interactions between the social world and the environment, as well as the role the environment may have had in the construction of local identities and community cohesion.

Harmonious Representations

The society and culture of the prehistoric lake dwellers was usually perceived as primitive and rudimentary compared to the technological and social developments of nineteenth century Switzerland, and comparisons were often made within the framework of the upward progress of civilization. However, when comparing the variety of representations of lake-dwelling communities and their environments, many present conflicting stories. Of these representations some depict the inhabitants of lake sites as prehistoric communities in harmony with the natural world. Appropriating alpine scenery to embellish the calm serenity of domestic scenes, these images were made suitable to the political ends they served. For example the painting *Village lacustre de l'âge de la Pierre* (1867) and *Village lacustre de l'âge du Bronze* (1867) by the Swiss historical painter Auguste Bachelin (1830–1890) were created to accompany the many artifacts and models from the Swiss lake sites to the Great Exhibition of 1867 in Paris, representing Switzerland and Swiss technology to the world (Müller-Scheesel 2001). These images presented lake dwelling communities as peace-loving and literally 'rooted' in the water. Alpine 'Nature' provided the appropriate background and scenery to this way of life, seen for example in Anton Seder's (1850–1916) *Pfahlbausiedlungen am Bodensee* (Figure 13.1). Similar images that emphasized picturesque Swiss scenery were produced in England. The painting *Lake Village* (Figure 13.2) by Ernest Griset (1844–1907) was commissioned by Sir John Lubbock, while Keller's (1866) account of the

Fig. 13.1. *Pfahlbausiedlungen am Bodensee* by Anton Seder (1877). (Used with permission of the Rosgartenmuseum, Konstanz, Switzerland.)

Fig. 13.2. *Lake Village* by Ernest Griset (*c.*1869–1871). (Used with permission of the Bromley Museum, copyright of Bromley Museum Service.)

Swiss lake sites displayed a frontispiece entitled '*Ideal sketch of a Swiss Lake Dwelling restored from latest discoveries*' (Figure 13.3).

The lake sites were not only represented in illustrative form but also in literature and poetry. One such work, produced in Switzerland by antiquarian Jakob Messikomer, owner of the prolific and well-known site of Robenhausen, was an 1860 song celebrating the lake dwellers entitled *Pfahlbauerlied* or *Chant lacustres*.[2] Similarly, archaeological artefacts, illustrations and reconstructions of lake dwellings served as a resource for literary creativity, providing a Romantic 'staging' for fantastic novels and contributing to the development of an already well established genre of literature—the prehistoric novel.[3] Antiquarians and the emerging archaeologists of the period also described these sites lyrically in their publications, emphasizing the romantic idea of dwellings or houses above water. For example, F. A. Forel, an antiquarian deeply involved in the recovery of artefacts from Lake Geneva, mused on the romance of living above water, how one might experience the seasons, and thus become profoundly attached to such a life:

[2] Displayed in the exhibition *Visions d'une Civilisation Engloutie* 2009, Museum Latenium, Switzerland.
[3] e.g. Berthet (1876) and Rosny (1897).

Fig. 13.3. *Ideal sketch of a Swiss Lake Dwelling restored from latest discoveries* by John E. Lee (Keller 1866).

These were wonderful dwellings for men with a taste for lakes, these wooden cabins built above the waters. To have the lake in front of you, around you, below you, to be surrounded by it, possessed by it; to only jump in to have a bath or to get into a boat; only to throw out a net to pull in an abundant catch of fish . . . to enjoy also the prodigious variety which must arise from the incessant modifications to the lake, sometimes calm, sometimes stirred by the storm, sometimes bathed in light, sometimes made sad by the grey taint of the fog. We, the lakeside residents, we know what powerful charm, always renewed, always refreshed, is given to us by the spectacle of those waters . . . we are seized by it, we are excited by it, we are profoundly attached to it . . .[4]

The Battle against Nature

In contrast to the images of the peace and productivity of the lake communities those in keeping with progressionist views of history posited prehistory as an upward struggle against pure nature, a trope extensively used in many depictions of prehistoric life. For example, many late nineteenth century paintings of prehistoric life show 'the hunt,' or 'man against the beasts'; the environment acting as the battleground between man and nature, seen for example in the *L'envahisseur* (1884) by L. M. Faivre. Similarly, plentiful

---

[4] Forel quoted in Ripoll 1994: 212 (Author's translation).

paintings and illustrations of lake sites depict the destruction of villages by fire and floods. One of these is the Swiss artist F. T. Aerni's depiction of a night-time attack on a lake village in his *Attaque nocturne d'une station lacustre* (1896), while a later image shows a similar event in the children's story book *Die Inselleute vom Bodensee* (Figure 13.4). Representations of these disasters were a direct consequence of archaeological evidence for the regularity with which such dwellings succumbed to the flames or waters.

Fig. 13.4. *Fire in a lake village.* Illustration from an early twentieth century German children's book (Keller-Tarnuzzer 1937).

This theme is also seen in the work of poet Josef Victor Scheffel. Whilst contemplating the lake site of Robenhausen on Lake Pfäffikon in 1865, Scheffel composed a poem musing on the icy wind and fog that covered the lake, concluding 'see how Europe was born, with rheumatism and a tooth ache'.[5] Moreover, the Chancellor's Gold Medal for English poetry at the University of Cambridge in 1868 was awarded for 'the best poem on the Lake Dwellings of Switzerland'.[6] Francis Henry Wood's lyrical exposition of both the joys and dangers of living on the lake was named the winner. Wood's descriptions range from a sublime description of the landscape around Zurich: 'branching pines have girt with shadowy zone yon pendant heights, that stand like monarchs o'er the plain and guard their realms—a mimic Eden,' to an account of the destructive might of the flames: 'when round these homes the scorching Föhnwind wrapt a sheet of flame! Then, like a molten shroud, the encircling blast enveloped in its folds the fated race' (Wood 1873: 29–38). This poem captures well the ambivalent and almost schizophrenic perception people had of this romantic yet 'primitive' way of life. The Swiss lakes were both idyllic in situation and yet perilous for the communities inhabiting them, living so closely with the threat of fire or flood.

What we see here are both views of the past being exhibited: that of the fight against nature and that of a peaceful, aquatic idyll. The fact that these sites inspired such opposing images was partly due to their importance in the Swiss national context. The peaceful images were meant to reflect well on the progenitors of contemporary Swiss society whilst the images of mankind's struggle against the elements reflect the parallel view held in the eighteenth and nineteenth centuries that prehistory was the start of an uphill struggle against nature on the long ladder of progress. Both these threads can clearly be seen in the representations that were produced of the Swiss lake villages.

CONTEMPORARY REPRESENTATIONS

More recent attempts to represent the lake villages have taken the form of heritage sites incorporating archaeological reconstructions (Figure 13.5), but some of the same themes explored above can be detected.

At the lake dwelling exhibition in Zürich in 1990 were two exhibits with sound effects, one showing a village flooding whilst the other is burning. The intention in representing these disasters was 'to show how prehistoric man was more or less at the mercy of natural forces which he could not control' (Ruoff 1992: 144). This exhibition provides us with a vignette of some of the

---

[5] Translated by E. Simon and cited in Paret 1958: 81.
[6] 'University Intelligence', *The Times*, 12th December 1868.

Fig. 13.5. Present-day reconstruction of a lake dwelling at Unteruhldingen, Lake Constance (photograph the author's own).

issues considered earlier. For example, the occurrence of an unexpected fire at a reconstructed lake village heritage site throws into relief the realities of lake dwelling, for the exhibition admitted that 'it is difficult for us to imagine how prehistoric people confronted these [natural] forces' (Ruoff 1992: 144). The desire to capture the event, and represent it as a way of perhaps understanding the risky environments of these prehistoric settlements, is highlighted by the media response to an accident at the exhibition. Archaeologist Ulrich Ruoff described the scene:

> A couple of weeks after opening the managing team of the exhibition was sitting in the restaurant built on the premises, when a thunderstorm broke out over Zürich. Storm clouds raced across the lake and the rain pelted down. A television crew, who had just been recording, was now obviously seeking shelter in the reconstructed Bronze Age village. We wondered whether the TV crew might actually take advantage of the situation because we kept seeing dark figures hurrying over the bridge, and indeed, they were creating the effects of a fire. Above the nearest row of houses a bright glow appeared . . . then a flame seemed to run across the gable. Whilst we were wondering how the film people had managed this in the midst of a downpour another flame blazed up. 'It's really burning' someone shouted. . . . We fought the flames from the outside and the inside . . . and finally the fire brigade arrived and set up their hoses. From the

outside all one could see was blackened thatch with a burnt out hole at the gable, but the incident had given us a good idea of what a fire really meant in a village where the houses stood very near to each other. In the Bronze age the village would certainly have burnt hopelessly to the ground. (Ruoff 1992: 144–5).

The film crew actually attempted to take advantage of the dramatic weather conditions and the storm increased the drama of their attempts to represent the sites. The fire was intended to further add to this. In fact, the site burnt down after an arson attack the following week raising some key questions in the minds of archaeologists: had the prehistoric settlers kept all their vital grain stores in houses which were such high risk? Why did they build the houses so close together? Where did people go after such an event?

RISK IN THE PAST

This exhibition and an accidental disaster at the reconstruction site highlight the way in which we can become too focused on representing events, like the burning of a prehistoric village, rather than considering the impact this event would have had on the community. This experimental site and the events described above raise interesting archeological questions. Archaeological evidence suggests that that these villages burnt down with terrifying regularity, almost every decade; the many wooden piles discovered around the alpine lakes are remains of recurring villages built on the same sites and evidence of frequent alterations to these structures (Ruoff 1992). This implies that members of these communities could in a single lifetime experience perhaps three or four of these disasters and the consequential destruction, rebuilding effort, and tensions that such events provoked.

Comparing the nature of nineteenth- and of twentieth-century research into the lake dwelling sites highlights two problems. Nineteenth-century interpretations were a mixture of progressive evolutionism and romantic imagination. Much research was heavily influenced by popular and archaeological illustrations that placed a great deal of emphasis on the location of the dwellings; whether they were picturesque villages situated over the water, or less romantically located in the littoral zone. Illustrations of the 'lake dwellers' from this time shows them either nonchalantly enjoying the beauty of the lake or escaping from one of the devastating infernos that seem occasionally to have destroyed these sites.

Throughout the twentieth century, in embarrassed reaction to such imaginative responses to these sites, new analyses and interpretations have been mainly confined to the use of techniques such as dendrochronology, archaeobotany, palaeoclimatology, micro-fauna, and computing methods, in order to present more scientific accounts (or representations) of these sites (Menotti 2001, 2004). The aim of such research has been to move toward the retrieval of hard 'facts' about the environmental and structural characteristics of the settlement sites. Such a microscopic focus on these sites has, however, been critiqued as lacking any attention to social archaeology. A review of a recent publication of current lake site archaeological research was criticized for 'its limited engagement with social theory and the archaeology of *people* . . . [and] consequently [has] surprisingly little to say about the people who actually built the lake-villages, and how they lived together, experienced, valued and identi-fied with them' (Skeates 2007: 96–7). So, despite new scientific analysis, there has been little progress in our understanding of social, visual, or symbolic elements to these societies.

Both 'imaginative' and 'scientific' approaches to these prehistoric settlements of the Alpine region have been directed partly in response to preconceived notions of prehistory, or in reaction to overly 'Romantic' interpretations of the past. It would seem that both however have missed the subtlety of how people actually lived with and managed risk. There seems to have been little consider-ation of the re-inscription of natural risk into the 'life-styles' and experiences of these communities, and its effect on their identity is an aspect of the social archaeology that is missing (see Rudiak-Gould, Chapter 14 this volume for a more recent examination of living with environmental risk).

LIVING IN A RISKY ENVIRONMENT: BEYOND REPRESENTATION

Although grossly generalizing and culture-historical in its approach, the interests that the nineteenth century had in prehistoric peoples' relationship to the structure of their habitations and ways of dwelling in their environment is interesting, and reminds us of an element of research that has perhaps been lacking for much of the last century. Associating a type of settlement structure and environmental habitat with an ethnic 'people,' as Keller did, was clearly simplistic and strongly influenced by prevalent culture-historical and nation-alist approaches to archaeological evidence that saw similar material practices (such as styles of pottery production or the structure of settlements and housing) as indicative of a racial or ethnic community. But it is a line of questioning, admittedly in the imaginative context of the paintings and poems, that shows an interest in the symbiosis between cultural characteristics and ways of inhabiting the environment. It is not a completely invalid line of archaeological questioning, particularly when reconsidering the place of the

environment in the construction of community identities and the daily process of 'living with nature'.

How do we connect such archaeological sites and their representations to
consider how communities experienced living in risk-prone environments?
How can we change our popular illustrations and images to gain a deeper
understanding of these experiences and processes of representation? As I have
previously intimated, these dichotomous representations ignore an intricate
and complex relationship that lake-dwelling communities would have had
with the environment. Being aware of the historical trajectories and agendas
giving rise to the representations that so often influence our archaeological
imaginations, we instead might use them as a starting point for considering
the interactions between the people and the environment that they depict.
Instead of our goal simply being the construction of a scenario or representation of past peoples in their specific environments, we need to ask deeper
questions that attempt to consider how the environment in which they lived
impinged on their own perceptions and identities. As such we can begin to
posit a lake dwelling life-way—a *habitus*—that was partially predicated on and
constructed from environmental risk. From this viewpoint, these settlement
forms can begin to be seen as 'vehicles of ritual expression and belief . . . a total
cultural creation, as well as a rational solution to the Neolithic occupance of
the areas around the Alps' (Sherratt 2004: 273).

We therefore need to re-evaluate dramatic representations of disaster in the
light of solid archaeological evidence. Fires and flood would certainly have had
a very severe effect on a community. It would seem that there is firm
archaeological evidence from microanalysis of the remains of these sites for
the total destruction of lake villages by fire and flooding, and this suggests that
complete rebuilding of villages occurred with regularity. What has not been
considered, however, is the immense community cohesion that would have
been required to cope with such contingencies and the need to reconstruct life-
ways on a regular basis. The importance of collective participation in the
rebuilding of structures and platforms affected by flooding or burning would
have been essential, suggesting that each lake-dwelling unit would have been a
cohesive and tightly knit community that faced such events as a group.

Paradoxically, rebuilding water-based dwellings served only to reinscribe
the potentiality of such threats. It might therefore be interesting to consider
how events that would have had such practical and social impact might have
become part of a community's cultural representations of itself: as part of their
oral histories or a cause for new negotiations of relationships and social roles
in the event of mass homelessness and the need to rebuild the community.
Such disasters may have been associated with a cosmological or religious
explanation that required libations, or may have forced the community to
interact with neighbouring unaffected communities. We might ask if people
commemorated such events, and if so, how? We may be able to address some

of these questions by considering how close the villages were to each other. This will require the application of archaeological experimentation or observation of the effect of natural disasters on small wetland communities and how such events become incorporated into oral histories or cosmologies.

Despite having more information on lake dwellings than ever before, in our studies of them we have become 'complacent' about our understanding (Sherratt 2004: 268). Andrew Sherratt has suggested that '[w]hat is perhaps missing is the artistic imagination. It is the integration of this quantity and diversity of information in terms of human experience and action which is the most necessary element of the nineteenth-century appreciation that is lacking today' (Sherratt 2004: 274). Despite the importance of being aware of the purposes and limitations of representations, both archaeological and imaginative, we might consider the scenarios and narratives they create to inject a new and creative line of questioning within the archaeological enterprise. Representations can be seen then not as a goal, but a process by which we begin to ask deeper questions about what we are representing.

Taking inspiration from imaginative approaches to prehistory that at least take the discussion out of the laboratory and into the realm of human experiences, we must consider the entwined relationship between humans and their environment and the place that risk and disaster had in these communities. We might also realize that such discussions can inform the ways in which present day communities will have to deal with future risks. Environmental disaster is not unique to the present, but we forget that peoples lived with and recovered from disasters in the past. If we really want to understand more about past and present human–environment relationships, we need to consider how communities responded to such processes and were, in turn, shaped by them.

ACKNOWLEDGEMENTS

Many thanks to Ben Morris and Trinidad Rico for convening the session at WAC 2008 where this paper was first presented, and to Matthew Davies and Freda Nkirote M'Mbogori for their editorial guidance and advice in putting this article together.

14

Memories and Expectations of Environmental Disaster: Some Lessons from the Marshall Islands

Peter Rudiak-Gould

INTRODUCTION: NEW THREATS MEET OLD VULNERABILITIES

The Republic of the Marshall Islands, an archipelago of low-lying coral atolls in eastern Micronesia, is one of four sovereign nations that may be rendered uninhabitable by climate change in the present century. It is not merely sea level rise which is expected to undermine life in these islands, but the synergy of multiple climatic threats (Barnett and Adger 2003). Rising oceans and increasingly frequent typhoons will exacerbate flooding at the same time that the islands' natural protection—coral reefs—will die from warming waters and ocean acidification. Fresh water resources will be threatened by both droughts and salt contamination from flooding. Although the reaction of the coral atoll environment to climate change is uncertain, it is likely that the islands will no longer be able to support human habitation within fifty or a hundred years (Barnett and Adger 2003: 326)—quite possibly within the lifetimes of many Marshall Islanders living today.

In the public imagination, climate change in vulnerable, remote locations is the intrusion of contamination into a formerly pristine environment, of danger into a once secure sanctuary, of change into a once static microcosm (see Lynas 2004: 81, 124). Archaeologists, of course, know better than this: every place has a history of environmental upheavals, and the Marshall Islands is no exception. Researchers agree that coral atolls are among the most precarious and marginal environments that humans have managed to inhabit (Weisler 1999; Yamaguchi et al. 2005: 27), existing only 'on the margins of sustainability' (Weisler 2001). The islands in fact only recently formed: while the reefs are tens of millions of years old, the islets that sit on them emerged

Fig. 14.1. Fisherman returning to land: Ujae Atoll.

from the sea only recently, probably around 2000 BP (Weisler et al. 2000: 194; Yamaguchi et al. 2005: 31–2), just before the first people arrived (Yamaguchi et al. 2005: 31–2). The new home that these early seafarers found was not so much an ancient safe haven as a fragile geological experiment—land whose very existence was tenuous long before humans were altering the global climate.

The islands presented a number of severe challenges to human occupants. The land is scarce and scattered: the archipelago totals a mere 180 square kilometres of land, divided into 1,225 individual islets spread over almost two million square kilometres of ocean. In addition, they are exceptionally low, with an average elevation of just two metres; the highest point in the archipelago is only ten metres above mean sea level. As a result, the archipelago is perpetually vulnerable to typhoons and flooding, and inhabitants have no possibility of fleeing to high ground or sheltered inland areas. Fresh water is also scarce: there are few lakes and no rivers, and freshwater lenses are found only on the larger islands; droughts are an ever-present danger, especially in the drier northern atolls.

Little is known about Marshallese prehistory, which for all intents and purposes extends into the early or mid-nineteenth century. Atolls were once considered poor sites for archaeological investigation, unlikely to yield significant finds (Weisler 2001). This view has changed, but the archaeological record of the Marshall Islands has only begun to be uncovered (Weisler et al. 2000: 194). What we do know, however, suggests the precariousness of human habitation. The paucity of fresh water was an essential limit on human population in this archipelago (Williamson and Sabath 1982). Archaeology confirms that several of the drier northern atolls were never permanently inhabited owing to a lack of fresh water, inhibiting crop growth (Yamaguchi et al. 2005). Land was scarce, and to preserve it, commoners (as opposed to chiefs) were usually buried at sea (Chamisso 1986 [1821]: 231): competition for land was a constant theme in traditional politics. Analyses of middens indicate that protein resources, initially abundant, declined over time because of over-exploitation, requiring the islanders to work harder, venture further, and become more creative in order to secure sufficient supplies (Weisler 1999). For all of these reasons, adequate nutrition may have been uncertain even for high-status individuals, as some archaeological findings suggest (Weisler et al. 2000: 215). Severe limitations on subsistence are also indicated by the old custom, now long since abandoned, of killing all children after the third (Chamisso 1986 [1821]: 231).

Marshallese history is riddled with dramatic climate-induced tragedies (Spennemann and Marschner 1994: 8–10). Here the evidence comes from the written accounts of Westerners, both their own observations and local oral history which they collected. The following examples are only some of those that we know about, and only a small percentage of all that have occurred since people settled the islands. In the mid-nineteenth century a typhoon destroyed all of the coconut and breadfruit trees on Ebon Atoll, leading to starvation; another storm hit this atoll in 1864, and was described as having torn away all of the vegetation. Another typhoon in the mid-nineteenth century caused such severe damage on Ujelang Atoll that a passing Westerner surmised that the island must have experienced a volcanic eruption. An 1875 typhoon caused all the inhabitants of Kili Island to move elsewhere. A typhoon in 1905 obliterated three uninhabited islands in Mili Atoll and several inhabited islands on Nadikdik Atoll, washing away all of the soil and vegetation so that only the reef platform remained (Spennemann 1996). Everyone on Nadikdik Atoll died as a result except for two children who floated on a log to nearby Mili Atoll. The storm also hit Arno, Majuro, and Jaluit. In total, 227 people drowned in the resulting floods, and around ninety more died afterwards from famine due to the destruction of fruit trees by salt spray, wind, and flooding. The waves were described as being as high as the coconut trees. Another typhoon in 1918 caused a flood in Majuro Atoll along thirty kilometres of its length; it breached the perimeter of the atoll, creating new channels from the outer ocean to the inner lagoon, and drowned 200 people (Spennemann 1996). In 1870, a cyclone reduced the population of Ujelang Atoll from a thousand to twenty (Spennemann and Marschner 1994: 9). Archaeological findings confirm that Marshall Islanders used to permanently inhabit only the lagoon shores of larger islands on the leeward side of atolls, as partial protection against such storms (Spennemann 1996). Although we have no direct data from the Marshall Islands, the archipelago may also have been severely affected by the AD 1300 event in which a drop in sea level killed shallow reefs and decimated marine resources, leading to desperation and warfare throughout the Pacific islands (Nunn 2003: 223–5).

Thus, all that we fear from future climate change in low-lying islands—droughts, storms, floods, coral mortality, and even the total obliteration of islands—has occurred before. As such, global climate change in the Marshall

Islands is not so much a new threat as it is an intensification of old threats that people have faced for thousands of years (Nunn 2003: 226; Weisler 2001). A passage from the first written account of Marshallese culture, from the early nineteenth century, shows that even the fear of catastrophic sea level rise did not begin in the era of global warming: 'In the case of transgression the sea would come over the island and all land would disappear. A well-known danger threatens all low islands from the sea, and religious belief often holds this rod above the people' (Chamisso 1986 [1821]: 278).

One commonly hears in discussions of human–environment interactions that the people of a particular region have 'coped with' or 'survived' local environmental risks for millennia (see for instance Green (2009) on indigenous Australians). This is true on the level of the regional population as a whole: they 'survived' these catastrophes in the sense that not everyone died—the populace did not die out *in toto*. But it is certainly not true on the level of the individual or the community, since many people did in fact die, and entire settlements were wiped out. Our focus on coping and resilience should not blind us to the fact that one of the most common human responses to disaster is death (Roland Fletcher, personal communication). Returning to the present case study, the fact that the Marshall Islands have been continuously inhabited for two thousand years does not entail that the inhabitants were always able to cope with disasters: they often died in large numbers. So climate change will not be the first environmental calamity to devastate the Marshall Islands, although it may be the last.

There is a risk here of overstating the precariousness of the islands (Yamaguchi et al. 2005) and underemphasizing the *dis*continuities between previous hazards and present-day climate change. It is certainly true that climate change poses a larger threat than anything that has come before. But it is not *categorically* distinct. Signs of climate change will not be different in kind from things people have dealt with before; and the first signs of climate change will not be different even in degree. It is easy to see then why these early warnings may fail to set off alarm bells.

This leads us to this chapter's case study: a flood that struck the Marshall Islands in December 2008. I will show that this event did nothing to increase local concern about the looming spectre of climate change, and I will offer an explanation for this fact based on Marshallese notions of natural environmental risk as built up over millennia of experience in a vulnerable landscape. While the example is a contemporary one, the lessons learned both draw on the past and can be applied to it.

Fig. 14.2. Vulnerable homes: Jenrōk neighbourhood, Majuro.

THE DECEMBER 2008 FLOOD

A few weeks before Christmas 2008, the Marshall Islands—in particular the capital city of Majuro—was impacted by three wave events in the space of a week. The onslaught began on 9 December as large waves pounded the eastern side of Majuro. The waves returned a few days later, then again in increased strength on 15 December. Several neighbourhoods of Majuro were flooded. Seawalls broke, more than 200 houses were damaged (BBC 2008), and at least twenty homes were destroyed (Radio Australia 2009), not insignificant numbers in this small town. At least 600 Majuro residents (Journal 2009b) were forced out of their homes—representing a little over 1 per cent of the country's population. They lived in churches, schools, a community center, and with relatives (Johnson 2008b). The flood eroded a cemetery in the Jenrōk neighbourhood, exposing two bodies which had to be returned to their graves and covered by a Public Works crew. Dead fish, coral, rocks, and enormous quantities of trash were washed onto streets and yards, causing concerns about sanitary conditions (Journal 2008b). Hundreds of tons of rubbish had to be removed from the roads (ABC 2008).

There were impacts outside of Majuro as well. On Arno Atoll, just to the east of Majuro, 130 people were forced to leave their homes temporarily (Hezel 2009). An island in Maloelap Atoll was reportedly split in two. Fish were swimming on the inundated airstrip of Roi, on Kwajalein Atoll. On Leb Island, big rocks were washed ashore, breaking coral in their path. Some food crops were damaged in the outer islands when salty water contaminated the soil. A causeway in Kwajalein Atoll experienced washouts.

Fig. 14.3. All that remains of a coastal graveyard after erosion from the December 2008 flood and other wave events: Jenrōk neighbourhood, Majuro.

The day before Christmas, the Marshallese government declared a state of emergency (Journal 2009b). At least $1.5 million of damage had been inflicted in Majuro, in particular to the College of the Marshall Islands (Journal 2009d). There were worries about the effect of the flood on food crops in the outer islands, causing officials from the US Federal Emergency Management Agency to visit the country to assess the situation (Journal 2009a). The government of Taiwan donated over 200,000 kilos of rice to the country in light of the flood and high cost of food, distributing them to various islands (Journal 2009c; Journal 2009e). Displaced families returned to their homes in two or three weeks in most cases.

The event could not be called devastating, but it touched the lives of a large majority of Majuro residents. In a survey I conducted, 70.6 per cent of survey respondents had witnessed the flood firsthand, 74.6 per cent reported that friends' or relatives' houses had been damaged, and 29.7 per cent had seen their own houses damaged.

A DRAMATIC EVENT?

These floods were reportedly the result of a low pressure system north of Majuro combined with expected high tides (Johnson 2008a). One could also perhaps point a finger at climate change, since the sea level rise that the country has already begun to experience (see Solomon et al. 2007: Section 5.5.2.5) makes any flooding event that much worse. But the scientific cause of the flood is irrelevant here. The important point is that, regardless of its cause, the flood is the kind of event that climate change is likely to make more frequent in the future, and thus could serve, for the local people, as vivid, visceral evidence of climate change's reality and the country's vulnerability. Psychologists and behavioural economists have demonstrated an 'availability heuristic' by which risks that are easier to bring to mind are considered more dangerous than equally threatening risks that are difficult to conceive (Patt and Schröter 2007; Sunstein 2006; Tversky and Kahneman 1982). Weinstein (1989) lists several reasons why dramatic, personally experienced events are more likely than impersonal statistics to raise concern and change behaviour: such events are more concrete, more detailed, more certain, easier to remember, and easier to apply to one's own situation without the need to extrapolate from another person's experience to one's own. We might therefore expect the December 2008 flood to increase local concern about the threat of climate change.

To determine if it did, I conducted a survey[1] among Majuro residents regarding perceptions of environmental change, and performed statistical analysis on the results. The answer was an unequivocal 'No'. Exposure to the flood did not boost the total amount of environmental change that the subject reported. It made people no more likely to say that the weather (*lañ*) or climate (*mejatoto*) had changed since the past, or that the ocean had changed in a way related to climate change. It made people no more likely to report that sea level rise was occurring, that flooding had increased, or that erosion had increased. Having been personally affected by the flood also made people no more likely to mention sea level rise, environmental change, or climate change when asked open-ended questions about the country's problems and its future. Nor did it make those who are familiar with scientists' predictions of climate change any more likely to say that they believed these predictions. This was true regardless of how I measured flood exposure: by whether the person had witnessed it, by whether the person's house was damaged by it, by whether

---

[1] I administered a survey orally in the Marshallese language to 146 adults in the D-U-D (downtown) area of Majuro. Seventy-six men and seventy women responded. Ages ranged from 18 to 84, with a mean of 42.2 and a median of 40. Education ranged from none at all to high school plus four years of tertiary education, with a mean of 11th grade and a median of 12th grade.

their friends' or relatives' houses were damaged by it, or by an aggregate measure including all three of these variables.

It is not the case that the survey yielded no results at all: the sample size (146 individuals) was large enough to reveal statistically significant effects. For instance, awareness of the scientific concept of climate change significantly boosted the amount of environmental change reported. Thus, the data did yield robust results. As such, the lack of any link between flood exposure and other variables is a good indication that the flood did nothing, or very little, to make people more concerned about the threat of sea level rise.

It is also worth noting that the overall level of local concern about climate change is only moderate at best. In the survey, only a small percentage—ranging from 4 per cent to 9 per cent depending on the question—spontaneously mentioned climatic or environmental change when asked general questions such as 'What problems are there nowadays in the Marshall Islands?', 'What problems will there be in the future in the Marshall Islands?', 'Are the Marshall Islands different now from the past? If yes, how?' and 'Will Marshall Islanders stay in the country in the future? Why or why not?' Comparing the frequency of different responses to these questions, we find that climate change is not the number one concern of Marshall Islanders, but the number five concern: the more pressing threats are economic hardship, the breakdown of traditional values, population growth, and health issues. When asked open-ended questions about environmental change, 35 per cent spontaneously mentioned sea level rise in their list of changes, while 5 per cent mentioned sea level *fall*; 16 per cent mentioned increased erosion while 0.7 per cent mentioned *decreased* erosion; 14 per cent mentioned increased flooding while 2 per cent mentioned *decreased* flooding. Thus, while individuals are far more likely to report changes that are consistent with global warming than changes that are not consistent (for instance, almost no one reported sea level *fall* or *decreased* erosion), only a fairly small minority report specific changes such as increased flooding.

Thus, the threat of climate change is only moderately salient to Marshall Islanders. This is in spite of the fact that sea level rise and other local manifestations of global warming have already begun in this country (Solomon et al. 2007: Section 5.5.2.5), and that radio announcements, newspaper articles, and local workshops have educated the populace about the threat, resulting in most Marshall Islanders (though by no means all) having heard of the theory and professing belief in it.

LOCAL EXPLANATIONS FOR THE FLOOD

Why did the flood fail to increase concern? Why was this not the '9/11 for climate change' (Sunstein 2006: 4) in the Marshall Islands? More generally, why is the salience of the threat only moderate even in a country whose very habitability is at stake? These sorts of questions are commonly asked by policymakers, activists, and researchers whenever a disaster fails to cause the sort of increased concern and preparedness that they hope for (see for instance Patt and Schröter 2007). The problem is this: when a calamity occurs, it is clearly a vivid example of something, but a vivid example of *what*? In some cases the answer is clear: the events of 9/11 were unambiguously attributable to terrorism, and they therefore caused an enormous increase in concern about this threat. But in other catastrophes the cause is not so clear: should we attribute the high death tolls of Hurricane Katrina and the 2003 European heatwave to global climate change, to government incompetence, or to nothing at all?

In terms of increasing concern about climate change, the timing of the Marshall Islands flood was fortuitous. The event occurred just as climate change was beginning to receive significant attention in the country's media: in the previous year there had been mentions of climate change in thirty of the fifty-two issues of the *Marshall Islands Journal,* and a month before the flood there had been a major article on the topic (Journal 2008a). In the time between the flood and when I started interviewing locals, there had been sixteen issues of the *Marshall Island Journal* with mentions of climate change (including many full articles), and between then and when I began conducting the survey, there had been thirty-one issues of the *Marshall Islands Journal* with mentions of climate change. During these periods there had also been many local workshops aimed at increasing awareness of climate change, in particular those organised by the women's NGO Women United Together Marshall Islands (WUTMI).

So did locals attribute the flood to global warming? A quick perusal of official statements on the subject seems to indicate that they did. The deputy director of the Office of Environmental Planning and Policy Coordination said of the flood, 'It shows that we're extremely vulnerable. If the tide had been two feet higher, it would have been much worse. At the global level, we're trying to explain that the smallest change in sea levels will have a big impact on our islands. Even a few centimetres increase in sea level will impact our islands' (Johnson 2008a). Similarly, Hirobo Obeketan, a local businessman and member of a disaster management group, stated that the flood was at least in part due to global climate change, and that it demonstrated the need for more aggressive protection of the shoreline (Australia Network 2008).

But most locals did not make the same connection. I asked thirty-two adults why the flood had happened. The most common answer was 'I don't know' (47 per cent). The second most common answer was that the flood was a result of natural cycles such as twice-monthly spring tides or seasonal changes in wave activity (22 per cent). The third most common answer was American military activity or radiation from erstwhile nuclear testing (19 per cent). Only 6 per cent mentioned sea level rise or the scientific concept of climate change; 3 per cent said the flood was due to a typhoon, and 3 per cent blamed local dredging.

This result leads to further questions. First, why did so many people have no theory as to why the flood happened? It is *unusual* events, those that are in the foreground rather than the background, which trigger the need for explanation or blame (Einhorn and Hogarth 1986: 5). What counts as unusual will depend on a community's experiences and expectations of variability (McIntosh et al. 2000b: 17). So did locals consider the flood to be out of the ordinary?

Most did not: 71 per cent of survey respondents said that events like the December 2008 flood had occurred in the past. In fact, when I asked about 'the flood' (*ibwijleplep eo*) six to nine months after the event, people were not always sure which flood I meant; this was not *the* flood, only *a* flood. Respondents were particularly likely to mention the flood of November 1979, which was more damaging than the December 2008 flood by any measure: it temporarily displaced five thousand Majuro residents and wreaked US$30 million in damage (Spennemann 1996). Another major flooding episode in living memory occurred on Jaluit Atoll in January 1958, inundating the land under two metres of water in some areas, felling 70 to 90 per cent of trees in other areas, destroying almost all of the property on the atoll, and killing thirty-one people (Blumenstock 1958; Hezel 2005: 9; Spennemann and Marschner 1994: 11). More recently, Majuro was impacted by a typhoon-induced flood in January 1992.

Compared to some of these floods—and to even more destructive disasters, further in the past—the 2008 event was inconsequential. Indeed, it was used as an argument *against* concern about climate change in a staged debate[2] in February 2009 over the inevitability of climate change-induced exodus: in an argument against migration, a debater said 'Last December . . . we faced a high tide which didn't even sacrifice a [single] life.'

We gain more insight into the lack of attribution by examining Marshallese notions of natural variability. In each day one sees two high tides (*ibwij*) and two low tides (*pāāt*). On a twice-monthly cycle, there are larger variations: periods of large tidal variation (spring tide) are called *iaḷap*, while periods of low tidal variation (neap tide) are called *idik*. *Iaḷap* times will produce very high tides (*ibwijleplep*) and very low tides (*pāāt mōṇakṇak*).

In addition to these twice-daily and twice-monthly cycles, there are yearly cycles. The Marshallese language names two seasons: *añōneañ* ('north wind') and *rak* ('south'). There is no clear dividing line between the two seasons, but *añōneañ* corresponds roughly to the period from September to April, and *rak* between May and August. Informants may disagree with each other about the

---

[2] This was between the College of the Marshall Islands and the University of the South Pacific, as part of the February 2009 Education Week with the theme of climate change, organized by the Ministry of Education.

exact timing of events, but there is very good general agreement about the characteristics of the two seasons.

The *rak* season is expected to be relatively windless (*lur*) with smooth seas (*ḷae*). This makes the season favourable for open-ocean activities like sailing. People say the rhyming phrase '*Juḷae bwe eḷae*' ('July because the water is smooth'), as July is in the heart of the *rak* season. This is also the season of breadfruit, a staple crop in the outer islands. In addition, rainfall is abundant, so there is no concern about fresh water availability. *Rak*, then, is the time of ease and plenty.

In contrast, the *aṅōneaṅ* season is windy (*ḷap kōto*) with a fairly constant wind from the northeast, causing large waves (*ḷap ṇo*). This makes the season unfavourable for boating in the open ocean, although the lagoon remains calm enough for many kinds of fishing. December and January are expected to bring the largest waves and highest tides. Some time during this season—perhaps as early as November or as late as May, according to different informants—one expects a *Kapiḷak*, a particular weather pattern that causes strong winds, rains, large waves, and high tides. *Aṅōneaṅ* is also the drier season, with water catchments running low and droughts an ever-present possibility. Breadfruit is not available in the same abundance as in the *rak* season, and not available at all during December and January, so people rely more on preserved food, in particular preserved breadfruit. So *aṅōneaṅ* is the season of relative danger and privation.

The most general point to glean from this is that a certain amount of variability is considered normal: not every period of high waves is seen as an anomaly or cause for rumination. A proverb expresses this: '*Ewōr tarlik tarar in bōkā*', which literally means 'there is a tidal movement towards the lagoon and towards the ocean', or 'the tide goes back and forth', referring to natural cyclical variation.[3] On this note, the word for 'very high tide' and the word for 'flood' are the same: *ibwijleplep*. Even the Biblical flood is called *ibwijleplep*. This underscores the fact that what we would call a 'flood' (a disaster, an unusual event) may be perceived by locals as merely a high tide (an expected, natural event). This is not to say that Marshallese people believe in a static universe—indeed, the discourse of changing culture is pervasive in the country—only that a certain amount of cyclical variability is part of the ordinary, unremarkable working of the world, and what outsiders may see as early warning signs of climate change may be perceived by insiders as part of that natural variation.

---

[3] The exact interpretation of this phrase varies according to the individual: some say it refers to the inevitability of retribution after being wronged, or to the inevitability of bad times to balance out the good. In all interpretations, however, there is reference to a natural cyclical balance in the world. Similarly, *ukōt bōkā* (literally 'turn the tide') means 'to return a favour', also referring to a rightful restoration of balance.

In addition to this general point, we also see that Marshallese weather concepts provide locals with several specific natural phenomena to which they can attribute floods. The December 2008 flood struck the country during the heart of the *añōneañ* season, when people expected danger from the sea, and privation in general, to be at its highest. Had the flood occurred a few months earlier or later, there might have been disagreement about whether the flood had occurred in *añōneañ* or *rak*, since, as I mentioned before, the cut-off between the two is fuzzy. But the period of December to January is the quintessential *añōneañ* time, with its rough waves, heavy winds, and droughts, so there was no doubt that the flood occurred during the expected season. (Note also that the three floods within living memory mentioned above all occurred during the *añōneañ* season, further reinforcing the idea that inclement weather is to be expected in this season.) Locals also could (and did) attribute the flood to the *iaḷap* (spring tide) and to the particular kind of weather pattern called the *Kapiḷak*. With three natural phenomena to pin the flood on, the event was hardly unexpected.[4]

Regarding the third of these explanations—the *Kapiḷak*—it is interesting to note that this weather pattern has extremely uncertain timing and characteristics, being said to occur anywhere between November and May and to involve anything from strong winds to high tides. Thus, almost any atmospheric or oceanic disturbance during more than half the year can be called a *Kapiḷak*. Whatever the reason for the vagueness of this term—whether it is an old characteristic of the *Kapiḷak* concept or merely a product of fragmenting and declining traditional knowledge in the modern day—it allows locals to regard as normal many weather events which otherwise might be seen as remarkable.

Putting this together, it becomes obvious why many people offered no theory as to why the flood happened, or attributed the flood to natural cycles: a sort of null attribution, saying that it happened because things are the way they are.

The other common attribution was to radiation or American military activity. This can be understood in light of the psychological and cultural effects of nuclear testing in the Marshall Islands, leading to an inclination among Marshall Islanders to attribute many sorts of ills to lingering radiation (see Rudiak-Gould 2009: 56–60). This discussion, however, is beyond the scope of this chapter. For our present purposes, the important point is this: blaming the December 2008 flood on military activity frames the event as being unnatural, yet also subsumes it under the heading of a fairly familiar

---

[4] A government official involved in climate change policy chose to frame the event differently, stating 'We weren't in our maximum high tide period, but [the waves] still impacted many areas in Majuro' (Johnson 2008a), thus portraying the flood as an unexpected event, indicative of a worrisome trend. Most of the populace, however, did not speak of the event in these terms.

threat which locals have faced for more than sixty years. Thus, this attribution could only increase concern about a pre-existing hazard, and not the newer threat that is climate change. Again we see that the flood failed to register as a sign of something new, being attributed instead to older and more familiar hazards.

CONCLUSION: THE PAST AND THE PRESENT IN DIALOGUE

Thus, the widespread inclination among Marshall Islanders was to 'normalize' the December 2008 flood: to regard it as unexceptional rather than indicative of a burgeoning catastrophe such as climate change. This is understandable in light of the fact that Marshall Islanders have always lived with high levels of environmental risk and that these ever-present threats are incorporated into their views of nature. It is therefore unsurprising thst the flood did nothing to increase concern about the country's environmental future.

What wider lessons about human response to environmental disaster can be gained from this case study? Most fundamentally, people do not react directly to disasters, but to their perceptions of them (Barnett and Busse 2002: 29). What an outsider sees as a clear sign of impending catastrophe is not necessarily what the insider sees as such; this is true whether the outsider is a climate change activist puzzling over lack of concern in a vulnerable nation, or an archaeologist wondering why a prehistoric community failed to prepare for a coming calamity. Presentism and ethnocentrism are essentially alike in missing this point.

More specifically, societies have always lived with environmental risk, and every society accepts a particular level of such risk as normal. If a new threat is to be perceived and confronted as such—if it is to convince people to discard their usual assumptions of what can happen and to change their behaviour accordingly—it must do more than simply cause harm: it must be perceptibly different in size or kind from that which preceded it, and it must be clearly part of a larger trend rather than a one-off event.

The early stages of climate change in the Marshall Islands fail all of these criteria: they are little different and hardly larger than the hazards which preceded them, and even a climatologist finds it difficult to attribute them directly and unambiguously to climate change. Such slow, 'creeping' threats— as opposed to sudden, 'exploding' ones—offer communities time to act before the situation becomes dire, but that same gradualness undermines the impetus for action by making it difficult to perceive that a new threat is at work. The catch-22 known as Giddens's paradox (Giddens 2009) points to the fact that the impacts of climate change will be obvious only after it is too late to avert them. This usually refers to the unlikelihood of polluting countries mending their ways in time to avert climatic self-destruction, but it can apply equally well to the case of adaptation in countries that are impacted by global warming yet have done little to cause it: by the time that the necessity of adaptation becomes obvious, it is too late to adapt. Giddens's paradox can be extended yet further, applying not just to global warming but to any creeping environmental hazard, past or present.

Thus we see how the past and the present can inform each other. Just as societies use their memories of previous disasters to interpret contemporary ones, archaeologists can apply their knowledge of prehistoric responses to the modern day. The application can flow in the other direction as well: researchers can use contemporary studies, even of apparently unprecedented threats such as global anthropogenic climate change, to inform their understanding of the past. If the barriers to action in the present day are essentially similar to those in the past, this indicates how deeply rooted they are and how difficult to overcome; but it also points to a practical and constructive role for archaeological knowledge in the twenty-first century.

15

Climate Change and Cultural Dynamics: Lessons from the Past for the Future[1]

David G. Anderson, Kirk A. Maasch, and Daniel H. Sandweiss

INTRODUCTION

As the twenty-first century winds onward, it is becoming increasingly clear that understanding how climate affects human cultural systems is critically important. Indeed, it has been argued by many researchers that how we respond to changing global climate is one of the greatest scientific and political challenges facing our planetary technological civilization, comparable and closely intertwined with concerns about biological or nuclear warfare, famine, disease, overpopulation, or environmental degradation. By any reasonable evaluation of the evidence, this century, and likely the several centuries that follow it, will be characterized by dramatic climate change, perhaps as significant in terms of its impact on our species as any climatic episodes that have occurred in the past.

What we don't know with much certainty is how these environmental changes will play out across the planet, and how individuals as well as nation states will respond to them. Archaeology has a major role to play in helping us move through this period of crisis, however, by showing us how human cultures in the past responded to dramatic changes in climate. As the work of many archaeological scholars has shown, climate change has not invariably proven to be a bad thing: it is how people respond to it that is critical (e.g. Anderson et al. 2007b; Cooper and Sheets 2012; Crumley 2000, 2006, 2007;

[1] This chapter has been based, in part, on work presented in an earlier paper on the subject (Anderson et al. 2007a), although the text here is original. The chapters in the book *Climate Change and Cultural Dynamics: A Global Perspective on Mid-Holocene Transitions* (Anderson et al. 2007b) cited throughout this chapter, it should be noted, are summaries of extensive prior work by palaeoclimatologists and archaeologists, and provide a much more comprehensive bibliography and discussion for the interested reader.

Hardesty 2007; McAnany and Yoffee 2010; McIntosh et al. 2000; Redman 2004a; Sandweiss and Quilter 2008; Sassaman and Anderson 1996; Tainter 2000). Archaeology working in tandem with a host of palaeoenvironmental and historical disciplines has lessons for our modern world and, as this volume demonstrates, we as a profession are making great strides in getting our message out. Perhaps the most important lesson from the past is that people, through their actions, are the drivers of cultural change, including response to climate change. Societies are not, however, monolithic entities that 'chose' to succeed or fail; people as individuals, groups, or factions through their actions generate outcomes, and often some demonstrate remarkable flexibility and resilience (Cooper and Sheets 2012; Diamond 2005; McAnany and Yoffee 2010). This is not to say optimal or happy endings are inevitable, only that they are possible. Likewise, change and diversification typify human response to climate change, not stasis or uniformity. Human response to climate change has varied, with some cultures striving to maintain the status quo in their current setting, sometimes unsuccessfully, others adapting their technology or organization to meet new conditions, and still others relocating to new areas.

This chapter was prepared during a period of record sustained low and then high temperatures in eastern North America in the winter, spring, and summer of 2010. The reasons for these unusual seasonal conditions were the subject of extensive informed and not so well informed public discourse, illustrating how varied humans' responses can be to conditions occurring right before their eyes. Interest in climate and climate change has attracted increasing attention in recent years among the scientific community as well as the general public, and research and publication on the subject as well as political debate about what to do about it has grown markedly. There is an old adage attributed to Mark Twain, but perhaps more appropriately to his collaborator Charles Dudley Warner, that 'everyone talks about the weather, but nobody does anything about it'. Unquestionably a lot of people are now talking about the weather, and a great many scientists are researching the subject. Doing something about the weather, either directly by attempting to change it, perhaps through reducing greenhouse gases, or indirectly by learning how to cope with new conditions, is now something facing everyone, and something that many people and nations are attempting to address.

Children being born today in developed nations are likely, given current life expectancy, to live until near the end of the century, and as a result will witness significant changes in many areas in temperature, sea level, glacier and ice sheet extent, and snow and rainfall patterns, mandating the relocation of and changes in plant and animal communities, including human populations (IPCC, 2007: 8, 16). Indeed, the well known migrations of peoples in the late prehistoric and early historic eras, like those of the Angles and Saxons in north-western Europe, the Huns or Mongols in Asia, or the Bantu-speaking peoples in Africa, may pale in comparison to the movements that may occur in the years to come, at least in terms of the sheer numbers of people involved and the geographic areas covered (see Stipp 2004). The occupation and use of whole regions will likely change markedly, particularly as rising sea levels or changing rainfall patterns affect settlement. To cite one example, as the Arctic Ocean becomes ice-free in the summer, it will likely come to serve as a new shipping route as well as become an area increasingly favourable for the exploitation of minerals, oil, and biota, mandating increased settlement along its margins (e.g. Schiermeier 2007; Screen and Simmonds 2010). The concomitant thawing of the permafrost will undoubtedly change the accessibility and utility of this terrain, as well as threaten an archaeological and palaeobiological record currently preserved in a deep freeze. In a like fashion, around the world, areas now thinly settled may become attractive, while regions of dense population, particularly in low-lying coastal areas, may have to be abandoned, all of which will create new archaeological sites or threaten existing ones.

The question is thus not will the climate change, for it always does, but what will we do about it. The record from the human past gives us numerous examples from which to work and to offer guidance. When presenting our archaeological narratives, however, we must be careful about what we say and how we say it. That is, we should avoid overdramatizing the positive or the negative, but instead document what happened, and why, and what would be the likely parallels in the modern world. Fortunately, archaeology is but one of a wide range of disciplines exploring the impact of climate change past and present. Indeed, modern archaeological research is first and foremost multi-disciplinary research, and its successful practice mandates consideration of a wide range of data and, ideally, a wide range of approaches. To cite a few examples, archaeologists having been working with palaeoclimatologists to determine the effects of past climate change on human societies, examining topics as diverse as the impacts of El Niño-induced rainfall and erosion in the Americas (e.g. Richardson and Sandweiss 2008; Sandweiss and Quilter 2008; Sandweiss et al. 1996, 2001, 2007); how variation in rainfall or temperature can affect agricultural productivity and surplus mobilization in the prehistoric American southeast and the Mayan area of Central America (Anderson et al. 1995; Freidel and Shaw 2000; Yaeger and Hodell 2008); and how changes in the ranges of floral and faunal resources in the Late Pleistocene Old and New Worlds, examined using procedures such as ecological niche modelling, can help determine where on the landscape past human populations might be found (Banks et al. 2006): this procedure is especially effective at documenting where new biotic ranges might be located given changing climate. The successful reconstruction of climate and culture change in the past involves working with information from multiple sources, and it is clear that multiple independent lines of evidence and argument yield greater insight than individual scholars or disciplines working alone (see Crumley, Chapter 17 this volume and Sandweiss and Kelley 2012 for further examples of similar work and discussion of the role of archaeologists in global environmental debates).

LESSONS FROM PAST EPISODES OF UNUSUALLY WARM GLOBAL CLIMATE

At present most researchers examining climate change are thinking about developments no more than a century or so into the future, although there are important and somewhat under-appreciated exceptions looking ahead hundreds and in some cases thousands of years (Berger and Loutre 2002; Loutre and Berger 2000; Zickfeld et al. 2010). Most projections, however, focus on change in the twenty-first century, within the lifetimes of people currently alive or their immediate descendants. Global surface temperatures in AD 2100 are assumed to be between 2° and 4.5°C warmer than at present, and sea level perhaps no more than a metre higher (IPCC 2007: 12). Archaeologists and palaeoclimatologists use comparisons with warm periods in the past to suggest possible outcomes of current trends. During the Eemian, the penultimate interglacial period *c.*120,000 years ago, for example, high latitude temperatures were some 3°–5°C above those at present and sea level was perhaps 4 to 6 m above current level (IPCC 2007:9). Unfortunately, the Eemian lies in the fairly remote past, and since it has not received anywhere near as much research attention as the current interglacial, it is difficult to draw detailed lessons for the modern world from it. The fact that sea level was several metres higher during that interglacial, in a period when climate was not being influenced by anthropogenic effects (greenhouse gas emissions), however, should give anyone pause, considering that much of the archaeological record of humanity's past as well as an appreciable portion of its current population is found on or near the coast.

Another episode of warmer global climate that is used to explore change in cultural systems in the near term is the Medieval Warm Period between about AD 800 and AD 1200. Only a millennium in the past, our climate and cultural records for this period are much better, and one clear lesson from archaeology and history is that climate conditions as well as cultural responses were highly varied, with conditions favourable for human population growth in some areas, such as among the agricultural Mississippian societies of the southeastern United States, and less favourable in other areas, such as among the coastal hunter-gatherers of California (Anderson 2001; Fagan 2008; Jones et al. 1999; Milner 2004). The period was only a few hundred years long, however, and global climate was similar to that at present, making it a useful analogue for a world in which climate conditions stabilize as they are at present. Unfortunately, stable climate does not seem likely in either the short or the longer term, barring a major and sudden change in human behaviour.

The Mid-Holocene warm period from about 9,000 to about 5,000 years ago offers (we argue) perhaps the best parallel from the past through which to explore the impacts of sustained global temperatures higher than those at present, something long noted in the technical and popular literature (e.g. Anderson et al. 2007a; deMenocal et al. 2000; Mitchell 1990). The Mid-Holocene period is not an exact parallel to modern circumstances, however, since the observed warming was due to orbital parameters resulting in greater solar radiation (insolation), and not to anthropogenic effects such as greenhouse gas production. For exploring changes in climate, biota, and human culture due to prolonged warmer temperatures, however, the period is the best we have, and a close parallel with what is likely to occur in the coming decades (e.g. Anderson et al. 2007a, 2007b; Ganopolski et al. 1998; Mitchell 1990: 1180–3). The remainder of this chapter briefly explores what happened during the Mid-Holocene, and how study of this period can help us prepare for the changes likely to occur in the decades and centuries to come.

THE MID-HOLOCENE AS A PROXY FOR THE CLIMATE AND CULTURE CHANGE IN THE COMING MILLENNIUM

Studying what happened during the Mid-Holocene in specific regions illustrates the kind and extent of changes in climate and biota in these areas, and how they could have influenced the human societies present. Correlation of climate and cultural phenomena does not equate with a causal linkage, of course, and relationships must be demonstrated rather than assumed to exist. To cite perhaps the most critical variable of interest to past and present human populations, Mid-Holocene precipitation conditions were of particular importance to agricultural populations then emerging or present in many areas, and having ready access to potable water was critical for human survival anywhere. Observed patterns in precipitation and in the availability of fresh water during the Mid-Holocene (e.g. Mitchell 1990; Ganopolski et al. 1998) are similar to those predicted for the future, when it is likely that there will be 'significantly increased precipitation in eastern parts of North and South America, northern Europe, and northern and central Asia [and drying] ... in the Sahel, the Mediterranean, southern Africa, and parts of southern Asia' (IPCC 2007: 7). Parts of the Sahara were grassland during the Mid-Holocene, and here and in other parts of the world, such as the Atacama Desert of coastal Peru and Chile, minor changes in rainfall and temperature had a major impact on the occurrence of resources important to human populations living in these areas. The origins of Egyptian as well as western South American civilizations have been attributed in some scenarios to peoples coalescing in river valleys like the Nile as deserts expanded and the ranges of flora and fauna shifted, resulting in the adoption of new forms of social organization to deal with higher population densities, as well as of new food sources such as agriculture and riverine or maritime fisheries (e.g. Grosjean et al. 2007; Moseley and Keefer 2008; Sandweiss et al. 2007; Wendorf et al. 2007). Small changes in climate appear to have had a far greater effect on biota and culture in desert and grassland regions than in areas with much greater vegetation cover. While the Sahara was green in the Mid-Holocene (Kuper and Kröpelin 2006; Wendorf et al. 2007), there were also regional trends toward greater aridity, particularly in southern Mesopotamia from about 5,000 years ago, after state-level societies had become widespread (Kennett and Kennett 2007; Rosen 2007). In the Atacama Desert, millennial-scale changes in water availability may have led to new religious practices built around artificial mummification (Marquet et al. 2012). Some classic cases of societal collapse, such as the end of the Old Kingdom in Egypt and the Akaddian empire in Mesopotamia, both events occurring about 4,200 years ago, may have been caused by climate change, and specifically by regional drying and changes in the flow of major drainages like the Nile, Tigris, and Euphrates (deMenocal 2001; Stanley et al. 2003; Weiss et al. 1993; but see Yoffee 2005:143; Zettler 2003:17–29).

As is happening again at present, extensive and sometimes fairly large changes in the ranges of plants and animals, both altitudinally and latitudinally, occurred worldwide during the Mid-Holocene (e.g. Delcourt and Delcourt 2004; Parmesan 2006; Walther et al. 2002). For example, the boundary between taiga and tundra (the furthest point at which trees occur) moved as much as 250 km in many areas, and many cold-tolerant species moved to higher elevations (e.g. Delcourt and Delcourt 2004; Ganopolski et al. 1998: 1918). These changes in distribution occurred over large areas and were the result of comparatively minor temperature changes—typically no more than one or two degrees Celsius—a lesson modern planners concerned with the effects of a changing climate would do well to remember. Major declines and range shifts in northern European elm (*Ulmus* spp.) and eastern North American hemlock (*Tsuga canadensis*) occurred during the Mid-Holocene: warmer conditions, drought and insect and pathogen infestations are implicated, illustrating how changing climate can produce a range of effects, including the introduction of diseases formerly foreign to a given area (e.g. Bennett and Fuller 2002; Digerfeldt 1997; Dincauze 2000:188–91; Foster et al. 2006; Parker et al. 2002). These broad changes in tree cover are associated with major changes in the human societies in these regions, with increased hunting–gathering activities observed in portions of northeastern North America and the initial adoption of agriculture in northern Europe (Dincauze 2000; Karlén and Larsson 2007; Sanger et al. 2007).

Other major changes in forest community composition and range that occurred during the Mid-Holocene include the expansion of western red cedar (*Thuja plicata*) in the Pacific northwest and coniferous longleaf pine (*Pinus palustris*) in the southeastern United States (Anderson et al. 2007b; Delcourt and Delcourt 2004; Fedje and Mathewes 2005: 57; Moss et al. 2007; Watts et al. 1996). The increase in red cedar is thought to have led to the classic northwest coastal adaptation characterized by the use of the wood in plank houses and boats and in totem poles. In the southeast, the pine forests replaced a formerly more mesic community across much of the coastal plain, leading to a reduction in mast for game and an apparent relocation of human populations to the margins of major rivers or well into the interior, where deciduous forests continued to occur. Shellfish began to be intensively used in both regions, and monumental architecture appeared in the southeast in some areas, indicating the emergence of more elaborate forms of social organization. The greater use of shellfish is attributed, in part, to a stabilization of sea level as well as a need to exploit a wider range of resources as human populations grew. Not long after the intensive use of shellfish became widespread in the southeast a number of local plants were domesticated. Changing conditions led to changes in technology, particularly related to food production, and the same is likely to happen in the twenty-first century and after. Palaeosubsistence debris from archaeological sites worldwide provides useful data on changes in the abundance of species that appear related to changes in climate; molluscan fauna are particularly sensitive to small changes in temperature and salinity, and are thus especially useful climate markers (Lutaenko et al. 2007; Sandweiss et al. 2007). Just as ecological and cultural refuges were critical to the survival of species and societies during periods of climate change in the past, comparable 'arks' are likely to be needed in the years to come.

Climate-based changes in range and productivity apply to domesticated plants and animals as well as to wild species like molluscs or anadromous fish. Variation in the number of frost-free days, the occurrence and amount of rainfall, and the intensity of wind or hail storms can profoundly affect the productivity of certain plant species. Agricultural populations past and present have been dependent upon their ability to create and store surplus production, and crop failures lasting more than a year or two in succession are frequently catastrophic (Fagan 2000; Le Roy Ladurie 1971). Our own diet will be affected by changes in climate and related changes in the ranges of plant and animal species, and consideration must be directed to ensuring the reliability of food sources, not just their location. Cold-adapted species will not only relocate toward higher latitudes but also to higher elevations, at least as long as such locations where they can thrive exist: a pattern of vertical movement of biota is already under way in the Appalachians (e.g. Delcourt and Delcourt 2004). Depending on local conditions there were sometimes lags between climate change and biotic response, in some cases with responses taking centuries to play out (Davis and Botkin 1985). This needs to be borne in mind when pollen and charcoal particle data are considered, since changes may not correspond temporally to changes in climate (R. Anderson and Smith 1997).

When it comes to climate change we must think globally, but also focus on how matters played out locally, since they may not correspond to expectations derived from proxy measures based on conditions over broad areas, such as oxygen isotope ratios in ice or ocean sediment cores (e.g. Kirch 2007; Maasch 2008; Mayewski 2008). Research focusing on the Mid-Holocene in particular regions indicates that climate change was not uniform or identical everywhere, in the sense that it was not characterized by directional trends toward warmer and dryer or cooler and wetter conditions. Within particular regions, such as the Amazon basin, the Mayan area, and southeastern North America, rainfall regimes differed appreciably in different areas over the course of the Mid-Holocene (Anderson et al. 2007b; Meggers 2007; Voorhies and Metcalfe 2007). Climate change must always be considered in terms of its effects at the local scale, both spatially within small areas and at intra-annual, inter-annual, and decadal temporal scales. Such variation can be as important as longer-term climate trends.

Perhaps the most intensively studied example of relatively short-term climate change and its effect on human society is the El Niño Southern Oscillation, or ENSO, whose effects are observed widely, with variation on an inter-annual to decadal scale but with changes also observed over much longer intervals. El Niño frequency and intensity increased for several centuries in the Mid-Holocene after about 6,000 years ago and again in the Late Holocene after about 3,000 years ago. The changes in precipitation regimes and biota led to increased runoff and erosion that created problems for complex societies in western South America but also occasionally led to new adaptations (Moseley and Keefer 2008; Richardson and Sandweiss 2008; Sandweiss and Quilter 2008; Sandweiss et al. 1996, 2001, 2007).

In the southeastern United States a similar pattern is observed during these two intervals, around 6,000 and 3,000 years ago, which are characterized by, respectively, the emergence of monumental architecture of shell or earth in several areas and the end of a number of complex Late Archaic societies, including Poverty Point, which had the largest monumental architecture found during the Archaic period in eastern North America (Kidder 2006, 2010; Thomas and Sanger 2010). Changes in precipitation regimes, flooding patterns, and fluctuations in sea level that affected the availability of subsistence resources are thought have played a role in bringing about the observed changes in culture (e.g. Kidder 2006, 2010), although many other factors are also implicated, such as regional population density, established traditions of behaviour, intensity of land use, and patterns of regional interaction (Anderson 2002, 2004, 2010; Gibson 2010; Hamilton 1999; Sanger 2010; Sassaman 2010a, 2010b; Thompson 2010). In both western South America and the

southeastern United States, moreover, diversity characterized local adaptations during the Middle and Late Holocene as well as the responses to
changing climatic conditions.

Evidence for warfare is observed during the Mid-Holocene for the first time
in many areas, although whether climate change had much to do with it is
uncertain. Some view warfare as a phenomenon dependent on population
density, although it is also a means by which individuals and societies can
obtain status and resources at the expense of others. That climate change has
the potential to lead to major conflict is something politicians and military
planners are taking seriously at the highest levels. As the US Department of
Defense noted in its most recent Quadrennial Defense Report:

> The U.S. Global Change Research Program, composed of 13 federal agencies,
> reported in 2009 that climate-related changes are already being observed in every
> region of the world, including the United States and its coastal waters. Among
> these physical changes are increases in heavy downpours, rising temperature and
> sea level, rapidly retreating glaciers, thawing permafrost, lengthening growing
> seasons, lengthening ice-free seasons in the oceans and on lakes and rivers, earlier
> snowmelt, and alterations in river flows.
>
> Assessments conducted by the intelligence community indicate that climate
> change could have significant geopolitical impacts around the world, contributing
> to poverty, environmental degradation, and the further weakening of fragile
> governments. Climate change will contribute to food and water scarcity, will
> increase the spread of disease, and may spur or exacerbate mass migration.
>
> While climate change alone does not cause conflict, it may act as an accelerant
> of instability or conflict, placing a burden to respond on civilian institutions and
> militaries around the world (DoD 2010: 84–5).

While it is hoped that conflict will be avoided, climate change will affect
critical areas such as freshwater supplies and crop yields. It will also result in
the opening of new areas as ice caps melt, and cause other regions to be
abandoned as agriculture becomes impractical or as sea levels rise. Changes in
wind patterns and ocean currents will influence maritime traffic, much as it
did earlier in the Holocene (A. Anderson et al. 2007).

Human populations have responded to climate change through changes in
organization or technology, or through migration, the relocation from one
area to another. They have also exploited new resources. Beginning in the
Mid-Holocene, and especially from about 6,000 years ago, human use of
shellfish and agriculture began to intensify in many areas and helped to
make possible the development of complex societies in many parts of the
world. Complex hunting–gathering cultures that emerged at this time include
the Jomon culture in Japan and the Russian Far East (Lutaenko et al. 2007), the
Shell Mound and coastal Archaic cultures of the southeastern United States
(Anderson et al. 2007b; Sassaman 2010b; Thomas and Sanger 2010), and
various societies along the western coast of North America (Jones 2010;

Kennett 2005; Moss et al. 2007). That minor fluctuations in sea level can have profound effects on the location of settlements is a lesson archaeology teaches well; in the southeastern United States, for example, coastal Archaic shell midden sites were often abandoned and their peoples displaced kilometres away by rises and falls encompassing no more than a metre or two (e.g. Sanger 2010). These relocations only affected a few hundreds of people, however, while similar shifts occurring today would affect millions of people in the southeast alone, and tens of millions worldwide. Minor changes in sea level in the area of the Persian Gulf appear to have played a role in the emergence of civilization in ancient Mesopotamia; cities fabled in history such as Eridu and Ur were apparently much closer to the sea when they first appear in the historical record (Kennett and Kennett 2006: 74, 78; 2007). Sea level rise is regarded with such interest that on Google Earth it is possible to find the area that each one metre increment would flood. The changes in sea level that will likely occur in the centuries to come will prove to be a major challenge for our civilization and in the process will damage or destroy countless archaeological and historic sites. Many archaeologists in the twentieth century worked in reservoir areas that were about to be flooded; in the twenty-first century and after, our profession may be focusing more on coastal areas.

THE FUTURE IS NOT FIXED, BUT IS UP TO US

How does studying climate and culture change during the Holocene help us in the modern world? In many ways. Lessons range from revealing the large-scale changes over time and space that can occur in vegetation and precipitation, and how humans have responded to them, to developing new ways of thinking about how we can best deal with similar changes that are likely to come. Climate change during the Mid-Holocene helped shape the development of complex societies in several parts of the world, not only when conditions favoured the aggregation of larger numbers of people but also when less favourable conditions required new social strategies to maintain existing populations. The Mid-Holocene record also shows how environmental change can trigger a range of cultural responses, from collapse to reorganization to expansion. It appears to have forced or necessitated culture change in some areas, deliberate efforts to maintain the status quo in others, and no obvious impact in yet others. The demonstration of spatio-temporal correlation between climate and culture change, of course, does not prove they are related. It does, however, mandate consideration of possible linkages.

To conclude, Holocene climate has been variable at spatial and temporal scales, a record receiving ever increasing attention by palaeoclimatologists and archaeologists alike. Climate cycles roughly 1,500 years in extent are well documented (e.g. Bond et al. 1997), and it is clear from archaeological, historical, and palaeoclimatic proxy records that climate change has had a significant impact on human culture as well as on natural ecosystems. Climate change since the Late Pleistocene has sometimes occurred rapidly, over decades and even within a few years, and, if the past is any guide, we can expect similar episodes of rapid change in the future (NRC 2002). The Mid-Holocene was a time of major change in human societies in many parts of the world, and included the rise of civilization in some areas, continuity with minimal change in other areas, and large scale movements of peoples in still others. The lessons are both sobering and comforting. When faced with significant environmental change, what was critical was how human societies reacted (McAnany and Yoffee 2010; Skinner 2008). Almost invariably, people responded as best they could to the changes occurring; we are a resilient species. While societal collapse or abandonment occurred in some areas, people typically relocated rather than died out, or reorganized their social systems. In some cases, environmental change led to growth and expansion occurred. We as individuals and as nations in the twenty-first century face dramatic changes in the world around us, and unlike earlier societies we have a pretty good idea how to address them. Whether we will not merely endure but prevail, as William Faulkner stated in his Nobel acceptance speech (see Frenz 1969), is up to us, and will depend on how we exercise our ability for perseverance, compassion, and sacrifice.

ACKNOWLEDGEMENTS

This chapter was initially presented as a paper in the session 'Human Responses to Mid-late Holocene Climate Change' organized by Val Attenbrow and John Gratton, at the Sixth World Archaeological Congress, Dublin, Ireland, 1 July 2008. The authors wish to thank Matthew Davies and Freda Nkirote M'Mbogori for inviting us to participate in this volume, and for helpful suggestions with the manuscript.

Part V

New Directions

In this final section three chapters emphasize new directions for the application of environmental archaeology. They also point to the need for archaeologists to re-centre aspects of their discipline and to engage more fully with cognate scholars and policy makers. In Chapter 16, James Fairhead presents a view of the potential of environmental archaeology from the vantage point of ecological anthropology. He argues strongly for the role of archaeology in breaking down accepted environmental norms and narratives and illustrates this potential through West African examples. In particular Fairhead shows how environmental narratives always draw on vague historical arguments yet, as he demonstrates, evidence in the present can often support multiple historical narratives and thus it is the narrative which best suits current political or popular theorizing which often becomes orthodox; archaeology and rigorous historical enquiry thus become essential foils to this kind of lazy historical reasoning. Fairhead's paper further emphasizes the ways in which West African landscapes are anthropogenically modified and reiterates the importance of their study as archaeological artefacts. As Fairhead states, all ecology is 'historical'; but in many parts of the world the historical record is so lacking that archaeologists must be involved in the broader study of ecology.

In Chapter 17 Crumley provides a wider overview of archaeology's potential role in global environmental debates and the new theoretical perspectives emerging to facilitate this role. She outlines a whole series of interdisciplinary environmental projects that involve strong archaeological components and presents information about the ways in which archaeologists are engaging with cognate disciplines and policy makers. Crumley's chapter is a timely and practical call to arms. Building on the chapter by Anderson et al. in the preceding section, Crumley and Fairhead's chapters both also highlight the range of global and local scales at which archaeologist operate and fruitfully emphasize archaeology's ability to translate between these scales.

In Chapter 18, Gosden offers a concluding review which points to the intersections between chapters and situates the volume more broadly within current anthropological thought. As he points out, the perspectives offered in the volume are complex and occasionally at variance, but he notes that what really brings them together is an emerging view of the world which breaks down the nature culture divide and recognizes the agency of both people and things. As Gosden also notes, the chapters in this book all represent an engagement with the present and future *through* archaeology.

16

Archaeology and Environmental Anthropology: Collaborations in Historical and Political Ecology

James Fairhead

INTRODUCTION

This chapter examines the importance of integrating archaeological per-spectives within contemporary environmental anthropology. It does this through exposing key questions raised by environmental anthropologists concerning West African relations with soil and forests that can only be addressed through collaboration with archaeological investigation (see also Balée, Chapter 3 this volume).

Environmental anthropological research has been particularly important in revealing the ecological knowledge and environmental practices of land users and how these practices interplay with ecological and economic processes in the shaping of landscapes.

This research has systematically undermined a paradigm of environmental reasoning that equates land use with the progressive degradation of otherwise 'natural', 'equilibrial', or 'pristine' environments (whether of soils, forests, or faunal assemblages). Whilst equilibrial ecology is apparently no longer upheld in ecological sciences either, in its shift to non-equilibrium ecology and recognition of path dependency, and whilst nature is no longer so easily configured simply as the absence of people, assumptions rooted in such simplistic ideas of nature still strongly inform and mislead the way West African environments are understood and problematized. Anthropologically derived critiques of the way landscapes are understood have been associated with a rereading of the history of those landscapes. Yet given how oral historical and anthropologically derived historical evidence can so easily be delegitimized and dismissed by apparently 'harder' sciences, environmental archaeology becomes a crucial player in these debates.

In this brief chapter I shall focus on two key debates which can only be resolved (or reconceptualized) through environmental archaeology. The first of these concerns the degradation (or otherwise) of soils and vegetation linked to farming in West Africa's Guinea savannah and forest-savannah transition zones. The second concerns the legacy of past land use on current 'old growth' forest in the Central and West African humid forest zones. These are not only interesting debates, but are at the heart of sustainable development policy deliberation in West Africa.

SOIL AND FOREST DEGRADATION: RELICT THINKING

The continued power of the paradigm in environmental reasoning that equates land use with the progressive degradation of otherwise 'natural' or 'pristine' environments is visible in the way that landscape features are often interpreted uncritically as 'relicts' of that nature. This has been common to the interpretation of landscape in the forest–savannah transition zone in West Africa. Table 16.1 shows the landscape features that have normally been understood to represent degradation, and alternative explanations.

Table 16.1. Contrasting interpretations of landscape features at the forest–savannah transition

Landscape Feature	Interpretation as a relict	Alternative reasoning
Patches of forest in otherwise savannah landscapes	Relicts of previously more extensive forest	Anthropogenic forest islands established in savannah
Bush fallows	Secondary forest thicket, regenerating following degradation of 'primary' forest	Improved bush fallows established in previous savannahs
Relatively infertile savannah soils found next to richer soils under forest patches.	Depleted savannah soils that have degraded from the initial 'natural' fertility under forest	Enriched forest soils rendered 'superfertile' through inhabitation and the establishment of forest in less fertile savannahs
Isolated trees in fields taking a 'forest form' (straight boles, without lower branches and with a high canopy)	Relict trees indicative of recently felled forest	Isolated trees that 'self prune' having established and been protected in farmers' fields.
Dense stands of oil palm ('Palm belt') on forest margins	Degraded forest, relict of a receded forest	First stage of forest transgression into savannahs (or established purposefully on forest margins)

Source: Fairhead and Leach 1998.

A case study can expose these varied readings. This is taken from anthropological fieldwork in the savannahs of Kissidougou Prefecture in the Republic of Guinea. Research there focused on agro-ecological practices and vegetation history (e.g. Leach and Fairhead 1995, Fairhead and Leach 1996a). Kissidougou has a largely savannah landscape, but around each of its eight hundred or so villages there is usually an island of high semi-deciduous forest, each covering tens of hectares. The houses of each village are built in a central clearing, and behind each house are small kitchen gardens (used for tobacco, vegetables, and other high value crops). These gardens are themselves surrounded by wooded home gardens in which fruit, nut, and other trees are encouraged to grow. The belt of woodland or forest surrounding each village is usually established purposefully, either in whole or in part. When a new village site is established, inhabitants transplant or otherwise nurture or encourage seedlings or cuttings of forest species to grow right around the village. This helps to keep the savannah fires out, and provides other benefits: in pre-colonial times, such peri-village forests served as vegetation fortifications, and more recently have been more useful as fruit and nut plantations, as a source of privacy for men's and women's private social associations, and more prosaically as a source of privacy for morning ablutions.

The sites of long-abandoned villages, hamlets, or farm camps are also scattered throughout any village's territory. Whilst there is little archaeology in this region, such evidence as there is suggests that the region has been inhabited and farmed for several thousand years (Andah 1992). The soils of these ruins are particularly appreciated for farming, as they have been enriched over their long years of habitation from the ash of hearth fires, the excreta of people, domestic animals and poultry, and the residues of processed harvests, fish and purchased dried fish, gathered products (palm, kola, and *Carapa procera* nuts) and cooking. Villagers sometimes protect these ruins for the tree crops growing in their forests or the grave sites and sacred spaces which they contain, but with time such forests are often reconverted to farmland.

Villagers explain not only how they prefer to farm on the sites of former settlements which have improved soils, but also how they improve other soils to make them more workable and productive. 'New' savannah land which has never been cultivated is said to be hard and impervious. The worst are 'elephant-compacted' soils (*senba gbere*). With regular use, new soils can be improved. The use of soil mounding in raised beds, and the incorporation of burnt and unburnt residues (of weeds, crops, and everyday wastes) year after year is said to 'open' hard 'new' savannah land, to let water in, and to make the soil oily (*tulu*), 'mature', or 'ripe' (*mo*). The soils become softer and easier to hoe and weed, have good infiltration, and because they enable deeper rooting and remain damp for longer, they allow crops to resist dry periods better. Farmers find especially that the soils under old habitation sites acquire these qualities and maintain them long after the site is abandoned. These sites can be identified from several indicators, such as the pottery that is found associated with them, their darker soil colour, and the different termite mounds that can be found on them.

Importantly, when farmers cultivate to improve new land, they liken the soils that they create to the soils of ruins. The ripened or mature soils 'will become like an abandoned site' (*a di ke tombondu di*). The concept of a ruined village is a powerful metaphor for the kind of improvements that farmers can make to soils. Soil 'ripening' not only transforms the soil, but also changes people's categorical relationship to that place. In effect, through this work— including the sweat that farmers drain off their faces with a powerful gesture during preparation of land, the blood spilt from the cuts and grazes of farming, and defecation in the areas at the back of the house—new land is 'initiated' into a mature and productively fertile status, of which its oiliness is a physical embodiment. This transformation parallels that of a girl's initiation and excision, when she is considered to become more purely female and to acquire fertility as a mature woman: oiliness is again the physical embodiment of this transformed state, and is accentuated in the festivities as initiated women are oiled.

People claim enduring rights over both the land of their ancestral villages and other land which they have improved and actively ripened to mimic it. These lands are thus distinct not only in terms of their character but also tenurially, in that they can be claimed by the patrilineal descent group whose members lived or worked there. This contrasts with unimproved land which is tenured at the village level.

Farms which become 'like ruins' need to be fallowed after 4–6 years of cultivation, but although they might have been established in savannah, their fallow vegetation will be a succession to forest thicket, not savannah. After about a decade, farmers return to cultivate these improved places, moving in a cycle of several years around them and leaving most of the rest of the land unfarmed. There are several reasons why these soils acquire a forest fallow and not a grassy one. First, tree seeds germinate and establish well on these soils which are less prone to drought. Second, for the same reasons, fires in the dry season are less intense. Third, the grasses that do germinate are more palatable to wild herbivores, which reduces fuel for the wild fires that pass. These improved soils thus develop further as the vegetation associated with their fallow recursively transforms the soils beneath them.

In discussing these soils, one informant likened villagers' farming activity to that of termites, which also transform the soils and whose mounds (settlements, villages), once 'ruined', are both prized for their fertility and support tree vegetation. Inhabitants also distinguish spirit 'villages' in their landscape that should not be entered. Spirits live in more or less the same ways as people, and their villages and farming are understood to have similar effects on soil and vegetation as people. Thus a pervasive assumption in this region is that it is settlement itself (of people, termites, spirits) which transforms initially infertile soils and brings them into fertility.

At a second fieldwork site, some 40 km further south east, within the more humid forest zone, the vegetation was not one of forest–savannah transition but of forest and forest fallow land. Here, again, people appreciated the same important legacy of former inhabitation sites on their soils. Our study village had at least twelve ruined village sites in its territory, and '*pulo cei pomdo*' (soil or earth of old villages) was particularly sought after. Not all of these were intensively farmed. Descendants of those who lived in at least five of them retained tree crop (cola, coffee) plantations on them, along with shade trees, although used parts of them also for gardens. The other ruined sites—some much older and others formerly inhabited by other peoples—had since been reconverted to farm land. The old village sites are recognized by all for their quality, and each ten years, when they are cultivated again, specific families have rights to return to them.

This is a region where statues are made from soft stone, and sculptures are sometimes dug up when farming in these old village sites. The statues are also called *pomdo*, after the ruined villages in which they are found. When they are dug up, they are (unsurprisingly) understood as a portent of agricultural fertility.

Despite an enormous volume of research on African soil fertility and African forests, there has been virtually no research on anthropogenic soils and anthropogenic forests. The research world has been silent on the legacy of past inhabitation and soil investments in these regions. Many researchers have appreciated the huge variety of 'fertilizing' practices developed by African farmers. Yet whilst they are appreciative of temporarily improved fertility, this has always been represented either as a transient improved state or as requiring the continuous import of fertility as in infields. There has been virtually no attention to the durable transformations to the soil that current research on Amazonia reveals can be made—transformations which take the soil to a qualitatively different state.

There are some exceptions. Mitja (1990) and Mitja and Puig (1991) describe how in Cote d'Ivoire, farmers transform humid savannahs into secondary forest thicket and improve infiltration characteristics and soil faunal activity. Mondjannagni (1969) shows the establishment of forest thicket in earlier baobab-rich savannahs of Benin, and describes the weeding and burning practices involved. In Togo, Guelly and colleagues show how farmers deflect ecological successions to create a forest formation in grassland savannahs, creating anthropogenic forest fallows (Guelly et al. 1993). Even though little research has focused on this logic of land improvement in farming practices in West Africa, such research as there is does highlight how farming can effect durable transformations on the soil. We can see this in the metaphors which speak of such transformations: just as farmers in

Guinea spoke of soil 'ripening', so farmers in Benin speak of 'waking up' their soils (Brouwers 1993).

These anthropological contributions to what has come to be called 'historical ecology'—broadly, the study of landscapes in relation to the unfolding interactions between social and ecological processes (Balée 2006)—reveal how the prevalent 'relict' readings of landscape might be incorrect. There is evidence from around the West African forest savannah transition zone supporting alternative readings of landscape processes (Fairhead and Leach 1998). These anthropologically derived rereadings of historical ecology can, however, be contested. It is in this that the methods of environmental archaeology become so important, perhaps not only to 'resolve' the salience of different readings in one way or another but also to reveal the more subtle, even recursive, interactions between the social and ecological factors that shape the nature of nature in the landscape (e.g. Blackmore et al. 1990).

Anthropology is not content only to address the historical ecology questions, but extends its reflections and inquiry to political ecology issues, asking when and why incorrect interpretive grids built around 'relict' thinking have arisen in the ecological and conservation sciences—grids which, as we have seen, cast African land users as exclusively destructive. It asks why these grids persist despite contradictory evidence, and what have been their effects—for example in removing landholders' rights over valuable trees and in creating a regime of fines that act as a tax on land-users. Once again, however, without strong archaeological evidence, critics of anthropologists could ask whether their questions derive more from post-colonial social science than from the landscape itself. Anthropological contributions to historical and political ecology will be more powerful (and potentially more nuanced) if conducted in conjunction with environmental archaeology.

THE FOREST ARCHIVE: NATURAL HISTORY
OR SOCIAL HISTORY?

A set of questions relating to high forest can exemplify in a different way the crucial importance of collaborations between environmental anthropology and archaeology. Climate ecologists have become interested in the extent to which the dynamics of 'old growth' forest in West and Central Africa actually reflect past land use. This has become a pressing question as evidence is accumulating that 'old growth' forests in Africa are increasing in biomass (as they are in South America). Some ecologists are hypothesizing that forests are putting on weight due to increased carbon dioxide concentrations in the atmosphere, which may be accelerating plant growth and turnover and shifting the 'old growth' forest to steady states of higher biomass (Lewis 2009; Phillips et al. 2008; also see Crumley, Chapter 17 this volume for further discussion of global anthropogenic effects). Critics suggest that increases in biomass are only to be expected as 'old growth' forests across both continents are still responding to earlier disturbance.

Environmental anthropology can help address this debate. Firstly, local readings of 'old growth' forests frequently reveal the presence of former settlements and claim rights to forest resources. This was the case, for example, in the Ziama forest of the Republic of Guinea, where inhabitants of enclave villages suggest that their ancestral, pre-colonial populations had been large and that the area that is now 'old growth' forest was intensively farmed as recently as the mid-nineteenth century. The villagers identified for us the 'look out' trees which they used to communicate from village to village—but these are now engulfed by the forest around. In this instance, historical sources could be used to validate local historical claims that the forest is recent and that it is only to be expected that it would be putting on weight (Fairhead and Leach 1994; Fairhead et al. 2003). In most instances historical sources are not available, and adjudicating between local readings of forest history and eco-logical deductions about it—and thus perhaps adjudicating claims to land and forest revenue—must rest on the work of environmental archaeologists.

This argument can be seen clearly in a second example, from the Oban forest reserve in Nigeria. Don Rosevear, a colonial forester who visited this forest in the 1920s returned there in the 1960s and, in his retirement, reflected on its history:

> What I had in my inexperience looked upon as glorious virgin growth, dating from the Flood, quickly revealed itself to my better experienced and disappointed eye as nothing more than secondary growth of moderately good quality.... But there was one curiosity. The abnormally large trees which had so impressed me in 1924 were still there, scattered throughout the forest in sufficient numbers to attract puzzled attention. I was still more perplexed when I discovered that they comprised two—and only two—species, the Sasswood, *Erythrophleum ivorense* and the Inoit Nut, *Pogaoleosa*. Why these two species? And why this young—in tropical terms—forest, indicating previous widespread destruction in a so mark-edly underpopulated area? And then it dawned on me. The forest made it clear to me, like reading a book, that the entire region had once been heavily populated, so densely in fact that the whole, except perhaps for the more inaccessible upper portions of the hills (which I myself never visited) had been intensely farmed, leaving no surplus area of undestroyed forest. What had become of this popula-tion; and why the two untouched species, obviously carefully preserved hang-overs from the original forest? (Rosevear 1979: 78).

In order to 'read' this landscape—to answer questions concerning the origin and predominance of Sasswood and Inoit nut in this forest, an understanding of the logics of past land use is necessary, and this can be illuminated by the environmental anthropological investigation.

Curiously, some of the 'permanent sample plots' that forest ecologists have been surveying at intervals and which reveal that African forests are increasing in biomass are actually to be found in this forest of Oban, which seems to have met forest ecologists' criteria for being 'old growth' forest (Clark 1996). It is assumed by those ecologists to be in an otherwise 'equilibrial' state, and any changes to its biomass are being attributed to external conditions, such as atmospheric carbon dioxide concentration. Yet according to Rosevear, the emergent trees in this forest are actually the very same ones that were present when the land was farmed—and presumably they are still growing. It is not surprising that the forest is putting on weight. Moreover, the continued growth of these emergent trees will certainly be influencing the productivity of the rest of the ecosystem. Emergent trees can act as 'ecosystem engineers', modulating the availability of resources to other species (e.g. Stinchcombe 2006) as their roots tap into new regions of the soil and aquifers.

Observations such as those by Rosevear call into question the definitions of 'old growth' that are currently used in modern forest ecology. The potential life span of particular trees is longer than the period required to achieve 'old growth'. Most tropical forests that have not been disturbed for 300 years meet the criteria that forest ecologists are using for 'old growth', and yet in most African forests, trees of 250–350 years are moderately common. Emergents of 450 years old have been felled (Anon 1976), and individuals in West and Central Africa can live for 800–1,000 years (White and Oates 1999; White 2001; Sheil et al. 2000). Carbon-dating studies in Amazonia suggest average mature tree ages in places of 500 years, with individuals up to 1,400 years (Chambers et al. 1998).

The case of the Oban forest reserve discussed here is not an exception but the norm. Anthropological and historical evidence suggests that, of the permanent sample plots located in 'old growth' forests in Africa and which have been used to discern biomass change, most are in forests where there is strong evidence of major forest disturbance in historical times (e.g. Fairhead and Leach 1998; Weber et al. 2001). Yet without precision from archaeological evidence, dating and characterizing the nature of the disturbance is weak.

The extent to which African forests are increasing in biomass, and the reasons for this, are increasingly important not only in global climate change research but also to the economic questions raised in carbon trading and around policies concerning the United Nations collaborative programme on Reducing Emissions from Deforestation and forest Degradation (REDD) in developing countries. Carbon is set to become a critical commodity in the twenty-first century. In the face of this, it is most important that environmental anthropologists link with environmental archaeologists to address questions which continue to be dominated by non-historical ecology.

Once again, however, environmental anthropologists are interested not only in addressing the 'historical ecology' questions concerning 'forest history' but also in the political ecology questions: how is the unfolding configuration of contemporary scientific research actually shaping knowledge about African tropical forests? How does the financing and institutional context of this research (for example within global governance regimes on climate change, biodiversity, forests, and so on) affect the content? Among other things, we might ask whether ecological research on forests is understating past land use in the African forests, thus downplaying the demographic impact of the slave trade, in the same way as it has understated past land use in the Amazonian forest thus downplaying the extraordinary mortality associated with the Hispanic encounter (contrast, for example, Phillips et al. 2008 with Nevle and Bird 2008). Yet the salience of these political ecology questions depends on the validity of historical claims. The forest and the soils beneath it are almost the only archive of these events. It will take a combination of environmental anthropology and environmental archaeology (and a more enlightened ecology) to read it.

CONCLUSION

It is impossible to review the myriad of ways in which contemporary environmental anthropology can work productively with archaeology in addressing the pressing issues at the heart of development studies. This chapter has focused on the nature and degradation of soils and forests, and on forest history. It highlights how one of the important contributions of environmental anthropology is in providing support for an analytical turn that renders all ecology historical—and yet for many of the regions of the world in which development institutions exert influence on environmental science and governance, the historical record is both short and contested. This perspective has necessarily become an interdisciplinary partnership of anthropology, history, and archaeology, in which the time depth and precision of archaeological approaches to the environment provide full force for this critique (and its limits).

Yet as this chapter has also made clear, once these historical ecology questions have been addressed they raise further questions concerning the contemporary politics of ecological knowledge; questions that have greater validity if built on archaeological as well as anthropological data.

17

The Archaeology of Global Environmental Change

Carole L. Crumley

INTRODUCTION

Recent, widely recognized changes in the Earth system are, in effect, changes in the coupled human–environment system. We have entered the Anthropocene, when human activity—along with solar forcing, volcanic activity, precession, and the like—must be considered a component (a 'driver') of global environmental change (Crutzen and Stoermer 2000; Levin 1998). The dynamic non-linear system in which we live is not in equilibrium and does not act in a predictable manner (see Fairhead, chapter 16 this volume for further discussion of non-equilibrium ecology). If humankind is to continue to thrive, it is of utmost importance that we identify the ideas and practices that nurture the planet as well as our species. Our best laboratory for this is the past, where long-, medium-, and short-term variables can be identified and their roles evaluated. Perhaps the past is our only laboratory: experimentation requires time we no longer have. Thus the integration of our understanding of human history with that of the Earth system is a timely and urgent task.

COLLABORATION AND APPLIED LEARNING

Archaeologists bring two particularly useful sets of skills to this enterprise: how to collaborate, and how to learn from the past. Archaeology enjoys a long tradition of collaboration with colleagues in both the biophysical sciences and in the humanities to investigate human activity in all planetary environments. Archaeologists work alongside one another in the field, live together in difficult conditions, welcome collaboration with colleagues in other disciplines—

and listen to them carefully—and tell compelling stories to an interested public. All are rare skills and precious opportunities.

Until recently few practitioners of biophysical, social science, and humanities disciplines had experience in cross-disciplinary collaboration. Many scholars who should be deeply engaged in collaboration to avert disaster (for example, specialists in tropical medicine with their counterparts in land use change) still speak different professional 'languages' and have very different traditions of producing information.

C. P. Snow, in *The Two Cultures* (1993 [1959]), was among the first to warn that the very structure of academia was leading to this serious, if unintended, outcome. A rift between the biophysical sciences and the humanities can be discerned at least as early as the nineteenth century (see Collini in Snow 1993), but only now, when we urgently need the exchange of information and ideas across the divide, are hastily built bridges and partially demolished barriers to be found everywhere.

Epistemological issues and unexamined academic prejudices impede the search for new ways to address global challenges. Some collaborative frameworks have appeared (e.g. Hoppe 2010; Newell et al. 2005), but the work is necessarily tailored to specific circumstances. By necessity, archaeologists sit on the fence: we are scientists in the trenches and the laboratory, but must become philosophers, historians, and qualitative social scientists when we interpret the past. This transformation is little discussed among us, but it is one of archaeology's most treasured, useful, and mind-expanding characteristics. Similarly, the conceptual glue that holds together archaeological practice, archaeological theory, and a good story can also hold together trans-disciplinary projects that search the past for insights.

The bulk of archaeological theory addresses what one learns about the past. It is quite different to ask how the past can make the future more resilient and equitable. Simply to understand what happened is hard enough. We try to discern basic characteristics of vanished societies—economy, governance, social stratification, and the like—from remains that are maddeningly partial, lack critical information, and compel us to filter our inferences through batteries of proxies. The material record available for analysis is only a part of the totality of the past; it is also only a part of the lives of vanished peoples. With these pitiful and partial witnesses, we attempt to reconstruct the life of the mind.

But attempt we do, and in many ways our efforts are quite successful. One of our most valuable tools is a standardized system for the scientific recovery of what does remain. Of course, there is inevitable variation in the research designs of the excavators and the rigour with which sites are excavated and analysed. Geographic coverage necessarily reflects the availability of funding and the research focus of the excavators. Nevertheless, in the last century a surprisingly detailed chronology of human activity in most parts of the world has emerged. So much work has been done on every continent that it is possible to sketch a tentative chronology and culture histories for even the least studied regions. While our knowledge of the past will always be incomplete, we can follow the development of many societies and estimate the human and environmental contributions to their trajectories.

What can be done with this record of the past? If it is possible to steer ourselves and the planet toward what has been termed a 'safe operating space for humanity' (Rockstrom et al. 2009), it is critical to know how this dynamic human–environment system operates. Fortunately, key features in complex biophysical systems (integration, communication, and the importance of the system's history, termed initial conditions) correspond to key features of social systems (the holistic nature of culture, knowledge sharing through the senses, and the formative power of traditions, structures and materials, strategies, and habits of mind).

A particularly important characteristic of dynamic systems (also termed complex adaptive systems (CAS)—such as the humans-in-the-environment Earth system—is how a system's history can offer clues to later sets of conditions to which the system can return, termed 'states'. Long-term history, the *longue durée* of the *Annales* school of history, can reveal the processes, decisions, and events that shape societies and frame the conditions (but not the precise situations) to which the system periodically returns (a spiral; see Jantsch 1982). While history does not 'repeat itself' there are indeed recurring conditions that are the result of a mixture of human behavioural history and shifting environmental circumstances; an example would be the conjuncture of unequal access to scarce resources, multiple ethnicities, and conflict. Insight into how such slow, medium, and fast-changing variables interact can allow archaeologists and their colleagues to examine the entire 'life-cycles' of societies in their environments.

Nothing lasts forever: people and societies eventually yield to forces that send them into another state. But as McAnany, Yoffee, and their colleagues have pointed out, human history is by and large a story of resilience—dispossession and cultural survival—not collapse (McAnany and Yoffee 2010; see also Diamond 2005; Tainter 2006). While dramatic stories of disaster are compelling, they offer little in the way of guidance for averting similar calamities. Only careful analysis of the circumstances and conditions that led to the event can hope to avoid recurrence.

In ecology the study of ecosystems and the conditions (including human activity) that produce shifts from one state to another is termed 'resilience thinking' (Gunderson and Holling 2002; Gunderson and Folke 2003; Walker and Salt 2006). While resilience thinkers have adopted many concepts from complex systems science (e.g. initial conditions, basins of attraction, path dependency, emergent properties) the history of entire coupled human–environment systems are of much less interest. In useful reviews of resilience for archaeologists, Redman and colleagues (Redman 2005; Redman and Kinzig 2003; van der Leeuw and Redman 2002) point out that the work of ecologists and others, who usually have years or decades of data, can be extended by the archaeological record to multiple 'adaptive cycles' (in resilience terminology, the adaptive cycle moves through periods of exploitation, conservation, release, reorganization) in the same geographical location. The adaptive cycle does not end with a mature system (conservation) but follows on through a fundamental reorganization of energy flows and structures. Resilience thinking replaced the temporally truncated climax theory of vegetation that dominated plant ecology in much of the twentieth century, but has yet to embrace system history beyond several decades. Despite the lack of interest in long-term history on the part of the Resilience Alliance, other ecologists have joined with archaeologists to use historical ecology in the study of coupled human–environment systems (e.g. Jackson and Hobbs 2009; Swetnam et al. 1999; see also Crumley 2013; Meyer and Crumley 2012). This framework is amenable to the long cycles archaeologists observe in regional chronologies and enables analysis of the acts, events, and circumstances that lead to prolonged resilience or reorganization of the coupled human-environment system.

In treating both the past and the future, archaeologists may need to adjust how to think about both, but we have a real opportunity to enlist archaeology in the quest for a viable future for humanity; the past can indeed improve the future.

SCALES OF ANALYSIS

Most of the models created to predict future changes in the Earth's climate have a short time depth (decades) and are missing climate history at the regional scale that is long enough (centuries or more) to register slower societal and ecosystem changes. This emphasis on time scales that are not long enough to include trends and events that significantly modify human behaviour leaves the social sciences and humanities with reduced opportunities to contribute to the study of the coupled human–Earth system. A focus on the human scale (e.g. communities, landscapes, regions) is essential for understanding how to plan future strategies that draw on the laboratory of the past.

The history of archaeology is one of increasingly broad spatial scales: artefacts, sites, exploitation zones (catchments) around sites, and, most recently, ancient landscapes. Thus, the next step in the growth of the discipline will be to construct regional chronologies. By 'region' I evoke the spatial scale(s) at which long-term change in an area over time can be studied; thus a region contains one or several landscapes but has a flexible upper spatial boundary.

The spatial scales at which one studies change over time can be multi-continental (Wolf 1982) or, with the onset of the Anthropocene, global. It is through the study of rhythms of expansion and contraction that we come to see the factors that shape regions' unique and shifting biophysical and cultural histories. Because our research can span these broad parameters of time and space, it is another role archaeology can play in the study of global environmental change.

The archaeological record yields considerable information about local and regional land cover, land use, and management strategies. Archaeological and palaeoecological sites can produce closely dated sequences from which may be read both the history of domesticated species and the 'background' environment from which people chose their preferred species. A variety of techniques makes it possible to develop an understanding of ancient landscapes, regional climate, and the human activity that took place in their context.

For example, the isotopic signature of plant remains can provide closely dated qualitative and quantitative assessments of past environmental changes and economic strategies employed in site catchments (Fiorentino et al. 2010). This interdisciplinary approach to the history of food production combines palaeoclimatic, palaeoagricultural, and palaeoeconomic data, inferred in part from plants' stable isotope analysis and an absolute chronological framework fine-grained enough to sequence annual variation.

Despite fascinating research by archaeologists, geographers, historians, and others on the historic impacts of climate (such as drought, hurricanes, el Niño events), there has been no systematic effort to incorporate these regional climate histories into scenario modelling of future climates. Over time the world's biomes (combinations of characteristic flora, fauna, and climate, governed by latitude, topography, and humidity) move about as a function of changes in global average temperature. For instance, with the very low global temperatures of the 2.5 million year Pleistocene, arctic and sub-arctic biomes moved far to the south of their current latitudes. In contrast, warm and cold Holocene excursions lasted only hundreds of years, but affected the range of flora and fauna, particularly those propagated by humans.

The point is that long periods like the Pleistocene, shorter periods like the Roman Warm Period and the Little Ice Age, geographically isolated, repetitive patterns like the Southern (el Niño and la Niña) and North Atlantic Oscillations, and other less predictable events such as hurricanes (Walker and Surge 2013), all leave archaeological and palaeoenvironmental records. Whether the future will be warmer (the consensus prediction) or colder (if Broecker (1997) is correct about the ocean 'conveyor belt') is perhaps not the issue. If we wish to identify regions favourable to human habitation and niches that can protect biodiversity, we would be wise to examine all excursions in past records. Analysis of climate change at finer scales than the global reveals continent- and region-sized phenomena that vary in temporal and spatial intensity, affecting bioregions. At these scales archaeologists can assess the resilience and vulnerability of societies.

Archaeologists are learning to read the conjoined history of climate and human activity and cautiously interpret how linked environmental and cultural circumstances furthered or checked the development of human societies. A growing number of case studies suggest that so-called 'slow' variables that build up over time (such as deteriorating pastureland in medieval Greenland) combine with more rapidly changing 'fast' variables (deteriorating sailing conditions to Europe) and rigidity 'traps' (colonists' clinging to an unsustainable way of life) so that the effects cascade throughout the society (Berglund 2010; Dugmore et al. 2007).

DERIVING PRACTICAL LESSONS

Projects are under way to build on archaeological practice and connect the historical sciences with contemporary work in ecology and complex adaptive systems. One promising approach, originating in the Earth system science community but aiming to cross the Two Cultures divide, is to foster collaboration among researchers—especially archaeologists—who work in the same region or who share a comparative interest such as ancient water management or the history of cities. The Integrated History and Future of People on Earth (IHOPE) facilitates an interdisciplinary network of scholars, fosters their projects, and offers a framework for integration at regional, continental, and global scales (Costanza et al. 2012; van der Leeuw et al. 2011). IHOPE is a special project of the International Geosphere–Biosphere Programme (IGBP). In addition to IGBP, IHOPE's sponsors are the International Human Dimensions Programme (IHDP) and two IGBP core projects: Analysis, Integration and Modelling of the Earth System (AIMES) and Past Global Changes (PAGES). To facilitate integration of scholarly research, all these organisations will soon be amalgamated into a global program called Future Earth.

IHOPE investigates the long-term dynamics among climate, economics, technology, disease, language, culture, conflict, and other variables; models these relationships and tests the models against the historical record; and uses knowledge of these dynamic systems to increase the viability of future societies and the Earth system which makes them possible. IHOPE is forming a global network of researchers and research projects; its International Program Office (IPO) is based at Uppsala University in Sweden. The key question is: In what ways do human activities foster or undermine the systems on which they depend?

IHOPE will facilitate discussion and adoption of perspectives, theories, tools, information, and knowledge from a variety of sources. From geographic scales where human activity is most easily understood (e.g. landscape, region) to continental and larger scales (e.g. el Niño/la Niña, the Indian subcontinental monsoon) and over long periods (hundreds and thousands of years), the IHOPE goal is to integrate relevant scholarship, whatever its source.

SOME ILLUSTRATIVE IHOPE PROJECTS

Over the past 3,000 years, the **US Southwest** has seen a succession of very different adaptations to extreme climatic circumstances. One group has been working together for decades to study different cultural responses to environmental change. Their project benefits from long tree-ring sequences that allow detailed reconstructions of fluctuations in annual average precipitation and temperature and the assignment of precise dates to the archaeological evidence. In addition, the project has developed dynamic (multi-agent) models of social-environmental interaction over thousands of years and a sophisticated historical GIS database. By comparing how the region's extreme environmental circumstances have been managed by different societies over the last 10,000 years, the group focuses on distinguishing cultural and economic factors from environmental conditions (Anderies and Hegmon 2011; Hegmon et al. 2010).

The **Yucatan region**, home to the Maya civilization, is being studied from 1000 BC to 1000 AD. The chronology is well-established through the presence of stelae with calendar dates. The region is important to the Earth system because such tropical wet–dry forests hold half of the planet's biodiversity. The region's historical ecology can help us understand how to maintain these ecosystems and the humans that live there. The Mayan archaeologists demonstrate what can be accomplished at the regional scale when investigators with large projects of their own agree to collaborate.

IHOPE research from the Yucatan combines archaeology, engineering, geology, ecology, cartography, architecture, linguistics, and more to trace the millennium-long history of water allocation and land use at the ancient Maya city of Tikal in Guatemala. There they unearthed and studied the largest dam in the Maya area, which revealed how water in the urban complex was successfully supplied and managed despite the region's frequent droughts. Researchers have identified low-technology adaptations (at least by current standards) that were nonetheless remarkable for their resilience and sustainability over deep time (Scarborough et al. 2012). These simple systems are consistent with today's conservation efforts and can prove useful in situations where energy sources are limited and state-of-the-art technologies are expensive and have greater environmental impact. Such research can offer more sustainable solutions to today's growing cities in similar environmental circumstances.

The ***Urban Minds*** project studies urban resilience across the Old World and over the long term, from the origins of urbanism 10,000 years ago until modern times. The development of urbanism is a global phenomenon that takes radically different forms in different times and places, with widely varying consequences. Following on the first Urban Mind book <http://www.arkeologi.uu.se/Research/Projects/Urban_Mind/Book/> researchers from various institutes in Europe, the Middle East, and Africa are collaborating on a project re-think relationships among environment, energy and food security, and the people who lived and will live in towns and cities. Through analysis, comparison, and modelling of urban experience, the programme is developing a theoretical framework to deal with the complexity of both past and future urban experiences, highlighting examples and solutions that are applicable to current and future urban challenges.

A part of the research focuses on histories of resources fundamental to urban life (such as water) and their management. Ancient engineering and architectural solutions have the advantage of being designed for the very places that can use them today: such designs can use local, non-polluting, and carbon-neutral materials and machines, employ local craftspeople and workforces, and engender a sense of pride in regional traditions and histories. Considerable collaboration is already occurring among hydrological engineers, anthropologists, and archaeologists (Lansing 2006; Scarborough 2003, 2010).

The IHOPE endeavour entails enormous intellectual, technical, and other challenges, but it also offers the opportunity to pursue intriguing questions with colleagues who share archaeologists' commitment to collaboration and a belief that the past can illustrate both the folly and the remarkable ingenuity of our species. The challenges we face are persistent: sustainable food production, prudent resource management, effective governance; the lessons of the past endure for us to retrieve and apply, and archaeology has a critical role to play in this process.

18

Humanized Environments

Chris Gosden

It is now well known that there is a spectrum of views about humans and the world they live in, ranging from the concept of the environment as an external force to the idea that people exist through a series of relations which it makes little sense to divide up as culture on the one hand and nature on the other. It is worth thinking through the implications of these varied views briefly (although I do not want to duplicate Davies's detailed introduction in Chapter 1), so that we can think about what is lost and gained when trying to combine nature and culture, my main aim in current work.

Let us start with views in which there is a radical separation of people and the physical world. In such views, which are in themselves varied, the physical world is seen as a series of energy budgets and nutrients that people have to extract in the most cost-efficient way possible in order to maintain life. Leslie White (1949) made a three-fold division between the physical, the biological, and the cultural. Academic study, in which physicists, chemists, or earth scientists probe the physical state of the universe, biologists investigate living things, and the social sciences and humanities focus on the human world, was not constructed around a series of heuristic divisions, but instead mirrored reality, White argued. Culture was also divided into three levels, of which the first, technology determined social organization and ideology. The primary function of culture for White was the harnessing of energy and the more efficiently this was done, the more it allowed for organizational complexity and multiple ideologies. Human history moved by revolutions in energy capture from early periods in which human muscles were key, to the agricultural revolution where plants and animals were domesticated to increase food supplies and animals could be used for traction, through to the industrial revolution (and the possibility of a future nuclear revolution) (see also Armstrong Oma, Chapter 11 this volume). Not only is there a desire to ground anthropology and archaeology as sciences in such views, but also an implicit split between mind and body, where the former is the seat and origin of culture and the latter our connection to the physical and biological worlds. Such views were introduced fully into archaeology through the so-called New Archaeology of Binford (1972) and others. Although 'culture' was acknowledged as a possible cause of change, when it came to actual analyses it was generally environmental change or population pressure (which came about due to more conducive environments) which were seen to cause the agricultural revolution and other key moments (Binford 1972: 421–9; see also Davies, Chapter 4 this volume). Much of the radical rethinking and excitement engendered by such new approaches was lost to environmental determinism, though in the middle of the last century they promised quite a different view of cultural history.

The excitement of the 'anthropology as science' polemics gave way the equally exciting possibility of culture as the key cause of human change. The common feature of both stances was that culture was a set of ideas, or a world view, which then shaped practical action. Lévi-Strauss's (1964, 1997) statement that food is good to think with as much as it is good to eat is a useful shorthand here for a broader set of ideas in which cultural categories of edible and inedible determine what is considered food rather than a pure drive for the efficient harvesting of energy and nutrients. But an all-in-the-mind view tends to leave out key issues like climatic and environmental change, focusing also on the more obviously creative aspects of human culture, leaving practical forms of food getting and mundane aspects of making a living less well examined.

Consequently, and to cut a long story very short, a need has been felt for a framework which includes both nature and culture or the body and the mind. Again these moves have many sources which are not currently well integrated. These include the practice-based anthropology of Pierre Bourdieu (1977) who, building on earlier work by Marcel Mauss and others, focused on the encultured nature of everyday actions. If French and English soldiers could not use each other's shovels to dig trenches in the First World War it must mean that their bodies had learned subtly different sequences of muscle actions, most likely when they were young. If two closely related cultures like the French and English enculturated their bodies differently then such differences must be writ even larger in more distant groups. An older model of culture, such as that of structuralism, made a distinction between the mind, which was the seat of culture, and the body which was more part of nature. Bourdieu's work showed that it was culture all the way down, with learned bodily actions being something we are rather than something we know. The body has its muscular mechanics, its biochemistry and sets of neurons firing, properties shared with many other organisms, which might make them natural. But the body and its brain are clearly plastic and able to use and develop these physical attributes in many ways.

More recently has come the influence of 'thing theory' (Hodder 2011) which develops the corollary to the plastic body—that materials have a clear influence on human actions, senses, and emotions. Things are not merely functional, but help define and shape the person and the group. An axe or a field system has a set of requirements that it brings with it, requirements which need to be followed if the tool is to be used effectively. The desire to chop down a tree may originate with a person, but the actions required of the body come partly from the axe, depending on its length of handle, the size, shape, and weight of the blade, and so on. A field system has even more requirements, in that it cannot be created, maintained, or effectively worked by one person on their own; only a group working cooperatively can effectively use a field system for a combination of animals and crops. The notion of domestication becomes a two-way process if thought of in those terms. A vegetatively propagated plant has a different set of needs and requirements from one grown from seed; requirements people ignore at their peril. The idea of subsistence quickly becomes too thin to be analytically useful. People are domesticated by their plants and animals as much as the other way round. This happens not just at the point of domestication but as the relationships unfold, as Armstrong Oma points out in the case of cattle in Bronze Age Scandinavia. She goes on to question the model of maximizing returns that underlies much discussion of ancient farming, feeling that a model that includes broader community sets of interests (a stakeholder model) is preferable. As in many of the chapters in this volume, the stress is put on understanding the range of values that are attached to relationships between humans and between people and other elements of the world, whether these be cows, houses, fields or forests.

Historical ecology is an approach used by a number of the writers in this volume (particularly Anderson, Maasch and Sandweiss, Balée and Crumley) as it recognizes the richness of relationships between humans, soil, climate, and other organisms. The old Childean story of hunter-gatherer to farmer to mass surplus production underwriting urbanism and industrialization is not now thought to be very helpful, for a number of reasons. This single, central trajectory to world history leaves too much out, though it works to some degree for temperate parts of the world where cereals and animals become the basis for life, such as in the central plains of China, northern India, Europe, the riverine urban systems of Mesopotamia and Egypt, some southern African systems, and a scattering of instances in North and South America. However, much gets left out, including an undifferentiated and passive set of hunter-gatherers as well as many tropical systems which have dynamics of their own. In his chapter Davies looks at Pokot agriculturalists in East Africa and considers the complexity of decision-making when people intensify: what we might call 'ecological' or population factors are only part of a spectrum of concerns. Indeed people rarely have knowledge of the full range of family structures, age sets, networking, and genealogy in which any one family is enmeshed. Kin groups make decisions on some of the more pressing factors, which may be as much cultural as ecological or economic. Fairhead argues that all ecology is historical: the concept has embedded within it notions of change and that people are always key agents of change. Humanly induced change, he argues, can often be seen as degradation of natural environments, whereas in cases like the West African savannah forests humans can be understood as bringing into being habitats with both positive and negative sets of character-istics. Villages in the Kissidougou Prefecture of the Republic of Guinea are often near islands of semi-deciduous forest, which are there because of the actions of the villagers, as the forests are full of useful trees, providing food, timber and fuel. The village is not located near the forest; the forest has grown up in the vicinity of the village.

A key empirical realization of the last thirty years is the domestication of the rainforests in the Amazon, central Africa, south-east Asia, and Melanesia. Rainforests are generally seen by the Western eye to be pristine natural wilderness, prior to modern logging. We are increasingly realizing that they are human creations to the same degree as *padi* fields or European arable and pasture systems (whether these be found in Europe itself or North America, Australia, or New Zealand). The processes by which the structure of the forest has been altered over many millennia, bringing in fruit and medicinal trees or those useful for building and boat making, are still a new topic for research (see Balée's excellent survey in Chapter 3). Different areas exhibit their own histories, so although all rainforests are humanly altered, each area has its own long-term trajectory, which includes temperate rainforests such as those of Canada's northwest coast (Braun 2002). In fact archaeology more broadly is moving from a concentration on food getting to a notion of ecological creation, in which the East African savannah can be seen as the product of human settlement and goat husbandry (Davies, Chapter 4 this volume; Lane 2010) and the growth of deserts, as well as the parkland savannahs of southern Britain, mainly as a result of deforestation and animal grazing (Roberts and Wrathmell 2002). Climates change, cycling through warmer and colder epi-sodes so that zones of vegetation expand and contract in any case. But such modes of expansion and contraction have been altered by humans, who have created quite new sets of communities of plants and animals in ways which are affecting the climate.

People and the world are entangled in many ways. It may be that the possessive individualism of capitalism has obscured our view of that entangle-ment, leading us to see the world as resources and potential commodities existing 'out there' (Harvey 1989). Western thought is trying to knit together these separated strands into a more seamless appreciation of the world. Other cultural forms can provide inspiration here as they have not separated cul-tured and nature in the first place, nor do they make the same judgements as to what has agency and what does not. Descola (1994) and Viveiros de Castro (1998) both draw from Amazonian ethnography to outline a world of animals considered to be persons with their own cultural lives. Viveiros de Castro (1998) points out that whereas we see a world with a single nature but many cultures, Amerindians feel that nature is diverse but that the cultures of all beings are variants of the human culture and in essence are one. Ingold (2000) adds instances from circumpolar ethnographies to highlight worlds in which stones, trees or animals can be animate and intentional in ways parallel to the agency of people. Sahlins's (2011) recent restatement of the importance of kinship studies to anthropology draws many of these insights together around the importance of mutuality. All human beings are given identity through a multiplicity of meaningful relationships and these might, with entities of a variety of kinds, include those we would take to be people. Here then is a historical ecology of an extended kind, where the notion of ecology includes a great range of relations. It is true to say that such studies have hitherto looked little at history, and there is work here for archaeology to do (Gosden 2008) such as is being started by Balée in his chapter on indigenous landscapes. Such work raises the question of what counts as heritage. In the Western world we tend to think of buildings, monuments, and cultivated landscapes; in many other parts of the world only the last of these would count, but the plants, animals, and ancestral spirits within them would count too (see the chapter by Kost on forms of Aboriginal care for the Australian landscape through burning).

Holmberg, in a thoughtful piece on disasters, focusing on the AD 79 eruption of Pompeii, talks of loss. Disasters of the natural kind are seen to be about the loss of life and property enacted on people by eruptions, earthquakes, floods and so on. Such dramatic occurrences help see the world not just as process, but also as event. But by acknowledging an event-like aspect to what we call nature, we can see more echoes between natural episodes and those in the human world, further eroding distinctions between the two. Holmberg echoes Marx and Engels in seeing relations we have taken to be solid melt into air. Disasters, she argues, bring loss, but they also can create a sense of lost distinctions that can initially be disorientating but eventually liberating. Leckie looks at modes of discourse which pit culture against nature, with the latter term being something that humans must emancipate themselves from. She concentrates on representations of Swiss Lake Villages from the nineteenth century onwards which locate so-called 'primitive' communities within a natural environment and at its mercy. Such representations are deeply embedded in all Western imaginations and hard to easily dismantle. Images, Leckie argues, may have more power than critique, so that it is easier to recognize conceptual impasses than it is to move beyond them. Threatening aspects of nature are most regularly highlighted in situations perceived to be difficult or fragile. Small Pacific islands are often cited such as the Marshall Islands examined by Rudiak-Gould and a key current trope of climate change is small islands disappearing beneath waves as the sea rises. Rudiak-Gould starts to examine the cultural bases for perceptions of flooding events in the Marshall Islands which we might see as disasters, but which the locals are inclined to attribute to overall cycles of tide and wind, or to external forces such as US military activity. Most people in the Marshall Islands consider change to be normal and are loath to attribute changes to disasters, leading us to question how different are the analyst's views from those of local people.

Fiore, Tivoli, and Zangrando look at the hunter-gatherer lifestyles of the ancestors of the Yamana people in the Beagle Channel of Tierra del Fuego, thinking about the interaction of fish and birds used as prey and those species appearing as art. Unsurprisingly those that were good to eat are not always those good to paint and vice versa. Ecological circumstances are not perceived through a neutral lens, but through complex layers of action and perception. The trick in any one case is to look at the modes of action in all domains in an interlinked manner, bringing together activities we might consider to concern subsistence with those creating art. Up in the Lurín valley on the Central Peruvian coast Chevalier considers the use of plants and their interactions with ceremonial activities within highly constrained ecological circumstances, in a valley surrounded by desert and ocean. The importation of starchy foods from the Andes and the Amazon reflects both ecological constraints and the social imperatives deriving from exchange and prestige. Plants here help develop a sense of identity and presumably issues of identity have had a considerable influence on the history of plants.

Not only is there considerable intellectual excitement around emerging views of people, things, plants, and animals but implications for policy and for our future. As Anderson, Maasch, and Sandweiss show, archaeology has an enormous contribution to make to an understanding of past climate change and its human effects. The concept of resilience as developed by Crumley and co-workers looks at the ability systems have to bounce back to a productive state after some perturbation. Although there is an attempt in this work to look at conjoined human–environmental systems, some tendency to divide the human and the ecosystem still exists and more theoretical work is needed in this regard, perhaps drawing on the broader literatures in geography and anthropology. Because of the present concentration on human degradation of the world, the emphasis in studies of the past is on periods of change and how people have reacted to climatic changes. Given our growing interest in sustainability, studies of where people have lived over the long-term in some sort of equilibrium with the world around them are also valuable, as are the occasions when people have instigated beneficial changes in the ecosystem. So-called applied archaeology is also prominent in the discussion by Isendahl, Sánchez, Calla, Irahola, Salvatierra, and Ticona when looking at the Yungas of the Bolivian Andes using earlier human responses to slope, soil, and water management to think of innovative approaches to agricultural problems and potentials in the present. Here they view landscapes as human products, using the term 'agronomy' to delineate the combination of cultivation practices and forms of knowledge which underlie human productive interactions with their worlds. Working with the Yungas, rather than researching them, has been key. Working in the central Andes, Kendall has focused on terracing and irrigation over the last 1,200 years. The excavation of bodies of knowledge on how to use and integrate these systems has been important to their physical regeneration. Furthermore, an understanding of past climate change can help mitigate the possible difficulties of contemporary changes. With the break-up of the Soviet Union new theoretical approaches are being developed and sought, as Smyntyna explores. In the process, she provides a most useful history of research in an area of the world still too little known outside the former Soviet Union. Here strong research traditions in ecology had often resulted in a rather environmentally deterministic slant to archaeology, which is now, as elsewhere, trying to balance human and other ecological effects.

The picture emerging in this volume is a complex one, but so too is the world we inhabit. It is important to maintain a sense of human agency, along with the agency of other entities in the world, and to feel that relationships can develop in a beneficial manner as well as for ill. There is an excitement evident in the approaches being developed in this volume, partly because a new picture of the world, and of the place of humans within it, is emerging, but also because of the practical implications developing out of a complicated relationship between people and the natural world. To paraphrase Marx: it is important to understand the world, but it is even more important to change it.

References

ABC (2008), 'Marshall Islands in "Major Clean-up"'. Australian Broadcasting Corporation 26 December. Available at http://www.abc.net.au/news/stories/2008/12/26/2455403.htm?site=news [Accessed on 25 March 2010].

Adams, R. McC. (1966), *The Evolution of Urban Society* (Chicago, IL: Aldine).

Adams, W. M. (1996), 'Irrigation, Erosion and Famine: Visions of Environmental Change in Marakwet, Kenya. pp. 155–67, in M. Leach and R. Mearns, eds, *The Lie of the Land: Challenging Received Wisdom on the African Environment* (London: James Currey).

——and Anderson, D. M. (1988), 'Irrigation Before Development: Indigenous and Induced Change in Agricultural Water Management in East Africa', *African Affairs* 87: 519–35.

——and Grove, A. T., eds (1984), *Irrigation in Tropical Africa—Problems and Problem-solving* (Cambridge: African Studies Centre).

——Potkanski, T. and Sutton, J. E. G. (1994), 'Indigenous Farmer Managed Irrigation in Sonjo, Tanzania', *Geographical Journal* 160(1): 17–32.

Agrawal, A. (1995), 'Dismantling the Divide Between Indigenous and Scientific Knowledge', *Development and Change* 26(3): 413–39.

Albarella, U. (2001), 'Exploring the Real Nature of Environmental Archaeology. An Introduction', in U. Albarella, ed., *Environmental Archaeology: Meaning and Purpose* (London: Kluwer), pp. 3–13.

Algaze, G. (2008), *Ancient Mesopotamia at the dawn of Civilisation: the Evolution of an Urban Landscape* (Chicago: University of Chicago Press).

Allison, P. (2002), 'Recurring Tremors: The Continuing Impact of the AD 79 eruption of Mt Vesuvius', in R. Torrence and J. Grattan, eds, *Natural Disasters and Cultural Change* (London and New York: Routledge), pp. 107–25.

Almond, P., Edwards, T., and Clark, I. (2003), 'Multinationals and Changing National Business Systems in Europe: Towards the "Shareholder Value" Model?', *Industrial Relations Journal* 34(5): 430–45.

Alrøe, H. F., Vaarst, M., and Kristensen, E. S. (2001), 'Does Organic Farming Face Distinctive Livestock Issues?—a Conceptual Analysis', *Journal of Agricultural and Environmental Ethics* 14: 275–99.

Alvarez, M. and Fiore, D. (1993), 'La Arqueología como Ciencia Social: Apuntes para un Enfoque Teórico-Epistemológico', *Boletín de Antropología Americana* 27: 21–38.

Amborn, H. (1989), 'Agricultural intensification in the Burji-Konso Cluster of South Eastern Ethiopia'. *Azania* 24: 71–83.

Andah, B. (1992), 'Identifying Early Farming Traditions of West Africa', in T. Shaw, P. Sinclair, B. Andah, and A. Okpolo, eds, *The Archaeology of Africa: Food, Metals and Towns* (London: Routledge), pp. 240–54.

Anderies, J. M. and Hegmon, M. (2011), 'Robustness and Resilience Across Scales: Migration and Resource Degradation in the Prehistoric US Southwest', *Ecology and Society* 16(2): 22.

Anderson, A., Gagan, M., and Shulmeister, J. (2007), 'Mid-Holocene Cultural Dynamics and Climatic Change in the Western Pacific', in D. G. Anderson, K. A. Maasch, and D. H. Sandweiss, eds, *Climate Change and Cultural Dynamics: A Global Perspective on Mid-Holocene Transitions* (Amsterdam: Academic Press), pp. 265–96.

Anderson, D. (1984), 'Depression, Dust Bowl, Demography and Drought: The Colonial State and Soil Conservation in East Africa during the 1930s', *African Affairs* 83:321–43.

——and Grove, R., eds (1987), *Conservation in Africa: People, Policies and Practice* (Cambridge: Cambridge University Press).

Anderson, D. G. (2001), 'Climate and Culture Change in Prehistoric and Early Historic Eastern North America', *Archaeology of Eastern North America* 29:143–86.

——(2002), 'Evolution of Tribal Social Organization in the Southeast', in W. A. Parkinson, ed., *The Archaeology of Tribal Societies* (Ann Arbor, MI: International Monographs in Prehistory), pp. 246–77.

——(2004), 'Archaic Mounds and the Archaeology of Southeastern Tribal Societies', in J. L. Gibson and P. J. Carr, eds, *Signs of Power: The Rise of Cultural Complexity in the Southeast* (University of Alabama Press: Tuscaloosa), pp. 270–99.

——(2010), 'The End of the Southeastern Archaic: Regional Interaction and Archaeological Interpretation', in D. H. Thomas and M. C. Sanger, eds, *Trend, Tradition, and Turmoil: What Happened to the Southeastern Archaic? Proceedings of the Third Caldwell Conference, St. Catherines Island, Georgia, May 9–11, 2008* (New York: Anthropological Papers of the American Museum of Natural History), pp. 273–302.

——Maasch, K. A., and Sandweiss, D. H. (2007a), eds, *Climate Change and Cultural Dynamics: A Global Perspective on Mid-Holocene Transitions* (Amsterdam: Academic Press).

————and Mayewski, P. A. (2007b), 'Climate and Culture Change: Exploring Holocene Transitions', in D. G. Anderson, K. A. Maasch, and D. H. Sandweiss, eds, *Climate Change and Cultural Dynamics: A Global Perspective on Mid-Holocene Transitions* (Amsterdam: Academic Press), pp. 1–23.

——Stahle, D. W. and Cleveland, M. R. (1995), 'Paleoclimate and the Potential Food Reserves of Mississippian Societies: A Case Study from the Savannah River Valley', *American Antiquity* 60: 258–86.

Anderson, D. M. (1984), 'Depression, Dust-Bowl, Demography and Drought: the Colonial State and Soil Conservation in East Africa During the 1930s', *African Affairs* 83: 196–210.

Anderson, R. S. and Smith, S. J. (1997), 'The Sedimentary Record of Fire in Montane Meadows, Sierra Nevada, California, USA: A Preliminary Assessment', in J. S. Clark, H. Cachier, J. G. Goldammer, and B. Stocks, eds, *Sediment Records of Biomass Burning and Global Change*, NATO ASI Series, vol. I 51, pp. 313–27.

Anon. (1833a), 'Account of the Country Intervening Between Augusta and Swan River', in J. Cross, ed., *Journals of Several Expeditions Made in Western Australia, during the years 1829, 1830, 1831, and 1832, Under the Sanction of the Governor, Sir James Stirling, Containing the Latest Authentic Information Relative to that Country* (London: J. Cross), pp. 110–13.

Anon, (1976), 'L'arrivée d'un Ancient'. *Bois et Forêts des Tropiques* 162: 37–8.

Antin, E. (2001), *The Last Days of Pompeii* (Chromogenic print series. Exhibit held February 16–March 16 2002, Feldman Gallery, New York City).

Ardiles Nieves, P. (1986), 'Sistema de drenaje subterráneo prehispánico', *Allpanchis Phuturinqa* 27: 75–97 (Cusco: Instituto de Pastoral Andina).

Argent, G. (2010), 'Do the Clothes Make the Horse? Relationality, Roles and Statuses in Iron Age Inner Asia', *World Archaeology* 42(2): 157–74.

Årlin, C. (1999), 'Under Samma Tak—Om "Husstallets" Uppkomst Och Betydelse under Bronsåldern Ur Ett Sydskandinaviskt Perspektiv', in M. Olausson, ed., *Spiralens Öga. Tjugo Artiklar Kring Aktuell Bronsåldersforskning.* (Avdelning För Arkeologiska Undersökningar Skrifter: Riksantikvarieämbetet), pp. 291–307.

Armstrong Oma, K. (2007), *Human-Animal Relationships: Mutual Becomings in the Household of Scandinavia and Sicily 900–500 BC* (Oslo: Unipub).

——(2010), 'Between Trust and Domination: Social Contracts Between Humans and Animals', *World Archaeology* 42(2): 175–87.

Arroyo-Kalin, M. (2010), 'The Amazonian Formative: Crop Domestication and Anthropogenic Soils', *Diversity* 2: 473–504.

Ascher, R. (1962), 'Ethnography for Archaeology: A Case from the Seri Indians', *Ethnology* 1: 360–9.

Atahan, P., Dodson, J. R., and Itzstein-Davey, F. (2004), 'A Fine-resolution Pliocene Pollen and Charcoal Record from Yallalie, South-Western Australia', *Journal of Biogeography* 31: 199–205.

Auden, W. H. (1940), 'Musée des Beaux Arts', *Another Time* (London & New York: Random House).

Australia Network (2008), 'High Tides Flood Marshall Islands and Palau', Australia Network News 18 December. Available at http://australianetworknews.com/stories/200812/2449669.htm?desktop [Accessed on 25 March 2010].

Baas, P. K. K. and Geesink, R., eds (1990), *The Plant Diversity of Malesia* (Dordrecht: Kluwer).

Balée, W. (1988), 'Indigenous Adaptation to Amazonian Palm Forests', *Principes* 32(2): 47–54.

——(1994), *Footprints of the Forest: Ka'apor Ethnobotany-The Historical Ecology of Plant Utilization by an Amazonian People* (New York: Columbia University Press).

——ed. (1998), *Advances in Historical Ecology* (New York: Columbia University Press).

——(2006), 'The Research Program of Historical Ecology', *Annual Review of Anthropology* 35: 75–98.

——(2008), 'Sobre a Indigeneidade das Paisagens', *Revista de Arqueologia* 21(2): 9–23.

——(2009), 'Culturas de distúrbio e diversidade em substratos amazônicos', in W. G. Teixeira, D. C. Kern, B. E. Madari, H. N. Lima, and W. Woods, eds, *As Terras Pretas de Índio da Amazônia: Sua Caracterização e Uso deste Conhecimento na Criação de Novas Áreas* (Manaus: Embrapa Amazônia Oriental), pp. 48–52.

——(2010), 'Contingent Diversity on Anthropic Landscapes', *Diversity* 2: 163–81.

——and Erickson, C. L., eds (2006), *Time and Complexity in Historical Ecology: Studies in the Neotropical Lowlands* (New York: Columbia University Press).

Balzac, Honoré de (1896), *The Work of Honoré de Balzac: Alkahest or the House of Claës*, trans. K. P. Wormeley, The Athenaeum Edition edn, vol. 17 (Cambridge, MA: Roberts Brothers).

Banks, W. E., d'Errico, F., Dibble, H. L., Krishtalka, L., West, D., Olszewski, D. I., Peterson, A. T., Anderson, D. G., Gillam, J. C., Montet-White, A., Crucifix, M., Marean, C. W., Sánchez-Goñi, M.-F., Wohlfarth, B., and Vanhaeran, M. (2006), 'Eco-Cultural Niche Modeling: New Tools for Reconstructing the Geography and Ecology of Past Human Populations', *PaleoAnthropology* 2006: 68–83.

Bannister, T. (1833), 'A report of Captain Bannister's Journey to King George's Sound, Over land', in J. Cross, ed., *Journals of Several Expeditions Made in Western Australia, During the years 1829, 1830, 1831, and 1832, Under the Sanction of the Governor, Sir James Stirling, Containing the Latest Authentic Information Relative to that Country* (London: J. Cross), pp. 98–109.

Barker, G. (1999), 'Cattle-Keeping in Ancient Europe: To Live Together or Apart?', in C. Fabeck and J. Ringtved, eds, *Settlement and Landscape* (Århus: Jutland Archaeological Society), pp. 273–80.

Barnard, A. (2000), *History and Theory in Anthropology* (Cambridge: Cambridge University Press).

Barnett, J. and Adger, W. N. (2003), 'Climate Dangers and Atoll Countries', *Climatic Change* 61: 321–37.

——and Busse, M., eds (2002), *Proceedings of APN Workshop on Local Perspectives on Climate Change and Variability in the Pacific Islands* (Christchurch: Macmillan Brown Centre for Pacific Studies).

Barrett, J. C. and Ko, I. (2009), 'A Phenomenology of Landscape: A Crisis in British Landscape Archaeology', *Journal of Social Archaeology* 9: 275–95.

Bartman, W., ed. (1995), Allan McCollum Interviewed by Thomas Lawson (New York: Art Resources Transfer).

Basso, K. (1996), *Wisdom Sits in Places* (Albuquerque, NM: University of New Mexico Pressax.

Bastien, J. W. (1978), *Mountain of the Condor: Metaphor and Ritual in an Andean ayllu* (St. Paul, MN: West Publishing Company).

Bateson, G. (1973), *Steps to an Ecology of Mind* (London: Fontana).

Bayliss-Smith, T., Hviding, E., and Whitmore, T. (2003), 'Rainforest Composition and Histories of Human Disturbance in Solomon Islands', *Ambio* 32(5): 346–52.

BBC (2008), 'Marshall Atolls Declare Emergency'. BBC 25 December. Available at <http://news.bbc.co.uk/1/hi/world/asia-pacific/7799566.stm> [accessed on 25 March 2010].

Beach, H. (2007), 'Self-determining the Self: Aspects of Saami Identity Management in Sweden', *Acta Borealia* 24(1): 1–25.

Beard, J. S. (1979), 'Phytogeographic regions', in Gentilli, J., ed., *Western Landscapes* (Nedlands: University of Western Australia Press), pp. 107–21.

——Chapman, A. R., and Gioia, P. (2000), 'Species Richness and Endemism in the Western Australian flora', *Journal of Biogeography* 27:1257–68.

Beck, R., Bolender, D. J., Brown, J. A., and Earle, T. K. (2007), 'Eventful Archaeology: The Place of Space in Structural Transformation', *Current Anthropology* 48(6): 833–60.

Beck, U. (2006), *Cosmopolitan Vision* (Cambridge: Polity Press).

Beech, M. W. H. (1911), *The Suk: their Language and Folklore* (Oxford: Oxford University Press).

Beinart, W. (1984), 'Soil Erosion, Conservation, and Ideas about Development: a Southern African Exploration, 1900–1960', *Journal of Southern African Studies* 11: 52–83.

Benavides, M. A. (2004), 'Andenes y riego en el Perú: un analisis de informes coloniales y republicanos', in C. A. Llerena, M. Imbar, and M. A. Benavides, eds, *Conservación y abandono de andenes* (Lima: Universidad Agraria La Molina y Universidad de Haifa), pp. 51–65.

Bender, B. (1978), 'Gatherer-Hunter to Farmer: A Social Perspective', *World Archaeology* 10: 204–22.

——(1993), *Landscapes: Politics and Perspectives* (Oxford: Berg).

——Hamilton, S., and Tilley, C. (1997), 'Leskernick: Stone Worlds; Alternative Narratives; Nested Landscapes', *Proceedings of the Prehistoric Society* 63: 147–78.

Benecke, N. (1994), *Archäozoologische Studien Zur Entwicklung Der Haustierhaltung in Mitteleuropa Und Südskandinavien Von Der Anfängen Bis Zum Ausgehenden Mittelalter. Schriften Zur Ur- Und Frühgeschichte* (Berlin: Akademie Verlag).

Benjamin, W. (1983), *Das Passagen-Werk*, 2 vols (Frankfurt: Suhrkamp).

Bennett, K. D. and Fuller, J. L. (2002), 'Determining the Age of the Mid-Holocene Tsuga canadensis (Hemlock) Decline, Eastern North America', *The Holocene* 12: 421–9.

Berger, A. and Loutre M.-F. (2002), 'An Exceptionally Long Interglacial Ahead?', *Science* 297: 1287–8.

Berglund, J. (2010), 'Did the Medieval Norse Society in Greenland Really Fail?', in P. A. McAnany and N. Yoffee, eds, *Questioning Collapse: Human Resilience, Ecological Vulnerability, and the Aftermath of Empire* (Cambridge: Cambridge University Press), pp. 45–70.

Berkes, F. (1999), *Sacred Ecology: Traditional Ecological Knowledge and Resource Managements* (Philadelphia, PA: Taylor and Francis).

Berthet, É. (1876), *Romans préhistoriques: le monde inconnu* (Paris: Dentu).

Bertonio, L. (2005 [1612]), *Vocabulario de la lengua aymara* (Arequipa: Ediciones Lector).

Bettinger, R. L. (1991), *Hunter-Gatherers: Archaeological and Evolutionary Theory* (New York: Plenum Press).

Binford, L. R. (1962), 'Archaeology as Anthropology', *American Antiquity* 28: 217–25.

——(1965), 'Archaeological Systematics and the Study of Culture Process', *American Antiquity* 31: 203–10.

——(1972), *An Archaeological Perspective* (New York: Seminar Press).

——(1978), *Nunamiut Ethnoarchaeology* (New York: Academic Press).

——(1981a), *Bones: Ancient Men and Modern Myths* (New York: Academic).

——(1981b), 'Behavioral Archaeology and the "Pompeii Premise"', *Journal of Anthropological Research* 37: 195–208.

——and Binford, L. R., eds (1968), *New Perspectives in Archaeology* (Chicago, IL: Aldine).

Bird, D. W., Bliege Bird, R., and Codding, B. F. (2009), 'In Pursuit of Mobile Prey: Martu Hunting Strategies and Archaeofaunal Interpretation', *American Antiquity* 74(1): 3–29.

Blackmore A. C., Mentis M. T., and Scholes, R. J. (1990), 'The Origin and Extent of Nutrient-Enriched Patches within a Nutrient-poor Savanna in South Africa', *Journal of Biogeography* 17: 463–70.

Blackmore, S. (1999), *The Meme Machine* (Oxford: Oxford University Press).

Blanchot, M. (1995), *The Writing of the Disaster*, trans. A. Smock (London: University of Nebraska Press).

Blix, G. (2009), *From Paris to Pompeii: French Romanticism and the Cultural Politics of Archaeology* (Philadelphia, PA: University of Pennysylvania Press).

Blumenstock, D. I. (1958), 'Typhoon Effects at Jaluit Atoll in the Marshall Islands', *Nature* 182(4645): 1267–9.

Bollig, M. (1990), 'An outline of Pre-Colonial Pokot History', *Afrikanistiche Arbeitspapiere* 23: 73–91.

Bond, G., Showers, W., Cheseby, M., Lotti, R., Almasi, P., deMenocal, P., Priore, P., Cullen, H., Hajdas, I., and Bonani, G. (1997), 'A Pervasive Millennial-Scale Cycle in North Atlantic Holocene and Glacial Climates', *Science* 278: 1257–66.

Börjeson, L. (2005), *A History Under Siege: Intensive Agriculture in the Mbulu Highlands, Tanzania, 19th Century to the Present* (Stockholm: Department of Human Geography, Stockholm University).

——(2007), 'Boserup Backwards? Agricultural Intensification as its own Driving Force in The Mbulu Highlands, Tanzania', *Geografiska Annaler* Series B, Human Geography 89(3): 249–67.

Boserup, E. (1965), *The Conditions of Agricultural Growth: the Economics of Agrarian Change under Population Pressure* (London: Allen and Unwin).

——(1970), *Women's Role in Economic Development* (London: Earthscan).

BOSTID [Board on Science and Technology for International Development] (1996), *Lost Crops of Africa* (Washington, DC: National Academy Press).

Boulanger, N.-A. (1766), *L'antiquité dévoilée par ses usages* (Amsterdam, Marc-Michel Rey).

Bourdieu, P. (1977), *Outline of a Theory of Practice* (Cambridge: Cambridge University Press).

——(1993), *Sociology in Question* (London: Sage).

Bowman, D. M. J. S. (1998), Tansley Review no. 101: 'The Impact of Aboriginal Landscape Burning on the Australian Biota', *New Phytologist* 140: 385–410.

Bradley, R. (1998), *The Significance of Monuments: On the shaping of human experience in Neolithic and Bronze Age Europe* (London: Routledge).

——(2000), *An Archaeology of Natural Places* (London: Routledge).

Braidwood, R. and Howe, B. (1960), *Prehistoric Investigations in Iraqi Kurdistan* (Chicago, IL: Chicago University Press).

Branch, N. P., Kemp, R. A., Silva, B., Meddens, F. M., Williams, A., Kendall, A., and Pomacanchari, C. V. (2007), 'Testing the sustainability and sensitivity to climatic change of terrace agricultural Systems in the Peruvian Andes: a pilot study', *Journal of Archaeological Science* 34: 1–9.

Braun, B. (2002), *The Intemperate Rainforest. Nature, Culture and Power on Canada's West Coast* (Minneapolis, MN: University of Minnesota Press).

Bridges, T. (1894), 'A Few Notes on the Structure of Yahgan', *Journal of the Anthropological Institute of Great Britain and Ireland* 23: 53–80.

Bridges, T. (1933), *Yamana-English Dictionary* (Ushuaia: Zagier y Urruty Publicaciones).

Bridges, T. (2001), Los Indios del Último Confín (Bueno Aires: Zaguier y Urruty).

Brillat-Savarin, A. (2009 [1825]), *Physiologie du goût*. (Paris: Flammarion).

Brncic, T. M., Willis, K. J., Harris, D. J., and Washington, R. (2007), 'Culture or climate? The Relative Influences of Past Processes on the Composition of the Lowland Congo rainforest', *Philosophical Transactions of the Royal Society B* 362: 229–42.

Brockington, D. and Homewood, K. (2001), 'Degradation Debates and Data Deficiencies: the Mkomazi Game Reserve, Tanzania', *Africa* 71: 449–80.

Broecker, W. S. (1997), 'Thermohaline Circulation, the Achilles heel of our Climate System: Will man-made CO2 Upset the Current Balance?', *Science* 278: 1582–8.

Brokensha, D., Warren, D. M., and Werner, O., eds (1980), *Indigenous Knowledge Systems and Development* (Lanham, MD: University Press of America).

Brookfield, H. C. (2001), 'Intensification and Alternative Approaches to Agricultural Change', *Asia Pacific Viewpoint* 42: 181–92.

——and Hart, D. (1971), *Melanesia: Geographical Interpretation of an Island World* (London: Methuen).

Broughton, J. M. (1994), 'Late Holocene Resource Intensification in the Sacramento Valley, California: The Vertebrate Evidence', *Journal of Archaeological Science* 21: 501–14.

Brouwers, J. H. A. M. (1993), *Rural People's Response to Soil Fertility Decline:The Adja Case (Benin)* (Wageningen:,Wageningen Agricultural University).

Brown, J. M. and Hopkins, A. J. M. (1983), 'The Kwongan (sclerophyllous shrublands) of Tutanning Nature Reserve, Western Australia', *Australian Journal of Ecology* 8: 63–73.

Brush, S. (1976), 'Man's use of an Andean Ecosystem', *Human Ecology* 4(2): 147–66.

Buck-Morss, S. (1999), *Dialectics of Seeing: Walter Benjamin and the Arcades Project* (Cambridge, MA: MIT Press).

Bulwer-Lytton, E. (2003 [1834]), *The Last Days of Pompeii* (Holicong, PA: Wildside Press).

Bunbury, H. W. (1930), *Early Days in Western Australia* (London: Oxford University Press).

Burger, R. (1987), 'U-shaped complex, Cardal, Peru', *National Geographic Research* 3(3) : 363–75.

——(1991), *Informe final de las investigaciones arqueológicas en Mina Perdida, temporada 1990, valle de Lurín, Departamento de Lima* (Lima: Instituto Nacional de Cultura).

——(1992), *Chavin and the origins of Andean civilization* (London: Thames and Hudson).

——and Salazar-Burger, L. (1993), 'The Place of Dual Organization in Early Andean Ceremonialism: a Comparative Review', in L. Millones and Y. Onuki, eds, *El Mundo Ceremonial Andino* (Osaka: National Museum of Ethnology), pp. 97–116.

——(1984), *The Prehistoric Occupation of Chavín de Huantar, Peru* (Berkeley, CA: University of California Press).

Burkill, I. H. (1966), *A Dictionary of the Economic Products of the Malay Peninsula*, 2 vols (Kuala Lumpur: Ministry of Agriculture and Co-operatives).

Burling, R. (1962), 'Maximization Theories and the Study of Economic Anthropology', *American Anthropologist* 64: 802–21.

——(1964), 'Cognition and Componential Analysis: God's Truth or Hocus-Pocus?', *American Anthropologist* 66: 20–8.

——(1976), 'Teorías de la Maximización y el Estudio de la Antropología Económica', in M. Godelier, ed., *Antropología y Economía* (Barcelona: Anagrama), pp. 101–24.

Bussell, J. C. (1833), 'Report of An Expedition to the Northward from Augusta', in J. Cross, ed., *Journals of Several Expeditions Made in Western Australia, During the Years 1829, 1830, 1831, and 1832, under the Sanction of the Governor, Sir James Stirling, Containing the Latest Authentic Information Relative to that Country* (London: J. Cross), pp. 178–85.

Butzer, K. W. (1982), *Archaeology as Human Ecology: Method and Theory for a Contextual Approach* (Cambridge: Cambridge University Press).

Calwell, J. (1959), 'The New American Archaeology', *Science* 129: 303–7.

Camino, A. (1982), 'Tiempo y Espacio en la Estrategia de Subsistencia Andina: Un caso de las vertientes Orientales Sud-Peruanas', in L. Millones and H. Tomoeda, eds, *En El Hombre y su Ambiente de los Andes Centrales* (Japan: C. International).

Carswell, G. (2007), *Cultivating Success in Uganda: Kigezi Farmers and Colonial Policies* (Oxford: James Currey).

Casimir, M. (2008), 'The Mutual Dynamics of Cultural and Environmental Change: An Introductory Essay', in M. Casimir, ed, *Culture and the Changing Environment: Uncertainty, Cognition, and Risk Management in Cross-cultural Perspective* (New York: Berghahn Books), pp. 1–58.

Chambers, J. Q., Higuchi, N., and Schimel, J. P. (1998), 'Ancient Trees in Amazonia', *Nature* 391: 135–6.

Chamisso, A. von (1986 [1821]), *A Voyage Around the World with the Romanzov Exploring Expedition in the Years 1815–1818 in the Brig Rurick, Captain Otto von Kotzebue*, trans. H. Kratz (Honolulu, HI: University of Hawaii Press).

Chepstow-Lusty, A. and Winfield, M. (2000), 'Agroforestry by the Inca: Lessons from the Past', *Ambio* 29: 322–8.

——Frogley, M. R., Bauer, B. S., Leng, M. J., Boessenkool, K. P., Carcaillet, C., Ali, A. A., and Gioda, A. (2009), 'Putting the rise of the Inca Empire within a Climatic and Land Management Context', *Climate Past* 5: 375–88.

Chevalier, A. (2002), 'L'exploitation des Plantes sur le Côte Péruvienne en Contexte Formatif'. Doctoral thesis, Faculté des Sciences, Université de Genève.

Childe, V. G. (1925), *The Dawn of European Civilisation* (London: Keegan Paul).

——(1942), *What Happened in History: A Study of the Rise and Decline of Cultural and Moral Values in the Old World up to the Fall of the Roman Empire* (Harmondsworth: Penguin).

Churchill, D. M. (1968), 'The Distribution and Prehistory of Eucalyptus Diversicolor F. Muell., E. Marginata Donn Ex Sm., and E. calophylla R.Br. in Relation to Rainfall', *Australian Journal of Botany* 16:125–51.

Clark, D. B. (1996), 'Abolishing Virginity', *Journal of Tropical Ecology* 12: 735–9.

Clark, J. G. D. (1939), *Archaeology and Society* (London: Methuen).

——*Prehistoric Europe: The Economic Basis* (London: Methuen).

Clarke, D. (1968), *Analytical Archaeology* (London: Methuen).

Clarke, D. (1977), 'Spatial Information in Archaeology', in D. L. Clarke, ed., *Spatial Archaeology* (London: Academic Press), pp. 1–32.

Clement, C. R. (1999a), '1492 and the Loss of Amazonian Crop Genetic Resources. I. The Relation Between Domestication and Population Decline', *Economic Botany* 53: 188–202.

——(1999b), '1492 and the Loss of Amazonian Crop Genetic Resources. II. Crop Biogeography at Contact', *Economic Botany* 53: 203–16.

——Cristo-Araújo, M. de, Coppens d'Eeckenbrugge, G., Pereira, A. A., and Picanço-Rodrigues, D. (2010), 'Origin and domestication of native Amazonian crops', *Diversity* 2: 72–106.

——and Junqueira, A. B. (2010), 'Between a Pristine Myth and an Impoverished Future', *Biotropica* 42(5): 534–6.

Collie, A. (1833), 'Account of an Excursion to the North of King George's Sound, Between the 26th of April and the 4th of May, 1831', in J. Cross, ed., *Journals of Several Expeditions Made in Western Australia, During the Years 1829, 1830, 1831, and 1832, Under the sanction of the Governor, Sir James Stirling, Containing the Latest Authentic Information Relative to that Country* (London: J. Cross), pp. 132–54.

——and Preston, W. (1833), 'Observations on the Coast, Country &c. From Cockburn Sound to Geographe Bay, Between the 17th and 30th of November 1829', in J. Cross, ed., *Journals of Several Expeditions Made in Western Australia, During the Years 1829, 1830, 1831, and 1832, Under the Sanction of the Governor, Sir James Stirling, Containing the Latest Authentic Information Relative to that Country* (London: J. Cross), pp. 35–50.

Conelly, W. T. (1994), 'Population Pressure, Labour Availability, and Agricultural Disintensification: The Decline of Farming on Rusinga Island, Kenya'. *Human Ecology* 22: 145–70.

Conservation Council of Western Australia (1997), 'Policy number 50: Fire in the natural environment', www.coagbushfireenquiry.gov.au/subs_word/67_schultz_cc-wa_fire_policy.doc [Accessed 25/02/09].

Cooper, J. and Sheets, P., eds (2012), *Surviving Sudeen Environmental Change: Answers from Archaeology* (Boulder, CO: University Press of Colorado).

Corrêa, C. (1985), 'Fases ceramistas não-sambaqueiras do litoral do Pará'. MA thesis, Universidade Federal de Pernambuco Recife, Brazil.

Costanza, R., Graumlich, L. J., and Steffen, W., eds. (2007a), *Sustainability or Collapse?: An Integrated History and Future of People on Earth (Report of the 96th Dahlem Workshop, Berlin, June 12–17, 2005)* (Cambridge, MA: MIT Press).

——————Crumley, C., Dearing, J., Hibbard, K., Leemans, R., Redman, C., and Schimel D. (2007b), 'Sustainability or Collapse: What can we Learn from Integrating the History of Humans and the Rest of Nature?' *Ambio* 36(7): 522–7.

—— van der Leeuw, S., Hibbard, K., Aulenbach, S., Brewer, S., Burek, M., Cornell, S., Crumley, C., Dearing, J., Folke, C., Graumlich, L., Hegmon, M., Heckbert, S., Jackson, S., Kubiszewski, I., Scarborough, V., Sinclair, P., Sorlin, S., and Steffen, W. (2012), 'Developing an Integrated History and Future of People on Earth (IHOPE)', *Current Opinion in Environmental Sustainability* 4: 106–14.

Counihan, C. and Kaplan, S., eds (1998), *Food and Gender: Identity and Power* (Amsterdam: Harwood Academic Publishers).

——and Van Esterik, P., eds (1997), *Food and Culture: a Reader* (London: Routledge).

Critchley, W. R. S., Reij, C., and Willcocks, T. J. (1994), 'Indigenous Soil and Water Conservation: a Review of the State of Knowledge and Prospects for Building on Traditions', *Land Degradation and Rehabilitation* 5: 293–314.

Cronon, W. (1992), 'A Place for Stories: Nature, History, and Narrative', *Journal of American History* 78(4): 1347–76.

Cruikshank, J. (2005), *Do Glaciers Listen? Local Knowledge, Colonial Encounters, and Social Imagination* (Toronto: University of British Columbia Press).

Crumley, C. L., ed. (1994), *Historical Ecology: Cultural Knowledge and Changing Landscapes* (Santa Fe, NM: School of American Research Press).

——(2000), 'From Garden to Globe: Linking Time and Space with Meaning and Memory', in R. J. McIntosh, J. A. Tainter, J. A., and S. K. McIntosh, eds, *The Way the Wind Blows: Climate Change, History, and Human Action* (New York: Columbia University Press), pp. 193–208.

——(2006), 'Archaeology in the New World Order: What We Can Offer the Planet', in E. C. Robertson, J. D. Seibert, D. C. Fernandez, and M. U. Zender, eds, *Space and Spatial Analysis in Archaeology* (Calgary, AB: University of Calgary Press), pp. 383–95.

——(2007), 'Historical Ecology: Integrated Thinking at Multiple Temporal and Spatial Scales', in A. Hornborg and C. L. Crumley, eds, *The World System and the Earth System: Global Socioenvironmental Change and Sustainability since the Neolithic* (Walnut Creek, CA: Left Coast Press), pp. 15–28.

——(2013), 'Historical Ecology in Archaeology', in C. Smith, ed., *Encyclopedia of Global Archaeology* (New York: Springer).

Crutzen, P. and Stoermer, E. F. (2000), 'The "Anthropocene"', *IGBP Newsletter* 41: 17–18.

Cullen, B. (1995), 'Living Artefact, Personal Ecosystem, Biocultural Schizophrenia: a Novel Synthesis of Processual and Post-processual Thinking', *Proceedings of the Prehistoric Society* 61: 371–92.

Cusichaca Trust (2005), 'Los andenes y su impacto en la agricultura sustentable' Pampachiri—Andamarca, 13–17 marzo de 2005, Memoria del Seminario Taller, Ayacucho: Mercantil Ayacucho E.I.R.L.

——(2006), *Informe: Proyecto de Rehabilitación del Patrimonio Vivo Agrícola en Laymecocha, Distrito de Larcay, Provincia de Sucre, Departamento de Ayacucho.* (Lima: Unpublished Report Presented to Instituto Nacional de Cultura).

——(2006), 'Inventario y mapeo de sitios arqueológicos en los valles de Chicha-Soras y Sondondo', Internal Report, Andahuaylas.

D'Altroy, T. N. (1992), *Provincial Power in the Inka Empire* (Washington, DC: Smithsonian Institution Press).

——and Hastorf, C. A. (1984), 'The distribution and contents of Inca state storehouses in the Xauxa region of Peru', *American Antiquity* 49: 334–49.

Dabbert, S., Häring, A. M., and Zanoli, R. (2004), *Organic Farming: Policies and Prospects* (London: Zed Books).

Dale, R. (1833), 'Mr. Dale's journal of an expedition from King George's Sound to the Koikyennuruff Range of mountains', in J. Cross, ed., *Journals of several expeditions made in Western Australia, during the years 1829, 1830, 1831, and 1832, under the sanction of the governor, Sir James Stirling, containing the latest authentic information relative to that country* (London: J. Cross).

Dannenmaier, E. (2008), 'Beyond Indigenous Property Rights: Exploring the Emergence of a Distinctive Connection Doctrine', *Washington University Law Review* 86: 53–110.

Darvill, T. (2008), 'Pathways to a Panoramic Past: A Brief History of European Landscape Archaeology', in B. David and J. Thomas, eds, *Handbook of Landscape Archaeology* (Walnut Creek, CA: Left Coast Press), pp. 60–76.

David, B. and Thomas, J., eds (2008a), *Handbook of Landscape Archaeology* (Walnut Creek, CA: Left Coast Press).

——— (2008b), Landscape Archaeology: 'Introduction', in B. David and J. Thomas, eds, *Handbook of Landscape Archaeology* (Walnut Creek, CA: Left Coast Press), pp. 27–43.

Davies, M. (2008), 'The Irrigation System of the Pokot, Northwest Kenya', *Azania* 43: 50–76.

——(2009a), 'An Applied Archaeological and Anthropological Study of Intensive Agriculture in the Northern Cherangani Hills, Kenya'. Unpublished DPhil thesis, University of Oxford.

——(2009b), 'Wittfogel's Dilemma: Heterarchy and Ethnographic Approaches to Irrigation Management in Eastern Africa and Mesopotamia', *World Archaeology* 41(1): 16–35.

——(2010), 'A View from the East: an Interdisciplinary "Historical Ecology" Approach to a Contemporary Agricultural Landscape in Northwest Kenya', *African Affairs* 69: 279–97.

Davies, M. I. J. (2012), 'Some thoughts on a "useable" African archaeology: settlement, population and intensive farming among the Pokot of northwest Kenya', *African Archaeological Review* 29: 319–53.

Davis, M. B. and Botkin, D. B. (1985), 'Sensitivity of Cool-temperature Forests and their Fossil Pollen Record to Rapid Temperature Change', *Quaternary Research* 23: 327–40.

Dawdy, S. L. (2009), 'Millennial Archaeology: Locating the Discipline in the Age of Insecurity', *Archaeological Dialogues* 16: 131–42.

Dawkins, R. (1976), *The Selfish Gene* (Oxford: Oxford University Press).

de Stael, Mme. (1998 [1805]), *Corinne, or, Italy.* Ed. and trans. Sylvia Raphael, Introduction by John Isbell (Oxford: Oxford University Press).

Dean, W. (1995), *With Broadax and Firebrand: The Destruction of the Brazilian Atlantic Forest* (Los Angeles, CA: University of California Press).

Dearing, J. A. (2007), 'Integration of World and Earth Systems: Heritage and Foresight', in A. Hornborg, and C. Crumley, eds, *The World System and the Earth System. Global Socioenvironmental Change and Sustainability since the Neolithic* (Walnut Creek, CA: Left Coast Press), pp. 38–55.

Deetz, J. (1996), *In Small Things Forgotten* (New York: Anchor, Doubleday).

Delcourt, P. A. and Delcourt, H. R. (2004), *Prehistoric Native Americans and Ecological Change: Human Ecosystems in Eastern North America Since the Pleistocene* (Cambridge: Cambridge University Press).

Demarest, A. A. (2004), *Ancient Maya: The Rise and Fall of a Rainforest Civilisation* (Cambridge: Cambridge University Press).

deMenocal, P. (2001), 'Cultural Responses to Climate Change during the Late Holocene', *Science* 292: 667–73.

——Ortiz, J., Guilderson, T., and Sarnthein, M. (2000), 'Coherent High- and Low-Latitude Climate Variability During the Holocene Warm Period', *Science* 288(5474): 2198–202.

Demeritt, D. (1994), 'Ecology, Objectivity and Critique in Writings on Nature and Human Societies', *Journal of Historical Geography* 20(1): 22–37.

Demian, M. and Wastell, S. (2007), 'Part II. Creative Appropriations and Institutional Contexts: Introduction', in Elizabeth Hallam and Ingold, T., eds, *Creativity and Cultural Improvisation* (Oxford: Berg), pp. 119–26.

Denevan, W. M. (1988), 'Causes of Terrace Abandonment in the Colca Valley', in W. M. Denevan, ed., *The Cultural Ecology, Archaeology and History of Terracing and Terrace Abandonment in the Colca Valley of Southern Peru. Technical Report to the National Science Foundation and the National Geographic Society*, vol. II (Madison, WI: University of Wisconsin, Madison Department of Geography), pp. 87–90.

——(1992), 'Native American Populations in 1492: Recent Research and a Revised Hemispheric Estimate', in W. E. Denevan, ed., *The Native Population of the Americas in 1492*, 2nd edn (Madison, WI: University of Wisconsin Press), pp. xvii–xxxviii.

——(2001), *Cultivated Landscapes of Native Amazonia and the Andes* (Oxford: Oxford University Press).

——(2006), 'Pre-European Forest Cultivation in Amazonia', in W. Balée and C. L. Erickson, eds, *Time and Complexity in Historical Ecology: Studies in the Neotropical Lowlands* (New York: Columbia University Press), pp. 153–63.

Denham, T. and White, P. (2007), *The Emergence of Agriculture: A Global View* (London: Routledge).

Desai, K. (2006), *The Inheritance of Loss* (New York: Grover Press).

Descola, P. (1994). *In the Society of Nature: a Native Ecology in Amazonia* (Cambridge: Cambridge University Press).

Desperret, A. (1833), 'Troisième Eruption de Volcan de 1789' (lithograph), *La Caricature*, no. 135, 6 June 1833.

Diamond, J. (1997), *Guns, Germs and Steel: A Short History of Everybody for the Last 13,000 years* (London: Vintage).

——(2005), *Collapse: How Societies Choose to Fail or Succeed* (New York: Viking).

Dickens, C. (1846), *Pictures from Italy* (Paris: A. and W. Galignant).

Dickenson, E. (1924), 'On My Volcano Grows the Grass', *The Complete Poems of Emily Dickenson, with an introduction by her niece, Martha Dickenson Bianchi* (Boston: Little, Brown, and Company).

Dietler, M. and Hayden, B., eds (2001), *Feasts: Archaeological and Ethnographic Perpectives on Food, Politics, and Power* (Washington, DC: Smithsonian Institution Press).

Dietz, T. (1987), *Pastoralists in Dire Straits: Survival Strategies and External Interventions in a Semi-arid Region at the Kenya-Uganda Border: West Pokot, 1900–1986* (Amsterdam: Institute Voor Sociale Greographie, Universiteit van Amsterdam).

Digerfeldt, D. (1997), 'Reconstruction of Holocene Lake-level Changes in Lake Kalvsjon, Southern Sweden, with a Contribution to the Local Palaeohydrology at the Elm Decline', *Vegetation History and Archaeobotany* 6: 9–14.

Dincauze, D. (1987), 'Strategies for Palaeoenvironmental Reconstruction in Archaeology. pp. 255–336, in M. B. Schiffer, ed., *Advances in Archaeological Method and Theory* (San Diego, CA: Academic Press).

——(2000), *Environmental Archaeology Principles and Practice* (Cambridge: Cambridge University Press).

Djegui, N. (1995), 'Les Stocks Organiques dans les sols Cultivés sous Palmeraie et Cultures et Cultures Vivrières dans le sud du Benin', in *Fertilité du Milieu et Stratégies Paysannes sous les Tropiques Humides. Report of Seminar, 13–17 November 1995* (Montpellier: CIRAD), pp. 189–93.

Dobres, M. A. (2000), *Technology and Social Agency* (Oxford: Blackwell).

Dodson, J. R. (2001), 'Holocene Vegetation Change in the Mediterranean-type Climate Regions of Australia', *The Holocene* 11: 673–80.

——and Lu, J. J. (2000), 'A late Holocene Vegetation and Environment Record from Byenup Lagoon, South-Western Australia', *Australian Geographer* 31: 41–54.

——Robinson, M., and Tardy, C. (2005), 'Two Fine-resolution Pliocene Charcoal Records and their Bearing on Pre-human Fire Frequency in South-western Australia', *Austral Ecology* 30: 592–9.

Donaldson, T. and Preston, L. E. (1995), 'The Stakeholder Theory of the Corporation: Concepts, Evidence, and Implications', *Academy of Management Review* 20: 65–91.

Donkin, R. A. (1979), *Agricultural Terracing in the Aboriginal New World*, Viking Fund Publications in Anthropology 56 (Tucson, AZ: University of Arizona Press for the Wenner-Gren Foundation for Anthropological Research).

Dortch, C. E. (2002), 'Modelling Past Aboriginal Hunter-gatherer Socio-economic and Territorial Organisation in Western Australia's Lower South-west', *Archaeology in Oceania* 37: 1–21.

Douglas, M. (1971), 'Deciphering a Meal', in C. Geertz, ed., *Myth, Symbol and Culture* (New York: Norton), pp. 61–82.

Dove, M. (2006), 'Indigenous People and Environmental Politics', *Annual Review of Anthropology* 35: 191–208.

——(2010), 'The Panoptic Gaze in a Non-Western Setting: Self-Surveillance on Merapi Volcano, Central Java', *Religion* 40: 121–7.

——and Carpenter, C. (2008), 'Introduction: Major Historical Currents in Environmental Anthropology', in M. Dove and C. Carpenter, eds, *Environmental Anthropology: A Historical Reader*, Blackwll Anthologies in Social and Cultural Anthropology (Malden, MA: Blackwell), pp. 1–85.

Dransart, P. Z. (2002), *Earth, Water, Fleece, and Fabric: An Ethnography and Archaeology of Andean Camelid Herding* (New York: Routledge).

Dugmore, A., Keller, C., and McGovern T. (2007), 'Norse Greenland Settlement: Reflections on Climate Change, Trade, and the Contrasting Fates of Human Settlements in the North Atlantic Islands', *Arctic Anthropology* 44(1): 12–36.

Duncan, N., Pearsall, D., and Benfer, R. (2009), 'Gourd and Squash Artifacts Yield Starch Grains of Feasting Foods from Preceramic Peru', *Proceedings of the National Academy of Science* 106(32): 13202–6.

Earle, T. (2002), *Bronze Age Economics: The Beginnings of Political Economics* (Cambridge, MA: Westview Press).

Earls, J. (2006), *Topo Climatología de la Alta Montaña : Una Experiencia en la Vertiente Oriental Andina* (Lima: Concejo Nacional de Ciencia, Tecnologia e Innovación Tecnológica).

Edwards, K. (2001), 'Environmental Reconstruction', in D. A. Brothwell, ed., *Handbook of Archaeological Sciences* (New York: John Wiley), pp. 103–10.

Einhorn, H. J. and Hogarth, R. M. (1986), 'Judging Probable Cause', *Psychological Bulletin* 99: 3–19.

Ellen, R. (2010), 'Why Aren't the Nuaulu Like the Matsigenka? Knowledge and Categorization of Forest Diversity on Seram, Eastern Indonesia', in L. M. Johnson and E. S. Hunn, eds, *Landscape Ethnoecology: Concepts of Biotic and Physical Space* (New York: Berghahn Books), pp. 116–40.

Erickson, C. L. (1985), 'Applications of Prehistoric Andean Technology: Experiments in Raised Field Agriculture, Huatta, Lake Titicaca, Peru, 1981–1983', in I. Farrington, ed., *Prehistoric Intensive Agriculture in the Tropics*, British Archaeological Reports International Series No. 232 (Oxford: British Archaeological Reports), pp. 209–32.

——(1994), 'Methodological Considerations in the Study of Ancient Andean Field Systems', in N. F. Miller, and K. L. Gleason, eds, *The Archaeology of Garden and Field* (Philadelphia, PA: University of Pennsylvania Press), pp. 111–52.

——(1998), 'Applied Archaeology and Rural Development: Archaeology's Potential Contribution to the Future', in M. B. Whiteford and S. Whiteford, eds, *Crossing Currents: Continuity and Change in Latin America* (Upper Saddle River, NJ: Prentice Hall), pp. 34–45.

——(2000a), 'The Lake Titicaca basin: A pre-Columbian Built Landscape', in B. Lentz, ed., *Imperfect Balance: Landscape Transformations in the Pre-Columbian Americas* (New York: Columbia University Press), pp. 311–56.

——(2000b), 'An Artificial Landscape-scale Fishery in the Bolivian Amazon', *Nature* 408: 190–3.

——(2006), 'The Domesticated Landscapes of the Bolivian Amazon', in W. Balée and C. L. Erickson, eds, *Time and Complexity in Historical Ecology: Studies in the Neotropical Lowlands* (New York: Columbia University Press), pp. 235–78.

——(2008), 'Amazonia: The Historical Ecology of a Domesticated Landscape', in H. Silverman and W. H. Isbell, eds, *Handbook of South American Archaeology* (New York: Springer), pp. 157–83.

——(2010), 'The Transformation of Environment into Landscape: The Historical Ecology of Monumental Earthwork Construction in the Bolivian Amazon', *Diversity* 2: 618–52.

——and Balée, W. (2006), 'The Historical Ecology of a Complex Landscape in Bolivia', in W. Balée and C. L. Erickson, eds, *Time and Complexity in Historical Ecology:*

Studies in the Neotropical Lowlands (New York: Columbia University Press), pp. 187–233.

Eshetu, Z. and Högberg, P. (2000), 'Reconstruction of a Forest Site History in the Ethiopian Highlands Based on 13-C Natural Abundance in Soils', *Ambio* 29: 83–9.

Espinoza Soriano, W. (1971), 'Los Huancas, aliados de la conquista : Tres informaciones sobre la participaci6n indigena en la conquista del Peru, 1558–1560–1561', *Anales Científicos de la Universidad del Centro del Peru* 1: 3–407.

Estévez Escalera, J. and Vila Mitjá, A., eds (1995), *Encuentros en los Conchales Fueguinos*, Treballs D'Etnoarqueología 1 (Barcelona: Consejo Superior de Investigaciones Científicas).

Ethelberg, P., Jørgensen, E., Meier, D., and Robinson, D. (2000), *Det Sønderjyske Landbrugs Historie: Sten- og Bronzealder* (Haderslev: Haderslev Museum og Historisk Samfund for Sønderjylland).

Evans, J. (1978), *An Introduction to Environmental Archaeology* (London: Paul Elek).

Fagan, B. (2000), *The Little Ice Age: How Climate Made History 1300–1850* (New York: Basic Books).

——(2004), *The Long Summer: How Climate Changed Civilisation* (New York: Basic Books).

——(2007), *People of the Earth: An Introduction to World Prehistory* 12th edn (New York: Harper Collins).

——(2008), *The Great Warming: Climate Change and the Rise and Fall of Civilizations* (New York: Bloomsbury Press).

Fairfield, S. L. (1832), *The Last Night of Pompeii* (New York: Elliot and Palmer).

Fairhead, J. and Leach, M. (1994), 'Contested Forests: Modern Conservation and Historical Land use in Guinea's Ziama Reserve', *African Affairs* 93: 481–512.

————(1996a), *Misreading the African Landscape: Society and Ecology in a Forest-Savanna Mosaic* (Cambridge: Cambridge University Press).

————(1996b), 'Rethinking the Forest-savannah Mosaic: Colonial Science and its relics in west Africa', in M. Leach and R. Mearns, eds, *The Lie of the Land: Challenging Received Wisdom on the African Environment* (London: James Currey), pp. 105–21.

————(1998), *Reframing Deforestation: Global Analysis and Local Realities-Cases from West Africa* (London: Routledge).

——Holsoe, S., Geysbeek, T., and Leach, M. (2003), *African-American Exploration of West Africa: Four Nineteenth Century Diaries* (Bloomington, IN: Indiana University Press).

Fall, P. L., Falconer, S. E., Lines, L., and Metzger, M. C. (2004), 'Environmental Impacts of the Rise of Civilization in the Southern Levant', in C. L. Redman, S. R. James, P. R. Fish, and J. D. Rogers, eds, *The Archaeology of Global Change: The Impact of Humans on their Environment* (Washington, DC: Smithsonian Institution Press), pp. 141–57.

FAO [Food and Agriculture Organization of the United Nations] (1990), *The conservation and rehabilitation of African lands: an international scheme* (Rome: FAO).

Farb, P. and Armelagos, G. (1983), *Consuming Passions: The Anthropology of Eating* (New York: Pocket Books).

Farrington, I. S. (1979), 'The vertical economy of the Cusichaca Valley (Dept. of Cuzco, Peru) and its prehistoric implications', Vancouver: XLIII International Congress of Americanists (ICA).

——(1980), 'The archaeology of Irrigation Canals, with Special Reference to Peru', *World Archaeology* 2: 287–305.

Fedje, D. and Mathewes, R. W. (2005), *Haida Gwaii: Human History and Environment from the Time of Loon to the Time of the Iron People* (Vancouver, BC: University of British Columbia Press).

Feierman, S. (1990), *Peasant Intellectuals. Anthropology and History in Tanzania* (Madison, WI: University of Wisconsin Press).

Ferguson, J. (1990), *The Anti-politics machine: 'Development', Depoliticization and Bureaucratic Power in Lesotho* (Cambridge: Cambridge University Press).

Fernandez, D. (2000), 'Caracterización Histoquímica, Distribución y Crecimiento de las Fibras Musculares en Nototénidos Subantárticos. Análisis Inicial de los Factores Relacionados con la Natación: Flotabilidad y Temperatura', PhD Thesis, Facultad de Ciencias Exactas y Naturales, Universidad de Buenos Aires.

Fiore, D. (2002), 'Body Painting in Tierra del Fuego. The Power of Images in the Uttermost Part of the World', PhD Thesis, Institute of Archaeology, University College London.

——(2006), 'Painted Genders: The Construction of Gender Roles Through the Display of Body Painting by the Selk´nam and the Yámana from Tierra del Fuego (Southern South America)', in S. Hamilton, R. D. Whitehouse, and K. I. Wright, eds, *Archaeology and Women: Ancient and Modern Issues* (California: Walnut Creek), pp. 373–403.

——and Zangrando, A. F. (2006), 'Painted Fish, Eaten Fish: Artistic and Archaeofaunal Representations in Tierra del Fuego, Southern South America', *Journal of Anthropological Archaeology* 25: 371–89.

Fiorentino, G., Caracuta, V., Volpe, G., Turchiano, M., Quarta, G., D'Elia, M., and Calcagnile, L. (2010), 'The First Millennium AD Climate Fluctuations in the Tavoliere Plain (Apulia, Italy): New Preliminary Data from the 14C AMS-dated Plant Remains from the Archaeological Site of Faragola', *Nuclear Instruments and Methods in Physics Research B* 268: 1084–7.

Fischler, C. (1985), 'Alimentation, Cuisine et Identité: l'identification des Aliments et l'identité du Mangeur', in P. Centlivres, ed., *Identité alimentaire et altérité culturelle: Actes du colloque de Neuchâtel 12–13 novembre 1984* (Neuchâtel: Institut d'Ethnologie), pp. 171–92.

——(1988), 'Food, Self and Identity', *Social Science Information* 27: 275–92.

Fisher, C. T. and Feinman, G. M. (2005), 'Landscapes over time: Resilience, Degradation and Contemporary Lessons', *American Anthropologist* 107: 62–9.

Flannery, K. (1972), 'The Cultural Evolution of Civilisations', *Annual Review of Ecology and Systematics* 3: 399–426.

——(1976), *The Early Mesoamerican Village* (London: Academic Press).

Fleming, A. (2005a), 'Post-processual Landscape Archaeology: a Critique', *Cambridge Archaeological Journal* 16:267–80.

——(2005b), 'Megaliths and Post-Modernism: the Case of Wales', *Antiquity* 79: 921–32.

Flenley, J. and Bahn, P. (2002), *The Enigmas of Easter Island* (Oxford: Oxford University Press).

Flores Ochoa, J. and Paz, P. (1986), 'La agricultura en lagunas (qocha)', in C. de la Torre and M. Burga, eds, *Andenes y camellones en el Perú Andino: Historia, presente y future.* (Lima: Consejo Nacional de Ciencias y Tecnologia), pp. 85–106.

Flüeler-Grauwiler, M. and Gisler, J., eds (2004), Pfahlbaufieber: von Antiquaren, Pfahlbaufischern, Altertümerhändlern und Pfahlbaumythen (Mitteilngen der Antiquarischen Gesellschaft in Zürich: Chronos).

Fokkens, H. (1999), 'Cattle and Martiality: Changing Relations Between Man and Landscape in the Late Neolithic and the Bronze Age', in C. Fabeck and J. Ringtved, eds, *Settlement and Landscape* (Århus: Jutland Archaeological Society), pp. 35–43.

Foley, R. A. (1981), 'Off-site Archaeology: An Alternative Approach for the Short-sighted', in I. Hodder, G. Isaac, and N. Hammond, eds, *Patterns of the Past: Essays in Honour of David Clarke* (Cambridge: Cambridge University Press), pp. 152–84.

Ford, A. and Emery, K. (2008), 'Exploring the Legacy Of The Maya Forest', *Journal of Ethnobiology* 28: 147–53.

Ford, J. A. and Willey, G. R. (1941), 'An Interpretation of the Prehistory of the Eastern United States', *American Anthropologist* 43: 325–63.

Forel, F. A. (1892–1904), *Le Léman: Monographie Limnologique* (Lausanne: Librairie de l'Université).

Foster, D. R., Oswald, W. W., Faison, E. K., Doughty, E. D., and Hansen, B. C. S. (2006), 'A Climatic Driver for Abrupt Mid-Holocene Vegetation Dynamics and the Hemlock Decline in New England', *Ecology* 87: 2959–66.

Fox, C. (1922), *The Archaeology of the Cambridge Region* (Cambridge: Cambridge University Press).

Frank, A. G. (1969), *Latin America: Underdevelopment or Revolution* (New York: New Left Books).

Franklin, A. (2002), *Nature and Social Theory* (London, Thousand Oaks).

Freeman, R. E. (1983), *Strategic Management: A Stakeholder Approach* (Boston, MA: Financial Times Prentice Hall).

Freidel, D. and Shaw, J. (2000), 'The Lowland Maya Civilization: Historical Consciousness and Environment', in R. J. McIntosh, J. A. Tainter, and S. K. McIntosh, eds, *The Way the Wind Blows Climate, History, and Human Action* (New York: Columbia University Press), pp. 271–200.

French, C., Sulas, F., and Madella, M. (2009), 'New Geoarchaeological Investigations of the Valley Systems in the Aksum Area of Northern Ethiopia', *Catena* 78: 218–33.

Freud, S. (1917), *Delusion and Dream: An Interpretation in the Light of psychoanalysis of Gradiva, a Novel, by Wilhelm Jensen, which is here Translated* (New York: Moffat, Yard and Company).

Fried, M. H. (1967), *The Evolution of Political Society* (New York: Random House).

Friend, M. A. (1931), 'The Diary of Mary Ann Friend', *Western Australian Historical Society Journal and Proceedings* 1:1–11.

Gade, D. W. (1975), 'Plants, Man and the Land in the Vilcanota Valley of Peru', *Biogeographica* 6: 240.

Ganopolski, A., Kubatzki, C., Claussen, M., Brovkin V., and Petoukhov, V. (1998), 'The Influence of Vegetation–atmosphere–ocean Interaction on Climate during the Mid-Holocene', *Science* 280: 1916–19.

Gibson, J. (1979), *The Ecological Approach to Visual Perception* (Boston, MA: Houghton Mifflin).

Gibson, J. L. (2010), ' "Nothing but the River's Flood": Late Archaic Diaspora or Disengagement in the Lower Mississippi Valley and Southeastern North America', in D. H. Thomas and M. C. Sanger, eds, *Trend, Tradition, and Turmoil: What Happened to the Southeastern Archaic? Proceedings of the Third Caldwell Conference, St. Catherines Island, Georgia, May 9–11, 2008* (New York: Anthropological Papers of the American Museum of Natural History), pp. 33–42.

Giddens, A. (1984), *The Constitution of Society* (Los Angeles, CA: University of California Press).

——(2009), *The Politics of Climate Change* (Cambridge: Polity Press).

Gillson, L., Sheridan, M., and Brockington, D. (2003), 'Representing Environments in Flux: Case Studies from East Africa', *Area* 35(4): 371–89.

Gilman, B. (2007), *Ashen Sky: The Letters of Pliny the Younger on the Eruption of Vesuvius*, illus. Barry Moser (Los Angeles, CA: The J. Paul Getty Museum).

Girault, L. (1984), *Kallawaya, Guérisseurs Itinérants des Andes: Recherches sur les Pratiques Médicinales et Magiques* (Paris: ORSTOM).

Glacken, C. (1967), *The Epoch of Man, Traces on the Rhodian Shore: Nature and Culture in Western Thought from Ancient Times to the end of the Eighteenth Century* (Berkeley, CA: University of California Press).

Glave, L. M. and Remy, M. I. (1983), *Estructura agraria y vida rural en una region Andina: Ollantaytambo entre los siglos XVI y XIX* (Cusco: Centro de Estudios Rurales Andinos, Bartolome de las Casas).

Godelier, M. (1976), *Antropología y economía* (Barcelona: Anagrama).

Godwin, H. (1933), 'British Maglemose harpoon sites', *Antiquity* 7: 36–48.

Goldstein, L. (1979), 'The Impact of Pompeii on the Literary Imagination', *Centennial Review* 23: 227–41.

Goldstein, P. S. (2005), *Andean Diaspora: The Tiwanaku Colonies and the Origins of South American Empire* (Gainesville, FL: University of Florida Press).

Golte, J. (1980), *La Racionalidad de la Organización Andina* (Lima: Instituto de Estudios Peruanos).

Goody, J. (1982), *Cooking, Cuisine and Class: a Study in Comparative Sociology* (Cambridge: Cambridge University Press).

Gosden, C. (2005), 'Ethnoarchaeology', in C. Renfrew and P. Bahn, eds, *Archaeology: The Key Concepts* (London: Routledge), pp. 95–101.

——(2008), 'Social Ontologies', *Philosophical Transactions of the Royal Society B* 363: 2003–10.

Gourou, P. (1991), *L'Afrique Tropical, Nain ou Géant Agricole?* (Paris: Flammarion).

Grant, A. (2002), 'Food, Status and Social Hierarchy', in N. Milner and P. Miracle, eds, *Consuming Passions and Patterns of Consumption* (Cambridge: McDonald Institute), pp. 17–23.

Grattan, J. and Torrence, R. (2007), 'Beyond Gloom and Doom: The Long-Term Consequences of Volcanic Disasters', in J. Grattan and R. Torrence, eds, *Living*

Under the Shadow: Cultural Impacts of Volcanic Eruptions, One World Archaeology Series (Walnut Creek, CA: Left Coast Press), pp. 1–18.

Grayson, D. and Delpech, F. (1998), 'Changing Diet Breadth in the Early Upper Paleolithic of Southwestern France', *Journal of Archaeological Science* 25: 1119–30.

Green, D. (1997), 'Tecnología tradicional y apropiada en la restauración de obras de irrigación', in A. Kendall, ed., *Restauración de sistemas agrícolas prehispánicos en la sierra sur, Perú: arqueología y tecnología indígena en desarrollo rural* (Cuzco: Cusichaca Trust, Editorial Amauta), pp. 85–9.

Green, D. (2009), 'Opal Waters, Rising Seas: How Sociocultural Inequality Reduces Resilience to Climate Change among Indigenous Australians', in S. A. Crate and M. Nuttall, eds, *Anthropology & Climate Change: From Encounters to Actions* (Walnut Creek, CA: Left Coast Press), pp. 218–27.

Gremillion, K. J. (2002), 'Foraging Theory and Hypothesis Testing in Archaeology: An Exploration of Methodological Problems and Solutions', *Journal of Anthropological Archaeology* 21: 142–64.

Grey, G. (1841), *Journals of two Expeditions of Discovery in North-west and Western Australia, During the years 1837, 38 and 39* (London: T. and W. Boone).

Grosjean, M., Santoro, C. M., Thompson, L. G., Núñez, L., and Standen, V. G. (2007), 'Mid-Holocene Climate and Culture Change in the South Central Andes', in D. G. Anderson, K. A. Maasch, and D. H. Sandweiss, eds, *Climate Change and Cultural Dynamics: A Global Perspective on Mid-Holocene Transitions* (Amsterdam: Academic Press), pp. 51–115.

Guelly, K. A., Roussel, B., and Guyot, M. (1993), 'Initiation of Forest Succession in Savanna Fallows in SW Togo', *Bois et Forêts des Tropiques* 235: 37–48.

Gumerman, G., IV. (1997), 'Food and Complex Societies', *Journal of Archaeological Method and Theory* 4: 105–39.

Gunderson, L. H. and Holling, C. S. (2002), *Panarchy: Understanding Transformations in Systems of Humans and Nature* (Washington, DC: Island Press).

——and Folke, C. (2003), 'Toward a "Science of the Long View"', *Conservation Ecology* 7(1): 15.

Gunn, J., Crumley, C. L., Jones, E., and Young, B. K. (2004), 'A Landscape Analysis of Western Europe during the Early Middle Ages', in C. L. Redman, S. R. James, P. R. Fish, and J. D. Rogers, eds, *The Archaeology of Global Change: The Impact of Humans on their Environment* (Washington, DC: Smithsonian Books), pp. 165–85.

Gusinde, M. (1986 [1937]), *Los Indios de Tierra del Fuego : Los Yámana*, 3 vols (Buenos Aires: Centro Argentino de Etnología Americana).

Hacking, I., ed., (1990), *The Taming of Chance* (Cambridge: Cambridge University Press).

Håkansson, N. T. (1995), 'Irrigation, Population Pressure, and Exchange in Precolonial Pare, Tanzania', *Research in Economic Anthropology* 162: 97–323.

——(2003), 'Rain and Cattle: Gendered Structures and Political Economy in Precolonial Pare, Tanzania' in G. Clark, ed., *Gender at Work in Economic Life* (Walnut Creek, CA: AltaMira), pp. 19–40.

Halbwachs, M. (1980 [1950]), *The Collective Memory (La Mémoire Collective)* (New York: Harper and Row Colophon Books).

Hallam, S. J. (1975), *Fire and Hearth—a Study of Aboriginal Usage and European Usurpation in South-Western Australia* (Canberra: Australian Institute of Aboriginal Studies).

Halstead, P. (1998), 'Mortality Models and Milking: Problems of Uniformitarianism, Optimality and Equifinality Reconsidered', *Anthropozoologica* 27: 3–20.

Hamilakis, Y. (2001), 'Re-Inventing Environmental Archaeology? A Comment on Economic Prehistory or Environmental Archaeology? On Gaining a Sense of Identity', in U. Albarella, ed., *Environmental Archaeology: Meaning and Purpose* (London: Kluwer), pp. 29–38.

Hamilton, F. E. (1999), 'Southeastern Archaic Mounds: Examples of Elaboration in a Temporally Fluctuating Environment?', *Journal of Anthropological Archaeology* 18: 344–55.

Hammond, J. E. (1933), *Winjan's People* (Perth: Imperial Printing Company).

Haraway, D. (1991), *Simians, Cyborgs, and Women: The Re-Invention of Nature* (London: Free Association).

——(2003), *The Companion Species Manifesto: Dogs, People, and Significant Otherness* (Chicago. IL: Prickly Paradigm Press).

——(2008), *When Species Meet* (Minneapolis, MN: University of Minnesota Press).

Hardesty, D. L. (2007), 'Perspectives on Global-Change Archaeology', *American Anthropologist* 109: 1–7.

Harding, A. (1980), *The Lake Dwellings of Switzerland: Retrospect and Prospect,* University of Edinburgh Department of Archaeology Occasional Paper 5 (Edinburgh: University of Edinburgh Department of Archaeology).

Harlan, J. R. (1993), 'The Tropical African Cereals', in T. Shaw, P. Sinclair, B. Andah, and A. Opoko, eds, *The Archaeology of Africa: Food, Metals and Towns* (London: Routledge), pp. 53–60.

Harris, O. (1985), 'Ecological Duality and the Role of the Center: Northern Potosí', in S. Masuda, I. Shimada, and C. Morris, eds, *Andean Ecology and Civilization: an Interdisciplinary Perspective on Andean Ecological Complementarity* (Tokyo: University of Tokyo Press), pp. 311–36.

Harris, R. (2003), *Pompeii* (New York: Random House).

Hart, T. B. and Hart, J. A. (1985), 'The Ecological Basis of Hunter-gatherer Subsistence in African Rain Forests: The Mbuti of Eastern Zaire', *Human Ecology* 14(1): 29–55.

Harvey, D. (1989), *The Condition of Postmodernity: An Enquiry into the Origins of Cultural Change* (Oxford: Blackwell).

Hasluck, A. (1965), *Thomas Peel of Swan River* (Melbourne: Oxford University Press).

Hastorf, C. (1990), 'The Effect of the Inka State on Sausa Agricultural Production and Crop Consumption', *American Antiquity* 55: 262–90.

——(1993), *Agriculture and the Onset of Political Inequality Before the Inka* (Cambridge: Cambridge University Press).

——(2003), 'Andean luxury foods: Special food for the Ancestors, Deities and the élite', *Antiquity* 77(297): 545–54.

——and Johannessen, S. (1993), 'Pre-Hispanic Political Change and the Role of Maize in the Central Andes of Peru', *American Anthropologist* 95: 115–38.

Hayashida, F. M. (2005), 'Archaeology, Ecological History, and Conservation', *Annual Review of Anthropology* 34: 43–65.

Head, L. (2008), 'Is the Concept of Human Impacts Past its Use-by Date?', *Holocene* 18(3): 373–7.

Hegmon, M., Peeples, M. A., Kinzig, A. P., Kulow, S. A., Meagan, C. M., and Nelson, M. C. (2008), 'Social Transformation and Its Human Costs in the Prehispanic U.S. Southwest', *American Anthropologist* 110: 313–24.

Hezel, F. X. (2005), 'The Catholic Centuries', *The Marshall Islands Journal* 16 December 2005, pp. 8–10.

——(2009), 'High Water in the Low Atolls', *Micronesian Counselor* 76. Available at <http://www.micsem.org/pubs/counselor/frames/highwaterfr.htm> [Accessed on 25 March 2010].

Higgs, E. S., ed., (1972), *Papers in Economic Prehistory* (Cambridge: Cambridge University Press).

——and Vita-Finzi, C. (1972), 'Prehistoric Economies: a Territorial Approach', in E. Higgs, ed., *Papers in Economic Prehistory* (Cambridge: Cambridge University Press), pp. 27–36.

Hinchliffe, S. (2003), ' "Inhabiting": landscapes and natures', in K. Anderson, M. Domosh, S. Pile, and N. Thrift, eds, *Handbook of Cultural Geography* (London: Sage), pp. 207–25.

Hirsch, E. and O'Hanlon, M., eds (1995), *The Anthropology of Landscape* (Oxford: Clarendon Press).

Hodder, I. (1978), *The Spatial Organisation of Culture* (London: Duckworth).

——(1982a), *The Present Past: An Introduction to Anthropology for Archaeologists* (London: Batsford).

——(1982b), *Symbols in Action: Ethnoarchaeological Studies of Material Culture* (Cambridge: Cambridge University Press).

——(1987), 'Converging Traditions: the Search for Symbolic Meanings in Archaeology and Geography', in M. Wagstaff, ed., *Landscape and Culture: Geographical and Archaeological perspectives* (Oxford: Blackwell), pp. 134–45.

——(1991), *The Domestication of Europe: Structure and Contingency in Neolithic societies* (Oxford: Blackwell).

——(2011), 'Human-thing entanglement: towards and integrated archaeological perspective', *Journal of the Royal Anthropological Institute* 17: 154–77.

——and Orton, C. (1976), *Spatial Analysis in Archaeology* (Cambridge: Cambridge University Press).

Hoffman, S. (2005), 'Katrina and Rita: A Disaster Anthropologist's Thought', *Anthropology News*, November 2005, <http://www.aaanet.org/press/an/1105/Hoffman.htm>.

Høgestøl, M. and Prøsch-Danielsen, L. (2006), 'Impulses of Agro-Pastoralism in the 4th and 3rd Millennia BC on the South-Western Coastal Rim of Norway', *Environmental Archaeology* 11: 19–34.

Holtorf, C. (2009), 'Archaeology: From Usefulness to Value', *Archaeological Dialogues* 16: 182–6.

——(2010), 'Meta-stories of Archaeology', *World Archaeology* 42(3): 381–93.

Hoppe, R. (2010), 'Lost in Translation?: Boundary Work in Making Climate Change Governable', in P. Driessen, P. Leroy, and W. van Vierssen, eds, *From Climate*

Change to Social Change: Perspectives on Science-Policy Interactions (Utrecht: International Books), pp. 109–30.

Hopper, S. D. (1979), 'Biogeographical Aspects of Speciation in the Southwest Australian Flora', *Annual Review of Ecology and Systematics* 10: 399–422.

——and Gioia, P. (2004), 'The Southwest Australian Floristic Region: Evolution and Conservation of a Global Hotspot of Diversity', *Annual Review of Ecology, Evolution, and Systematics* 35: 623–50.

Hornborg, A. and Crumley, C., eds (2007), *The World System and the Earth System: Global Socioenvironmental Change and Sustainability Since the Neolithic* (Walnut Creek, CA: Left Coast Press).

Horst, F. (1969), *Nobel Lectures: Literature 1901–1967* (Amsterdam: Elsevier).

Hosmer, L. T. (1995), 'Trust: The Connecting Link between Organizational Theory and Philosophical Ethics', *Academy of Management Review* 20(2): 379–403.

Hulme, M. (2008), 'The Conquering of Climate: Discourses of Fear and their Dissolution', *Geographical Journal* 174: 5–16.

——(2010), 'Cosmopolitan Climates: Hybridity, Foresight and Meaning', *Theory, Culture, and Society* 27: 267–76.

Hyslop, J. (1984), *The Inka Road System* (New York: Academic Press).

Ingold, T. (1993), 'The Temporality of the Landscape', *World Archaeology* 25: 152–74.

——(1996), *Key Debates in Anthropological Theory* (London: Routledge).

——(2000), *The Perception of the Environment: Essays on Livelihood, Dwelling and Skill* (London: Routledge).

International Society of Ethnobiology (2006). *ISE Code of Ethics* (with 2009 additions). <http://ise.arts.ubc.ca/global_coalition/ethics.php>. Date of access: 21 April 2010.

IPCC (2001), *Climate Change 2001: The Scientific Basis. Contribution of Working Group I to the Third Assessment Report of the Intergovernmental Panel on Climate Change*, ed. J. T. Houghton, Y. Ding, D. J. Griggs, M. Noguer, P. J. van der Linden, X. Dai, K. Maskell, and C. A. Johnson (Cambridge: Cambridge University Press).

——(2007), 'Summary for Policymakers', in *Climate Change 2007: The Physical Science Basis. Contribution of Working Group I to the Fourth Assessment Report of the Intergovernmental Panel on Climate Change*, ed. S. Solomon, D. Qin, M. Manning, et al. (Cambridge: Cambridge University Press), pp. 1–18.

Irwin, F. C. (1835), *The State and Position of Western Australia; Commonly Called the Swan-River Settlement* (London: Simpkin, Marshall).

Isbell, B. J. (1978), *To Defend Ourselves: Ecology and Ritual in an Andean Village* (Austin, TX: Institute of Latin American Studies, University of Texas).

Isendahl, C. (2008), 'Applied Agro-Archaeological Research in the Bolivian Yungas'. *SAA Archaeological Record* 9: 24–7.

——Sanchez, W., Calla, S., Irahola, M., Orozco, G., Pérez, J. A., Salvatierra, D., Sandivar, G., and Ticona, T. (2009), 'Tablas Montes un trabajo conjunto entre arqueólogos y comunidad', paper presented at the Museo Arqueológico de la Universidad Mayor de San Simón (UMSS), Cochabambas, Bolivia, November 2009.

—— —— ——Salvatierra, D., and Ticona, M. (2008), 'Cultivando el pasado: Resultados iniciales del proyecto agro-arqueológico en los Yungas de Cochabamba-Tablas Monte', paper presented at the Tercera Reunión Anual de la Sociedad de Arqueología La Paz, Bolivia, November 2008.

Jackson, S. and Hobbs, R. (2009), 'Ecological restoration in the light of ecological history', *Science* 325: 567–9.

James, P. E. and Martin, G. J. (1981), *All Possible Worlds: a History of Geographical Ideas*, 2nd edition (New York: John Wiley).

Jantsch, E. (1982), 'From Self-Reference to Self-Transcendance: The Evolution of Self-Organization Dynamics', in W. Schieve and P. Allen, eds, *Self-Organization and Dissipative Structures: Applications in the Physical and Social Sciences* (Austin: University of Texas Press).

Jarman, M. R., Higgs, E. S., and Vita-Finzi, C. (1972), 'Site Catchment Analysis in Archaeology', in P. Ucko, R. Tringham, and G. W. Dimbleby, eds, *Man, Settlement and Urbanism* (London: Duckworth), pp. 61–6.

Jasanoff, S. (2010), 'A New Climate for Society', *Theory, Culture, and Society* 27: 233–53.

Jensen, W. H. (2001 [1903]), *Gradiva: A Pompeiian Fantasy* (*Gradiva: Ein Pompejanisches Phantasiestuck*) (Boston, MA: Adamant Media).

Johns, R. J. (1990), 'The illusionary concept of the climax', in P. Baas, K. Kalkman, and R. Geesink, eds, *The Plant Diversity of Malesia* (Dordrecht: Kluwer), pp. 133–46.

Johnson, G. (2008a), 'Weather Event Shows Vulnerability of Atolls', *Marshall Islands Journal* 12 December 2008, p. 4.

——(2008b), 'Wild Waves Force 300 into Shelters', *Marshall Islands Journal* 19 December 2008, pp. 10–11.

Jones, A. and Richards, C. (2003), 'Animals into Ancestors: Domestication, Food and Identity in Late Neolithic Orkney', in M. Parker Pearson, ed., *Food, Culture and Identity in the Neolithic and Early Bronze Age* (Oxford: Archaeopress), pp. 45–52.

Jones, T. M. (1995), 'Instrumental Stakeholder Theory: A Synthesis of Ethics and Economics', *Academy of Management Review* 20(2): 404–37.

Jones, T. L. (2010), *California Prehistory: Colonization, Culture, and Complexity* (Lanham, MD: AltaMira Press).

——Brown, G. M., Raab, L. M., McVickar J. L., Spaulding, W. G., Kennett, D. J., York, A., and Walker, P. L. (1999), 'Environmental Imperatives Reconsidered: Demographic Crises in Western North America During the Medieval Climatic Anomaly', *Current Anthropology* 40: 137–70.

Journal (2008a), 'Teens' Comments on Climate', *Marshall Islands Journal* 14 November 2008, p. 12.

——(2008b), 'The Wavy Secret', *Marshall Islands Journal* 19 December 2008, p. 7.

——(2009a), 'Atoll Damage Survey', *Marshall Islands Journal* 23 January 2009, p. 4.

——(2009b), 'Emergency Set for Wave Damage', *Marshall Islands Journal* 2 January 2009, p. 2.

——(2009c), 'Free Rice for Outer Isles', *Marshall Islands Journal* 23 January 2009, p. 4.

——(2009d), 'Outer Island Crops an Issue After High Waves', *Marshall Islands Journal* 9 January 2009, p. 3.

——(2009e), 'Taiwan Donates 10 Containers of Rice', *Marshall Islands Journal* 9 January 2009, p. 3.

Kaeser, M.-A. (2001), 'Villages palafittiques et défis identitaires d'une nation en construction. Nature et fonction du "mythe lacustre" Suisse', *ArScAn CNRS, Universités de Paris-I et Paris-V. Cahiers des thèmes transversaux* 2(1): 227–30.

—— (2004), *Les Lacustres: Archéologie et Mythe National* (Lausanne: Presses Polytechniques et Universitaires Romandes).

—— (2008), *Visions d'une Civilisation Engloutie: La representation des Villages Lacustres, de 1854 à nos jours* (Hauterive/Zürich: Laténium/Schweizerisches Landesmuseum).

—— (forthcoming), 'Collective Representations and Identity Construction: the Material Constraints of Archaeology', in A. Coudart, ed., *Constructing Identity: the Role of the Historical and Social Sciences* (Cambridge: Cambridge University Press).

Karlén, W. and Larsson, L. (2007), 'Mid-Holocene Climatic and Cultural Dynamics in Northern Europe' in D. G. Anderson, K. A. Maasch, and D. H. Sandweiss, eds, *Climate Change and Cultural Dynamics: A Global Perspective on Mid-Holocene Transitions* (Amsterdam: Academic Press), pp. 407–34.

Keeley, H. (1984), 'The soils and terraces of the Cusichaca Valley, Perú', in A. Kendall, ed., *Current archaeological projects in the Central Andes* (Oxford: British Archaeological Reports), pp. 323–43.

Keller, F. (1854), 'Die keltischen Pfahlbauten in den Schweizerseen', *Mittheilungen der Antiquarischen Gesellschaft in Zurich* 9(3): 65–100.

—— (1866), *Lake Dwellings of Switzerland and other Parts of Europe*, 1st edn (London: Longmans, Green).

Keller-Tarnuzzer, K. (1937), *Die Inselleute vom Bodensee* (Stuttgart: Thierieman).

Kelly, G. (1999), 'Karla Wongi: a Nyungar Perspective on Forest Burning', *Landscope* 14(2), Summer 1998-99 (Special Fire Edition).

Kemp, R., Branch, N., Silva, B., Meddens, F., Williams, A., Kendall, A., and Vivanco, C. (2006), 'Pedosedimentary, cultural and environmental significance of paleosols within pre-hispanic agricultural terraces in the southern Peruvian Andes', *Quaternary International* 158: 13–22.

Kendall, A. (1991), *Los patrones de asentamiento y desarrollo rural prehispánico entre Ollantaytambo y Machu Picchu* (Cuzco: Proyecto Cusichaca and Editorial Universitaria of the Universidad Nacional San Antonio Abad de Cuzco (UNSAAC).

—— ed. (1997a), Restauración de sistemas agrícolas prehispánicos en la sierra sur, Perú: Arqueología y tecnología indígena en desarrollo rural (Cuzco: Cusichaca Trust).

—— ed. (1997b), Restoration and Rehabilitation of Pre-Hispanic Agricultural Systems in the Southern Highlands of Peru (Bellbroughton, UK: Cusichaca Trust).

—— (2005), 'Applied Archaeology: Revitalising Indigenous Agricultural Technology Within an Andean Community', *Public Archaeology* 4: 205–21.

—— Aguirre-Morales, M., and Aramburu, D. (2005/6), Excavaciones en Andamarca. Informe, Cusichaca Trust, Andahuaylas, Perú. (Report to Instituto Nacional de Cultura in 2005 and 2006).

—— Miguel, R., Adripino, R., and Aramburu, J. D. (2008), Tecnología Tradicional Andina: Rehabilitación agrícola y ambiental para el desarrollo rural del sector comunal. (Lima: Cusichaca Trust).

—— and Rodríguez, A. (2009), *Desarrollo y perspectivas de los sistemas de andenerías en los Andes Centrales del Perú* (Cusco: Centro Bartolomeo de las Casas).

Kennett, D. P. (2005), *The Island Chumash: Behavioral Ecology of a Maritime Society* (Berkeley, CA: University of California Press).

Kennett, D. P. and Kennett, J. P. (2006), 'Early State Formation in Southern Mesopotamia: Sea Levels, Shorelines, and Climate Change', *Journal of Island and Coastal Archaeology* 1: 67–99.

—— —— (2007), 'Influence of Holocene Marine Transgression and Climate Change on Cultural Evolution in Southern Mesopotamia', in D. G. Anderson, K. A. Maasch, and D. H. Sandweiss, eds, *Climate Change and Cultural Dynamics: A Global Perspective on Mid-Holocene Transitions* (Amsterdam: Academic Press), pp. 229–64.

Kern, D. C., D'Aquino, G., Rodrigues, T. E., Frazão, F. J. L., Sombroek, W., Myers, T. P., and Neves, E. G. (2003), 'Distribution of Amazonian Dark Earths in the Brazilian Amazon', in J. Lehmann, D. C. Kern, B. Glaser, and W. I. Woods, eds, *Amazonian Dark Earths: Origins, Properties, Management* (Dordrecht: Kluwer), pp. 51–75.

—— Lima da Costa, M. and Lima Frazão, F. J. (2004), 'Evolution of the Scientific Knowledge Regarding Archaeological Black Earths of Amazonia', in B. Glaser and W. I. Woods, eds, *Amazonian Dark Earths: Explorations in Space and Time* (Berlin: Springer), pp. 19–28.

Kershaw, A. P., Clark, J. S., Gill, A. M., and D' Costa, D. (2002), 'A History of Fire in Australia', in R. A. Bradstock, J. E. Williams, and A. M. Gill, eds, *Flammable Australia: The Fire Regimes and Biodiversity of a Continent* (Cambridge: Cambridge University Press), pp. 3–25.

Kidder, A. V. (1924), *An Introduction to the Study of Southwestern Archaeology* (New Haven, CT: Phillips Academy).

Kidder, T. R. (2006), 'Climate Change and the Archaic to Woodland Transition (3000–2600 cal B.P.) in the Mississippi River Basin', *American Antiquity* 71: 195–231.

—— (2010), 'Trend, Tradition, and Transition at the End of the Archaic' in D. H. Thomas and M. C. Sanger, eds, *Trend, Tradition, and Turmoil: What Happened to the Southeastern Archaic? Proceedings of the Third Caldwell Conference, St. Catherines Island, Georgia, May 9–11, 2008* (New York: Anthropological Papers of the American Museum of Natural History).

Kirch, P. V. (2007), 'Hawaii as a Model System for Human Ecodynamics', *American Anthropologist* 107: 8–26.

Knight, J. (2005), 'Introduction', in J. Knight. ed., *Animals in Person: Cultural Perspectives on Human-Animal Intimacies* (Oxford: Berg). pp. 1–13.

Kohler, T. A. and van der Leeuw, S. E., eds (2007), *The Model-Based Archaeology of Socionatural Systems* (Santa Fe, NM: SAR Press).

Kolata, A. L., ed. (1996), *Tiwanaku and Its Hinterlands: Archaeology and Paleoecology of an Andean Civilization*, vol. 1: *Agroecology* (Washington, DC: Smithsonian Institution Press).

Koponen, J. (1988), *People and Production in Late Pre-Colonial Tanzania: History and Structures* (Helsinki: Finnish Society for Development Studies).

Koppers, W. (1997 [1924]), *Entre los Fueguinos* (Punta Arenas: Universidad de Magallanes y Programa Chile Austral de la Unión Europea).

Kraemer, F. L. (1967), 'Eduard Hahn and the End of the "Three Stages of Man"', *Geographical Review* 57: 73–89.

Kreike, E. (2003), 'Hidden Fruits: A Social Ecology of Fruit trees in Manibia and Angola, 1880s–1990s', in W. Beinart and J. McGregor, eds, *Social History and African Environments* (Athens, OH: Ohio University Press), pp. 27–42.

Kuper, R. and Kröpelin, S. (2006), 'Climate-Controlled Holocene Occupation in the Sahara: Motor of Africa's Evolution', *Science* 313: 803–7.

Lagerås, P. and Regnell, M. (1999), 'Agrar Förändring under Sydsvensk Bronsålder', in M. Olausson, ed., *Spiralens Öga: Tjugo Artiklar Kring Aktuell Bronsåldersforskning* (Stockholm: Avdeling För Arkeologiska Undersökningar, Riksantikvarieämbetet), pp. 263–76.

Lambin, E. F. et al. (2001), 'The Causes of Land-Use and Land-Cover Change: Moving Beyond the Myths', *Global Environmental Change* 11: 261–9.

Lane, P. J. (2009), 'Environmental Narratives and the History of Soil Erosion in Kondoa District, Tanzania: An Archaeological Perspective', *International Journal of African Historical Studies* 42: 457–83.

—— (2010), 'Developing landscape historical ecologies in eastern and southern Africa: opportunities and challenges', *African Studies* 69: 299–322.

Langstroth, R. (1996), 'Forests Islands in an Amazonian Savanna of Northeastern-Bolivia', unpublished PhD dissertation. University of Wisconsin, Madison, WI.

Lansing, J. S. (2006), *Perfect Order: Recognizing Complexity in Bali* (Princeton, NJ: Princeton University Press).

Latinis, D. K. (2000), 'The Development of Subsistence System Models for Island Southeast Asia and Near Oceania: The nature and Role of Arboriculture and Arboreal-based Economies', *World Archaeology* 32: 41–67.

Latour, B. (2007), 'A Plea for Earthly Sciences' (<http://www.bruno-latour.fr/sites/default/files/102-BSA-GB_0.pdf>), Keynote lecture, Annual Meeting of the British Sociological Association.

Le Roy Ladurie, E. (1971), trans. B. Bray, *Times of Feast, Times of Famine: a History of Climate since the Year 1000* (Garden City, NY: Doubleday and Company).

Leach, M. and Fairhead, J. (1995), 'Ruined Settlements and New Gardens: Gender and Soil Ripening Among Kuranko Farmers in the Forestsavanna Transition Zone', *IDS Bulletin* 26: 24–32.

—— and Mearns, R. (1996), 'Challenging Received Wisdom in Africa', in M. Leach and R. Mearns, eds, *The Lie of the Land: Challenging Received Wisdom on the African Environment* (Oxford: James Currey), pp. 1–33.

Leckie, K. (2011), 'Collecting Swiss Lake Dwellings in the UK, 1850–1900', unpublished PhD thesis, Department of Archaeology, University of Cambridge.

Lee, K. (1979), '7,000 años de Historia del hombre de Mojos: Agricultura en Pampas estériles: Informe Preliminar'. Universidad Beni: 23–6.

Legge, A. J. (1981a), 'Aspects of Cattle Husbandry', in R. Mercer, ed., *Farming Practice in British Prehistory* (Edinburgh: Edinburgh University Press), pp. 169–81.

—— (1981b), 'The Agricultural Economy', in R. Mercer, ed., *Grimes Graves, Norfolk: Excavations 1971–72* (London: HMSO), pp. 79–103.

Lepofsky, D. (1992), 'Arboriculture in the Mussau Islands, Bismarck Archipelago', *Economic Botany* 46: 192–211.

Leroi Gourhan, A. (1968), *The Art of Prehistoric Man in Western Europe* (London: Thames and Hudson).

Levin, S. A. (1998), 'Ecosystems and the Biosphere as Complex Adaptive Systems', *Ecosystems* 1: 431–6.

Lévi-Strauss, C. (1964), *Le Cru et le Cuit* (Paris: Plon).

——(1974), 'Structuralism and Ecology', *Social Science Information* 12: 7–23.

——(1997), 'The Culinary Triangle', in C. Counihan and P. Van Esterik, eds, *Food and Culture: a Reader* (London: Routledge), pp. 28–35.

Lewis, S. M. et al. (2009), 'Increasing Carbon Storage in Intact African Tropical Forests', *Nature* 457: 1003–6.

Lillehammer, G. (2007), 'The Past in the Present. Landscape Perception, Archaeological Heritage and Marginal Farmland in Jæren, South-Western Norway', *Norwegian Archaeological Review* 40: 159–78.

Lima da Costa, M, Kern, D. C., and Kämpf, N. (2003), 'Pedogeochemical and mineralogical analysis of Amazonian Dark Earths', in J. Lehmann, D. C. Kern, B. Glaser, and W. I. Woods, eds, *Amazonian Dark Earths: Origins, Properties, Management* (Dordrecht: Kluwer), pp. 333–52.

Lock, G. (2003), *Using Computers in Archaeology* (London: Routledge).

Loiske, V. M. (2004), 'Institutionalized Exchange as a Driving Force in Intensive Agriculture: an Iraqw Case Study', in M. Widgren and J. E. G. Sutton, eds, *'Islands' of Intensive Agriculture in Eastern Africa* (Oxford: James Currey), pp. 105–13.

Løken, T. (1998), 'Bofaste Bønder Eller Jordbrukere På Flyttefot? Hus Og Bosetning I Bronsealderen På Opstad I Tune, Østfold', in E. Østmo, ed., *Fra Østfolds Oldtid. Foredrag Ved 25-Års-Jubiléet for Universitetets Arkeologiske Stasjon* (Oslo: Universitetets Oldsaksamlings), pp. 173–97.

Loutre, M. F. and Berger, A. (2000), 'Future Climatic Changes: Are We Entering an Exceptionally Long Interglacial?', *Climate Change* 46: 61–90.

Lovelock, J. (1992 [1991]), *Gaia: Søkelys På Jordens Helsetilstand* (Oslo: Cappelen).

Lowry, M. (1961), 'The Present Estate of Pompeii', in *Hear Us O Lord From Heaven They Dwelling Place* (Philadelphia, PA: Lippincott).

Lubbock, J. (1865), *Pre-historic Times, as Illustrated by Ancient Remains and the Manners and Customs of Modern Savages* (London: Williams and Norgate).

Lucas, G. (2005), *The Archaeology of Time*. Themes in Archaeology (London: Routledge).

——(2008), 'Time and the Archaeological Event', *Cambridge Archaeological Journal* 18: 59–65.

Lund, V. (2002), 'Ethics and Animal Welfare in Organic Animal Husbandry—an Interdisciplinary Approach', Department of Animal Environment and Health. Unpublished doctoral thesis, Skara, Swedish University of Agricultural Sciences.

——(2005), 'The Human–Animal Relationship in Organic Farming', in F. de Jonge and R. van den Bos, eds, *The Human–Animal Relationship: Forever and a Day* (Assen: Royal van Gorcum), pp. 231–46.

——and Röcklinsberg, H. (2001), 'Outlining a Concept of Animal Welfare for Organic Farming Systems', *Journal of Agricultural and Environmental Ethics* 14: 391–424.

——Anthony, R. and Röcklinsberg, H. (2004a), 'The Ethical Contract as a Tool in Organic Animal Husbandry', *Journal of Agricultural and Environmental Ethics* 17: 23–49.

——Hemlin, S. and White, J. (2004b), 'Natural Behaviour, Animal Rights, or Making Money—a Study of Swedish Organic Farmers' View of Animal Issues', *Journal of Agricultural and Environmental Ethics* 17: 157–79.

Lutaenko, K. A., Zhushchikhovskaya, I. S., Mikishin, Y. A., and Popov, A. N. (2007), 'Mid-Holocene Climatic Changes and Cultural Dynamics in the Basin of the Sea of Japan and Adjacent Areas', in D. G. Anderson, K. A. Maasch, and D. H. Sandweiss, eds, *Climate Change and Cultural Dynamics: A Global Perspective on Mid-Holocene Transitions* (Amsterdam: Academic Press), pp. 331–406.

Lynas, M. (2004), *High Tide: How Climate Crisis is Engulfing Our Planet* (London: Harper Perennial).

Lynott, M. J. and Wylie, A., eds (2000), *Ethics in American Archaeology* 2nd edn (Washington, DC: Society for American Archaeology).

Maasch, K. A. (2008), 'El Niño and Interannual Variability of Climate in the Western Hemisphere', in D. H. Sandweiss and J. Quilter, eds, *El Niño, Catastrophism, and Culture Change in Ancient America* (Washington, DC: Dumbarton Oaks Research Library and Collection, Harvard University Press), pp. 33–55.

MacClancy, J. (2004), 'Food, Identity, Identification', in H. Macbeth and J. MacClancy, eds, *Researching Food Habits: Methods and Problems* (Oxford: Berghahn Books), pp. 63–73.

Macie-Taylor, C. G. N. and Boyce, A. J., eds (1988), *Human Mating Patterns* (Cambridge: Cambridge University Press).

Mackenzie, F. (1992), 'Development from Within? The Struggle to Survive', in D. R. F. Taylor and F. Mackenzie, eds, *Development from Within. Survival in Rural Africa* (London: Routledge), pp. 1–32.

Macnaghten, P. and Urry, J. (1998), *Contested Natures* (London: Sage Publications).

Madsen, D. B. and Schmitt, D. (1998), 'Mass Collecting and the Diet Breadth Model: a Great Basin example', *Journal of Archaeological Science* 25: 445–55.

Maley, J. (2002), 'The Catastrophic Destruction of African Forests Around 2500 years ago Still Exerts a Major Influence on Present Vegetation Form and Distribution', *IDS Bulletin* 33: 1–15.

Malinowski, B. (1922), *Argonauts of the Western Pacific* (New York: Dutton).

Mameli, L. and Estévez Escalera, J. (2004), *Etnoarqueozoología de Aves: el Ejemplo del Extremo Sur Americano*, Treballs D'Etnoarqueología 5 (Madrid: Consejo Superior de Investigaciones Científicas).

Marquet, P. A., Santoro, C. M., Latorre, C., Standen, V. G., Abades, S. R., Rivadeneira, M. M., Arriaza, B., and Hochberg, M. E. (2012), 'Emergence of Social Complexity among Coastal Hunter-Gatherers in the Atacama Desert of Northern Chile', *Proceedings of the National Academy of Sciences* 109(37): 14754–14760.

Marx, K. and Engels, F. (1969 [1848]), 'The Communist Manifesto', trans. S. Moore in cooperation with F. Engels, 1888, in Marx/Engels Selected Works, vol. 1, (Moscow: Progress Publishers), pp. 98–137.

Mason, O. T. (1895), *The Origins of Invention* (New York: Scribner).

Massey, D. (2006), 'Landscape as a Provocation: Reflections on Moving Mountains', *Journal of Material Culture* 11: 33–48.

Masson, L. (1992), 'Articulo Sobre Resultados y Suspensión del Proyecto de ONERN, en la revista Debate', *Agrario* 19: 1–27.

Mayewski, P. A. (2008), 'Paleoclimates from Ice Cores: A Framework for Archaeological Interpretation', in D. H. Sandweiss and J. Quilter, eds, *El Niño, Catastrophism, and Culture Change in Ancient America* (Washington, DC: Dumbarton Oaks Research Library and Collection, Harvard University Press), pp. 15–32.

Mazoyer, M. and Roudart, L. (2006), *A History of World Agriculture: From the Neolithic Age to the Current Crisis* (London: Earthscan).

McAnany, P. A. and Yoffee, N., eds (2010), *Questioning Collapse: Human Resilience, Ecological Vulnerability, and the Aftermath of Empire* (Cambridge: Cambridge University Press).

McClatchey, W., Mynkee, B. S., Jr, Kaleveke, L., and Pitanapi, C. (2006), 'Differential Conservation of Two Species of *Canarium* (Buseraceae) Among the Babatana and Ririo of Laur (Choiseul), Solomon Islands', *Economic Botany* 60(3): 212–26.

McCollum, A. (1991), *The Dog from Pompei* (New York: Cast polymer-enhanced Hydrocal).

McIntosh, R. J., Tainter, J. A., and McIntosh, S. K., eds (2000a), *The Way the Wind Blows: Climate, History and Human Action* (New York: Columbia University Press).

——————(2000b), 'Climate, History, and Human Action', in R. J. McIntosh, J. A.Tainter, and S. K. McIntosh, eds, *The Way the Wind Blows: Climate, History, and Human Action* (New York: Columbia University Press), pp. 1–44.

McKey, D, Rostain, S., Iriarte, J., Glaser, B., Birk, J. J., Holst, I., and Renard, D. (2010), 'Pre-Columbian Agricultural Landscapes, Ecosystem Engineers, and Self-organized Patchiness in Amazonia', *Proceedings of the National Academy of Sciences* 107(17): 7823–8.

McKibben, B. (1989), *The End of Nature* (New York: Anchor Books).

McLean, S. (2009), 'Stories and Cosmogonies: Imagining Creativity beyond "Nature" and "Culture"', *Cultural Anthropology* 24: 213–45.

Mead, M. (1997), 'The Changing Significance of Food', in C. Counihan, and P. Van Esterik, eds, *Food and Culture: a Reader* (New York: Routledge), 11–19.

Meggers, B. J. (2007), 'Mid-Holocene Climate and Cultural Dynamics in Brazil and the Guianas', in D. G. Anderson, K. A. Maasch, and D. H. Sandweiss, eds, *Climate Change and Cultural Dynamics: A Global Perspective on Mid-Holocene Transitions* (Amsterdam: Academic Press), pp. 117–55.

Mejia, A. (1992), 'Rehabilitación del sistema de andenerías en la margen derecha del valle del Colca'. Ponencia presentada en el Seminario Taller Infraestructura Agroecológica Prehispánica—Sostenibilidad y Competitividad del Relacionamiento de Andenes, Chivay, Cañón del Colca, Arequipa, 26–7 June 2001.

Mennell, S. (1985), *All Manners of Food: Eating and Taste in England and France from the Middle Ages to the Present* (Oxford: Blackwell).

——Murcott, A. and Van Otterloo, A. (1992), *The Sociology of Food: Eating, Diet, and Culture* (London: Sage).

Menotti, F. (2001), '*The Missing Period': Middle Bronze Age Lake-Dwellings in the Alps*, BAR Archaeopress 968 (Oxford: Oxbow Books).

——(2004), *Living on the Lake in Prehistoric Europe: 150 years of Lake Dwelling Research* (London: Routledge).

Merlan, F. (2009), 'Indigeneity: Global and Local', *Current Anthropology* 50: 303–33.

Merleau-Ponty, M. (1964), 'Eye and Mind', trans. C. Dallery, in J. Edie, ed., *The Primacy of Perception: and Other Essays on Phenomenological Psychology, the Philosophy of Art, History and Politics* (Evanston, IL: Northwestern University Press).

Mesía Montenegro, C. J. (2000), 'Anchucaya: Aproximación Teórica Sobre un Complejo con Planta en U en el Valle Medio del río Lurín', *Arqueológicas* 24: 45–52.

Meyer, W. J. and Crumley, C. (2011), 'Historical Ecology: Using what Works to Cross the Divide', in T. Moore and X.-L. Armada, eds, *Atlantic Europe in the First Millennium BC: Crossing the Divide* (Oxford: Oxford University Press).

Milner, G. R. (2004), *The Moundbuilders: Ancient Peoples of Eastern North America* (New York: Thames and Hudson).

Milton, K. (2002), *Loving Nature: Towards an Ecology of Emotion* (London: Routledge).

Minnis, P. E. (2006), 'Answering the Skeptic's Question', *SAA [Society for American Archaeology] Archaeological Record* 6: 17–20.

Mintz, S. W. (1996), *Tasting Food, Tasting Freedom* (Boston. MA: Beacon Press).

Mitchell, J. F. B. (1990), 'Greenhouse Warming: Is the Mid-Holocene a Good Analogue?', *Journal of Climate* 3: 1177–92.

Mitchell, P. (2008), 'Practising Archaeology at a Time of Climatic Catastrophe', *Antiquity* 82: 1093–103.

Mitja, D. (1990), 'Influence de la Culture Itinérante sur la Vegetation d'une Savane Humide de Côte d'Ivoire'. Unpublished PhD Thesis, University of Pierre et Marie Curie, Paris.

——and Puig, H. (1991), 'Essartage, Culture Itinérante et Reconstitution de la Végétation dans les Jachères en Savane Humide de Côte d'Ivoire (Booro-Borotou, Touba)', in C. Floret and G. Serpantié, eds, *La Jachère en Afrique de l'Ouest. Report of International Workshop, Montpellier, 2–5 December 1991.* (Paris, ORSTOM Editions).

Mohr Chávez, K. L. (1989), 'The significance of Chiripa in Lake Titicaca Basin developments', *Expedition* 30: 17–26.

Mondjannagni, A. (1969), *Contribution à l'étude des Paysages Vegetaux du Bas-Dahomey*, Annales de l'Université d'Abidjan, série G vol. 1 part 2.

Montanari, M. (2000), 'Food Models and Cultural Identity'. in J.-L. Flandrin and M. Montanari, eds, *Food: a Culinary History from Antiquity to the Present* (New York: Penguin), pp. 189–93.

Mooney, S. D., Black, M. P., and Haberle, S. (2007), 'The Fire, Human and Climate Nexus in the Sydney Basin, Eastern Australia', *The Holocene* 17: 469–80.

Morales, F. C. (2004), 'Balance de las investigaciones sobre andenes en el Perú', in C. A. Llerena, M. Inbar, and M. A. Benavides, eds, *Conservación y abandono de andenes* (Lima: Universidad Agraria La Molina y Universidad de Haifa), pp. 66–9.

Morcote-Rios, G. and Bernal, R. (2001), 'Remains of Palms (Palmae) at Archaeological Sites in the New World: A Review', *Botanical Review* 67: 309–50.

Morgan, L. H. (1877), *Ancient Society* (New York: Holt).

Morphy, H., ed. (1989), *Animals Into Art*. One World Archaeology 7 (London: Unwin Hyman).

Morrison, K. (1994), 'The Intensification of Production: Archaeological Approaches', *Journal of Archaeological Method and Theory* 1: 111–59.

Mortillet, G. de (1897), *Formation de le Nation Française* (Paris: Alcan).

Moseley, M. E. (1989), 'Large Monuments and Precocious Formative Development', *Quarterly Review of Archaeology* 10(1): 186–91.

——(2001), *The Incas and their Ancestors: The Archaeology of Peru* (New York: Thames and Hudson).

——and Keefer, D. K. (2008), 'Deadly Deluges in the Southern Desert: Modern and Ancient El Niños in the Osmore Region of Peru', in D. H. Sandweiss and J. Quilter, eds, *El Niño, Catastrophism, and Culture Change in Ancient America* (Washington, DC: Dumbarton Oaks Research Library and Collection, Harvard University Press), pp. 129–44.

Moser, S. (1998), *Ancestral Images: the Iconography of Human Origins* (Ithaca, NY: Cornell University Press).

——(2001), 'Archaeological Representation: the Visual Conventions for Constructing Knowledge about the Past', in I. Hodder, ed., *Archaeological Theory Today* (Cambridge: Polity Press), pp. 262–83.

——(2009), 'Archaeological representation: the consumption and creation of the past', in B. Cunliffe, C. Gosden, and R. Joyce, eds, *The Oxford Handbook of Archaeology* (Oxford: Oxford University Press), pp. 1048–77.

——and Gamble, C. (1997), 'Revolutionary Images: the iconic vocabulary for representing human antiquity', in B. Molyneaux, *The Cultural Life of Images: Visual Representation in Archaeology* (London: Routledge), pp. 184–212.

Moss, M. L., Peteet, D. M., and Whitlock, C. (2007), 'Mid-Holocene Culture and Climate on the Northwest Coast of North America', in D. G. Anderson, K. A. Maasch, and D. H. Sandweiss, eds, *Climate Change and Cultural Dynamics: A Global Perspective on Mid-Holocene Transitions* (Amsterdam: Academic Press), pp. 491–529.

Moutarde, F. (2006), 'L'évolution du Couvert Ligneux et de son Exploitation par l'homme dans la Vallée du Lurín (côte central du Pérou), de l'Horizon Ancien (900–100 av. J.-C.) à l'Horizon Tardif (1460–1532 ap. J.-C.). Approche anthracologique'. Doctoral thesis, Université Paris I—Panthéon-Sorbonne.

Müller-Scheessel, N. (2001), 'Fair Prehistory: Archaeological Exhibits at French Expositions Universelles', *Antiquity* 75: 391–401.

Mulvaney, D. J. and Green, N. (1992), [Barker, C. n.d.], *Commandant of Solitude: The diaries of Captain Collet Barker 1828–1831* (Carlton: Melbourne University).

Murra, J. (2002), *El mundo andino: población, medio ambiente y economía* (Lima: IEP-PUC).

——(1985), '"El archipielago Vertical" Revisited', in S. Masuda, I. Shimada, and C. Morris, eds, *Andean Ecology and Civilization: an Interdisciplinary Perspective on Andean Ecological Complementarity* (Tokyo: University of Tokyo Press), pp. 3–14.

Myers, N., Mittermeier, R. A., Mittelmeier, C. G., da Fonseca, G. A. B., and Kent, J. (2000), 'Biodiversity Hotspots for Conservation Priorities', *Nature* 403: 853–8.

Nagaoka, L. (2002), 'The Effects of Resource Depression on Foraging Efficiency, Diet Breadth, and Patch Use in Southern New Zealand', *Journal of Anthropological Archaeology* 21: 419–42.

Navarrete A. A., Cannavan, F. S., Taketani, R. G., and Tsai, S. M. (2010), 'A Molecular Survey of the Diversity of Microbial Communities in Different Amazonian Agricultural Model Systems', *Diversity* 2: 787–809.

Nazarea, V. D. (2006), 'Local Knowledge and Memory in Biodiversity Conservation', *Annual Review of Anthropology* 35: 317–35.

——ed. (1999), *Ethnoecology: Situated Knowledge/Located Lives* (Tucson, AZ: Univsity of Arizona Press).

Neusius, S. W. (2009), 'Changing the Curriculum: Preparing Archaeologists for Careers in Applied Archaeology', *SAA Archaeological Record* 9: 18–22.

Nevle, R. J. and Bird, D. K. (2008), 'Effects of Syn-pandemic Fire Reduction and Reforestation in the Tropical Americas on Atmospheric CO_2 During European Conquest', *Palaeogeography, Palaeoclimatology, Palaeoecology* 264: 25–38.

Newell, B., Crumley, C. L., Hassan, N., Lambin, E. F., Pahl-Wostl, C., Underdal, A., and Wasson, R. (2005), 'A Conceptual Template for Integrative Human-Environment Research', *Global Environmental Change* 15: 299–307.

Newsome, J. C. and Pickett, E. J. (1993), 'Palynology and Palaeoclimatic Implications of two Holocene Sequences from Southwestern Australia', *Palaeogeography, Palaeoclimatology, Palaeoecology* 101: 245–61.

Nielsen, A. (1995), 'Architectural Performance and the Reproduction of Social Power', in J. Skibo, W. Walker, and A. Nielsen, eds, *Expanding Archaeology* (Salt Lake City, UT: University of Utah Press), pp. 47–66.

Niemeijer, D. (1996), 'The Dynamics of African Agricultural History: is it time for a New Development Paradigm?', *Development and Change* 27: 87–110.

Nietschmann, B. (1992), *The Interdependence of Biological and Cultural Diversity* (Kenmore, WA: Center for World Indigenous Studies).

Nind, S. (1831), 'Description of the Natives of King George's Sound (Swan River Colony) and Adjoining Country', *Journal of the Royal Geographical Society of London* 1: 21–51.

NRC [National Research Council Committee on Abrupt Climate Change] (2002), *Abrupt Climate Change Inevitable Surprises* (Washington, DC: National Academy Press).

Nunn, P. (2003), 'Nature–Society Interactions in the Pacific Islands', *Geografiska Annaler B* 85: 219–29.

Nygren, A. (1999), 'Local Knowledge in the Environment Development Discourse: From Dichotomies to Situated Knowledge', *Critique of Anthropology* 19: 267–88.

O'Connor, T. and Evans, J. G. (2005), *Environmental Archaeology: Principles and Methods* (Stroud: Sutton Publishing).

Oliver-Smith, A. (2002), 'Theorizing Disasters: Nature, Power, and Culture', in S. Hoffman and A. Oliver-Smith, eds, *Catastrophe and Culture: the Anthropology of Disaster* (Santa Fe, NM: School of American Research Press), pp. 23–48.

Olsen, B. (1997), *Fra Ting Til Tekst. Teoretiske Perspektiv I Arkeologisk Forsking* (Oslo: Universitetsforlaget).

Olwig, K. R. (2002), *Landscape, Nature, and the Body Politic: From Britain's Renaissance to America's New World* (Madison, WI: University of Wisconsin Press).

O'Neill, R. V. (2001), 'Is it Time to Bury the Ecosystem Concept? (with full military honours, of course!)', *Ecology* 82: 3275–84.

Orlove, B. S. and Godoy, R. (1986), 'Sectoral Fallowing Systems in the Central Andes', *Journal of Ethnobiology* 6: 169–204.

Orquera, L. A. (1999), 'El Consumo de Moluscos por los Canoeros del Extremo Sur', *Relaciones de la Sociedad Argentina de Antropología* 24: 307–27.

——and Piana, E. L. (1995), La Imagen de los Canoeros Magallánicos-Fueguinos: Conceptos y Tendencias. Runa XXII: 187–245.

————(1999a), *Arqueología de la Región del Canal Beagle (Tierra del Fuego, República Argentina)* (Buenos Aires: Sociedad Argentina de Antropología).

————(1999b), *La Vida Material y Social de los Yámana* (Buenos Aires: Editorial Universitaria de Buenos Aires).

————(2005), 'La Adaptación al Litoral Sudamericano Sudoccidental: Qué es y Quiénes, Cuándo y Dónde se adaptaron', *Relaciones de la Sociedad Argentina de Antropología* 30: 11–32.

————(2009), 'Sea Nomads of the Beagle Channel in Southernmost South America: Over Six Thousand Years of Coastal Adaptation and Stability', *Journal of Island and Coastal Archaeology* 4: 61–81.

Osily, R. (2001), 'The History of Human Settlement in the Middle Ogooué Valley (Gabon): Implications for the Environment', in W. Weber, L. J. T. White, A. Vedder, and L. Naughton-Treeves, eds, *African Rain Forest Ecology and Conservation: an Interdisciplinary Perspective* (New Haven, CT: Yale University Press), pp. 101–18.

Ossio, J, M. (1978), 'El simbolismo del agua y la representación del tiempo y el espacio en la fiesta de la acequia de la comunidad de Andamarca', *Actes du XLIIe Congrés International des Americanistes* 4: 355–96.

——(1987), 'Las andenerías de la comunidad de Andamarca (Ayacucho-Perú)', Seminario sobre Tecnologías Tradicionales. Primera Reunión: Manejo de Suelos y Aguas en la Sociedad Andina Cienaquilla.

Östberg, W. (2004), 'The Expansion of Marakwet Hill-Furrow Irrigation in the Kerio Valley of Kenya', in M. Widgren and J. E. G. Sutton, eds, *Islands of Intensive Agriculture in Eastern Africa* (Oxford: James Currey), pp. 19–48.

Paret, O. (1958), *Le Mythe des Cites Lacustres et les Problemes de la Construction Neolithique* (Paris: Dunod).

Parker, A. G., Anderson, D. E., Robinson, M. A., and Bonsall, C. (2002), 'A Review of the Mid-Holocene Elm Decline in the British Isles', *Progress in Physical Geography* 26: 1–45.

Parmesan, C. (2006), 'Ecological and Evolutionary Responses to Recent Climate Change', *Annual Review of Ecology, Evolution, and Systematics* 37: 637–69.

Pärssinen, M., Schaan, D. P., and Ranzi, A. (2009), 'Pre-Columbian Geometric Earthworks in the Upper Purús: a Complex Society in Western Amazonia', *Antiquity* 83: 1084–95.

Patt, A. G. and Schröter, D. (2007), *Perceptions of Environmental Risks in Mozambique: Implications for the Success of Adaptation and Coping Strategies* (Policy

Research Working Paper 4417, The World Bank Development Research Group, Sustainable Rural and Urban Development Team).

Patterson, T. C. (1994), 'Toward a Properly Historical Ecology', in C. L. Crumley, ed., *Historical Ecology: Cultural Knowledge and Changing Landscapes* (Santa Fe, NM: School of American Research Press), pp. 223–37.

——(2008), 'A Brief History of Landscape Archaeology in the Americas', in B. David and J. Thomas, eds, *Handbook of Landscape Archaeology* (Walnut Creek, CA: Left Coast Press), pp. 77–84.

Payne, S. (1973), 'Kill-Off Patterns in Sheep and Goats: The Mandibles from Asvan Kale', *Anatolian Studies* 23: 281–303.

Pennington, R. T., Lavin, M., Särkinen, T., Lewis, G. P., Klitgaard, B. B., and Hughes, C. E. (2010), 'Contrasting Plant Diversification Histories within the Andean Biodiversity Hotspot', *Proceedings of the National Academy of Sciences* 107: 13783–7.

Peristiany, J. G. (1951), 'The Age-set System of the Pastoral Pokot: the *Sapana* Initiation Ceremony', *Africa* 21: 188–206.

Pétrequin, P. and Bailly, M. (2004), 'Lake Dwelling Research in France: from climate to demography', in F. Menotti, ed., *Living on the Lake in Prehistoric Europe: 150 years of Lake-Dwelling Research* (London: Routledge), pp. 36–49.

Phillips, O. L., Lewis, S. L., Baker, T. R., Chao, K. J., and Higuchi, N. (2008), 'The changing Amazon Forest', *Philosophical Transactions of The Royal Society B-Biological Sciences* 363: 1819–27.

Piana, E. L., Estévez Escalera, J., and Vila, A. (2000), 'Lanashuaia: un Sitio de Canoeros del Siglo Pasado en la Costa Norte del Canal Beagle', in *Desde el país de los gigantes. Perspectivas en arqueología* (Río Gallegos UNPA), pp. 455–69.

Pieroni, A. and Price, L., eds (2006a), *Eating and Healing: Traditional Food as Medicine* (New York: Haworth Press).

——and Quave, C. (2006b), 'Functional Foods or Food Medicine? On the Consumption of Wild plants Among Albanians and Southern Italians in Lucania', in A. Pieroni and L. Price, eds, *Eating and Healing: Traditional Food as Medicine* (New York: Haworth Press), pp. 101–30.

Polanyi, K. (1957 [1944]), *The Great Transformation: the Political and Economic Origins of Our Time* (Boston, MA: Beacon Press).

Politis, G. G. (2007), *Nukak: Ethnoarchaeology of an Amazonian People* (Walnut Creek, CA: Left Coast Press).

——and Saunders, N. J. (2002), 'Archaeological Correlates of Ideological Activity: Food Taboos and Spirit-Animals in an Amazonian Hunter-Gatherer Society', in P. Miracle and N. Milber, eds, *Consuming Passions and Patterns of Consumption* (Cambridge: McDonald Institute for Archaeological Research), pp. 113–30.

Pollock, S. (1999), *Ancient Mesopotamia: The Eden that Never Was* (Cambridge: Cambridge University Press).

Pozorski, S. (1976), 'Prehistoric Subsistence Patterns and Site Economics in the Moche Valley, Peru'. Unpublished PhD Thesis, University of Texas, Austin.

——(1987), 'Theocracy vs. Militarism: the Significance of the Casma Valley in Understanding Early State Formation', in J. Haas, S. Pozorski, and T. Pozorski, eds, *The Origins and Development of the Andean State* (Cambridge: Cambridge University Press), pp. 15–30.

Pozorski, S. and Pozorski, T. (1992), 'Early Civilization in the Casma Valley, Peru', *Antiquity* 66: 845–70.

Prance, G. T., ed. (1982), *Biological Diversification in the Tropics* (New York: Columbia University Press).

Prescott, C. (1991), *Kulturhistoriske Undersøkelser I Skrivarhelleren* (Bergen: Historisk Museum, Universitetet i Bergen).

——(1994), 'Paradigm Gained—Paradigm Lost? 150 Years of Norwegian Bronze Age Research', *Norwegian Archaeological Review* 27: 87–109.

——(1995), 'Aspects of Early Pastoralism in Sogn, Norway', *Acta Archaeologica* 66: 163–90.

Preston, W. (1833), 'A journal of the proceedings of a party of officers and men, belonging to his majesty's ship Sulphur, landed on the 8th of September, 1829, for the purpose of crossing the Darling Range of mountains, under the orders of Lieutenant Preston, R.N.', in J. Cross, ed., *Journals of several expeditions made in Western Australia, during the years 1829, 1830, 1831, and 1832, under the sanction of the governor, Sir James Stirling, containing the latest authentic information relative to that country* (London: J. Cross).

Prøsch-Danielsen, L. and Simonsen, A. (2000a), 'The Deforestation Patterns and the Establishment of the Coastal Heathland of South-Western Norway', *AmS-Skrifter* 15: 1–52.

—— ——(2000b), 'Palaeoecological Investigations Towards the Reconstruction of the History of Forest Clearances and Coastal Heathlands in South-Western Norway', *Vegetation History and Archaeobotany* 9: 189–204.

Proust, M. (1990 [1927]), *Le Temps Retrouvé* (Paris: Gallimard).

Pulgar Vidal, J. (1981), Geográfica del Perú: Las ocho regiones naturales del Perú Lima: Editorial Universo.

Pumpelly, R. (1908), *Explorations in Turkestan* (Washington, DC: Carnegie Institution).

Puri, R. K. (2005), 'Postabandonment Ecology of Penan Forest Camps: Anthropological Approaches to the History of a Rain-forested Valley in East Kalimantan', in M. R. Dove, P. E. Sajise, and A. A. Doolittle, eds, *Conserving Nature in Culture: Case Studies from Southeast Asia*, Yale Southeast Asia Studies Monograph Series, vol. 54. (New Haven, CT: Yale University Press), pp. 25–82.

DoD [Department of Defense] (2010), *Quadrennial Defense Review Report February 2010*. Available online at <http://www.defense.gov/qdr/> (Washington, DC: US Department of Defense).

Quilter, J. and Stocker, T. (1983), 'Subsistence Economies and the Origins of Andean Complex Societies', *American Anthropologist* 85: 545–62.

Radcliffe-Brown, A. R. (1922), *The Andaman Islanders* (Cambridge: Cambridge University Press).

Radio Australia (2009), 'Marshall Islands Continues Cleanup After Floods', Radio Australia News 2 January. Available at <http://www.radioaustralianews.net.au/stories/200901/2458235.htm?desktop> [Accessed on 25 March 2010].

Rainbird, P. (2004), *The Archaeology of Micronesia* (Cambridge: Cambridge University Press).

Ramage, N. (1992), 'Goods, Graves, and Scholars: 18th-century Archaeologists in Britain and Italy', *American Journal of Archaeology* 96: 653–61.

Ranke, J. (1895), *Diluvium und Urmensch* (Leipzig: Bibliographisches Institut).

Rasmussen, M. (1999), 'Livestock Without Bones: The Long House as Contributor to the Interpretation of Livestock Management in the Southern Scandinavian Early Bronze Age', in C. Fabeck and J. Ringtved, eds, *Settlement and Landscape* (Århus: Jutland Archaeological Society), pp. 281–90.

——and Adamsen, C. (1993), 'Bebyggelsen', in J. Jensen, ed., *Da Klinger I Muld* (Århus: Jysk Arkæologisk Selskab), pp. 136–41.

Ratzel, F. (1896–8), *The History of Mankind*, trans. A. J. Butler, 3 vols (London: Macmillan).

Raymond, G., Jr., ed. (2005), *Ethnologue: Languages of the World*, 15th edn (Dallas, TX: SLL International).

Redman, C. L. (2004a), 'Introduction: Human Impacts on Past Environments', in C. L. Redman, S. R. James, P. R. Fish, and J. D. Rogers, eds, *The Archaeology of Global Change: The Impact of Humans on their Environment* (Washington, DC: Smithsonian Institution Press), pp. 1–8.

——(2004b), 'Effects of Agriculture and Urban Society', in C. L. Redman, S. R. James, P. R. Fish, and J. D. Rogers, eds, *The Archaeology of Global Change: The Impact of Humans on their Environment* (Washington, DC: Smithsonian Institution Press), pp. 89–93.

——(2004c), 'Environmental Degradation and Early Mesopotamian Civilization', in C. L. Redman, S. R. James, P. R. Fish, and J. D. Rogers, eds, *The Archaeology of Global Change: The Impact of Humans on their Environment* (Washington, DC: Smithsonian Institution Press), pp. 158–64.

——(2005), 'Resilience Theory in Archaeology', *American Anthropologist* 107: 70–7.

——and Kinzig, A. P. (2003), 'Resilience of Past Landscapes: Resilience Theory, Society, and the *Longue Durée*', *Conservation Ecology* 7(1): 14.

Richards, P. (1985), *Indigenous Agricultural Revolution: Ecology and Food Production in West Africa* (London: Hutchinson).

——(1993), 'Cultivation: Knowledge or Performance?', in M. Hobart, ed., *An Anthropological Critique of Development: the Growth of Ignorance* (London: Routledge), pp. 61–78.

Richardson, J. B., III, and Sandweiss, D. H. (2008), 'Climate Change, El Niño, and the Rise of Complex Society on the Peruvian Coast during the Middle Holocene', in D. H. Sandweiss and J. Quilter, eds, *El Niño, Catastrophism, and Culture Change in Ancient America* (Washington, DC: Dumbarton Oaks Research Library and Collection, Harvard University Press), pp. 59–75.

Ripoll, D. (1994), 'Nos Ancêtres Les Lacustres: Images d'un Mythe d'origine', *Genava* 42: 203–18.

Rivière, G. (1983), 'Quadripartition et Idéologie dans les Communautés Aymaras de Carangas (Bolivie)', *Bulletin de l'Institut français d'études andines* 12: 41–62.

Roberts, B. and Wrathmell, S. (2002), *Region and Place: A Study of English Rural Settlement* (London: English Heritage).

Rocheleau, D. E., Steinberg, P. E., and Benjamin, P. A. (1995), 'Environment, Development, Crisis, and Crusade: Ukambani, Kenya, 1890–1990', *World Development* 23: 1037–51.

Rockström, J., Steffen, W., Noone, K., Persson, Å., Chapin, III, F. S., Lambin, E., Lenton, T. M., Scheffer, M., Folke, C., Schellnhuber, H., Nykvist, B., De Wit, C. A., Hughes, T., van der Leeuw, S., Rodhe, H., Sörlin, S., Snyder, P. K., Costanza, R., Svedin, U., Falkenmark, M., Karlberg, L., Corell, R. W., Fabry, V. J., Hansen, J., Walker, B. H., Liverman, D., Richardson, K., Crutzen, C., and Foley. J. (2009), 'A Safe Operating Space for Humanity', *Nature* 461: 472–5.

Roe, J. S. (1852), 'Report of an expedition under the Surveyor-General, Mr. J. S. Roe, to the south-eastward of Perth, in Western Australia, between the months of September, 1848, and February, 1849, to the Hon. Colonial Secretary. Communicated by the Colonial Office', *Royal Geographical Society* 22: 1–57.

——Dunning, N. P., Tankersley, K. B., Carr, C., Weaver, E., Grizioso, L., Lane, B., Jones, J. G., Buttles, P., Valdez, F., and Lentz, D. L. (2012), 'Water and sustainable land use at the ancient tropical city of Tikal, Guatemala', *PNAS* 109(31): 12408–13.

Roosevelt, A. C. (1991), *Moundbuilders of the Amazon: Geophysical Archaeology on Marajó Island, Brazil* (San Diego, CA: Academic Press).

Roscoe, P. (2008), 'Catastrophe and the Emergence of Political Complexity: A Sociological Model', in D. H. Sandweiss and J. Quilter, eds, *El Niño, Catastrophism, and Culture Change in Ancient America* (Washington, DC: Dumbarton Oaks Research Library and Collection, Harvard University Press), pp. 77–100.

Rosen, A. M. (2007), *Civilizing Climate Social Responses to Climate Change in the Ancient Near East* (Plymouth: AltaMira Press).

Rosenberg, M. (1990), 'The Mother of Invention: Evolutionary Theory, Territoriality, and the Origins of Agriculture', *American Anthropologist* 92: 399–415.

Rosevear, D. R. (1979), 'Oban Revisited', *The Nigerian Field* 44: 75–81.

Rosny, J. H. (1897), *Nomaï, Amours Lacustres* (Paris: Librairie Borel).

Rostain, S. (2010), 'Earthworks in Coastal Amazonia', *Diversity* 2: 331–52.

Rostow, W. W. (1960), *The Stages of Economic Growth: a Non-communist Manifesto* (Cambridge: Cambridge University Press).

Rostworowski De Diez Canseco, M. (1989), *Costa Peruana Prehispánica* (Lima: Instituto de Estudios Peruanos).

Rowe, J. H. (1962), 'Stages and Periods in Archaeological Interpretation', *Southwestern Journal of Anthropology* 18: 40–54.

Roymans, N. (1999), 'Man, Cattle and the Supernatural in the Northwest European Plain', in C. Fabeck and J. Ringtved, eds, *Settlement and Landscape* (Århus: Jutland Archaeological Society), pp. 291–300.

Rudiak-Gould, P. (2009), *The Fallen Palm: Climate Change and Culture Change in the Marshall Islands* (Saarbrücken: VDM Verlag).

Ruoff, U. (1992), 'The Pfahlbauland Exhibition, Zurich 1990', in B. Coles, ed., *The Wetland Revolution in Prehistory. Proceedings of a Conference Held by the Prehistoric Society and WARP at the University of Exeter, April, 1991* (London: The Prehistoric Society and WARP), pp. 134–46.

Ruskin, J. (1893), *The Poetry of Architecture, or, The Architecture of the Nations of Europe Considered in its Association with Natural Scenery and National Character* (Orpington: George Allen).

Russell-Smith, J., Lucas, D., Gapindi, M., Gunbunuka, B., Kapirigi, N., Namingum, G., Lucas, K., Giuliani, P., and Chaloupka, G. (1997), 'Aboriginal Resource Utilization and Fire Management Practice in Western Arnhem Land, Monsoonal Northern Australia: Notes for Prehistory, Lessons for the Future', *Human Ecology* 25: 159–95.

Rykwert, J. (1972), *On Adam's House in Paradise: the Idea of the Primitive Hut in Architectural History* (New York: Museum of Modern Art).

Sahlins, M. D. (1968), *Tribesmen* (Englewood Cliffs, NJ: Prentice Hall).

——(2011), 'What Kinship is (part one)', *Journal of the Royal Anthropological Institute* 17: 2–19.

Sánchez, W. (2008), *Inkas, "flecheros" y mitmaykuna: Cambio social y paisajes cultur- ales en los Valles y en los Yungas de Inkachaca/Paracti y Tablas Monte (Cocha- bamba-Bolivia, siglos XV–XVI)* (Uppsala: Department of Archaeology and Ancient History, Uppsala University).

Sandweiss, D. H. and Kelley, A. R. (2012), 'Archaeological Contributions to Climate Change Research: The Archaeological Record as a Paleoclimatic and Paleoenviron- mental Archive', *Annual Review of Anthropology* 41: 371–91.

——Maasch, K. A., Andrus, C. F. T., Reitz, E. J., Riedinger-Whitmore, M., Richardson, J. B., III, and Rollins, H. B. (2007), 'Mid-Holocene Climate and Culture Change in Coastal Peru', in D. G. Anderson, K. A. Maasch, and D. H. Sandweiss, eds, *Climate Change and Cultural Dynamics: A Global Perspective on Mid-Holocene Transitions* (Amsterdam: Academic Press), pp. 25–50.

————Burger, R. L., Richardson, J. B., III, Rollins, H. B., and Clement, A. (2001), 'Variation in Holocene El Niño Frequencies: Climate Records and Cultural Conse- quences in Ancient Peru', *Geology* 29: 603–6.

——Richardson, J. B., III, Reitz, E. J., Rollins, H. B., and Maasch, K. A. (1996), 'Geoarchaeological Evidence from Peru for a 5000 years B. P. Onset of El Niño', *Science* 273: 1531–3.

——and J. Quilter (2008), 'Climate, Catastrophe, and Culture in the Ancient Amer- icas', in D. H. Sandweiss and J. Quilter, eds, *El Niño, Catastrophism, and Culture Change in Ancient America* (Washington, DC: Dumbarton Oaks Research Library and Collection, Harvard University Press), pp. 1–11.

Sanger, D., Almquist, H., and Dieffenbacher-Krall, A. (2007), 'Mid-Holocene Cultural Adaptations to Central Maine', in D. G. Anderson, K. A. Maasch, and D. H. Sandweiss, eds, *Climate Change and Cultural Dynamics: A Global Perspective on Mid-Holocene Transitions* (Amsterdam: Academic Press), pp. 435–56.

Sanger, M. C. (2010), 'Leaving the Rings: Shell Ring Abandonment and the End of the Late Archaic', in D. H. Thomas and M. C. Sanger, eds, *Trend, Tradition, and Turmoil: What Happened to the Southeastern Archaic? Proceedings of the Third Caldwell Conference, St. Catherines Island, Georgia, May 9–11, 2008* (New York: Anthropological Papers of the American Museum of Natural History), pp. 201–15.

Sassaman, K. E. (2010a), 'Getting from the Late Archaic to Early Woodland in Three Middle Valleys (Those Being the Savannah, St. Johns, and Tennessee)', in D. H. Thomas and M. C. Sanger, eds, *Trend, Tradition, and Turmoil: What Happened to the Southeastern Archaic? Proceedings of the Third Caldwell Confer- ence, St. Catherines Island, Georgia, May 9–11, 2008* (New York: Anthropological Papers of the American Museum of Natural History), pp. 229–35.

——(2010b), *The Eastern Archaic Historicized* (Lanham, MD: AltaMira Press).

Sassaman, K. E. and Anderson, D. G., eds (1996), *The Archaeology of the Mid-Holocene Southeast* (Tuscaloosa, AL: University of Alabama Press).

Sauer, C. (1963), 'The Morphology of Landscape (1925)', in *Land and Life: A Selection from the Writings of Carl Ortwin Sauer*, ed. John Leighly (Berkeley, CA: University of California Press), pp. 315–50.

Scarborough, V. L. (2003), *The Flow of Power: Ancient Water Systems and Landscapes* (Santa Fe, NM: School of American Research Press).

——(2010), *Water and Humanity: A Historical Overview*, History of Water and Civilization Book Series, vol. VII (Paris: UNESCO).

——Dunning, N. P., Tankersley, K. B., Carr, C., Weaver, E., Grizioso, L., Lane, B., Jones, J. G., Buttles, P., Valdez, F., and Lentz, D. L. (2012), 'Water and sustainable land use at the ancient tropical city of Tikal, Guatemala', *PNAS* 109(31): 12408–13.

Scarre, C., ed. (2005), *The Human Past: World Prehistory and the Development of Human Societies* (London: Thames and Hudson).

Schaan, D. P. (2006), 'São Tartarugas até lá Embaixo! Cultura, Simbolismo e espacialidade na Amazônia pré-Colombiana', *Revista de Arqueologia Americana* 24: 99–124.

——(2008), 'The nonagricultural Chiefdoms of Marajó Island', in H. Silverman and W. H. Isbell, eds, *Handbook of South American Archaeology* (New York: Springer), pp. 339–57.

——(2010), 'Long-term Human Induced Impacts on Marajó Island Landscapes, Amazon Estuary', *Diversity* 2: 182–206.

Scheele, H. G. (1970), 'The Chavin Occupation of the Central Coast of Peru'. Unpublished PhD thesis, Harvard University.

Schiavini, A. M. (1990), 'Estudio de la Relación entre el Hombre y los Pinnípedos en el Proceso Adaptativo Humano del Canal Beagle (Tierra del Fuego, Argentina)'. PhD Thesis, Facultad de Ciencias Exactas y Naturales, Universidad de Buenos Aires.

——(1993), 'Los Lobos Marinos como Recurso Para Cazadores-Recolectores Marinos: El Caso de Tierra del Fuego', *Latin American Antiquity* 4: 346–66.

Schiermeier, Q. (2007), 'Polar Research: The New Face of the Arctic', *Nature* 446: 133–5.

Schiffer, M. (1972), 'Behavioral Archaeology', *American Antiquity* 37: 156–65.

——(1976), *Behavioral Archaeology* (New York: Academic Press).

Schladt, M. (1997), *Kognitive struckturen von körpoerteilvokabularien in Kenianischen sprachen*, Africanistische Monographien 8 (Köln: Institut für Afrikanistik, Universität zu Köln).

Schlichtherle, H. (1997), *Pfahlbauten rund um die Alpe* (Stuttgart: Theiss).

——(2004), 'Lake-Dwellings in South-Western Germany: History of Research and Contemporary Perspectives', in F. Menotti, ed., *Living on the Lake in Prehistoric Europe: 150 years of Lake-Dwelling Research* (London: Routledge), pp. 22–35.

Schofield, J. (2010), 'Archaeology and Contemporary Society: Introduction', *World Archaeology* 42: 325–7.

Scholliers, P., ed. (2001), *Food, Drink and Identity* (New York; Oxford: Berg).

Schreiber, K. (1987), 'Conquest and consolidation: a comparison of the Wari and Inka occupation of a highland Peruvian valley', *American Antiquity* 52: 266–84.

——(1991), 'Jincamocco: a Huari Administrative Center in the South Central high-lands of Peru', in W. Isbell and G. McEwan, eds, *Huari Administrative Structure: Prehistoric Monumental Architecture and State Government* (Washington DC: Dumbarton Oaks Research Library and Collection), pp. 199–213.

Screen, J. A. and Simmonds, I. (2010), 'The Central Role of Diminishing Sea Ice in Recent Arctic Temperature Amplification', *Nature* 464: 1334–7.

Sebald, W. G. (1988), *After Nature* (Canada: Knopf).

Semeniuk, V. (1986), 'Holocene Climate History of Coastal South-western Australia Using Calcrete as an Indicator', *Palaeogeography, Palaeoclimatology, Palaeoecology* 53: 289–308.

Serjeantson, D. (2007), 'Intensification of Animal Husbandry in the Late Bronze Age? The Contribution of Sheep and Pigs', in C. Haselgrove and R. Pope, eds, *The Earlier Iron Age in Britain and the near Continent* (Oxford: Oxbow), pp. 80–93.

Service, E. R. (1962), *Primitive Social Organisation* (New York: Random House).

Sewell, W. (2005), *The Logics of History: Social Theory and Social Transformation* (Chicago, IL: University of Chicago Press).

Shady, R. and Leyva, C., eds (2003), *La ciudad sagrada de Caral-Supe: Los origines de la civilización andina y la formación del estado prístino en el antiguo Perú* (Lima: Instituto Nacional de Cultura, Proyecto Especial Arqueológico Caral-Supe).

Shandy, D. J. (2007), *Nuer-American Passages: Globalizing Sudanese Migration* (Gainesville, FL: University Press of Florida).

Sheil, D., Jennings, S., and Savill, P. (2000), 'Long-term Permanent Plot Observations of Vegetation Dynamics in Budongo, a Ugandan Rainforest', *Journal of Tropical Ecology* 16: 765–800.

Shellenberger, M. and Nordhaus, T. (2005), 'The Death of Environmentalism: Global warming politics in post-environmental world', *The Daily Grist Online* 01/13, <http://www.grist.org/article/doe-reprint/>.

Shennan, S. (2002), *Genes, Memes and Human History: Darwinian Archaeology and Cultural Evolution* (London: Thames and Hudson).

Sheridan, M. J. (2002), 'An Irrigation Intake is Like a Uterus: Culture and Agriculture in Precolonial North Pare, Tanzania', *American Anthropologist* 104: 79–92.

Sherratt, A. (2004), 'The Importance of Lake Dwellings in European Prehistory', in F. Menotti, ed., *Living on the Lake in Prehistoric Europe: 150 years of Lake Dwelling Research* (London: Routledge), pp. 267–76.

Sillitoe, P. (1998), 'The Development of Indigenous Knowledge: a New Applied Anthropology', *Current Anthropology* 39: 223–52.

Skeates, R. (2007), Book review of 'Living on the Lake in Prehistoric Europe: 150 years of lake-dwelling research', ed. F. Menotti, London: Routledge, 2004. *Environmental Archaeology* 12: 95–7.

Skinner, L. (2008), 'Facing Future Climate Change: Is the Past Relevant?', *Philosophical Transactions of the Royal Society* 366: 4627–45.

Sluyter, A. (2010), 'The Geographical Review's Historical Dimensions and Recentism', *Geographical Review* 100: 6–11.

Smith, E. A. (1983), 'Anthropological Applications of Optimal Foraging Theory: a Critical Review', *Current Anthropology* 24(5): 625–51.

Smith, M. E. (2010), 'Sprawl, Squatters, and Sustainable Cities: Can Archaeological Data Shed Light on Modern Urban Issues?', *Cambridge Archaeological Journal* 20: 229–53.

Smyntyna, O. V. (2004), 'Ecological explanation of Hunter-Gatherers Behavior: an attempt of historical overview', *Social Evolution and History* 3(2): 3–24.

Snow, C. P. (1993 [1959]), *The Two Cultures*, 2nd edn (Cambridge: Cambridge University Press).

Solomon, S. et al., eds, (2007), *Climate Change 2007: The Physical Science Basis. Contribution of Working Group I to the Fourth Assessment Report of the Intergovernmental Panel on Climate Change* (Cambridge: Cambridge University Press).

Soltvedt, E.-C., Løken,T., Prøsch-Danielsen, L., Børsheim, R., and Oma, K. (2007), *Bøndene På Kvålehodlene. Boplass-, Jordbruks-, Og Landskapsutvikling Gjennom 6000 År På Jæren, Sv Norge*. AmS-Varia 47 (Stavanger: Arkeologisk Museum i Stavanger).

Sontag, S. (2001), 'The Imagination of Disaster', in *Against Interpretation: And Other Essays* (New York: Picador).

Spector, J. (1996), 'What this Awl Means: Toward a Feminist Archaeology', in R. Preucel and I. Hodder, eds, *Contemporary Archaeology in Theory* (Cambridge: Blackwell), pp. 485–500.

Spennemann, D. H. R. (1996), 'Non-traditional Settlement Patterns and Typhoon Hazard on Contemporary Majuro Atoll, Republic of the Marshall Islands', *Environmental Management* 20: 337–48.

——and Marschner, I. (1994), *Stormy Years: On the Association Between the El Niño/Southern Oscillation Phenomenon and the Occurrence of Typhoons in the Marshall Islands (Report to the Federal Emergency Management Agency Region IX, San Francisco)*.

Ssennyonga, J. W. (1983), 'The Marakwet Irrigation System as a Model of a Systems-Approach to Water Management', in B. E. Kipkorir, R. C. Soper, and J. W. Ssennyonga, eds, *Kerio Valley: Past, Present and Future* (Nairobi: University of Nairobi Press, Institute of African Studies), pp. 96–111.

Stahl, A. B. (2001), *Making History in Banda: Anthropological Visions of Africa's Past* (Cambridge: Cambridge University Press).

Stanley, J.-D., Krom, M. D., Cliff, R. A., and Woodward, J. C. (2003), 'Nile Flow Failure at the End of the Old Kingdom, Egypt: Strontium Isotopic and Petrologic Evidence', *Geoarchaeology* 18: 395–402.

Stavenhagen, R. (1998), 'Indigenous Organizations: Rising actors in Latin America', *CEPAL Review* 63–75.

Stern, S. J. (1982), *Peru's Indian Peoples and the Challenge of the Spanish Conquest* (Madison, WI: University of Wisconsin Press).

Steward, J. (1955a), *Theory of Culture Change: the Methodology of Multilinear Evolution* (Chicago, IL: University of Illinois Press).

——ed. (1955b), *Irrigation Civilisations, a Comparative Study: a Symposium on Method and Result in Cross-cultural Regularities* (Washington, DC: Pan American Union).

Stinchcombe, J. R. (2006), 'Ecosystem Engineers as Selective Agents: the Effects of Leaf Litter on Emergence Time and Early Growth in Impatiens Capensis', *Ecology Letters* 9: 258–70.

Stipp, D. (2004), 'The Pentagon's Weather Nightmare', *Fortune* 149(3): 100–8.

Stocking, M. and Perkin, S. (1992), 'Conservation-with-development: an Application of the Concept in the Usambara Mountains, Tanzania', *Transactions of the Institute of British Geographers* 17: 337–49.

Stoczkowski, W. (2002), *Explaining Human Origins: Myth, Imagination and Conjecture* (Cambridge: Cambridge University Press).

Stokes, J. L. (1846), *Discoveries in Australia; with an Account of the Coasts and Rivers Explored and Surveyed During the Voyage of H.M.S. Beagle in the Years 1837–38–39–40–41–42–43* vol. 2 (London: T. and W. Boone).

Stone, G. D. (2005), 'A Science of the Gray: Malthus, Marx and the Ethics of Studying Crop Biotechnology', in L. Meskell and P. Pells, eds, *Embedding Ethics: Shifting Boundaries of the Anthropological Profession* (Oxford: Berg Press), pp. 197–217.

Strang, V. (2008), 'Uncommon Ground: Landscapes as Social Geography', in B. David and J. Thomas, eds, *Handbook of Landscape Archaeology* (Walnut Creek, CA: Left Coast Press), pp. 51–9.

Strathern, M. (1992), *After Nature: English Kinship in the Late Twentieth Century* (Cambridge: Cambridge University Press).

Stump, D. (2006), 'The Development and Expansion of the Field and Irrigation System at Engaruka, Tanzania', *Azania* 41: 69–94.

——(2010), '"Ancient and Backward or Long-lived and Sustainable?" The Role of the Past in Debates Concerning Rural Livelihoods and Resource Conservation in Eastern Africa', *World Development* 38: 1251–62.

——and Tagseth, M. (2009), 'The History of Precolonial and Early Colonial Agriculture on Kilimanjaro: a Review', in T. Clack, ed., *Culture, History and Identity: Human-Environmental Relations in the Mount Kilimanjaro Area, Tanzania* (Cambridge Monographs in African Archaeology) (Oxford: Archaeopress), pp. 107–24.

Sunstein, C. R. (2006), *On the Divergent American Reactions to Terrorism and Climate Change*, John M. Olin Law & Economics Working Paper No. 295 (Chicago, IL: University of Chicago Law School).

Sutter, R. (2000), 'Prehistoric Genetic and Culture Change: a Bioarchaeological Search for pre-Inka Altiplano Colonies in the Coastal Valleys of Moquegua, Peru, and Azapa, Chile', *Latin American Antiquity* 11: 43–70.

Sutton, J. E. G. (1991), 'Agricultural History in East Africa: Purpose, Progress and Prospects', in L. E. Leakey and L. J. Slikkerveer, eds, *Origins and Development of Agriculture in East Africa: the Ethnosystems Approach to the Study of Early Food Production in Kenya* (Ames, IA: Iowa State University), pp. 95–101.

——(1998), 'Engaruka: An Irrigation Agricultural Community in Northern Tanzania Before the Maasai', *Azania* 33: 1–33.

——(2004), 'Engaruka: The Success and Abandonment of an Integrated Irrigation System in an Arid Part of the Rift Valley, c.15th to 17th centuries', in M. Widgren and J. E. G. Sutton, eds, *Islands of intensive agriculture in Eastern Africa* (Oxford: James Currey), pp. 114–32.

Swetnam, T. W., Allen, C., and Betancourt, J. (1999), 'Applied historical ecology: Using the past to manage for the future', *Ecological Applications* 9(4): 1189–206.

Szerszynski, B., Wallace, H., and Waterton, C., eds (2003), *Nature Performed: Environment, Culture and Performance* (Oxford: Blackwell).

Tainter, J. A. (2006), 'Archaeology of Overshoot and Collapse', *Annual Review of Anthropology* 35: 59–74.

——(2000), 'Global Change, History and Sustainability', in R. J. McIntosh, J. A. Tainter, and S. K. McIntosh, eds, *The Way the Wind Blows: Climate, History and Human Action* (New York: Columbia University Press), pp. 331–56.

Tajfel, H. and Turner, J. (1979), 'An Integrative Theory of Intergroup Conflict', in S. Worchel and W. Austin, eds, *The Social Psychology of Intergroup Relations* (Monterey, CA: Brooks/Cole), pp. 33–48.

————(1986), 'The Social Identity Theory of Intergroup Behavior', in S. Worchel and W. Austin, eds, *Psychology of Intergroup Relations* (Chicago: Nelson-Hall), pp. 7–24.

Taylor, W. (1948), *A Study of Archaeology*, American Anthropological Association Memoir No. 69 (Washington DC: American Anthropological Association).

Terrell, J. E., Hart, J. P., Barut, S., and Cellinese, N. (2003), 'Domesticated Landscapes: The Subsistence Ecology of Plant and Animal Distribution', *Journal of Archaeological Method and Theory* 10(4): 323–68.

Tesch, S. (1992), 'House, Farm and Village in the Köpinge Area from Early Neolithic to the Early Middle Ages', in L. Larson, J. Callmer, and B. Stjärnquist, eds, *The Archaeology of the Cultural Landscape. Field Work and Research in a South Swedish Rural Region* (Stockholm: Almqvist and Wiksell), pp. 283–344.

——(1993), 'Houses, Farmsteads and Long Term Change. A Regional Study of Prehistoric Settlements in the Köpinge Area, in Scania, Southern Sweden'. Unpublished PhD thesis, University of Uppsala.

Thomas, D. H. and Sanger, M. C., eds (2010), *Trend, Tradition, and Turmoil: What Happened to the Southeastern Archaic? Proceedings of the Third Caldwell Conference, St. Catherines Island, Georgia, May 9–11, 2008* (New York: Anthropological Papers of the American Museum of Natural History).

Thomas, J. (2004), *Archaeology and Modernity* (London: Routledge).

Thomas, K. (1984 [1983]), *Man and the Natural World: Changing Attitudes in England 1500–1800* (London: Penguin).

Thompson, I. I. G. and Mosley-Thompson. E. (1987), 'Evidence of Abrupt Climate Change During the Last 1500 years Recorded in Ice Cores from the Tropical Quelccaya Ice cap, Peru', in W. H. Berger and L. D. Labeyrie, eds, *Abrupt Climate Change* (Dordrecht: D. Reidel), pp. 99–110.

Thompson, V. D. (2010), 'The Rhythms of Space-Time and the Making of Monuments and Places during the Archaic', in D. H. Thomas and M. C. Sanger, eds, *Trend, Tradition, and Turmoil: What Happened to the Southeastern Archaic? Proceedings of the Third Caldwell Conference, St. Catherines Island, Georgia, May 9–11, 2008* (New York: Anthropological Papers of the American Museum of Natural History), pp. 217–28.

Thornberry, P. (2002), *Indigenous Peoples and Human Rights*, Melland Schill Studies in International Law (Manchester: Manchester University Press).

Tiffen, M. (1996), 'Land and Capital: Blind Spots in the Study of the "Resource-Poor" Farmer', in M. Leach and R. Mearns, eds, *The Lie of the Land: Challenging Received Wisdom on the African Environment* (Oxford: James Currey), pp. 168–85.

Tilley, C. (1981), 'Conceptual Frameworks for the Explanation of Sociocultural Change', in I. Hodder, ed., *Patterns of the Past: Studies in honour of David Clarke* (Cambridge: Cambridge University Press), pp. 363–86.

——(1994), *A Phenomenology of Landscape: Places, Paths and Monuments* (Oxford: Berg).

——(2004), *The Materiality of Stone* (Oxford: Berg).

——(2008), *Body and Image*, Explorations in Landscape Phenomenology 2 (Walnut Creek, CA: Left Coast Press).

Tivoli, A. M. (2008), 'Tendencias Temporales en el Aprovechamiento de las Aves en la Región del Canal Beagle: Nuevos Resultados y Perspectivas Futuras'. Paper presented at the VII Jornadas de Arqueología de la Patagonia, Ushuaia (Argentina).

——(2010a), 'Las Aves en la Organización Socioeconómica de Cazadores-Recolectores-Pescadores del Extremo Sur Sudamericano'. PhD Thesis. Facultad de Filosofía y Letras, Universidad de Buenos Aires.

——(2010b), 'Temporal Trends in Avifaunal Resource Management by Prehistoric Sea Nomads of the Beagle Channel Region (Southern South America)', in W. Prummel, J. T. Zeiler, and D. C. Brinkhuizen, eds, *Birds in Archaeology: Proceedings of the 6th Meeting of the ICAZ Bird Working Group*, Groningen Archaeological Studies 10 (Groningen: Barkhuis), pp. 131–40.

——(2010c), 'Exploitation of bird resources among prehistoric sea-nomad societies of the Beagle Channel region, southern South America', *Before Farming* 2: 1–12.

——(2012), '¿Intensificación? en el aprovechamiento de aves entre los cazadores-recolectores-pescadores de la región del canal Beagle', *Archaeofauna* 21: 121–37.

——and Pérez, A. F. (2009), 'Rendimiento Económico del Cauquén Común (Chloephaga picta, Fam.: Anatidae)', in M. Salemme, F. Santiago, M. Álvarez, E. Piana, M. Vázquez, and E. Mansur, eds, *Arqueología de Patagonia: Una Mirada Desde el último Confín* (Ushuaia: Utopías), pp. 853–64.

——and Zangrando, A.F. (2011), 'Subsistence variations and landscape use among maritime hunter-gatherers. A zooarchaeological analysis from the Beagle Channel (Tierra del Fuego, Argentina)', *Journal of Archaeological Science* 38: 1148–56.

Torrence, R. (2002), 'What Makes a Disaster? A Long-term View of Volcanic Eruptions and Human Responses in Papua New Guinea', in R. Torrence and J. Grattan, eds, *Natural Disasters and Cultural Change*, One World Archaeology 45 (London: Routledge), pp. 1–18.

Treacy, J. M. (1994), *Las chacras de Coporaque : Andenería y riego en el Valle del Colca* (Lima: Instituto de Estudios Peruanos).

Trigger, B. (1989), *A History of Archaeological Thought* (Cambridge: Cambridge University Press).

——(2006), *A History of Archaeological Thought*, 2nd edn (Cambridge: Cambridge University Press).

Trypanis, C. A. (1964), *Pompeian Dog, Pompeian Dog* (New York: Chilmark Press).

Tsai, S. M., O'Neill, B., Cannavan, F. S., Saito, D., Falcão, N. P. S., Kern, D. C., Grossman, J., and Thies, J. (2009), 'The Microbial World of Terra Preta', in W. I. Woods, ed., *Terra Preta Nova: A Tribute to Wim Sombroek* (New York: Springer), pp. 299–308.

Turner, J. (1982), 'Toward a Cognitive Redefinition of the Social Group', in H. Tajfel, ed., *Social Identity and Intergroup Relations* (Cambridge: Cambridge University Press), pp. 15–40.

Tversky, A. and Kahneman, D. (1982), 'Availability: A Heuristic for Judging Frequency and Probability', in D. Kahneman, P. Slovic, and A. Tversky, eds, *Judgment Under Uncertainty: Heuristics and Biases* (Cambridge: Cambridge University Press), pp. 163–78.

Twain, M. (2007 [1869]), 'The Buried City of Pompeii', *Innocents Abroad: or, The New Pilgrims' Progress* (Whitefish, MT: Kessinger Publishing).

Ucko, P. (1999), *The Archaeology and Anthropology of Landscape* (London: Routledge).

——and Rosenfeld, A. (1967), *Paleolithic Cave Art* (London: World University Library).

Valdez, L. M. (1994), 'Approach to the Pre-Wari occupation of the Huamanga Regions. Ayacucho, Peru', *Willay* 41: 24–5.

——(2004), 'Huarpa, la Cultura Local del Valle de Ayacucho', *Revista Arqueológica Warpa* 7: 3–8.

van der Leeuw, S., ed. (1981), *Archaeological Approaches to the Study of Complexity* (Amsterdam: University of Amsterdam).

——(2008), 'Climate and Society: Lessons from the Past 10,000 Years', *Ambio* 37: 476–82.

——and the ARCHAEOMEDES Research Team (2000), 'Land Degradation as Socionatural Process', in R. J. McIntosh, J. A. Tainter, and S. K. McIntosh, eds, *The Way the Wind Blows: Climate, History and Human Action* (New York: Columbia University Press), pp. 357–84.

——and Redman, C. L. (2002), 'Placing Archaeology at the Centre of Socio-Natural Studies', *American Antiquity* 67(4): 597–605.

——Costanza, R., Aulenbach, S., Brewer, S., Burek, M., Cornell, S., Crumley, C. L., Dearing, J. A., Downy, C., Graumlich, L. J., Heckbert, S., Hegmon, M., Hibbard, K., Jackson, S. T., Kubiszewski, I., Sinclair, P., Sörlin, S., and Steffen, W. (2011), 'Toward an integrated history to guide the future', *Ecology and Society* 16(4): 2.

van der Veen, M. (2003), 'When is food a luxury?', *World Archaeology* 34: 405–27.

Vita-Finzi, C. and Higgs, E. S. (1970), 'Prehistoric Economy in the Mount Carmel Area of Palestine: Site Catchment Analysis', *Proceedings of the Prehistoric Society* 36: 1–37.

Viveiros de Castro, E. (1998), 'Cosmological Deixis and Amerindian Perspectivism', *Journal of the Royal Anthropological Institute* 4: 469–88.

Vivian, R. G. (1990), *The Chacoan Prehistory of the San Basin* (San Diego, CA: Academic Press).

Vogt, A. M. (1998), *Le Corbusier: the Noble Savage* (Cambridge, MA: MIT Press).

Voorhies, B. and Metcalfe, S. E. (2007), 'Culture and Climate in Mesoamerica during the Middle Holocene', in D. G. Anderson, K. A. Maasch, and D. H. Sandweiss, eds,

Climate Change and Cultural Dynamics: A Global Perspective on Mid-Holocene Transitions (Amsterdam: Elsevier), pp. 157–87.

Vradenburg, J. A. (1992), 'Analysis of the Human Skeletal Remains from the Late (1150–800BC) Initial Period site of Cardal, Lurin valley, Peru'. Unpublished MA Thesis, Department of Anthropology, University of Missouri.

Wagner, R. (1981), *The Invention of Culture* (Chicago. IL: University of Chicago Press).

Wagstaff, J. (1987), *Landscape and Culture: Geographical and Archaeological Perspectives* (Oxford: Blackwell).

Walker, B. and Salt, D. (2006), *Resilience Thinking: Sustaining Ecosystems and People in a Changing World* (Washington DC: Island Press).

——Holling, C. S., Carpenter, S. R., and Kinzig, A. (2004), 'Resilience, Adaptability and Transformability in Social–Ecological Systems', *Ecology and Society* 9: 5. [online] URL<http://www.ecologyandsociety.org/vol9/iss2/art5/>.

Walker, K. J. and Surge, D. (forthcoming), 'Late Holocene climate change and human response in the Calusa region of coastal southwest Florida: developing geochemical proxies from archaeological sources', *Quaternary International*.

Walther, G. R., Post, E., Convey, P., Menzel, A., Parmesan C., Beebee, T. J. C., Fromentin, J.-M., Hoegh-Guldberg, O., and Bairlein, F. (2002), 'Ecological Responses to Recent Climate Change', *Nature* 416: 389–95.

Ward, D. J., Lamont, B. B., and Burrows, C. L. (2001), 'Grasstrees Reveal Contrasting Fire Regimes in Eucalypt Forest Before and After European Settlement of South-Western Australia', *Forest Ecology and Management* 150: 323–9.

Warren, D. M. (1989), 'The Impact of Nineteenth Century Social Science in Establishing Negative Values and Attitudes Towards Indigenous Knowledge Systems', in D. M. Warren, L. J. Slikkerveer, and S. O. Titilola, eds, *Indigenous Knowledge Systems: Implications for Agriculture and International Development*. Studies in Technology and Social Change 11 (Ames, IA: Iowa State University Press), pp. 171–83.

Watson, E. E. (2009), *Living Terraces in Ethiopia: Konso Landscape, Culture and Development* (Oxford: James Currey).

Watts, W. A., Grimm, E. C., and Hussey, T. C. (1996), 'Mid-Holocene Forest History of Florida and the Coastal Plain of Georgia and South Carolina', in K. E. Sassaman and D. G. Anderson, eds, *Archaeology of the Mid-Holocene Southeast* (Gainesville, FL: University Press of Florida), pp. 28–38.

Weber, W., White, L. J. T., Vedder, A., and Naughton-Treeves, L. (2001), *African Rain Forest Ecology and Conservation: an interdisciplinary perspective* (New Haven, CT: Yale University Press).

Webster, D. L. (2002), *The Fall of the Ancient Maya: Solving the Mystery of the Maya* (London: Thames and Hudson).

Weinstein, N. D. (1989), 'Effects of Personal Experience on Self-protective Behavior', *Psychological Bulletin* 105: 31–50.

Weisler, M. (1999), 'Atolls as Settlement Landscapes: Ujae, Marshall Islands', *Atoll Research Bulletin* 460: 1–51.

——(2001), *On the Margins of Sustainability: Prehistoric Settlement of Utrok Atoll, Northern Marshall Islands* (Oxford: Archaeopress).

Weisler, M. Lum, J. K., Collins, S. L., and Kimoto, W. S. (2000), 'Status, Health, and Ancestry of a Late Prehistoric Burial from Kwajalein Atoll, Marshall Islands', *Micronesica* 32: 191–220.

Weiss, H., Courty, M.-A., Wetterstrom, W., Senior, L., Meadow, R., Guichard, F., and Curnow, A. (1993), 'The Genesis and Collapse of Third Millennium North Mesopotamian Civilization', *Science* 291: 995–1004.

Wendorf, F., Karlen, W., and Schild, R. (2007), 'Middle Holocene Environments of North and East Africa, with Special Emphasis on the African Sahara', pp. 189–227, in D. G. Anderson, K. A. Maasch, and D. H. Sandweiss, eds, *Climate Change and Cultural Dynamics: A Global Perspective on Mid-Holocene Transitions* (Amsterdam: Academic Press), pp. 189–227.

Wengrow, D. (2006), *The Archaeology of Early Egypt: Social Transformations in North East Africa, 10,000 to 2650 BC* (Cambridge: Cambridge University Press).

Wessels Boer, J. G. (1965), 'Palmae', in J. Lanjouw, ed., *Flora of Suriname*, vol 5, part 1 (Leiden: E. J. Brill).

White, L. (1949), *The Science of Culture: a Study of Man and Civilization* (New York: Farrar, Straus and Giroux).

——(1959), *The Evolution of Culture: the Development of Civilization to the Fall of Rome* (New York: McGraw-Hill).

White, L. J. T. (2001), 'The African Rainforest: climate and vegetation', in W. Weber, L. J. T. White, A. Vedder, and L. Naughton-Treeves (2001), *African Rain Forest Ecology and Conservation: an Interdisciplinary Perspective* (New Haven, CT: Yale University Press), pp. 3–29.

——and Oates, J. F. (1999), 'New Data on this History of the Plateau Forest of Okomu, Southern Nigeria: an Insight into how Human Disturbance has Shaped the African Rainforest', *Global Ecology and Biogeography* 8: 355–61.

Whittle, A. (2003), *The Archaeology of People: Dimensions of Neolithic Life* (London: Routledge).

Widgren, M. (2000), 'Islands of Intensive Agriculture in African Drylands: Towards an Explanatory Framework', in G. Barker and D. Gilbertson, eds, *The Archaeology of Drylands: Living at the Margin* (London: Routledge), pp. 252–66.

——(2004), 'Towards a Historical Geography of Intensive Farming in Eastern Africa', in M. Widgren and J. E. G. Sutton, eds, *Islands of Intensive Agriculture in Eastern Africa* (Oxford: James Currey), pp. 1–18.

——and Sutton, J. E. G., eds (2004), *Islands of Intensive Agriculture in Eastern Africa* (Oxford: James Currey).

Willey, G. (1953), *Prehistoric Settlement Patterns in the Viru Valley, Peru*. Bureau of American Ethology Bulletin 155 (Washington DC: Smithsonian Institution).

Williams León, C. (1985), 'A scheme for the early monumental architecture of the Central Coast of Peru', in C. Donnan, ed., *Early ceremonial architecture in the Andes* (Washington: Dumbarton Oaks), pp. 227–40.

Williams, P. R. (1997), 'The role of disaster in the development of agriculture and the evolution of social complexity in the South Central Andes'. Unpublished doctoral thesis, University of Florida.

Williamson, I. and Sabath, M. D. (1982), 'Island Population, Land Area, and Climate: A Case Study of the Marshall Islands', *Human Ecology* 10: 71–84.

Willis, K. J., Gillson, L., and Brncic, T. M. (2004), 'How "Virgin" is Virgin Forest?', *Science* 304: 402–3.

Wilson, E. (1975), *Sociobiology: The New Synthesis* (Cambridge, MA: Harvard University Press).

Winckelmann, J. J. (1762), Open Letter on the Discoveries of Herculaneum [Sendschreiben von den herculanischen Entdeckungen] (Dresden).

Winterhalder, B. (1981), 'Foraging Strategies in the Boreal Forest: an Analysis of Cree Hunting and Gathering', in B. Winterhalder and E. A. Smith, eds, *Hunter-Gatherer Foraging Strategies* (Chicago, IL: University of Chicago Press), pp. 66–98.

——and Smith, E. A., eds, (1981), *Hunter-Gatherer Foraging Strategies* (Chicago, IL: University of Chicago Press).

————(2000), 'Analyzing adaptive strategies: human behavioural ecology at twenty-five', *Evolutionary Anthropology* 9:51–72.

Wittfogel, K. A. (1957), *Oriental Despotism: a Comparative Study of Total Power* (New Haven, CT: Yale University Press).

Wolf, E. (1982), *Europe and the Peoples Without History* (Los Angeles, CA: University of California Press).

Wood, F. H. (1873), 'The Lake-dwellings of Switzerland', in F. H. Wood, *Echoes of the night, and Other Poems* (London: E. Moxon), pp. 29–38.

Woods, W. I. and McCann. J. M. (1999), 'The Anthropogenic Origin and Persistence of Amazonian Dark Earths' in C. Caviedes, ed., *Conference of Latin Americanist Geographers Yearbook 25* (Austin TX: University of Texas Press), pp. 7–14.

——(2003), 'Development of Anthrosol Research', in J. Lehmann, D. C. Kern, B. Glaser, and W. I. Woods, eds, *Amazonian Dark Earths: Origins, Properties, Management* (Dordrecht: Kluwer), pp. 3–14.

Worsaae, J. J. A. (1849), *The Primeval Antiquities of Denmark*, trans. W. J. Thoms (London: Parker).

Yaeger, J. and Hodell, D. A. (2008), 'The Collapse of Mayan Civilization: Assessing the Interaction of Culture, Climate, and Environment', in D. H. Sandweiss and J. Quilter, eds, *El Niño, Catastrophism, and Culture Change in Ancient America* (Washington, DC: Dumbarton Oaks Research Library and Collection, Harvard University Press), pp. 187–242.

Yamaguchi, T., Kayanne, H., Yamano, H., Najima, Y., Chikamori, M., and Yokoki, H. (2005), 'Excavation of Pit-Agriculture Landscape on Majuro Atoll, Marshall Islands, and Its Implications', *Global Environmental Research* 9: 27–36.

Yoffee, N. (2005), *Myths of the Archaic State: Evolution of the Earliest Cities, States, and Civilization* (Cambridge: Cambridge University Press).

Zangrando, A. F. (2003), *Ictioarqueología del Canal Beagle: Explotación de Peces y su Implicación en la Subsistencia Humana* (Buenos Aires: Sociedad Argentina de Antropología).

——(2007), 'Long Term Variations of Marine Fishing at the Southern End of South America: Perspectives from Beagle Channel Region', in H. Hüster Plogmann, ed., *The Role of Fish in Ancient Time; Proceedings of the 13th Meeting of the ICAZ Fish Remains Working Group* (Rahden: Verlag Marie Leidorf), pp. 17–23.

——(2009a), *Historia Evolutiva y Subsistencia de Cazadores-Recolectores Marítimos de Tierra del Fuego* (Buenos Aires: Sociedad Argentina de Antropología).

Zangrando, A. F. (2009b), 'Is Fishing Intensification a Direct Route to Hunter-Gatherer Complexity? A Case Study from the Beagle Channel Region (Tierra del Fuego, Southern South America)', *World Archaeology* 41: 589–608.

Zent, E. L. and Zent, S. (2004), 'Amazonian Indians as Ecological Disturbance Agents: The Hotí of the Sierra de Maigulaida Venezuelan Guayana', in L. Maffi and T. Carlson, eds, *Ethnobotany and Conservation of Biocultural Diversity* Advances in Economic Botany 15 (Bronx, NY: New York Botanical Garden Press), pp. 79–111.

Zettler, R. (2003), 'Reconstructing the World of Ancient Mesopotamia: Divided Beginnings and Holistic History', *Journal of the Economic and Social History of the Orient* 46(1): 3–45.

Zickfeld, K., Morgan, M. G., Frame, D. J., and Keith, D. W. (2010), 'Expert Judgments about Transient Climate Response to Alternative Future Trajectories of Radiative Forcing', *Proceedings of the National Academy of Sciences* 107(28): 12451–6.

Zimmermann, W. H. (1999), 'Why Was Cattle-Stalling Introduced in Prehistory? The Significance of Byre and Stable and of Outwintering', in C. Fabeck and J. Ringtved, eds, *Landscape and Settlement* (Århus: Jutland Archaeological Society), pp. 301–18.

Žižek, S. (2008), *Unbehagen in der Natur* (London: Verso).

Андрианов Б.В. (1991), Закономерности географической среды и хозяйственно-культурная дифференциация народов мира//Этническая экология.—М.: Наука.—1991.—С. 149–73 [Andrianov, B. V. (1991), 'Regularities of geographic habitat and economic and cultural differentiation of peoples of the world', in V. E. Kozlov, ed., *Ethnic Ecology* (Moscow: Science), pp. 49–173] (In Russian).

Антонович В.Б. (1901), Археологическая карта Волынской губернии//Труды XI Археологического Съезда.—Том 1.—С. 1–140 [Antonovych, V. B. (1901), Archaeological map of Volynian province, in Proceedings of XI Archaeological Congress, vol. 1, pp. 1–140] (In Russian).

Арутюнов С.А. (1989), Народы и культуры. Развитие и взаимодействие.—М.: Наука, 243 с. [Arutyunov, S. A. (1989), *Peoples and cultures: Development and interaction* (Moscow: Science)] (In Russian).

——(1993), Адаптивное значение культурного полиморфизма//Этнографическое обозрение.—1993.—№ 4.—С. 41–56 [Arutyunov, S. A. (1993), 'Adaptive significance of cultural polymorhism', *Ethnographic Review* 4: 41–56] (In Russian).

Балакин С.А. (1985), Концепция хозяйственно-культурного типа: современное состояние проблемы и перспективы применения в археологическом исследовании//Археология и методы исторической реконструкции.—К.: Наукова думка.—1985.—С. 91–106. [Balakin, S. A. (1985), 'Concept of economic and cultural phylum: state-of-the-art and perspectives of application in archaeological investigation', in V. F. Gening, ed., *Archaeology and methods of historical reconstruction* (Kiev: Naukova Dumka), pp. 91–106] (In Russian).

Бибиков С.Н. (1969), Некоторые аспекты палеоэкономического моделирования палеолита//Советская археология, № 4.—С. 5–22. [Bibikov, S. N. (1969), 'Some aspects of palaeoeconomic modelling of the Palaeolithic', *Soviet Archaeology* 4: 5–22] (In Russian).

——(1971), Плотность населения и величина охотничьих угодий в палеолите Крыма//Советская археология, № 4.—С. 11–22. [Bibikov, S. N. (1971),

'Population density and size of hunting grounds in the Palaeolithic of Crimea', *Soviet Archaeology* 4: 11–22] (In Russian).

Бібіков С.М. (1977), Епоха мезоліту//Історія Української РСР.—К.: Наукова думка.—1977.—Т. 1.—С. 41–50. [Bibikov, S. M. (1977), 'Mesolithic epoch', in Y. Y. Kondufor et al., eds, *History of Ukrainian SSR*, vol. 1 (Kiev: Naukova Dumka), pp. 41–50] (In Ukrainian).

Бонч-Осмоловский Г.А. (1934), Итоги изучения Крымского палеолита//Труды II Международной конференции Ассоциации по изучению Четвертичного периода—Вып. 5, с. 114–83 [Bonch-Osmolovskiy, G. A. (1934), 'Summary of Crimean Palaeolithic Studies', *Proceedings of 2nd International conference of the Association of Quaternary Studies* 5: 114–83] (In Russian).

Бэр К. Э. (1848), О влиянии внешней природы на социальные отношения отдельных народов и историю человечества//*Карманная книжка для любителей землеведения, издаваемая от Русского географического общества*, за 1848, 2 изд., СПБ. 1849. [Baer, K. E. von (1848), 'On the influence of external nature on social relations of certain peoples and on history of humankind', in *Pocket book for amateurs of physical geography, published by Russian geographic society, for 1849*, 2nd edn (St Petersburg: Russian Geographic Society)] (In Russian).

Веклич М.Ф. (1987), Проблемы палеоклиматологии.—К.: Наукова думка, 189 с. [Veklich, M. F. (1987), *Problems of Palaeoclimatology* (Kiev: Naukova Dumka).] (In Russian).

——(1990), Основы палеоландшафтоведения.—К.: Наукова думка, 189 с. [Veklich, M. F. (1990), *Fundamentals of Palaeolandscape Studies* (Kiev: Naukova Dumka)] (In Russian).

Величко А.А. (1971), Связь динамики природных изменений в плейстоцене с развитием первобытного человека//Вопросы антропологии, Вып. 37.—С. 3–19. [Velichko, A. A. (1971), 'The relationship of the dynamics of natural changes in the Pleistocene to the development of prehistoric humans, *Questions of Anthropology* 37: 3–19] (In Russian).

Верещагин В.Ю. (1988), Философские проблемы теории адаптации человека.—Владивосток: Изд-во Дальневосточного ун-та, 163 с. [Vereschagin, V. Y. (1988), *Philosophical Problems of the Theory of Human Adaptation* (Vladivistok: Far Eastern University Publishing House)] (In Russian).

Герасимов И.П. (1979), Методологические проблемы экологизации современной науки//Новые идеи в географии: географические аспекты экологии человека.—М.: Прогресс, С. 9–24. [Gerasimov, I. P. (1979), 'Methodological problems of environmentalization of contemporary science', in Y. V. Medvedkov, ed., *New ideas in geography: geographical aspects of human ecology* (Moscow, Progress), pp. 9–24] (In Russian).

Дмитриев В.Е., Белокобыльский Ю.Г. (1989), Палеогеографические аспекты археологии каменного века//Методические проблемы реконструкции в археологии и палеоэкологии.—Новосибирск: Наука, с. 261–3. [Dmitriev, V. E. and Belokobylskiy, Y. G. (1989), 'Palaeogeographical aspects of Stone Age archaeology', in Y. P. Kholyushkin, ed., *Methodological Problems of Reconstructions in Archaeology and Palaeoecology* (Novosibirsk: Nauka), pp. 261–3] (In Russian).

Долуханов П.М. (1985), Верхний палеолит и мезолит Европы: опыт многомерного анализа//Проблемы реконструкций в археологии.—Новосибирск: Наука.—1985.—С. 55–62. [Dolukhanov, P. M. (1985), 'Upper Paleolithic and Mesolithic of Europe: an experience of multidimensional analysis', in R. S. Vasilevskiy, ed., *Problems of reconstructions in archaeology* (Novosibirsk: Nauka), pp. 55–62] (In Russian).

Залізняк Л.Л. (1998), Передісторія України X–V тис. до н.е.—К.: Бібліотека українця, 306 с. [Zalizniak, L. L. (1998), *Protohistory of Ukraine X—V mill. BC* (Kiev: Ukrainian Library)] (In Ukrainian).

Кабо В.Р. (1979), Теоретические проблемы реконструкции первобытности//Этнография как источник реконструкции истории первобытного общества.—М.: Наука. С. 60–107. [Kabo, V. R. (1979), 'Theoretical problems of reconstruction of the primitive state', in A. I. Pershits, ed., *Ethnography as source for reconstruction of the history of prehistoric society* (Moscow: Science), pp. 60–107] (In Russian).

——(1986), Первобытная доземледельческая община.—М.: Наука, 302 с. [Kabo, V. R. (1986), *Prehistoric Pre-agricultural Community* (Moscow: Nauka)] (In Russian).

Калайков И.Д. (1984), Цивилизация и адаптация.—М.: Прогресс, 240 с. [Kalaykov, I. D. (1984), *Civilization and adaptation* (Moscow: Progress)] (In Russian).

Левин М.Г., Чебоксаров Н.Н. (1955), Хозяйственно-культурные типы и историко-этнографические области//Советская этнография, № 4, с. 3–17. [Levin, M. G. and Chtboksarov, N. N. (1955), 'Economic and cultural phylums and historical and ethnographic regions', *Soviet Ethnography* 4: 3–17] (In Russian).

Леонова Н.Б., Несмеянов С.А., Матюшкин И.Е. (1993), Региональная и локальная палеоэкология каменного века//Проблемы палеоэкологии древних обществ.—М.: Изд-во Россий. Открытого ун-та, С. 5–19. [Leonova, N. B., Nesmeyanov, S. A., and Matyusshkin, I. E. (1993), 'Regional and Local Palaeoecology of the Stone Age', in N. B. Leonova, ed., *Problems of Palaeoecology of Ancient Societies* (Moscow: Publishing house of Russian Open University), pp. 5–19] (In Russian).

Маркарян Э.С. (1975), К пониманию специфики человеческого общества как адаптивной системы//Географические аспекты экологии человека.—М.: Институт географии АН СССР, С. 139–49. [Markarian, E. S. (1975), 'Understanding the specificity of human society as an adaptive system', in A. D. Lebedev, ed., *Geographical Aspects of Human Ecology* (Moscow: Institute of Geography of USSR Academy of Sciences), pp. 139–49] (In Russian).

Массон В.М. (1971), Метод палеоэкономического анализа в археологии//Краткие сообщения Института археологии Академии наук СССР, Вып. 127.—С. 3–10. [Masson, V. M. (1971), 'Method of palaeoeconomic analysis in archaeology', *Short reports of Institute of Archaeology of USSR Academy of Sciences*, no. 127, pp. 3–10] (In Russian).

——(1996), Палеолитическое общество Восточной Европы. Вопросы палеоэкономики, культурогенеза и социогенеза.—С.-Пб., 1996.—73 с. [Masson, V. M. (1996), *Palaeolithic society in Eastern Europe: Questions of palaeoeconomics, cultural genesis and sociogenesis.* (St Petersburg)] (In Russian).

Мережковский К.С. (1880), Отчет о предварительных исследованиях каменного века в Крыму//Известия Императорского Русского географического общества, Т. 16. С. 106–46. [Merezhkovskiy, K. S. (1880), 'Report on the preliminary investigations of the Stone Age in Crimea', *Proceedings of Imperial Russian Geographic Society* 16: 106–46] (In Russian).

Обермайер Г. (1913), *Человек в его прошлом и настоящем*. Москва: Брокгауз и Ефрон. 690 с. [Obermaier, H. (1913), *Man in his past and present* (Moscow: Brokhaus & Efron)] (In Russian).

Проблемы. (1989), Проблемы культурной адаптации в эпоху верхнего палеолита (по материалам Восточной Европы и США): Тезисы докладов советско-американского симпозиума.—Л.: Наука.—1989.—67 с. [Problems (1989), *Problems of cultural adaptation in the Upper Palaeolithic (based on Eastern Europe and the USA).* Abstract of proceedings of the Soviet–American symposium (Leningrad: Science)] (In Russian).

Радищев А.Н. (1941), О человеке, его смертности и бессмертии//Радищев А.Н. Полное собрание сочинений.—Том 2.—Москва-Ленинград: Издательство АН СССР, с. 39–145 [Radischev, A. N. (1941), 'On Man, his Mortality and Immortality', in A. N. Radischev, *Complete Works,* vol. 2 (Moscow-Leningrad: Publishing House of USSR Academy of Sciences), pp. 39–145] (In Russian).

Рухин Л.Б. (1959), Основы общей палеогеографии.—Л.: Гостоптехиздат.—557 с. [Rukhin, L. B. (1959), *Fundamentals of General Palaeogeography* (Leningrad: Gostoptekhizdat)] (In Russian).

Сминтина О.В. (2001), Зональність ранньопервісних культур: дослідження, факти, гіпотези.—Одеса: Астропринт, 2001. – 312 с. [Smyntyna, O. V. (2001), *Zonal features of Early Prehistoric cultures: studies, facts, hypotheses* (Odessa: Astroprint)] (In Ukrainian).

Уваров А.С. (1881), Археология России. Том 1. Каменный период.—М.: Синодальная типография, 1881. – 474 с. [Uvarov, A. S. (1881), *Archaeology of Russia.* vol. 1: *Stone Age* (Moscow: Synodal Press)] (In Russian).

Фисуненко О. (2000), Эволюция ландшафтов в истории Земли // Ландшафти і сучасність. - К.-Вінниця: Гіаніс. - 2000. - С. 38–41. [Fisunenko, O. (2000), 'Evolution of Landscapes in the History of the Earth', in V. M. Paschenko, ed., *Landscapes and the Present* (Kiev: Hyppanis), pp. 38–41] (In Russian).

Хвойко В.В. (1913), *Древние обитатели среднего Приднепровья и их культура в доисторические времена*. Киев: Типография товарищества "Е. Синькевич" 157 с. [Khvoiko, V. V. (1913), *The Ancient Inhabitants of the Middle Dnieper Region and their Culture in Prehistoric Times* (Kiev: E. Sinkivych Publishing)] (In Russian).

Хлебович И.А., Чуднова В.И., Чупанова Г.С. (1975), Экологический подход при исследовании формирования адаптации населения//Географические аспекты экологии человека.—М.: Институт географии АН СССР, с. 150–61. [Khlebovich, I. A., Chudnova, V. I., and Chupanova, G. S. (1975), 'Ecological approach to investigation of formation of human adaptation', in A. D. Lebedev, ed., *Geographical aspects of human ecology* (Moscow: Institute of Geography of USSR Academy of Sciences), pp. 150–61] (In Russian).

Швебс Г.И. (1993), Схемы экологического прогноза и методика принятия решения//Методологические проблемы современной географии.—К.: Наукова думка, С. 29–35. [Schvebs, G. I. (1993), 'Schemas of ecological prognosis and methodic of decision-making' in A. M. Marinich, ed., *Methodological Problems of Contemporary Geography* (Kiev: Naukova Dumka), pp. 29–35] (In Russian).

Index

abandonment:
  of land 63, 67–9, 72, 73, 135, 154–6, 163–4,
    68, 177, 182, 253
  of settlement 51, 64–7, 176, 247, 254, 255,
    261–2
Aboriginal 35, 117, 120, 121, 123, 126,
    131, 261
accumulation of goods/wealth 102
adaptation:
  co-adaptation 34
  concept 8, 9, 21, 34, 36, 37
  theory 33, 38
adaptive cycle 272
affection 79
Africa:
  central 218, 260, 264, 266, 280
  East 133, 171–82, 279, 280
  south 175, 249, 279
  West 257, 259, 260, 263, 264, 280
agency, *see* agency theory 17, 18, 28, 34, 39,
    40, 57, 58, 61, 96, 143, 152, 194, 236, 258,
    281, 283
age-sets 67
agricultural calendar 144
agriculture:
  growth of 60
  intensification of 54, 58, 62, 70, 73, 171,
    176, 185, 253
  surplus 70, 71, 102, 247, 251, 265, 279
  terracing 49, 51, 62, 141, 144, 152,
    153–68, 283
agro-archaeology 9, 135, 136
agronomy:
  agronomic knowledge 143, 144, 150,
    152, 156
  agrosystems 137, 151
  agro-technology 143
Akaddian 250
albatross 88
alpha diversity 46, 52
alpine 218, 220, 226, 227
altiplano 140, 141, 150, 153, 154, 155
Amazon:
  Amazonia 46, 49, 50–3, 54, 263, 266
  Dark Earths 53, 54
  estuary 51, 54
America 3–25, 33, 35, 47, 53, 77, 78, 87, 100,
    136, 153, 182, 201, 239, 242, 246, 247,
    249, 250, 252, 253, 264, 279, 280

Amuna (water collection systems) 161
Analysis Integration and Modelling of the
    Earth System (AIMES) 274
Andamarca 159, 162–5
andenerías (terrace systems) 156
andenes (stone walled terraces) 159
Andes:
  Andean culture 156, 168
  Andean people 103, 113, 115
annales:
  history 271
  school 271
añōneañ (north wind) 240, 241, 242
anthropocene 269, 273
anthropogenic:
  landscape transformations 17, 24, 41,
    42, 43, 46, 49, 50, 52, 54, 55, 58,
    119, 126, 127, 128, 204, 257,
    260, 263
  soils 53, 263
anthropology of food 97, 115
anthropology:
  anthropological 6, 7, 58, 115, 217, 258, 259,
    261, 264, 266, 267
  cultural 16, 39
  ecological 257
  environmental 259, 261, 263, 264,
    265, 267
  social 12, 18, 36, 39
antiseptic 109
Antonovich, Vladimir 29
Appalachians 251
applied archaeology 133, 134, 135, 136, 137,
    138, 144, 146, 149, 151, 152, 153–69, 177,
    180, 182, 282
  applied environmental archaeology 19, 133
Apurimac 156, 159, 162, 167
archaeofauna 42, 80, 81, 82, 84, 89, 90, 91, 93,
    94, 95
archaeology
  applied 133, 134, 135, 136, 137, 138, 144,
    146, 149, 151, 152, 153, 155, 157, 159,
    161, 163, 165, 167, 169, 177, 180, 181,
    182, 282
  environmental 12, 13, 19, 32, 33, 133, 257,
    259, 260, 264, 267
  historical 119, 178
  New Archaeology 5, 15, 16, 34, 278
  processual archaeology 5, 16, 208